INTERNATIONAL LAW IN POST-COLONIAL AFRICA

Studies and Materials on the Settlement of International Disputes

Volume 4

Series Editor
Professor Peter Malanczuk, *Chair of International Law, Erasmus University Rotterdam*

INTERNATIONAL LAW IN POST-COLONIAL AFRICA

by

Tiyanjana Maluwa

Legal Counsel and Head of Legal Division, OAU, Ethiopia;
Professor of Law, University of Cape Town, South Africa

KLUWER LAW INTERNATIONAL
THE HAGUE / LONDON / BOSTON

A C.I.P. Catalogue record for this book is available from the Library of Congress

ISBN 90-411-1089-5

Published by Kluwer Law International,
P.O. Box 85889, 2508 CN The Hague, The Netherlands.

Sold and distributed in North, Central and South America
by Kluwer Law International,
675 Massachusetts Avenue, Cambridge, MA 02139, U.S.A.

In all other countries, sold and distributed
by Kluwer Law International, Distribution Centre,
P.O. Box 322, 3300 AH Dordrecht, The Netherlands.

Printed on acid-free paper

Printed in the Netherlands.

CONTENTS

NOTE BY THE SERIES EDITOR

The present series Studies and Materials on the Settlement of International Disputes (SMSID) started as a contribution to the United Nations Decade of International Law (the programme announced by the UN General Assembly for the period 1990–1999) which attaches particular importance to the issue of dispute settlement. The series intends to address the issue of international dispute settlement and prevention from an interdisciplinary perspective – law, economics, history and politics – with the primary objective, however, to search for answers to the question of how to strengthen the rule of law in international relations. For practical purposes, this objective requires a broad perspective and must cover not only the analysis of the peaceful settlement of international disputes, but also the role of the use of force and its legitimacy. Furthermore, while the traditional focus of studies in this area has been limited to interaction between states, the series encourages the analysis also of international dispute settlement involving international organizations and non-state actors, including individuals, minorities, indigenous people, non-governmental organizations, and transnational companies. Finally, the series will also assist in exploring more in depth the linkages between dispute settlement in "public international law" and "international commercial arbitration" and their significance for enhancing the international rule of law.

The first volume of the series was published in 1996 by Dr. Mojtaba Kazazi on the topic Burden of Proof and Related Issues, an excellent study on evidence before international tribunals. The second volume, which also appeared in 1996, was written by Professor Karel Wellens and undertook a functional and well-researched analysis of the hitherto widely unknown field of Economic Conflicts before the World Court (1922–1995). The third volume of the series, published in 1998, by Professor Juliane Kokott continued research into the area explored by Dr. Kazazi and addressed The Burden of Proof in Comparative and International Human Rights Law comparing civil law and common law approaches in an in-depth study with a focus on the American and German legal systems.

The present fourth volume by Professor Tiyanjana Maluwa deals with International Law in Post-Colonial Africa. It is an illuminating and scholarly written analysis, including a number of case studies, of the contribution of

African States to the development of international law in a variety of areas. These areas relate to the formation and sources of international law; the relationship between international law and municipal law; state succession; human rights; refugee law; the peaceful settlement of disputes; the law of international watercourses; the position of land-locked states under the law of the sea; and the legal relationship between environment and development. Covering such a large territory of research requires patience and time and indeed this book is the product of many years of work that led to previous publications by the author in a number of distinguished international law journals. While some of these publications have been revised to be included in this volume, others appear for the first time. Nevertheless, a common thread emerges throughout the book resulting in very interesting conclusions regarding the particular areas in which Africa has taken part in forming new rules and principles of international law and enhanced existing ones (see Author's Preface).

Professor Maluwa, born and raised in Malawi, studied Law at the University of Malawi. Subsequently, completing his graduate studies in international law in the United Kingdom, he received his L.LM. from the University of Sheffield and a Ph.D. from the University of Cambridge. In the following years, Professor Maluwa taught international law at universities in Malawi and Botswana and then became a Professor of Law at the University of Cape Town, South Africa. He also has been a Visiting Research Fellow at the distinguished Max Planck Institute for Comparative Public Law and International Law in Heidelberg, Germany. In 1998, Professor Maluwa took sabbatical leave from the University of Cape Town to assume the position of Legal Counsel and Head of the Legal Division of the Organization of African Unity. He has published extensively on different subjects of international law and, in 1997, has co-edited (with Hugh Corder) a book on Administrative Justice in Southern Africa.

The present volume is a brilliant contribution from an African perspective to the general discussion on the influence of developing countries on the formation and contents of international law.[1] The general attitude of developing countries towards international law has been described in the existing literature, and it is often seen as conditioned primarily by the history of European international law (after the Peace of Westphalia 1648) and its extension throughout the world in the process of colonization, as well as by the economic situation of most developing countries.[2] There are, of course, many other very important scholarly contributions to the topic of Africa and international law.[3] However, the studies by Prof. Maluwa add to this literature significantly by addressing also specifically new areas of modern international law.

I am very pleased to include this impressive work in the SMSID. This is not merely due to the lucid analysis in the part specially relating to dispute settlement in Africa. At the same time the book also offers a valuable broader perspective, at least implicitly enabling the reader to better understand the problems of application of peaceful dispute settlement mechanisms in a number of substantive areas of international law in Africa. Finally, as Chairman of the new Study Group on State Responsibility, established by the International Law Association (ILA) as of 1999, I would like express my gratitude to Professor Maluwa that he has agreed to share his expertise with the Study Group as African member.[4]

Peter Malanczuk
Series Editor

The Hague, February 1999

Notes

1. See A.A. Fatouras, Developing States, in: R. Bernhardt (ed.), *Encyclopedia of Public International Law*, Vol. I (1992), pp. 1017-1024 with a bibliography.

2. See, for example, Wang Tieya, The Third World and International Law, in: R.St.J. Macdonald/D.M. Johnston (eds.), *The Structure and Process of International Law*, 1983, pp. 955-976; M. Shahabuddeen Developing Countries and the Idea of International Law, in: R.St.J. Macdonald (ed.), *Essays in Honour of Wang Tieya*, 1994, pp. 877-891; P. Malanczuk, Akehurst's *Modern Introduction to International Law*, 7th ed. 1997, pp. 9 et seq. and 233 et seq. with further references.

3. Such as T.O. Elias, *Africa and the Development of International Law*, 2nd ed. 1988, only to mention one example. For further literature see Elias, History of the Law of Nations Regional Developments: Africa, in: R. Bernhardt (ed.), *Encyclopedia of Public International Law*, Vol. II (1995), pp. 793-802.

4. See *ILA Newsletter*, No. 11 January 1999, pp. 5-6.

ABOUT THE AUTHOR

Tiyanjana Maluwa was born and raised in Malawi, where he read law at the University of Malawi. He subsequently pursued graduate studies in International Law in the United Kingdom, obtaining an LL.M. from the University of Sheffield and a Ph.D. from the University of Cambridge. He has taught at universities in Malawi and Botswana. He is currently Professor of Law at the University of Cape Town, South Africa. In 1998 he took up a sabbatical post as the Legal Counsel and Head of the Legal Division of the Organization of African Unity. He has also been a Visiting Research Fellow at the Max Planck Institute for Comparative Public Law and International Law in Heidelberg, Germany. He has published extensively on various aspects of International Law, and recently co-edited (with Hugh Corder) *Administrative Justice in Southern Africa* (1997).

PREFACE

> "In the early 1960s, the concept of an African international law might legitimately have been dismissed as [premature]. Although in an embryonic phase of development, African international law is currently being investigated by means of different approaches. It is as multifaceted as international law, its parent discipline."
>
> *A.K. Mensah-Brown*[1]

> "Because of its marginalization, Africa has generally been a recipient of, rather than a contributor to, the development of international law. This marginalization will likely continue as long as the African states remain weak. In a legal system in which the principal actors are still nation-states, the fragile African states will continue to play a limited role in shaping new international legal norms so long as these weaknesses persist."
>
> *A. Peter Mutharika*[2]

The two epigraphs above, separated in time by some twenty years, bring out two important aspects of a debate that has for some time now occupied the minds of those interested in the history and development of international law in Africa. The first aspect concerns the proposition regarding the existence of an African international law, as a sub-species of international law, its "parent discipline". The second concerns the more limited claim regarding Africa's contribution to the development of international law in general. The two issues are, of course, related, but they entail different considerations. As questions posed for both conceptual analysis and practical assessment, they yield different conclusions. The essays assembled in this collection are largely concerned with the second question.

The essays in the volume edited by Mensah-Brown referred to above were first presented at a UNITAR-sponsored symposium held in Accra, Ghana, a little over twenty years ago. The symposium had a twin-objective. First, to examine both the pre-colonial and contemporary history of international law in Africa. Second, to situate Africa's contribution to the development of international law and to identify the broad outlines of the emerging corpus of African international law. These discussions thus ranged from explorations of the "authenticity of African experience in international law in pre-colonial Africa"[3] and bold assertions about the existence of an African international law predating the colonization of the continent, on the one hand, to more tentative assessments of the contribution of the newly independent African states to the development of international law, on the other.

Not surprisingly, one of the major currents in these debates has been the repudiation of the notion that international law was a law made exclusively by a handful of European powers for exportation and transplantation to far flung corners of the "less civilized" world. For, as a number of commentators have argued, there is ample historical evidence to support the proposition that other States and nations outside Europe, including some in pre-colonial Africa, contributed to the evolution of some of the basic rules that have governed relations between States for centuries; and that this non-European infusion into the development of international law has become even more evident in modern times, especially in the post-colonial era, since the establishment of the United Nations.

There are at least two ways of assessing the contribution of African States to the development of modern international law. The first would be to examine the actual practice of these States in their interactions with each other, and with other States in the wider international community, on various matters which have a bearing on the creation of legal rules for the international community. Secondly, one could investigate the role played by these States within the United Nations, especially in the context of the organization's activities which have a bearing on the formation and development of new rules of international law, for example through the processes of progressive development or codification. Moreover, a whole range of developments which have occurred in the international community since the creation of the United Nations in 1945 have both been influenced by certain real and claimed rules and principles of international law and have, in their turn, affected the further development of some of these rules and principles. Almost all these developments have had a significant relevance to Africa and African peoples. Thus, the very process of decolonization in Africa, in which the United Nations played not an insignificant role, gave birth to one of the fundamental principles of modern international law, the right to self-determination. But African States may also stake an equally valid claim regarding their contribution to the shaping or strengthening of other rules and principles of modern international law. Some of the more important examples are: the broadening of the definition of "refugee" and the principle of *non-refoulement* in the area of refugee law; the rights of access and transit to the sea and the concept of the exclusive economic zone in the law of the sea; the principle of *uti possidetis*, which was adopted by the Organization of African Unity at its Heads of State and Government summit in 1964; the concept of peoples' rights, as opposed to that of human rights; the very expansion of the traditional scheme of human rights to embrace the so-called third generation rights, such as the right to development; the "Nyerere doctrine" of State succession; and, in general, certain principles in the area of international fluvial law concerning the common management and utilization of shared watercourses.

Moreover, some of the more specific historical events which have been at the centre of United Nations concerns and operations in Africa in the last thirty-five years or so have had, or may yet have, a tremendous impact on the development of certain norms of international law in the modern era: UN peace-keeping (first in the newly independent Congo (Kinshasa) in the early 1960s and, more recently, in Angola, Mozambique, Rwanda and Somalia); the UN mandate system (Namibia); collective non-recognition of States and governments (Rhodesia and the former South African "Bantustans"); as yet unresolved decolonization issues (Western Sahara), and the eradication of apartheid and racist minority rule in South Africa. From all this, it is obvious that post-colonial Africa has been, in various significant ways, an active participant in the continuing process of developing new rules of international law while strengthening existing ones. The view that African States, especially in the pre-independence era, were merely objects and recipients of an international law which was a monopoly of a Euro-centric world order can no longer be maintained.

The discussions on the various topics covered in this book seek to identify the proper limits and significance of this contribution by African States. The twelve essays contained here have been clustered in six sections, each dealing with a specific theme. However, although the twelve chapters do not reflect one continuous argument or sets of arguments, they are all connected in the sense that each discussion represents an exploration of the contribution of African States, singularly or collectively, through policy pronouncements and practice, to the ever expanding compass and scope of international law. The exception is the opening essay in Chapter 1, in which I address a general philosophical argument about custom as a law-creating phenomenon in the international community. Overall, the evidence that emerges from this exploration categorically refutes the extravagant claim made by Julius Stone almost forty years ago, when he wrote that:[4]

> "International law has grown from the law of European Christendom to the law of nearly a hundred States, most of which are African or Asian, and non-Christian, or even anti-Christian, and many of whom regard it with

> suspicion, as biased in favour of the former colonial powers. *The price of its expansion has been a continuous dilution of its content, as it is re-interpreted for the benefit of the newcomers.*" [Emphasis added]

The expansion of the international community, and the various contributions of the so-called newcomers to this community, have enriched rather than diluted the content of international law. Julius Stone wrote at a time when certain areas of international law which are today taken for granted (human rights, refugee law, air and space law, environmental law, to mention only a few examples) were either non-existent or only in their embryonic stages of development. The role played by the new States of Africa and other previously colonized parts of the world in these developments can no longer be seriously doubted.

I owe a lot of people various debts of gratitude. In fact, my debts are too numerous to be recorded here. However, a number of people deserve specific mention: Paul Tiyambe Zeleza, for almost three decades of friendship, and for his inspiring conversations and scholarship; Clement Ng'ong'ola, who has from time to time provided an invaluable sounding board for some of my thoughts on these subjects, without once letting our friendship stand in the way of honest criticism; Chuma Himonga, for generously acceding to my unreasonable demands for instant views and opinions on various questions; Evance Kalula for being such a supportive friend and colleague within the "internal" African diaspora; and Peter Kazembe, for our long years of friendship and shared concerns over Malawi, Africa and the world. A number of people have both encouraged and strengthened my initial interest in international law over the years. In particular, Derek Bowett will always be remembered not only as a sympathetic teacher and intellectual guide, but also as a rigorous critic who challenged me to rethink and refine ideas I might otherwise have thought self-evident. More recently, I have had the good fortune of sharing occasional, but enriching, conversations with John Dugard and Edward Kwakwa. They have both become, in their respective ways, a source of both intellectual support and encouragement. Again to all these people, and the many others whose names I cannot enumerate here, I am immensely grateful.

The essays in this volume have been conceived and written over a period of time. Some have appeared in periodical publications previously and are reproduced here in some revised form or other. Others are new pieces that have not been published before. I am indebted to all the editors and publishers of the journals concerned: *African Journal of International and Comparative Law*, *African Yearbook of International Law*, *International and Comparative Law Quarterly*, *International Journal of Refugee Law*, *International Law Review*, *Journal of African Policy Studies* and *Netherlands International Law Review*.

Notes

1. A.K. Mensah-Brown (Ed.), *African International Legal History*, (1975) p. 3.
2. A.P. Mutharika, "The Role of International Law in the Twenty-First Century: An African Perspective", *18 Fordham Int'l LJ 1706* (1995) at p. 1759.
3. Mensah-Brown, *op. cit.* p. 153.
4. J. Stone, *The Quest for Survival: The Role of Law and Foreign Policy*, (1961) p. 88.

I

CREATING AND SITUATING INTERNATIONAL LAW

1

CUSTOM, AUTHORITY AND THE CREATION OF INTERNATIONAL LAW

Introduction

Arguments regarding the definition and status of "custom" as a source of law and, indeed, the nature of customary law itself are not new. The latter question has been the subject of copious debate, particularly in relation to discussions concerning the nature of traditional or indigenous African legal systems (as opposed to the "received" Western law), for example. It is not proposed to re-open this debate, which some commentators would, in any case, regard as somewhat hackneyed, sterile and, in some cases, even misdirected.[1] Rather, the present discussion is aimed at a different, but related, question concerning the very normative basis of customary rules. Or, to put the matter differently, this chapter is concerned with the following question: how do authoritative customary rules emerge, and thus begin to regulate human communities as *legal* norms, without either the benefit of any agreed manner of generating such rules or, more importantly, the existence of any particular person or body of persons empowered or recognized as having the authority to make such rules? In itself, this is not a novel question either; legal philosophers and other theorists have addressed, or at least posed, the question directly or indirectly on many occasions. The most recent discussion, from a philosophical perspective at least, aimed at addressing the question in the form in which it has been framed here is that offered by Finnis in his book, *Natural Law and Natural Rights*.[2] The present discussion is, in part, an attempt to highlight some of the advantages offered by Finnis's treatment of this question over earlier analyses by other theorists, mostly international legal scholars.

The question has been thought particularly worth pursuing by international lawyers, for whom the proposition that custom represents, in historical terms at least, the most original and important source of law, holds an especial significance. It should be pointed out from the outset, however, that no attempt will be made in this chapter to address all issues concerning customary international law, let alone the wider debate regarding the sources of international law as such. Treatment of these issues in the scholarly literature is both numerous and comprehensive.[3]

But, of course, to say that the question has been raised repeatedly by legal scholars and commentators is not to say that it has often been answered satisfactorily. Quite the contrary; the general approach has been to regard the question as more or less self-evident. Allott acknowledges this problem squarely:[4]

> "Custom is a, or the major, source of law in customary laws. But what do we mean when we make this self-evident remark, and what sort of source is custom? [Custom] = practice, is what people do; law = norm, is what people ought to do. By what mysterious process does the normal become the normative? Not every practice engenders a norm; not all custom 'is' law."

This differentiation suggests a two-tier categorization: practice which is undertaken in the belief that it is binding (so-called legal custom, "the normative") as opposed to conduct followed without such belief or conviction (sometimes termed social custom, comity, or mere usage, "the normal"). Similar theoretical approaches are to be found in the vast literature devoted to the examination of custom as a source of law. Oppenheim, writing from the perspective of international law, put usage and custom in different orders of merit: he regarded usage as something legally less relevant than custom, connoting a habit followed without conviction of obligation, while granting that such usage may be transformed into custom when the habit is followed with a conviction of obligation.[5] Parry subsequently put the issue succinctly when he wrote:[6]

> "[Repetition] is significant. If a course of conduct is repeatedly followed, the only presumption, or at least a fair presumption, is that it was so followed, and another course not followed, because of the existence of a conviction of obligation. Repetition may, however, arise from mere imitation. But repetition may in time generate conviction."

Implicit in these statements is the notion that custom consists of (human or State) practices which, however, go beyond the fact of mere habitual conduct, not by reason only of their constant repetition, but as a result of the positive disposition which accompanies the conduct in question. Thus, Bos defines custom as "what one is in the habit of doing, convinced that such behaviour is legally obligatory, (*opinio juris*), although not ordered by a written rule".[7] Definitions of this nature are quite common, at least within the context of discussions of customary international law.

The preoccupation of international lawyers with attempts to explain the nature of custom as a source of international law goes back to the classical authorities. Thus, in his *De legibus ac deo legislatore*, which appeared in 1612, Suarez proposed two requirements for the existence of custom: consensus, and compliance with reason. The former, in Suarez's definition, meant the sovereign's (rather than the entire community's) consent to the given practice; and the latter signified *ratio*, or God's will as revealed to man. This was an interesting conception of custom, for it combined both positivist and natural law theorizing. On the other hand, that other acclaimed "father" of international law, Hugo Grotius, regarded custom as no more than a practice which had met with the peoples', or the community's, tacit consent, the *tacitus consensus popularum*. Apparently it was left to later theorists, in particular the German legal scholars Von Savigny and Puchta, to lay down the doctrine now routinely adopted by modern writers on the subject: that custom is based on two factors, namely: durable and constant repetition of a particular practice or conduct, and the psychological disposition of feeling bound to engage in the practice in question, the *opinio juris*.[8]

Following the above doctrine, and the scheme adopted in Article 38(1) of the Statute of the International Court of Justice, the late Judge Hudson, in his "Working Paper" on Article 24 of the Statute of the International Law Commission, summarized the requirements for the existence of custom as follows:[9]

> "(a) concordant practice by a number of States with reference to a type of situation falling within the domain of international relations;
>
> (b) continuation or repetition of the practice over a considerable period of time;
>
> (c) conception that the practice is required by, or consistent with, prevailing international law; and
>
> (d) general acquiescence in the practice by other States."

Formulations of this tenor are not uncommon in the standard treatises by international lawyers and legal philosophers. Kelsen, in an early work on this subject, identified both the constitutive elements of custom and the "unanswerable paradox" regarding the true relationship between *usus* and *opinio juris*.[10] But, as Finnis quite rightly observes, most of the accounts in this vast literature are confused insofar as the analysis of custom as a source of international law, and more particularly the element of *opinio juris*, is concerned.

Finnis sets out to clear up this confusion by proposing his own analysis which is dependent on an understanding of two other concepts: "authority" and "community". The connection is this: that a discussion of custom demonstrates how an authoritative rule can emerge (i.e. begin to regulate a community) without being made by anyone with authority to make it, and even without the benefit of any authorized way of generating rules. Such a discussion, Finnis argues, enables us to deepen our understanding of the relation between acknowledging the authority of a rule and following the principles of practical reasonableness.[11]

But why should the discussion be located in the context of international law, in particular? According to Finnis:[12]

> "It will be convenient to conduct our discussion of the formation of custom by reference to the international community and the formation of customary rules of international law. For this is the context in which the problem of custom arouses most interest today, has been most debated, and found most difficult to explain satisfactorily."

As has already been noted, there is an abundance of literature on this issue. It is generally agreed, as Judge Hudson's enumeration demonstrates, that (i) custom involves some concurrence, convergence or regularity of practice amongst States; (ii) such concurrence, convergence and regularity of practice is not enough, unless it is a deliberate practice not induced by force or fraud or mistake; (iii) this practice must be accompanied by a certain attitude, belief, intention or disposition: a positive feeling of being bound, or the *opinio juris*.

It is argued that the problems encountered in the attempts to explain the nature of custom as a source of international law arise precisely with respect to the last element mentioned above. For it is said that the classical accounts of the required content of the *opinio juris* are openly question-begging or paradoxical, but that alternative accounts have not been forthcoming either.[13] The paradoxical nature of these classical accounts can be seen, for example, in Oppenheim's observation that:[14]

> "International jurists speak of a custom when a clear and continuous habit of doing certain actions has grown up under the aegis of the conviction that these actions are, according to international law, obligatory or right."

This was also the approach adopted by the International Court of Justice in the *North Sea Continental Shelf* cases, probably the Court's most explicit pronouncement on the question of custom as a source of international law:[15]

> "Not only must the acts concerned amount to a settled practice, but they must also be such, or be carried out in such a way, as to be evidence of a belief that this practice is rendered obligatory by the existence of a rule of law requiring it. The need for such a belief, i.e. the subjective element, is implicit in the very notion of the *opinio juris sive necessitatis*. The States concerned must therefore feel that they are conforming to what amounts to a legal obligation. The frequency, or even habitual character of the acts is not in itself enough."

Parry, in an apt, if cynical, observation had earlier expressed the view that:[16]

> "[The] transformation of custom which is not law into custom which is can be judged of only after the event. We find that what we have done binds us. *[But] we also find that only that which we have done in the conviction that it is already binding so binds us.*"

This, then, is the crux of the problem: it is not disputed that, in international law at least, custom involves some concurrence or convergence or regularity of practice, not induced by force or fraud or mistake, among States; and furthermore, that the practice in question must be accompanied by a certain attitude, belief, intention, or disposition. This positive element is what was earlier termed the *opinio juris sive necessitatis*. But, as Finnis argues, and as most international lawyers would readily concede, the classical accounts of the required content of the *opinio juris* are openly paradoxical and involve a certain degree of circularity of logic; for they propose, by and large, that a customary norm can come into existence (i.e. become authoritative) only by virtue of the necessarily erroneous belief that it is already in existence (i.e. authoritative). Kunz[17] demonstrated this circularity of logic when he observed that custom is creative of new law and not declaratory of existing law, and also that it requires to be accompanied by a belief that the conduct in question is *already* law.

Custom as a Law-Creating Process

Almost all theories on customary international law bear out the major point that has just been alluded to above: that the role of custom as a law-creating phenomenon turns on the relationship between State practice, *usus*, and the accompanying psychological disposition, the *opinio juris.* And in this regard, it has been suggested that the requirement of simultaneousness or synchronization of *usus* and *opinio juris* in most of these theories has resulted in demanding the impossible and in efforts to "square the juridical circle".[18] In an effort to get out of this dilemma, some authorities have then opted for extreme, even diametrically opposed, interpretations of the relationship between the two elements of custom. On the one hand, there are those who argue that *usus* is not a necessary requirement, but that emphasis should be placed on *opinio juris* alone; on the other hand, others advocate the view that *usus* is the all-important requirement, and *opinio juris* need not enter into our analysis of customary rules. Strupp[19] was among the earlier advocates of the former view. In fact, some exponents of this view adopt the extreme position that rules of customary international law may emerge on the basis of a fairly short-lived, or even single-instance, practice and within a short space of time, provided that the States participating in such practice, and those acquiescing in it, display the necessary *opinio juris.* This is referred to in the legal literature as a case of "instant custom".[20] On the whole, these so-called single-element theories have not commanded widespread support among international legal scholars.[21]

The dilemma involved in the analysis of custom as a source of law was, as was noted above, identified in an early discussion of the issue by Kelsen.[22] Subsequently, a number of scholars have voiced similar observations. Kunz's observation is fairly representative of these views:[23]

> "On the one hand it is said that usage plus *opinio juris* leads to such a norm [i.e. a norm of customary international law], and that, on the other hand, in order to lead to such a norm, the States must already practice the first cases with the *opinio juris.* Hence, the very coming into existence of such norm would presuppose that States acted in legal error."

The question-begging nature of this debate has led one commentator to make the apt observation that the so-called pre-existing rule of law, entailing legal obligation by customary practice, is itself a product of customary practice.[24] In the words of Villiger:[25]

> "The conclusions to be drawn from this are, either, that a customary rule will never arise, or, if it has arisen, that the first States engaging in practice upon the rule did so in the erroneous belief that the rule was law when, in fact, it was not."

Of course, the first possibility may be disregarded outright, for it is not disputed that all the major legal systems of the world today, including the international legal system, recognize customary rules as valid rules within these legal systems.

The juridical circle that needs to be squared, therefore, exists only in relation to the second possibility intimated above: do the first States engaging in a practice which leads to the creation of a rule in fact do so in the mistaken belief that the rule is *already* law?

Some of the more recent attempts by leading international legal scholars to explain this apparent conundrum are those offered by D'Amato, Meijers, Walden and Verdross.[26] In his celebrated study on the subject, D'Amato takes issue with Judge Hudson's proposed four elements of customary law, quoted *in extenso* above, and proposes his own alternative formulation. In essence, D'Amato poses three related questions: (a) how can a new rule of customary international law ever come into existence if it has to be required by, or be consistent with, already existing law?; (b) how, in Hudson's view, can an existing rule of customary law ever change?; and (c) how can an international authority establish the existence of an international custom the existence of which depends on its establishment precisely by such an authority?[27]

D'Amato, in fact, proposes a two-stage approach to the ascertainment of the existence of a customary rule: first, identify a claim that a given line of conduct not only reflects a social habit or political expediency, but that it is also a matter of legal obligation; second, determine whether the determinative force of such a claim has been enhanced by successful repetition, consent, estoppel, or reasonableness.

D'Amato's attempts to reformulate the traditional theory of customary international law is partly reflected in his rejection of the traditional terminology: D'Amato substitutes "commitment" in place of *usus* and "articulation" for *opinio juris*. But the divergence of approach goes beyond a mere variation of terminology here; the idea of an internal reflective attitude, the psychological conviction or feeling of being bound, is discarded, in favour of the view that:[28]

> "[There] is no need for the acting State itself, through its officials, to have articulated the legal rule. [A] writer on international law, a court, or an international organization may well provide the qualitative component of custom."

This alternative approach to the concept of *opinio juris* is rather difficult to support. D'Amato goes on to group together "leading journals in international law, the leading textbooks, reports of leading decisions affecting international law, resolutions of international organizations"[29] as the likely sources for the articulation of rules. All these are regarded as media which State officials and their counsel would have reason to consult; logically, therefore, a State may be taken to have notice of any rule, or proposed rule, articulated therein, and if the subsequent conduct of such a State conforms to the proposed rule in question, such a State will be adjudged to have displayed the necessary *opinio juris* (or, in D'Amato's terminology, "articulation") to justify the conclusion that the conduct of the State in question has generated, or contributed to, the formation or emergence of a (new) rule of customary international law.

It is submitted that this account must be rejected as distorting the whole notion of *opinio juris*: viz., the psychological conviction of feeling bound by (emerging) rules from the participant's (i.e. the individual's or State's) own "internal point of view". Now, it is obvious that being an abstract entity, the State can only manifest its convictions through its human agents (State officials acting in their official capacities); indeed, it is precisely through the official acts of these agents that State practice is ascertained. But is it not a gross exaggeration to say that if a State adopts a certain course of conduct which happens to be in line with a rule (or putative rule) advocated by, for example, a writer on international law, some kind of *opinio juris* may be imputed to such State conduct merely because the alleged or proposed rule has been published in a medium (such as a journal or a textbook) or advanced at a forum (for example, a conference) of which the State's officials are presumed to have been aware? On the whole, D'Amato's account does not seem to provide a clear philosophical explanation that would offer us a way out of this dilemma. In fact, in a more recent work, D'Amato has dismissed the concept of *opinio juris* as "at best otiose".[30]

Verdross also advocates a reformulation of the traditional theory of custom in a way which is apparently intended to circumvent the paradox identified above. Verdross's argument, which proposes a three-stage schema, may be summarized thus: during the first stage, one or more States consciously (i.e. not as a result of mistake, fraud or duress) engage in a given practice, or make claims; such a course of conduct or claims may be the result of self-interest, gain, comity, courtesy, and so on. At the second stage, other States react to the initial practice or claims with their own claims and counter-claims; in the process, these other States may uphold the initial conduct in the *expectation* that yet other States will in their turn accord reciprocity. Thus, a situation arises in which reliance is placed by one or more States upon the conduct of other States and the latter are regarded as bound by the expectations which their conduct has raised in others. At the third and final stage, these relations and scheme of expectations begin to harden into a general rule; the *conviction* on the part of the States that they are adhering to an *emerging* customary rule may then gradually begin to accompany the practice in question. After this stage, as the practice or the claims become more wide-spread, or are acquiesced in by more States, so too the conviction that the type of conduct in question is obligatory (*ought to be done*) or permissible (*may be done*) in the scheme of inter-State relations becomes more wide-spread and more generally accepted. It is argued that this three-stage approach eliminates the need to enquire into the exact moment at which the customary rule arises. And the relationship between the material practice (*usus*) and the psychological conviction (*opinio juris*) becomes more integrated. The chronological separation of the two elements becomes somewhat slightly blurred.[31]

A similar three-stages theory respecting the creation of rules of international law in general has been advanced by Meijers.[32] These stages operate as follows: during the first stage the content of the rule is being delineated, that is to say there is an identification of a certain type of conduct without any reference to whether or not this conduct is a result of the existence of a rule which will become binding or not. At the second stage, the States participating in the practice shape their "will" in such a way as to transform the rule into law: "what is taking place during this stage is the development of the will to make a rule into law".[33] And, finally, during the third stage the "will" developed during the second stage has to become cognizable for all States for whom the practice or rule in question may, or is to, become law.

Both Verdross's and Meijers's theories point to the same thing: that the development of customary rules involves a chronological process of fact-situations and the internalization of behavioural patterns which in turn generate expectations and, subsequently, generally recognized norms in respect of future or recurring instances of such fact-situations and patterns of conduct. Somewhere along this scheme, States are either presumed to have formed certain convictions about the desirability and appropriateness of the conduct in question, or to have developed a "will" in respect of the required conduct; such conviction and "State-will" in turn lead to the emergence of binding rules. Both theories suggest that somewhere between stages one and three the juridical watershed that separates "binding customary practices" from "mere habits" is crossed, sometimes consciously, but often unconsciously and without proclamation. But both theories leave rather vague the question of when exactly, and why, the *opinio juris* arises: this could happen either at stage two or stage three.

The two so-called three-stages theories examined above do not, despite the lucidity of exposition and analysis involved, fully clear up the lingering questions left over from earlier discussions by other writers concerning custom as a source of international law, and in particular the attempted elucidations of *opinio juris*.

All the views surveyed in the foregoing discussion can generally be grouped together as belonging to Western legal thought or international legal scholarship. Is socialist (or formerly Soviet) doctrine different in this regard? It would seem not. In a fairly recent discussion of Soviet thinking on customary international law, Mullerson made the following categorical observation:[34]

> "[Soviet] doctrine and approach to customary law is not entirely different from Western doctrines, at least from most of them. If it were otherwise, there would be no general international law, obligatory for all States."

This observation is instructive, given the general tendency to assume that there exist (or existed), on most issues, fundamental differences of approach and substance between Western and Soviet conceptions of international law. Thus, Soviet scholars recognized that like all forms of international law-making, the process of creating norms of customary international law involves two stages. In the first stage, a rule or pattern of behaviour of subjects of international law takes shape. In the second stage, this rule is recognized by States or other subjects as legally binding on them.[35] From this, Mullerson goes on to conclude that:[36]

> "[Soviet] doctrine recognizes, as many Western lawyers do, the need for two elements in the process of forming a customary norm: practice and *opinio juris*."

Elsewhere in the same work, the learned scholar goes on to note, in relation to the role of custom in domestic law and under international law, that:[37]

> "In domestic law, custom is formed as a result of the acts of millions of individuals, none of whom really understands that his or her behaviour will ultimately lead to the formation of a customary rule. States, however, are usually more or less conscious of what they are doing and what the result (including also the legal rules) of their behaviour will be in the international arena. Consequently, while there are certain elements of spontaneity in customary lawmaking, especially during the first stage of the formation of a customary rule (when so-called usage, which is not legally binding, appears), the process of formation of customary norms does result from the concurrence of wills of States."

These observations are in order, and the great majority of international legal scholars (including Western scholars) would have no difficulty concurring with them. Yet, even the most sympathetic reading of this and similar socialist or Soviet views does not seem to explain fully and clearly the philosophical problems involved in the paradox identified earlier: how do authoritative (customary) rules emerge and begin to regulate a community (of individuals or States) as legal rules in the absence of any person or body endowed with the power or authority to make such rules, or without the benefit of any agreed method of generating such rules? As stated earlier, Finnis's discussion is an attempt to answer this question. A slightly earlier attempt at a jurisprudential analysis was undertaken by Walden.[38] A brief summary of his discussion would be in order.

In his analysis of custom-formation Walden adopts Hart's well-known model of custom: the model of the legal structure of a primitive society which is without "a legislature, courts, or officials of any kind". According to Hart, such a society only enjoys primary rules of obligation, and the question as to what rules exist in such a society is a purely factual one; a given rule exists if: (i) most people generally behave in a certain manner; (ii) deviations from such behaviour are regarded as lapses or faults and open to criticism, and threatened deviations meet with pressure for conformity; (iii) deviation from the conduct is generally accepted as a good reason for making such criticism, even by those against whom the criticism is directed; and (iv) there exists an "internal attitude" towards such behaviour on the part of the individual members of the society.[39]

In the Hartian model, the type of society described above is one in which the only rules available are customary rules. Such rules, then, come into being not through any process of law-making, but simply by virtue of their being complied with as a matter of fact. These rules, which Walden terms "fact-created custom", are primary rules imposing obligations to act or to forbear in various ways, and do not give us a full picture of an advanced legal system unless complemented by secondary rules of various types.[40]

Having adopted Hart's model of custom, however, Walden rejects Hart's conclusion, that systems of customary law (including customary international law) are systems of primary rules only. Instead, he advances the proposition that custom also involves both primary and secondary rules. He argues that Hart's account of the nature of fact-created custom must be supplemented with an account of the conditions under which a customary secondary rule can be said to exist analogous to that of the existence of a customary primary rule.[41] As a first step in his analysis, Walden thus proposes that the first truth-condition posited by Hart ("most people generally behave in a certain manner") must be recast in the following terms: "on the performance by a specified person or body of a specified act which stipulates a certain course of conduct, most people generally behave in the manner so stipulated"; the other truth-conditions remain unchanged. Walden goes on to observe thus:[42]

> "As an illustration, one may imagine a primitive society in which customary legislative powers are conferred on a Council of Elders. Of the truth-conditions for the existence of such powers, condition (i) will be, that on the

> issuing of prescriptions in the recognized manner by the Council of Elders most people generally comply with such prescriptions.
>
> [The] general compliance with the course of conduct indicated only gives rise to a customary secondary rule if the *reason* for that compliance is that the course of conduct in question has been indicated in the appropriate manner by the appropriate person or body."

The difficulty with this analysis is that it is predicated on the assumption that there is, indeed, a person or body of persons (the Council of Elders) *empowered* to issue prescriptions for the general compliance of all the other members in the society. But, as has already been pointed out above, the paradoxical question which all these analyses claim to be clarifying is precisely this: how do customary rules emerge and become accepted as legal rules without the existence of any particular person or body of persons empowered to prescribe such rules? Once we import into the debate, as Walden has done, the assumption that there exists in the society a person or body of persons recognized by the society as possessing the authority to make such rules then, of course, we can no longer claim to be dealing with the question as originally framed. In this case, there is simply no paradox calling for resolution.

Walden's analysis becomes clearer and more illuminating a little later, when he employs Hart's notion of the "internal point of view" to explain the binding character of customary legal rules. It is instructive in this regard to quote Walden *in extenso*:[43]

> "We must now turn to the case of law-created primary rules. Here, as we have seen, it is the secondary rule itself which stipulates how and under what conditions a rule of customary law comes into being, and it is therefore to the secondary rule that we must turn, in order to ascertain the role played by the internal point of view in generating the rules of customary law. This can be explained by the formula that practice treated by States as a legal standard of behaviour will generate customary law. [It] means that the conduct of the subjects of a legal system is only recognized as generating customary law, if, in addition to the other conditions that have to be fulfilled, the practice is treated as a standard of *legal* behaviour by those who pursue it. This seems paradoxical, since it seems to mean that a practice can only become law if (among other conditions) those who follow it already, (and at first wrongly) believe it to be law. But what is involved may be, not a belief that the practice is *already* legally binding, but a claim that it *ought* to be legally binding. In other words, those who follow the practice, and treat it as a legal standard of behaviour, may be doing so with the deliberate legislative intention."

It is submitted here that Walden's analysis goes further than most of the earlier attempts towards explaining the alleged philosophical paradox concerning the nature of customary law, including customary international law. For, according to this analysis, in order to understand custom-formation we need not lock ourselves into the vicious circle of proposing that "only that which we have done in the conviction that it is already binding so binds us". Custom-formation can be seen as a process which, at bottom, involves conduct relating to assertions of claim-rights, privileges, powers, immunities, and so on, on the part of one or more individual(s) or State(s), and countervailing claims, acquiescence or even non-committal silences, by other individuals or States. In following the particular pattern of conduct in question the individual(s) or State(s) need not believe that the conduct is *already* obligatory or required by (international) law, but merely that the conduct is, in the circumstances, right, worth pursuing and providing in itself a justification for wide recognition and subscription by all other individuals or States in the particular community. Where all, or most, individuals or States in the given community do in fact generally share this perception (or conviction) with regard to the conduct in question, and do therefore, converge in their actual patterns of conduct, there arises a basis for saying that such conduct has led to the emergence of a customary rule requiring (or permitting) the conduct to be followed. The basis for such a claim or conclusion is simply that the widespread convergence of practice and the shared conviction about the practical necessity and rightness of the conduct in question (for all individuals, States) creates an *expectation* that everybody else will, and *ought* to, behave accordingly. The argument can be restated in more familiar language as follows: consistent practice yields a *presumption* of shared conviction which, if the practice is ever put to the test (for example in court), throws the evidential burden onto the other party to prove non-existence of the alleged *opinio juris*, an admittedly impossible task.[44] When recast in this way, the traditional accounts of *opinio juris* need not present any paradox or lead to the usual question-begging conclusions. Probably the most accomplished philosophical elucidation of the issues involved here is that presented by Finnis.[45] It is to a consideration of his analysis that I now propose to turn.

Finnis's Account of Custom-Formation

Finnis's attempt to clarify the "openly question-begging or paradoxical" accounts of *opinio juris* is predicated upon a differentiation between what he terms practical judgments, on the one hand, and empirical judgments, on the other hand, about the existence and extent of practices.[46] These may be human practices (in the context of the practices of individuals within a given community) or State practice (in the international legal order). A practical judgment in this scheme refers to a judgment made by any person, whether privately or in some official capacity, which explicitly or implicitly states that some action (or omission or forbearance) by some (potential) agent should (not) be done, or could (not) appropriately or justifiably be done, etc. Finnis's analysis of practical judgments is itself rooted in other related philosophical discussions concerning the concepts of "authority" and "community".

Finnis presents his schema (employing some *ad hoc* notation) as follows:

> PJ_0 – (a) it is desirable that in this domain there be some determinate, common, and stable pattern of conduct and corresponding authoritative rule;
>
> (b) this particular pattern of conduct, x, is (or would be if generally acquiesced in) an appropriate pattern for adoption as an authoritative common rule.
>
> EJ_1 – there is widespread concurrence and acquiescence in this pattern of conduct, x, by States.
>
> EJ_2 – the *opinio juris* (i.e. PJ_0) is widely subscribed to by States.
>
> PJ_1 – the widespread subscription to PJ_0, and the widespread concurrence or acquiescence in the pattern of conduct x, are sufficient to warrant the judgment (PJ_2) that there is now an authoritative customary rule requiring (or permitting) x...
>
> PJ_2 – x is required (or permitted), by virtue of an authoritative customary rule of international law.
>
> EJ_3 – States generally accept the rule that x is to be done (or may be done)...
>
> JJ_1 – according to international law, x is required (or permitted)...

In this schema PJ signifies a practical judgment, in the sense explained above, EJ an empirical judgment, and JJ a juristic judgment. Furthermore, to paraphrase Finnis, the three types of judgment may be described in the following terms: a practical judgment treats a given rule or practice as authoritative not only for others but for the speaker of the statement as an exclusionary reason for action; an empirical judgment is a statement which may be made by someone who does not regard the rule or practice in question as authoritative for himself or in relation to him, but one who can demonstrate that some other people treat it as such; a juristic judgment is a statement asserted by someone neither in recognition of the authoritativeness of a given rule or practice in relation to himself, nor by way of report about other people's attitudes to the rule or practice, but rather by way of stating what is the case from the point of view of those who treat the rule or practice as authoritative, yet without either endorsing or rejecting such point of view.

Finnis claims that this analysis has four virtues. First, by differentiating between PJ_0 and PJ_1 the analysis enables us to see that there need be no paradox or circularity in the classic notion that a course of practice must be accompanied by a particular sort of attitude or opinio in order to amount to an authoritative custom. Secondly, by differentiating between PJ_0 and PJ_2, we can see that the legal judgment PJ_2, while in various ways dependent upon prior political or moral judgments PJ_0 (not necessarily made by the person – or State – now making the legal judgment), is quite distinct and positive; it points to the existence of *lex lata* and not merely *lex feranda*. Thirdly, by separating out the various empirical judgments (EJ_1, EJ_2 and EJ_3) from the other judgments, the relation of authoritative rules to facts is clarified: an authoritative rule can be said to be a fact which is treated as an exclusionary reason for action (i.e. a reason for judging or acting in the absence of understood reasons, or for disregarding at least some reasons which are understood and relevant and would in the absence of the exclusionary reason have sufficed to justify proceeding in some other way[47]). Finally, the analysis enables us to see clearly the real problems involved in explaining the formation of custom: for PJ_1 not to be a *non sequitur*, it must have a suppressed practical premiss. Finnis calls this premiss, PJ^m, the "meta-legal or framework principle".[48]

The central case of Finnis's analysis lies in the proper understanding of this meta-legal or framework principle. Finnis himself posits this premiss as follows:[49]

> "The emergence and recognition of customary rules (by treating a certain degree of concurrence or acquiescence in a practice and a corresponding *opinio juris* as sufficient to create such a norm and to entitle that norm to recognition even by States not party to the practice or the *opinio juris*) is a desirable or appropriate method of solving interaction or co-ordination problems in the international community."

The virtues claimed for this analysis can only be appreciated if certain assumptions are borne in mind, and more particularly if the entire schema is understood within the wider context of the principles of practical reasonableness which underpin Finnis's natural law theory. In particular, the formation of custom, when viewed in this light, can only be possible if the meta-legal principle PJ^m enjoys wider favour among States than does the PJ_0

relating to any specific aspect or particular problem of conduct. Thus, according to Finnis:[50]

> "Just as it is easier to get agreement that *some* rule would be desirable (PJ_o(a)) than to get agreement that *this* particular rule is desirable (PJ_o(b)), so it is easier still to get agreement that the international community needs methods of solving its interaction and co-ordination problems and that custom, if there is sufficient acceptance that custom is an appropriate method, is an appropriate method (since it is often the only practicable method). And this way of expressing PJ^m shows that the desirability or appropriateness of accepting PJ^m is conditional upon a sufficient number of other States also accepting PJ^m. This is not a paradox or vicious circle!"

Thus, the argument partly turns on the related propositions about "justice as reciprocity": the idea that the requirements of justice, fairness and equity in human communities necessitate co-ordination in resolving interaction problems, and reciprocation by all members of their mutual sacrifices, obligations, forebearances, and so on, for the common good. But before one even turns to a consideration of these related propositions, one must recognize, as Finnis himself readily does, that in order for custom-formation to work well as an instrument for generating binding legal rules in the (international) legal community, and in order for us to make sense of the apparent paradoxes entailed in the various theories or explanations of custom as a source of law, certain lingering questions need to be resolved. Among these the most important are: (a) what actions of what persons in what contexts count as State practice? (b) what degree of practice counts as widespread in a given domain, and for how long? (c) what expressions or silences, and whose, count as subscribing to the *opinio juris* (PJ_o(a) and (b)? (d) to what extent can custom be localized geographically, granted that the interaction and co-ordination problems of the international community, in a given domain, are perhaps not peculiar to a particular geographical area (but perhaps have local variations)?

In general, it may be said that most international lawyers would have little difficulty reaching agreement on answers to these questions, even if there may not be as much agreement on the notion of *opinio juris* itself, as has, in part, been demonstrated in this discussion. Besides, there is a respectable body of jurisprudence from the World Court itself in which some of these questions have been addressed both directly and indirectly. This jurisprudence need not be examined in any detail here[51]; rather, a few pertinent observations regarding Finnis's schema will be made.

Finnis is arguably the most influential and eloquent advocate of natural law theory today, at least in the English-speaking world. It has been observed that most earlier natural law theorists sought to reason out philosophical consequences from observed characteristics of the human condition, or to deduce moral principles from rational argument, or from imagined states of nature existing before societies or governments came into existence.[52] Finnis's approach is regarded as a radical departure from these earlier approaches. In this regard, Cotterrell has observed that:[53]

> "These approaches have usually been considered vulnerable to the criticism that an unacceptable sleight of hand is involved in seeking to deduce what morally *ought* to be from speculation about what *is*. [Finnis's] approach appears to bypass these traditional difficulties by grounding natural law not in reason but in intuition; in what is 'self-evident', requiring no rational justification."

Thus, Finnis, partly echoing St. Thomas Aquinas, and partly following his contemporary and collaborator Germain Grisez, posits seven objects of human striving which he regards as self-evidently good ("basic human goods"): life, knowledge, play, aesthetic experience, friendship or sociability, practical reasonableness and religion.[54] These basic goods are not derived from rational speculation on what is the case in nature, but rather they are intuitively recognized as self-evidently "good"; this makes it equally self-evident that they should be pursued and promoted.[55]

Earlier above it was pointed out that the virtues which Finnis claims for his analysis can best be appreciated if the schema is understood within the wider context of the principles of practical reasonableness which underpin his theory of natural law. Practical reasoning is, for Finnis, one of the basic goods which provides general prescriptions of reason (or "basic methodological requirements") which should guide the pursuit of the other goods. In brief, practical reasonableness entails being able to bring one's intelligence and judgment to bear in choosing how to live one's life.[56]

What bearing or relevance does this have upon our discussion of custom-formation? It is this: for Finnis, the seven basic forms of human good can only be sought in communal life, in interaction with other people. A legal system is required to secure these goods. In order to understand fully the relation of the legal system to the basic goods we need to bring into focus the three related concepts alluded to earlier: "community", "authority" and "law". Finnis paints a philosophical ideal of a "complete community" as:[57]

> "[An] all-round association in which would be co-ordinated the initiatives and activities of individuals, of families, and of the vast network of intermediate associations. The point of this all-round association would be to secure the whole ensemble of material and other conditions, including forms

of collaboration, that tend to favour, facilitate and foster the realization by each individual of his or her personal development."

To Aristotle, the Greek *polis* was the paradigmatic form of a complete and self-sufficient community for securing the all-round good of its members. Modern political philosophy takes as its paradigmatic form the territorial State. The State, as understood in this sense, is also the starting point for all discourse in international law, for States form the basic and fundamental units of the international community which provides the very *raison d'être* of the system of international law. One of the conclusions which can be drawn from Finnis's account is that the moral and rational strength of law is grounded in its purposive contribution to the continuance and fulfilment of a complete community.[58] The connection between law and community is postulated in the following terms:[59]

> "[As] the common understanding of the unqualified expressions 'law' and 'the law' indicates, the central case of law and legal system is the law and legal system of a complete community. That is why it is characteristic of legal systems that (i) they claim authority to regulate all forms of human [behaviour]; (ii) they therefore claim to be the supreme authority for their respective community, and to regulate the conditions under which the members of that community can participate in any other normative system or association; (iii) They characteristically purport to 'adopt' rules and normative arrangements (e.g. contracts) from other associations within and without the community, thereby 'giving them legal force' for that [community]."

The postulates outlined in the preceding paragraph have their foundation in the requirement that the activities of individuals (or States) be co-ordinated. This requirement itself derives partly from the requirement of impartiality as between persons and of impartiality as between the basic values or basic forms of human good and openness to all of them. These considerations of course arise within the framework of practical reasonableness, and suggest the idea of "justice as reciprocity" referred to earlier above.

A community, then, flourishes as a grouping of individuals with shared objectives and with a common interest in their interaction and co-ordination problems. The participants in such a community (whether family, club, enterprise, State) look out for practices, usages, conventions, or norms for solving their co-ordination problems and, in some cases, for someone with authority to select among the available solutions. Consequently:[60]

> "Such norms will then be thought of as norms *of* and *for* the group, and the leader(s) will be thought of as having authority *in* and *over* the group. The 'existence' of the group, the 'existence' of social rules, and the 'existence' of authority tend to go together. And what makes sense of these ascriptions of existence is in each case the presence of some more or less shared objective or, more precisely, some shared conception of the point of continuing co-operation. This we may call the common good."

The picture that Finnis paints is thus one of the law as a "coercive" system (though not in the Kelsenian sense), but more fundamentally, a system of rules. It "brings clarity and predictability to human interactions, regulates its own creation and modification, allows individuals to adjust their circumstances rationally within a rule-governed environment, provides reasons for future actions, and postulates a gapless framework of regulation".[61] Under certain circumstances, custom-formation then becomes a methodological substitute for the "leader(s) with authority *in* and *over* the community" (of individuals, States) with regard to the creation and modification of (some of) the community's rules.

This analysis of custom as a source of law urges us to accept at least five broad propositions which may be briefly stated as follows: first, the general authoritativeness of custom depends upon the fact that custom-formation has been adopted in the (international) community as an appropriate method of rule-creation. Second, recognition of the authoritativeness of particular customs affords all members of the community (individuals, States) the opportunity of advancing the common good of the community by solving (otherwise insoluble) interaction and co-ordination problems. Third, the requirements, pre-conditions, and forms of custom-formation are themselves determined, in large part, by custom (a "framework custom"). Fourth, acceptance of this framework custom should not lead us to conclude that the framework custom authorizes States (or individuals, etc.) to make custom, or that it is the "source" of the authority of particular customs: rather, both the framework custom and the particular customs which have become authoritative within its framework derive their authoritativeness directly from the fact that, if treated as authoritative, they enable States to solve their co-ordination problems. Finally, the solving of such co-ordination problems has a normative significance in that the common good of the (international) community requires that those co-ordination problems be solved.[62]

Concluding Observations: A Brief Interpretation of Finnis's Schema

It is true, to paraphrase the well known statement by Williams[63] a little more than half a century ago, that the Rubicon which divides custom from law is often crossed silently, unconsciously, and without proclamation. It is equally true that numerous pronouncements by tribunals (both national and international) and jurists in the intervening period have not always satisfactorily clarified this transformational process which turns custom into law. Nor, more fundamentally, have the various accounts by both international legal scholars and legal philosophers fully resolved the debate concerning the apparently paradoxical nature of *opinio juris* which, as we have seen, lies at the bottom of the whole process of custom-formation. But it is the view here that among the more recent accounts, Walden's and, much more fundamentally, Finnis's analyses of the notion of *opinio juris* provide a powerful juristic light which, if properly focussed, would show the way out of the philosophical tunnel into which the paradoxical and openly question-begging accounts by other writers and commentators have tended to lead the debate. In particular, Finnis's account of *opinio juris* (PJ_0) shows that this notion need not be expressed in the vague and elusive language of the "psychological disposition of feeling bound", but may be regarded simply as an expression of some kind of (moral or political) *desideratum* which forms the starting point of an emerging pattern-of-conduct.

The *opinio juris* (in the sense of the undifferentiated PJ_0) need not have been formed by the State, S_1, which subsequently makes the legal judgment, PJ_2, about the existence of a particular customary rule. But as was seen above, the initial practical judgment, or first-order practical judgment, which forms the *opinio juris* in this analysis operates at two levels: the first-level *opinio juris* (PJ_0(a)) expresses a desire for the adoption of some pattern of conduct in a very *general* sense; the second-level *opinio juris* (PJ_0(b)) is more specific and points to a particular pattern of conduct as justifying the adoption of a specified common rule. But where a particular State, S_1, along with other States (S_2, S_3, S_4, ...), shares the *opinio juris*, PJ_0(b), its participation in the formation of such *opinio juris* is predicated merely on the *expectation* that other States (S_5, S_6, S_7 ...) will similarly view the particular pattern of conduct as both *desirable* and *appropriate* for adoption as a common rule. At this stage there is no claim that those States which share this view and begin to engage in the desired conduct are doing so *because* they labour under the psychological feeling or disposition of being bound to do so. Or, to borrow Oppenheim's words, because they regard their conduct as being either right or obligatory, according to international law; merely that the conduct or practice in question is *desirable* and *appropriate*. Thus, no paradox or circularity of logic is involved in this conception of *opinio juris*.[64]

In the schema outlined above, the formation of the *opinio juris* is then followed by the making of two related but separate empirical judgments which, in sum, affirm the factual observance or non-observance of the desired pattern of conduct: do States, both those that formed the *opinio juris* (S_1, S_2, S_3, S_4, ...) and those that did not (S_5, S_6, S_7 ...), actually follow the pattern of conduct in question? The motives for compliance or non-compliance are not, as such, relevant to this question; but the magnitude and extent of the compliance by States (in addition to other recognized pre-conditions, such as the absence of duress, fraud or mistake in securing such compliance, etc.) will determine the making of the second-order practical judgments: the legal judgments represented by PJ_1 and PJ_2: that a customary rule requiring or permitting the conduct in question has emerged (or is emerging); this rule is, in essence, a crystallization of the expectations generated by the initial *opinio juris*, PJ_0, and buttressed by the subsequent convergent practice of States encapsulated in the related empirical judgments EJ_1 and EJ_2. The State(s) making the legal judgment PJ_2 may include those that participated in the PJ_0 and/or the EJ_1 and EJ_2 and those that did not participate (S_8, S_9, S_{10} ...S_i). Thus, we see that (as most international lawyers would agree) the recognition of the binding nature of a customary rule by a particular State need not depend upon the participation by that State in the customary practice upon which the rule is based, nor in the *opinio juris* which preceded the practice in question. Conversely, the participation by a State in the *opinio juris* need not imply that the State already recognizes the conduct which follows that *opinio juris*, and forms the basis of an authoritative rule, as binding upon it prior to the making of the legal judgments in PJ_1 and PJ_2.[65]

Finally, the legal judgment PJ_2 operates as a preliminary step to the making of a further, third-level, empirical judgment, EJ_3: recognition of the fact that States generally *accept* the rule that...(etc.). But for the international lawyer, the crucial judgment is the last one in the schema: JJ_1 is a juristic judgment which asserts or records the observation that according to (a rule of) international law, such and such conduct is required or permitted...(etc.). This is a judgment that may be made by someone, a neutral jurist, by way of stating what is the case from the point of view of the States which recognize the existence of the rule in question. Whether or not the neutral jurist (a textbook writer or a legal adviser, for example) accepts or rejects the existence of the alleged rule may be quite irrelevant, unless he or she is under a judicial duty (for example, as a judge) to pronounce authoritatively upon the existence (and validity) of the alleged rule.

The interpretation of Finnis's schema briefly sketched out here is not, as such, a wholly original conceptual or jurisprudential insight into the central issue discussed in this paper, the analysis of the notion of *opinio juris*. Of course, this interpretation essentially adopts Finnis's own suggested lines of analysis, but it attempts to elaborate on some of the assumptions which may only be implicit in the schema itself. It is the view here that if interpreted along the lines suggested above, Finnis's analysis would provide a much clearer solution to the jurisprudential conundrum posed by the vexed question of custom-formation in international law, and the role, indeed the meaning, of *opinio juris*, in this process.[66]

In the context of the international community, custom works, or can only work, as a method of creating normative rules if there is prior agreement in the community that custom provides an acceptable method of generating such normative rules, as a legitimate substitute for an authoritative leader, for the common good of the international community. This is what in Walden's analysis is referred to as "the formula that practice treated by States as a legal standard of behaviour will generate customary law"; Finnis terms this "a suppressed practical premiss" or "a meta-legal or framework principle". As already intimated above, the acceptance of such a formula or framework principle itself by the international community can only be presumed on the basis of a prior customary practice or rule. To say this is not to import into the debate concerning custom-formation further paradoxes or circularity of logic, no more than Hart's postulate of a master rule of recognition or Kelsen's *Grundnorm* imply paradoxical reasoning in their respective theories of law and legal system.

Notes

1. See, for example, E.K.M. Yakpo's "Editorial Comment" in *1 African J Int'l & Comp L* (1989) p. xiv, where he questions the relevance and usefulness of such concepts and terminology as "customary law", "African customary law", and so on, in modern legal discourse. For other fairly recent critical studies on African customary law, in particular, see M. Chanock, *Law, Custom and Social Order: the colonial experience in Malawi and Zambia* (1985) *passim*; I. Hamnett, *Chieftainship and Legitimacy: an anthropological study of executive law in Lesotho*, (1975) pp. 9–16; see also T.W. Bennett, *A Sourcebook of African Customary Law for Southern Africa*, (1991), especially Ch. 1 and the literature cited therein; see also S. Roberts, "Introduction: Some Notes on African Customary Law", *28 JAL 1* (1984);

M. Mamdani, *Citizen and Subject: Contemporary Africa and the Legacy of Late Colonialism*, (1996) pp. 109–137.

2. See J. Finnis, *Natural Law and Natural Rights*, (1980) p. 238.

3. Among the more recent works devoted to discussions of the sources of international law in general are: G.J.H. van Hoof, *Rethinking the Sources of International Law*, (1983); M. Bos, A *Methodology of International Law*, (1986) *passim*; R. Kearney, "Sources of Law and the International Court of Justice", in L. Gross (Ed.), *The Future of the International Court of Justice*, Vol. II, (1967); R. Pathak, "The General Theory of Sources of Contemporary International Law", *19 Indian J Int'l L 483* (1979); also G. Tunkin, "General Theory of Sources of International Law", *ibid.* at pp. 474–482. As regards custom as a source of international law, see G.M. Danilenko, "The Theory of International Customary Law", 31 GYIL 10 (1988); A. D'Amato, *The Concept of Custom in International Law*, (1971); M. Akehurst, "Custom as a Source of International Law", 47 BYIL 1 (1974–1975); H. Mosler, *The International Society as a Legal Community*, (1980) especially Ch. VI; H. Thirlway, *International Customary Law and Codification*, (1972); W. M. Reisman, "The cult of custom in the late 20th century", *17 Calif W Int'l L.J. 133* (1987); M. Bos, "Prolegomena to the identification of custom in International Law", in *Essays on International and Comparative Law: In Honour of Judge Erades*, (Presented by the Board of the Netherlands International Law Review, 1983); K. Skubiszewski, "Elements of Custom and the Hague Court", *31 Zaö RV 810* (1971); T.S. Rao, "International Custom", *19 Indian J Int'l L 515* (1979); O. Elias, "The Nature of the Subjective Element in Customary International Law", *44 ICLQ 501* (1995); see also M. Lobo de Souza, "The Role of State Consent in the Customary Process", *44 ICLQ 521* (1995). For some earlier views see K. Wolfke, *Custom in Present International Law*, (1964); L. Kopelmanas, "Custom as a Means of the Creation of Customary International Law", *18 BYIL 127* (1937).

4. A. Allott, "The people as law-makers: custom, practice, and public opinion as sources of law in Africa and England", *21 JAL 1* (1977) at p. 5.

5. L. Oppenheim, *International Law*, Vol.1, (8th ed., H. Lauterpacht, 1955) p. 26.

6. C. Parry, *Sources and Evidences of International Law*, (1965) p. 62.

7. M. Bos, A *Methodology of International Law*, (1986) p. 62. See also Mosler, *op. cit.* note 3 *supra* p. 107.

8. For a summary of these views, see discussion in Bos, *ibid*. As has been noted by Danilenko, for example, the traditional interpretation of *opinio juris* was influenced by various natural law theories according to which law in general, and international law in particular, emerges and operates independently of any formal

sources. According to this approach, *opinio juris* was defined as the feeling or belief that a given practice corresponds to an already existing legal obligation, and its traditional function was thus to draw a distinction between legally binding customary norms and other social norms, such as comity, in the process of ascertaining and applying international law. See Danilenko, *op. cit.* note 3 *supra*, p. 31.

9. ILC Yrbk, Vol. II, (1950) p. 26.

10. H. Kelsen, "Théorie du droit international coutumier", *1 Revue Int'l de la Théorie de Droit 253* (1939) 263 *et seq*.

11. Finnis, *op. cit.* note 2 *supra*, p. 238; see especially Ch. V for Finnis's account of the requirements of practical reasonableness. See also same author's "Human Good(s) and Practical Reasoning", *58 Proceedings of the Amer Cath Phil Assoc 23* (1984).

12. *Ibid.* p. 238.

13. *Ibid.*

14. See note 5 *supra*, p. 26.

15. 1969 ICJ Rep. 3 at p. 44. See also the Court's pronouncements in the *Military and Paramilitary Activities In and Against Nicaragua* case (*Nicaragua* v *United States*), 1986 ICJ Rep. 14 *passim*.

16. Parry, *op. cit.* p. 61 (Emphasis added).

17. J.L. Kunz, "The Nature of Customary International Law", 47 AJIL 662 (1953) *passim*. See also Akehurst, note 3 *supra*, who observes at p. 32: "However, the traditional approach gives rise to difficulties. It seems to require that States must believe that something is *already* law before it can *become* law".

18. See Thirlway, *op. cit.* p. 47.

19. K. Strupp, "Les Reglès Générales du Droit de la Paix", *47 Hague Recueil 263* (1934).

20. See, for example, B. Cheng, "United Nations Resolutions on Outer Space: 'Instant' International Customary Law?", *5 Indian J Int'l L 23* (1965) at p. 36, where he argues: "[Consequently] international customary law has in reality only one constitutive element, the *opinio juris* [which] in appropriate cases can be found in General Assembly resolutions". See also same author's "Custom: The Future of General State Practice in a Divided World", in R. St. J. Macdonald & D.M. Johnston (Eds.), *The Structure and Process of International Law: Essays in Legal Philosophy, Doctrine and Theory*, (1983) p. 513 at 531. Although the International

Court of Justice did acknowledge, in the *Military and Paramilitary Activities In and Against Nicaragua* case (*Nicaragua* v *United States*), the possibility that *opinion juris* may be deduced from the attitude of States towards certain General Assembly resolutions, it clearly did not adopt the view that there can be *opinio juris* leading to the creation of custom (i.e. a binding customary norm) in the absence of accompanying usage or practice (*usus*). Rather, at various points in its judgment, the Court observed that "the mere fact that States declare their recognition of certain rules is not sufficient for the Court to consider these as being customary international law", and that "the *opinio juris* [must] be confirmed by practice". See 1986 I.C.J. Rep. 14 at pp. 97–98.

21. See van Hoof, *op. cit.* pp. 85–87.

22. See Kelsen, note 10 *supra.*

23. Kunz, *op. cit.* p. 667.

24. K.V. Raman, "Toward a General Theory of International Customary Law", in M. Reisman and B.H. Weston (Eds.), *Toward World Order and Human Dignity*, (1976) p. 365 at 367.

25. M.E. Villiger, *Customary International Law and Treaties*, (1985) p. 29; see also Thirlway, *op. cit.* p. 47; *supra.*

26 D'Amato, *op. cit.* note 3 *supra*; A. Verdross, "Entstenhungsweisen und Geltungsgrund des universellen volkerrechtlichen Geworhnheitsrechts", *29 Zaö RV 635* (1969); H. Meijers, "How is international law made? – The stages of growth of international law and the use of its customary rules", *19 NYIL 3* (1978); R. Walden, "Customary International Law: A Jurisprudential Analysis", *13 Israel L. R.* 866 (1978).

27. *Ibid.* pp. 6–10.

28. *Ibid.* p. 85.

29. *Ibid.*

30. See D'Amato, "Custom and Treaty: A Response to Professor Weisburd", *21 Vand. J. Transnat'l L. 459* (1988) at p. 471.

31. Verdross, *op. cit.* note 26 *supra*; also quoted in Villiger, *op. cit.* pp. 29–30.

32. Meijers, *op. cit.* note 26 *supra*, pp. 5–7. A similar, but much earlier, "three-stages" theory was presented by I. MacGibbon in his "Customary International Law and Acquiescence", *33 BYIL 115* (1957).

33. Meijers, *ibid.* p. 7.

34. R.A. Mullerson, "Sources of International Law: New Tendencies in Soviet Thinking", 83 *AJIL* 494 (1989) at p. 501.

35. *Ibid.* p. 502.

36. *Ibid.* Mullerson thus conclusively rejects the categorical assertion by Erickson that Soviet scholars reject *opinio juris*; see also, generally, Danilenko, *op. cit.* note 3 *supra*, and his excellent account of the concept of *opinio juris* at pp. 31–36; cf. R. Erickson, *International Law and the Revolutionary State*, (1972) p. 35.

37. Mullerson, *op. cit.* pp. 502–503.

38 Walden, *op. cit.* note 26 *supra*; see also same author's "The Subjective Element in the Formation of Customary International Law", *12 Israel L. R. 344* (1977).

39. H.K.A. Hart, *The Concept of Law*, (1961) pp. 54–55.

40. These are: (i) the rule of recognition, which provides criteria for conclusive identification of the rules of the legal system; (ii) rules of change, which confer public or private powers upon officials or persons at large to enact, abrogate or alter the incidence of the primary rules; (iii) and rules of adjudication, empowering authorities to determine the violations of all the other rules, and the procedures and penalties to be applied in such adjudicatory processes. See Hart, *ibid.* pp. 89–96.

41. Walden, *op. cit.* note *supra*, p. 91.

42. *Ibid.*

43. *Ibid.* p. 97.

44. On the question of the shifting of the evidential burden of proof see, for example, the *Lotus* case (*France* v *Turkey*), 1927 PCIJ Rep., Ser. A, No. 10.

45. It must be borne in mind here that Finnis's discussion of custom-formation in international law and his analysis of the notion of *opinio juris* is only a small aspect of his larger discussion of "authority" and other related concepts: "community" and "law". His principal work, *Natural Law and Natural Rights*, cited in note 2 *supra*, is concerned with rather more profound philosophical objectives. First, to present St. Thomas Aquinas's natural law theory in a way that avoids the standard objections which have beset the theory since the eighteenth century, and in a way that also rectifies some of the deficiencies in St. Thomas Aquinas's own theory. Second, the book also aims at retrieving that systematic core of natural law theory in a way that is not only consonant with the older tradition, but is also persuasive to contemporary moral and legal philosophers. For a full-length critique of the new natural law theory advanced by Finnis and Germain Grisez see R. Hittinger,

A Critique of the New Natural Law Theory, (1987); see also the deconstructionist critique by C. Douzinas & R. Warrington, "On Deconstruction of Jurisprudence: Fin(n)is Philosophiae", in P. Fitzpatrick & A. Hunt (Eds.), *Critical Legal Studies*, (1987) pp. 33–46.

46. Finnis, *op. cit.*, especially Ch. IX. Statements which express practical and/or empirical judgments are species of "normative statements" or what Joseph Raz terms "existential statements about norms"; see J. Raz, *Practical Reasons and Norms*, (1975) pp. 80, 171–177.

47. Raz, *ibid.* pp. 35–48; 58–73.

48. Finnis, *op. cit.* p. 243.

49. *Ibid.*

50. *Ibid.*

51. Among these cases are: *Asylum* case (*Colombia* v *Peru*), 1950 ICJ Rep. 266; *Anglo-Norwegian Fisheries* case (*United Kingdom* v *Norway*) 1951 ICJ Rep. 116; *Lotus* case (*France* v *Turkey*), 1927 PCIJ Rep., Ser. A, No. 10; *North Sea Continental Shelf* cases (*Federal Republic of Germany* v *Denmark*; *Federal Republic of Germany* v *The Netherlands*), 1969 ICJ Rep. 3; *Military and Paramilitary Activities In and Against Nicaragua* case (*Nicaragua* v *United States*), 1986 ICJ Rep. 14; *Right of Passage over Indian Territory* case (*Portugal* v *India*), 1960 ICJ Rep. 6. For a discussion of the treatment of custom by the World Court in these and other cases, see P. Haggenmacher, "*La doctrine des deux éléments du droit coutumier dans la pratique de la Cour internationale*", 90 R.G.D.I.P. 5 (1980).

52. R. Cotterrell, *The Politics of Jurisprudence: A Critical Introduction to Legal Philosophy*, (1989) p. 146.

53. *Ibid.*

54. Finnis, *op. cit.* pp. 85–90.

55. Finnis *op. cit.* p. 92. But see Hittinger, *op. cit.* pp. 46–47, where he questions the assertion that all the seven basic goods are equally self-evident; thus he observes (at p. 46): "In the case of the good of knowledge, the self-referential method is cogent; from a philosophical standpoint that regards itself as a natural law method, it is certainly more cogent than anthropological surveys. Nonetheless, it is significant that Finnis makes no effort to account for the other six basic goods or principles in this fashion. Reason, after all, is transparently present in any conscious pursuit".

56. Finnis, *ibid.* p. 88.

57. *Ibid.* p. 147.

58. Cotterrell, *op. cit.* p. 148.

59. Finnis, *op. cit.* p. 148.

60. *Ibid.* p. 153.

61. Cotterrell, *op. cit.* p. 148.

62. Finnis, *op. cit.* p. 244.

63. F. Williams, *Some Aspects of International Law*, (1939) p. 44.

64. This interpretation of *opinio juris* is not too far removed from Thirlway's, who characterizes it thus: "[The] requirement of *opinion juris* is equivalent to the need for the practice in question to have been accompanied by either a sense of conforming with the law, or *the view that the practice was potentially law, as suited to the needs of the international community*". See work cited in note 3 *supra* at pp. 53–54. (Emphasis added). But cf. Akehurst, *op. cit.* p. 37: "It is important to note, however, that *opinio juris* is to be found in assertions that something is already law, not in statements that it ought to be law, or that it is required by morality, courtesy, comity, social needs, etc".

65. Cf. the observations by Akehurst, *ibid.*: "The traditional view [implies] that *opinio juris* consists of the *genuine* beliefs of States. It is submitted, however, that a statement by a State about the content of customary law should be taken as *opinio juris* even if the State does not believe in the truth of the statement". It is quite clear that the major factor which inclines Akehurst to this conclusion is simply the practical difficulty of having to prove that a particular State did or did not believe in the truth of its statements.

66. This discussion has been concerned with the question of custom as a source of law, and more specifically the role of *opinio juris* in the generation of rules among States. In his fairly recent work, *The Power of Legitimacy Among Nations*, (1990), Thomas Franck discusses the concept of legitimacy, and provides a taxonomy of factors that contribute to, and explain, "rule legitimacy" in the international legal order. Thus, although the book is not about the sources of international law as such, there is much in this work that is of pertinence and relevance to the debate about rule-creation in the international community and the normative basis of State behaviour.

2

SITUATING INTERNATIONAL LAW IN MUNICIPAL LEGAL SYSTEMS IN AFRICA

Introduction

The Constitution of the Republic of South Africa of 1996[1] expressly provides for the incorporation of both treaties and customary international law into the municipal law of South Africa, under Sections 231 and 232 respectively. In so doing, it largely confirms the innovative approach which had earlier been embodied in Sections 231(3) and 231(4) of the interim Constitution of 1993. It also reaffirms in Section 39(1) the role of international law, previously provided for in Section 35(1) of the interim Constitution, in the interpretation of the fundamental rights and freedoms enshrined in Chapter 2 of the Constitution (the Bill of Rights). As I have observed elsewhere[2], these constitutional provisions are almost unparalleled elsewhere in Africa, at least insofar as they concern the incorporation of customary international law. For, as will be argued in this chapter, all other instances regarding the incorporation of international law in the constitutions of African States have hitherto been limited to treaties and have not embraced customary international law as such. The question of whether customary international law is thus part of the municipal law of these States is one that has had to be answered on the basis of a consideration of the competing theories relating to the relationship between international law and municipal law, there being no constitutional provisions to provide guidance on the matter. Similarly, the question of whether or not the courts may invoke international law as an aid to interpretation is one that has mostly depended on the particular rules governing statutory or constitutional interpretation in the legal systems concerned. The inclusion of express provisions in both the 1996 Constitution and the interim Constitution of 1993 relating to the status and interpretational role of international law in the South African legal system renders such theoretical considerations and arguments unnecessary.

The incorporation of general international law in national constitutions in post-colonial Africa really begins with the Namibian Constitution of 1990, which provides in Article 144 as follows:

> "Unless otherwise provided by this Constitution or Act of Parliament, the general rules of public international law and international agreements binding upon Namibia under this Constitution shall form part of the law of Namibia."

It has been persuasively argued by one writer, following similar constructions of Article 25 of the German Constitution of 1949 (the *Grundgesetz*), that the reference to "general rules of public international law" in the Namibian Constitution should be understood to include both customary rules and general principles of law.[3] By contrast, the formulation adopted in Section 231(4) of the interim Constitution of South Africa expressly provided for the incorporation of customary international law. This formulation was shortly afterwards emulated in the Constitution of Malawi of 1995, where Section 211 expressly declares both customary international law and duly ratified treaties to be part of the law of Malawi. Thus, it is possible to conclude that among the more common characteristics shared by these three Southern African constitutions is the status accorded to public international law in the respective municipal legal orders. Moreover, in the case of South Africa and Malawi, public international law has specifically been accorded a role in the interpretative process. The courts in both countries are obligated to have regard to or consider international law in interpreting the provisions of the Bill of Rights or any legislation (Sections 39(1) and 233 of the South African Constitution of 1996) or the constitution itself as a whole (Section 11(2) of the Malawian Constitution). Indeed, one outstanding feature of all these constitutions is that they are, to borrow the words of one commentator, "international law-friendly".[4]

But, of course, not all constitutions in Africa are as international law-friendly as the Malawian, Namibian and South African constitutions. In fact, altogether, only twenty-one national constitutions in the whole of Africa currently contain provisions which refer to international law, broadly speaking, or to treaties or international agreements, in particular. And, as has already been indicated, these provisions are largely concerned with the incorporation of international agreements into the corpus of the national law. The question regarding the place and role of international law in the municipal legal systems of the various African countries, and in the interpretative process, is therefore one that needs to be investigated within the specificity presented by each national constitutional scheme.

The principal aim of this chapter is two-fold: first, to explore the place or status of international law within the municipal legal systems of African countries. To what extent has international law been received as part of the law of the land in these countries? Secondly, I aim to explore the role and relevance of international law in the interpretation and application of law and legal principles in municipal legal systems in Africa. To what extent, and in what contexts, is international law regarded as a tool of interpretation by the courts? Thus, there are two separate but related questions: that of the incorporation of international law into municipal law, and the question of international law as an aid to statutory and constitutional interpretation.

In a sense, the exercise being undertaken here can modestly be said to be part of the debate among international legal scholars regarding the relationship between international law and municipal law in the various States in Africa. Although the debate is not as such new, it has a particular relevance and currency for African States, especially given the fact that the last five years or so have witnessed the emergence of new constitutional democracies on the African continent.[5] In the legal and judicial fields, a common concern has been with the role of international human rights law in the interpretation and protection of the various fundamental rights and freedoms now generally enshrined in the constitutions of these new multi-party democracies. In the first place, I intend to examine the relationship between international law and municipal law in general. I will then provide a brief comparative overview of the constitutional provisions of a number of African States which can be regarded as representing the two major legal cultures or traditions of the continent: the common law and civil law systems. It will be argued that the various approaches to the relationship between international law and municipal law in the respective countries reflect the traditional approaches adopted by courts and constitutions in the former metropolitan colonial powers on whose legal cultures and traditions the post-colonial African legal systems are largely based. Where a national constitution specifically provides for the incorporation of international law into the municipal law of the country, as in the case of South Africa, all these questions resolve themselves, and the only issue for concern might be the extent to which the courts are sufficiently conversant with the relevant substantive rules of international law to be able to import them into the judicial process in interpreting and applying the law. However, it will also be shown that even although some of these States have not accorded international law any explicit role in their constitutional schemes, they have nevertheless developed a constitutional jurisprudence which takes account of the relevant norms of public international law in the interpretation not only of constitutionally protected rights, but of the law and legal principles in general.

This discussion does not pretend to be a comprehensive account of the legal position in all African States. Such an undertaking would be quite monumental, and in any case one that cannot be accomplished within the scope of the present discussion. The treatment here is thus purposefully selective. I propose to devote particular attention to the judicial developments in the Southern African region, for two major reasons. First, as already indicated above, it is in this region that the incorporation of international law into national constitutions has been most manifest. Second, it is also here that courts have begun to develop a jurisprudence that actively draws upon international law, especially international human rights law, in the process of interpreting and applying the respective constitutions and other legislation affecting the fundamental rights and freedoms of individuals in these countries.[6] In essence, this is only an exploratory survey.

International Law and Municipal Law

The Theoretical Issue

The major propositions regarding the relationship between international law and municipal law are reflected in the opposing doctrines commonly known as the monist and dualist theories.[7] It is not necessary to give a detailed account of these well-known theories here, or to trace their historical and philosophical origins, except to make the following brief observations.

Advocates of monism see all law as a unified body of rules; and since international law is law, it is regarded as being automatically part of this corpus of rules. In this scheme of things, international law and municipal law are thus related parts of the same legal structure. It is generally agreed that monism had its origins in the medieval unity of western Europe, which at the time fell under the twin hegemony of Pope and Emperor, and in the natural law philosophy of the Scholastics, which proposed an ultimate authority for all law. Monism was subsequently embraced by both Kantian philosophy and Kelsenian positivism. Dualists, on the other hand, building upon Hegel's theory of state, argue that while municipal law is a manifestation of sovereign will directed internally, international law is a manifestation of sovereign will directed externally; thus, the two legal orders are separate, not only in origin but also in purpose. Monist theory, proceeding as it does on the postulate of the hierarchical order of legal norms, asserts the supremacy of international law in both international and municipal spheres. Dualism, on the other hand, proclaims that the question of which of the two separate legal orders should prevail over the other is relative, depending on the forum in which the matter arises, whether it is a domestic court or an international tribunal. As a general rule, dualists accord international law primacy over municipal law in the international sphere, while municipal law has primacy over international law in the municipal sphere. Simply put, dualists take the view that international law can never be assumed to be automatically part of municipal law.

However, it must be cautioned that the standard treatment of these opposing doctrines in most treatises on the subject is apt to misrepresent the picture. For example, the neat characterization of the two approaches as, respectively, natural law and positivist approaches, can be challenged. In fact, as some authorities have rightly pointed out, the antithesis between monist and dualist approaches to the relationship between international and municipal law is something that must be viewed with some caution. Moreover, these theories must be approached with three general observations in mind.[8]

First of all, it should be emphasized that the effect of international law generally, and that of treaties in particular, will for the most part depend on a rule of municipal law. The fundamental principle in almost all legal systems is that the internal application of treaties is governed by domestic constitutional law. Secondly, between the extreme versions of monism, on the one hand, and dualism, on the other, as opposing approaches or doctrines there lies, in reality, a whole range of intermediate relationships which do not lend themselves to easy labelling. Alternative doctrines have even been proposed to describe these intermediate positions, for example the so-called radical monism, inverted monism and harmonization theories.[9] Finally, it has also been suggested that a facile distinction between monist and dualist systems may conceal the fact that the practice of the courts even in monist systems may fail to give effect to treaties which are binding under international law. Conversely, in dualist systems the courts may sometimes give limited effect even to unincorporated treaties, by applying to their domestic legislation the principle that such legislation should, wherever possible, be so construed as not to conflict with the international obligations of the State.[10] In any event, most scholars are of the view that the two theories alluded to above – monism and dualism – are of relevance only in the specific context of *customary* international law. In the final analysis, the more pertinent question is not so much the theoretical argument between monists and dualists, but the more practical one: under what circumstances should a municipal court apply international law to solve a problem or as an aid to interpretation?[11]

English Common Law and Civil Law Approaches

The practice of African States regarding the incorporation of international law into municipal law, or the use of international law as an aid in the interpretation and application of law and legal principles, has partly been determined by their respective colonial experiences and the inherited colonial legal cultures and systems. Thus, one notices an immediate distinction between the approach followed by countries falling within the English common law tradition, namely the former British colonies, and those belonging to the civil law tradition. In the latter category, one can place the former colonies of the continental European powers: France, Germany, Portugal and Spain.

As is well known, under the British practice, which has traditionally influenced judicial approaches in Anglophone Africa, because of the shared common law experience and perceptions, the relationship between international law and municipal law depends on whether what is involved is a rule of customary international law or treaty law[12]. As regards treaty law, English courts have consistently held that a treaty concluded by the United Kingdom does not become part of the municipal law except and insofar as it is made so by Parliament, since, under the unwritten British Constitution, an Act of Parliament is paramount over any other source of law, including even the common law. There is a general presumption, however, that Parliament does not intend to violate international law; thus, whenever possible, British statutes are interpreted in such a way as to be in harmony with international law, including treaty obligations. The ruling by Banda CJ in the Malawian case of *Chakufwa Chihana* v *The Republic*[13] exemplifies Commonwealth African practice in this regard. The Malawian Supreme Court had been called upon to consider, *inter alia*, the question of whether or not the African Charter on Human and Peoples' Rights was part of the law of Malawi. Malawi had ratified the Charter on 17 November 1989, some three years prior to this case. The court pronounced that:[14]

> "Malawi may well be a signatory to the Charter but until Malawi takes legislative measures to adopt it, the Charter is not part of the municipal law of Malawi and we doubt whether in the absence of any local statute incorporating its provisions the Charter would be enforceable in our Courts."

The approach of the English courts to customary international law has been, at times, problematic and controversial. The Blackstonian doctrine of incorporation, that "[the] law of nations, wherever any problem arises which is properly the object of its jurisdiction, is here adopted in its full extent by the common law, and is held to be part of the law of the land"[15], has never been consistently and universally accepted by the English courts. One approach follows the doctrine of full incorporation: rules of international law are automatically part of English law unless they are in conflict with an Act of Parliament. The opposing approach holds to the doctrine of transformation: rules of international law are not to be considered part of English law unless they have been specifically adopted by decisions of judges, long established custom or an Act of Parliament. A long line of cases stretching back two and a half centuries, from the early case of *Buvot* v *Barbuit*[16], decided in 1735, to Lord Denning's more recent rulings in *R* v *Immigration Officer, Ex Parte Thakrar*[17] and *Trendtex Trading Corporation v Central Bank of Nigeria*[18], reveals that the courts have vacillated between the two doctrines. Indeed, Lord Denning's own diametrically opposed decisions in these two cases, handed down within three years of each other, best exemplify the equivocal and uncertain approach of the English courts. Having advocated the transformation doctrine in *Thakrar*, the learned judge made a complete *volte face* in *Trendtex*, now accepting the doctrine of incorporation as the more correct approach.[19]

In Anglophone Africa, on the few occasions when domestic courts have been seized with the question, they have tended to follow the approach currently favoured by the English courts at the material time. Thus, the courts in Ghana and Uganda, for example, have adopted the incorporation doctrine in accepting the applicable rules of customary international law as part of the municipal law of those countries.[20] In South Africa, after some initial uncertainties, the courts finally settled on the incorporation approach insofar as customary international law was concerned, while employing the transformation approach in relation to treaties. In the pre-1993 Constitution era, Rumpff CJ's *dictum* in *Nduli* v *Minister of Justice* was acknowledged as authority for the proposition that customary international law formed part of South African law without any need for transformation – a position derived, according to Rumpff CJ, from the principles of Roman-Dutch law.[21] Any uncertainties that may have remained after the Nduli decision have now been cleared up by the adoption of specific constitutional provisions governing the status of both customary international law and treaties under both the interim Constitution and the 1996 Constitution.

The approach of the civil law countries is quite different from the British approach, although even within this grouping there is no uniformity as such. First, with regard to customary international law: some countries have constitutional provisions expressly stipulating that rules of general (or customary) international law are part of the municipal law of the particular

State and that they take precedence over domestic legislation. The constitutions of Italy, Germany, Greece, the Netherlands and Portugal belong to this category. Thus, Article 10 of the Italian Constitution of 1947 partly provides that "the Italian [legal] system conforms to generally recognized principles of international law". Courts in Italy have interpreted this provision to mean that customary international law forms part of Italian law. It has been pointed out that acceptance of this harmonization of international law and municipal law, in fact, pre-dates the 1947 Constitution.[22] Article 25 of the German Constitution of 1949 provides as follows:

> "The general rules of international law shall be an integral part of federal law. They shall override laws and directly establish rights and obligations for the inhabitants of the federal territory."

As was noted above, the expression "general rules of international law" is regarded as embracing customary international law (in addition to other sources of international law, such as general principles of law), and thus rendering it part of German law.[23]

French practice regarding the relationship between customary international law and municipal law is the most relevant here, since the courts in Francophone Africa squarely follow the approach of the French courts on this matter. The starting point is Paragraph 14(1) of the Preamble to the French Constitution of 1946, which reads: "The French Republic, faithful to its traditions, abides by the rules of international public law". The Preamble to the Constitution of 1958 subsequently reaffirmed this commitment by declaring that it "[solemnly] proclaims its attachment to [the] principles of national sovereignty as defined by the Declaration of 1789, reaffirmed and complemented by the Preamble of the Constitution of 1946". After surveying a number of French decisions pre-dating the 1946 Constitution, O'Connell rightly concluded that:[24]

> "It would seem that the proclamation of adherence to the rules of international public law in 1946 is descriptive of the attitude of municipal courts. French judges have never doubted that they were bound to apply rules of customary international law whenever appropriate, although no constitutional rule enjoined them to do so."

This continues to be the case today, as the more recent studies by Carreau, Dinh and Favoreu, among other writers, amply testify.[25] Understandably, other sources of international law do not receive as much attention in decided cases as the law derived from treaties. However, as one writer has observed, at least "[customary] international law is often referred to by the *juge judiciaire*, particularly where the rule is certain (as in questions of diplomatic immunity, the immunity of foreign states from jurisdiction and execution, and the international law of the sea)".[26] Furthermore, although French courts acknowledge the supremacy of the legislative will, as do courts in other countries, they have always endeavoured to construe such legislative will as not being in conflict with international law. In other words, when interpreting the law, Parliament is presumed not to intend to violate international law or France's international legal obligations.[27]

The incorporation of treaties into municipal law in civil law countries is also generally governed by specific constitutional provisions. Some national constitutions, notably those of France and Spain, provide that treaties to which the State concerned is a party, and which have been duly ratified or approved, shall have the force of law even if they are in conflict with domestic legislation. Article 55 of the French Constitution of 1958 contains what has become the prototypical provision in this regard. The formulation employed therein has been adopted verbatim in the constitutions of almost all the former French colonies in Africa which contain a clause relating to this issue. It reads:[28]

> "Treaties or agreements duly ratified or approved shall, upon their publication, have an authority superior to that of [domestic] legislation, subject, for each agreement or treaty, to [reciprocal] application by the other party."

In commenting upon this provision, De la Rochere has made the pertinent observation that the French Constitution recognizes three kinds of treaties or agreements: those subject to ratification with legislative approval; those subject to ratification without the need for legislative approval; and, finally, those needing publication. He further notes that to become applicable, an international agreement needs only one formality, publication; and that this requirement is liberally construed, since French law sometimes relies on publication made by international institutions. In a sense, therefore, what publication requires is merely that the treaty or international undertaking must be brought to the notice of those affected by it, whether through the *Journal Officiel* or via some other media. As regards the other requirement of reciprocity, De la Rochere has noted that since, in reality, French courts cannot be expected to enquire into and adjudicate upon "application by the other signatory State", they exercise considerable circumspection as to the condition of reciprocity. It would be highly inappropriate for the courts in a particular State to have to pass judgment on the reciprocal application of a treaty by a fellow signatory State. This requires a factual rather than a legal judgment, and thus one for the executive authorities to make.[29]

Constitutional Incorporation of International Law in Africa

Presently, only twenty-one States in Africa have constitutions that contain provisions which relate to international law. These States may be divided into two categories.

First, there are those constitutions which incorporate international law generally. Here one records, first and foremost, the three constitutions of Malawi, Namibia and South Africa, which, as was stated at the outset, incorporate both customary international law and treaties as part of the municipal law. As has already been pointed out, Namibia has followed the German example by adopting the broad term "general rules of public international law", whereas Malawi and South Africa provide for customary international law and treaties under separate provisions. The Constitution of Cape Verde of 1992, while belonging to this category, nevertheless stands out as the only instrument which goes beyond the limited reference to treaties and customary international law. It also incorporates, in Article 11, as part of Cape Verdian internal law, "judicial acts emanating from competent offices of supranational organizations to which Cape Verde belongs", and "rules and principles of international law, validly approved and ratified internationally and nationally, and in force". This provision casts the net rather widely, and raises more questions than it answers. What, for example, is meant by "supranational organizations"? And how is one to construe phrases such as "judicial acts emanating from competent offices" and "rules and principles [validly] approved and ratified internationally [and internally]", etc.?[30] Article 11 requires both conceptual and semantic clarity.

The second and larger category consists of States which, with the exception of Ethiopia and the Democratic Republic of Congo (former Zaire), are all former French colonies. All these States have followed the French approach, including a verbatim adoption of Article 55 of the French Constitution already reproduced above, with only minor variations in the case of three States.[31] In this category are: Algeria (Article 123 of Constitution of 1989); Benin (Article 147 of Constitution of 1990); Burkina Faso (Article 151 of Constitution of 1991); Central African Republic (Article 69 of Constitution of 1995); Chad (Article 106 of Constitution of 1993); Congo (Article 176 of Constitution of 1992); Cote d'Ivoire (Article 56 of Constitution of 1960); Democratic Republic of Congo (former Zaire; Article 109 of Constitution of 1978); Djibouti (Article 37 of Constitution of 1992); Ethiopia (Article 9 of Constitution of 1994); Guinea (Article 79 of Constitution of 1990); Mali (Article 116 of Constitution of 1992); Mauritania (Article 80 of Constitution of 1991); Niger (Article 120 of Constitution of 1992); Senegal (Article 79 of Constitution of 1963); Tunisia (Article 32 of Constitution of 1996). The

Ethiopian Constitution of 1994 merely declares that all international agreements ratified by Ethiopia are an integral part of the laws of the country (Article 9(4)), without ascribing any hierarchical order as between treaties and domestic legislation. By contrast, a 1993 amendment to the Zimbabwean Constitution of 1980 adopts a typical transformation approach by providing that treaties shall not form part of the law of Zimbabwe unless they have been made part of Zimbabwean law by or under an Act of Parliament (Article 111B(1)).

As can be seen, apart from Malawi and Zimbabwe, none of the former British colonies stipulates any specific role or status for international law, whether customary or treaty. Ghana's Constitution of 1992 merely provides in Article 40(c), as one of the 'Directive Principles of State Policy', that in its dealings with other nations, the Government shall "[promote] respect for international law, treaty obligations and the settlement of international disputes by peaceful means". In the case of Malawi, the inclusion of Section 211 in the 1995 Constitution was no doubt inspired by the similarly worded Section 231 in the South African interim Constitution of 1993. It is not without coincidence that some of the constitutional experts involved in the drafting of the South African Constitution were also later involved, albeit marginally, in the earlier stages of the consultations leading to the drafting of the new constitution in Malawi.

As a general proposition, therefore, one could argue that State practice in Anglophone Africa has been one of avoiding the constitutional incorporation of international law altogether. These States have preferred to leave the matter to be determined by the common law approaches developed in the English case law.

By contrast, a good proportion of States in Francophone Africa have, as already pointed out, followed France in at least expressly incorporating treaties into the municipal law and according them a superior authority to domestic legislation under the stipulated conditions of ratification or approval, publication and reciprocity. The longest surviving constitutional provision of this nature in Francophone Africa is to be found in Article 56 of the Constitution of Cote d'Ivoire of 1960. Although the paucity of recorded court decisions and law reports does not make possible a comprehensive analysis of the judicial trends, as a general proposition it can be said that the approach by the courts in these countries towards both customary international law and treaty law has also been in line with that of the French *juge judiciaire*, as described above. In the early Moroccan case of *Ecoffard* v *Cie Air France*, the court affirmed the "[rule] according to which international law is hierarchically superior to internal law, and prevails over it in case of conflict, particularly in case of multilateral agreements relating to private law".[32] The case concerned the supremacy of the 1929 Warsaw Convention for the Unification of Certain Rules regarding Air Transport over a municipal enactment. A later example from Francophone Africa comes from Gabon. In *Re: Draft Ordinance Modifying Law 6/61 Governing Expropriation*, the Supreme Court held that according to Article 54 of the Gabonese Constitution of 1961 (modelled on Article 55 of the French Constitution) treaties have priority over any internal law or ordinance.[33] Among the former British African colonies, Sierra Leone stands alone in adopting the principle that an incorporated treaty must prevail over other municipal legislation, according to a decision handed down by the country's Court of Appeal in 1971.[34]

International Law and Constitutional Interpretation: A Southern African Perspective

From the foregoing brief survey, it is clear that the majority of African States are reluctant to incorporate international law directly into their constitutions and thereby make it an integral part of their municipal law. This reluctance, in part at least, seems to result from the perceived uncertainty of both the existence and interpretation of relevant principles of international law, especially customary international law, in certain contested situations. No doubt various other explanations may be adduced. For example, Partsch has observed:[35]

> "National judges may prefer to apply a provision of domestic law with which they are familiar instead of making considerable effort to find out whether a rule of customary international law may perhaps be in conflict with this provision."

A number of commentators have also emphasized the relevance of certain political considerations. In particular, it has been argued that account must be taken of the fact that among newly-born States there exists a certain level of mistrust of legal rules created at a time when they were not yet able to participate in the creation of international law. This argument has been particularly cogent in relation to the evolution of customary international law, largely a product of the colonial era. This was especially true of the attitude of many African and Asian States in the 1960s.[36]

The difficulty here is compounded by the fact that even those constitutions which incorporate international law (or, at least, treaties and international agreements) do not contain any interpretation clauses enjoining domestic courts to use or have regard to international law as an aid in interpreting and applying the law. But, of course, this is not to say that the courts in these countries do not pay regard to international law when faced with issues of constitutional or statutory interpretation. Reference has already been made to the presumption of statutory interpretation, that courts will not only assume that Parliament did not intend to violate international law, but that legislation will be interpreted, whenever possible, in such a way as to give it a meaning which is consistent with international law. This presumption is equally respected in common law as in civil law jurisdictions. Recourse to this presumption is going to grow as the interpretation and application of international human rights law increasingly becomes a familiar field of judicial disputation and discourse in the new constitutional orders being established in the various African States. This is already the case in Southern Africa, at least.

In fact, the Malawian Constitution of 1995 and the South African Constitution of 1996 stand out as the only constitutions on the whole continent with interpretation clauses that specifically call upon the courts to have regard to international law when deciding matters. Section 11(2) of the Malawian Constitution provides that:

> "In interpreting the provisions of this Constitution a court of law shall –
>
> (a) promote the values which underlie an open and democratic society;
>
> (b) take full account of the provisions of Chapter III and Chapter IV; and
>
> (c) where applicable, have regard to current norms of public international law and comparable foreign case law."

The similarity of the above provision to Section 35(1) of the South African interim Constitution of 1993 is immediately noticeable, but there was a subtle difference in approach between the two provisions. Under the latter, recourse to "public international law" was mandatory, whereas recourse to "foreign case law" was only permissive; under the Malawian provision, recourse to both "norms of public international law" and "foreign case law" is couched in mandatory terms. Already, the emerging jurisprudence from South Africa's Constitutional Court demonstrates how, in keeping with these new constitutional requisites, the South African judiciary can use international law as an aid in the interpretation and application of domestic legislation and the constitution itself. Although the Constitutional Court has adverted to this issue in a number of judgments, it is enough, for our purposes, to draw attention only to the two leading *dicta* in this regard. In *S v Makwanyane and Another*[37], easily the most famous and most controversial of the court's decisions to date, Chaskalson P addressed the significance of international law and comparative law, relating to the death penalty, at some length. Having noted that international and foreign authorities are of value because they analyze arguments for and against the death sentence and show how courts of other jurisdictions have dealt with this vexed issue, he went on to conclude:[38]

> "For that reason alone they require our attention. They may also have to be considered because of their relevance to Section 35(1) of the [Constitution]. In the context of Section 35(1), public international law would include binding as well as non-binding law. They may both be used under this section as tools of interpretation. International agreements and customary international law accordingly provide a framework within which Chapter 3 can be evaluated and understood, and for that purpose decisions of tribunals dealing with comparable instruments, such as the United Nations Committee on Human Rights, the Inter-American Court of Human Rights, the European Commission on Human Rights, and the European Court of Human Rights, and in appropriate cases, reports of specialized agencies such as the International Labour Organization may provide guidance as to the correct interpretation of particular provisions of Chapter 3." [References omitted.]

There can be no doubt that the scope of international law envisioned by Chaskalson P in the above statement encompasses not only the "hard" law of customary rules, treaty provisions and judicial decisions, but also the "soft" law contained in resolutions, declarations and guidelines drawn up by appropriate international bodies. It also encompasses international law not binding on South Africa. This apparently liberal approach is, however, tempered with the caveat that:[39]

> "In dealing with comparative law, we must bear in mind that we are required to construe the South African Constitution, and not an international instrument or the constitution of some foreign country, and that this has to be done with due regard to our legal system, our history and circumstances, and the structure and language of our own Constitution. We can derive assistance from public international law and foreign case law, but we are in no way bound to follow it." [Reference omitted.]

Perhaps this is as it should be, although it may respectfully be argued that this approach unfortunately seems to collapse *international* law and *comparative* law into one and the same thing. The South African judiciary needs to be more careful in drawing a distinction between international law and foreign case law or comparative law. The *dictum* by Mohamed DP in the Constitutional Court's later decision in *Azanian Peoples Organization (AZAPO) and Others* v *President of the Republic of South Africa and Others* reiterated the court's acceptance of international law as a tool of interpretation. He stated thus (although, arguably, the Court's treatment of the relevant substantive rules and principles of international law *in casu* was misconceived):[40]

> "International law and the contents of international treaties to which South Africa might or might not be a party at any particular time are, in my view, relevant only in the interpretation of the Constitution itself, on the grounds that the lawmakers of the Constitution should not lightly be presumed to authorise any law which might constitute a breach of the obligations of the state in terms of international law."

In any case, the role of international law in the interpretative process has now been given constitutional reaffirmation under the South African Constitution of 1996. Section 39(1), the clause governing the interpretation of the Bill of Rights, provides that:

> "When interpreting the Bill of Rights, a court, tribunal or forum –
>
> (a) must promote the values that underlie an open and democratic society based on human dignity, equality and freedom;
>
> (b) must consider international law; and
>
> (c) may consider foreign law."

In addition, Section 233, the general interpretation clause, goes on to provide as follows:

> "When interpreting any legislation, every court must prefer any reasonable interpretation of legislation that is consistent with international law over any alternative interpretation that is inconsistent with international law."

Sections 11(2) of the Malawian Constitution and Sections 39(1) and 233 of the South African Constitution all strengthen the role of international law in the interpretative process since they require the courts to apply international law where it is applicable. In fact, as one commentator has rightly noted, in one respect, Section 39(1) extends the interpretational role of international law even further than that contained in the interim Constitution, since it requires not only "courts" but other "tribunal(s)" and "forum(s)" to consider international law in interpreting the Bill of Rights.[41] Almost every provision in the Bills of Rights in the two respective constitutions has some corresponding provision in one international human rights convention or another, or is governed by general principles of international law; thus, it would be difficult to conceive of any situations in which public international law would not be applicable under these provisions. And since the reference in these provisions is to "[public] international law" in the broad sense of the term, it may be concluded that in interpreting these constitutions (or any other legislation, in the case of South Africa) courts are therefore required to have regard to international law contained in general treaties, custom, general principles of law, the writings of publicists and the decisions of international and municipal courts. In brief, recourse will be had to all the sources of international law enumerated in Article 38(1) of the Statute of the International Court of Justice.

The new constitutions in Malawi and South Africa provide the courts with an opportunity to develop a constitutional jurisprudence in which international law will play a major part. In fact, whenever courts in these countries employ international law in constitutional and statutory interpretation, they will be following the precedents already established by other courts in the Southern African sub-continent. The following examples will suffice.

The question of relying upon international law was canvassed by the Court of Appeal in Botswana in *Attorney General of Botswana* v *Unity Dow*[42]. The court *a quo* had relied upon the international legal obligations incumbent upon Botswana in support of its decision that sex-based discrimination was prohibited by the Botswana Constitution. The appellant objected to this reliance upon international conventions, *inter alia*, the African Charter on Human and Peoples' Rights, The European Convention on Human Rights, and the Convention on the Elimination of All Forms of Discrimination against Women] some of which had not even been ratified by Botswana at the time of the hearing. However, Amissah JP held:[43]

> "Even if it is accepted that those treaties and conventions do not confer enforceable rights on individuals within the state until Parliament has legislated its [*sic*] provisions into the law of the land, in so far as such relevant international treaties and conventions may be referred to as an aid to the construction of an enactment, including the Constitution, I find myself at a loss to understand the complaint made against their use in that manner in interpretation of what no doubt are some difficult provisions of the Constitution. The reference made by the learned judge *a quo* to these materials amounted to no more than that."

A similar approach had been taken by the same court (per Aguda JA) in an earlier case, *S* v *Petrus and Another*[44]. The Supreme Court of Zimbabwe has also had occasion to examine similar issues and arguments, starting with the case of *A Juvenile* v *State*[45], which considered the constitutionality of imposing corporal punishment upon a juvenile. Furthermore, the constitutionality of corporal punishment in schools was also considered. The court held that the imposition of corporal punishment on school children was degrading, and in violation of section 15(1), which forms part of Chapter 3 (sections 11–26, styled the "Declaration of Rights") of the Constitution of Zimbabwe. However, it is interesting to note that in his judgment Dumbutshena CJ invoked the jurisprudence of the European Court of Human Rights as an aid to interpreting not only the constitutional provision in Zimbabwe, but also Article 5 of the African Charter on Human and Peoples' Rights, to which Zimbabwe is a party. The wording of this article is virtually identical to that of Article 3 of the European Convention on Human Rights and section 15(1) of the Constitution of Zimbabwe.

Another case which confirms this emerging regional jurisprudence also concerned the constitutionality of corporal punishment. In *Ex Parte Attorney-General, Namibia: In Re Corporal Punishment by Organs of State,*[46] the question was whether or not corporal punishment was constitutional under Article 8(2)(b) of the Namibian Constitution. This article provides that "no persons shall be subject to torture or to cruel, inhuman or degrading treatment or punishment". Mohamed AJA, as he then was, relied, in part, on Article 3 of the European Convention on Human Rights (as well as on provisions in other national constitutions and on the Zimbabwean case law) in order to establish that corporal punishment is now widely regarded as a violation of human rights.[47]

It bears pointing out that in all these cases the courts were only too ready to use, as an aid to the interpretation of fundamental rights entrenched in national constitutions, international human rights norms located in a regional convention to which the respective States concerned are not parties (and can never be, given the geographical scope of the convention in question). As has been noted above, Chaskalson P's judgment in the *Makwanyane* case suggests that the Constitutional Court is already inclined towards this wider construction of international law. There have been instructive decisions from outside the Southern African region as well. One example is the Tanzanian case of *Ephraim* v *Pastory and Another.*[48] Here, the High Court of Tanzania had occasion to invoke international human rights law, in the form of the provisions of the Convention on the Elimination of All Forms of Discrimination Against Women, the International Covenant on Civil and Political Rights, and the African Charter on Human and Peoples' Rights, to determine, *inter alia,* whether a Haya customary law which denied women, but not men, the right to sell clan land was compatible with the guarantee of equality and non-discrimination enshrined in Articles 13(4) and 13(5) of the Tanzanian Constitution. At the time of the hearing, Tanzania was a party to all these treaties, although none of them had been incorporated into Tanzanian municipal law. The court nevertheless declined to uphold the alleged customary law, holding that such a law was inconsistent not only with the country's constitution but also with international law.

Conclusion

Some commentators have recently suggested that there is a correlation between democracy within States and their peace- and international-law-oriented foreign policy[49]. Writing a little earlier, in 1985, Cassese had conjured up another, related correlation between the efforts to establish democracy following the defeat of authoritarian and undemocratic systems in wars or revolutions, on the one hand, and "the opening of state constitutions" to the international community generally and international law in particular, on the other[50]. Cassese perceived four historic stages in this process: the first extending from 1887 to the First World War; the second, from the Weimar Constitution of 1919 to the Second World War; the third, from the French Constitution of 1946 to the late 1950s; and the fourth commencing in the early 1960s.[51] To this correlative scheme, Stein has proposed a fifth stage: the era of post-communist constitution-making in Central-Eastern Europe[52]. I would suggest that the recent constitution-making processes in Southern Africa represent another stage, but one quite unrelated to the post-communist experience of Central-Eastern Europe.

As has been observed here, Namibia represents the first case of constitutional incorporation of general international law into municipal law in post-colonial Africa. The reasons for this are not too hard to find. Namibia emerged into independent statehood through the direct involvement of the international community, after decades of protracted negotiations and South African defiance and procrastination. This took place on the basis of a package of international agreements and United Nations resolutions which sought to ensure that Namibia emerged as a democratic State in which fundamental human rights were protected. Namibian independence was secured after a long drawn-out struggle for the realization of one of the most fundamental principles of international law, namely the right to self-determination. Yet, at the same time, this independence was predicated on the need for the new State to respect international law and the international rule of law. This much is implied in Article 144 of the Namibian Constitution.

Similar considerations come into play in relation to South Africa. The apartheid order in South Africa represented a negation of some of the most fundamental principles of international law: self-determination, equality, non-discrimination, and so on. During this era, the South African government was also a major violator of human rights and refused to subject itself to either constitutional or international law restraints in the field of human rights.[53] It is a commonplace that apartheid South Africa developed a remarkable degree of antipathy towards international law and the international community, especially the international human rights movement. To a lesser extent, this antipathy towards international law was shared by the pre-1994 regime in Malawi. The long years of isolation and paranoia which characterized the autocratic one-party rule of Dr. Hastings Banda had been accompanied by a veritable disdain for international human rights law and the international human rights movement as well. It goes without saying that any meaningful transition to new democratic orders in both countries was one that required a commitment to the acceptance of the need to protect human rights by both national and international mechanisms. The entrenchment of justiciable Bills of Rights and the express incorporation of international law into the South African and Malawian legal systems represent an obvious acknowledgment of this need.

These three Southern African constitutions confirm what Stein, in his study of the new democracies of Central-Eastern Europe, has termed "the tendency toward heightened recognition of the problem of internal effect of international law"[54] (or, in Cassese's model, the interaction between post-revolutionary democratization and an "opening" of new constitutions to the international system). However, this tendency has not been replicated in the other "democratic openings" elsewhere in Africa. As has been demonstrated in this discussion, with the exception of the Cape Verdian Constitution, none of the new or recently revised constitutions have followed the approach of the three Southern African States. In particular, Francophone African States have continued to limit themselves to reproducing the provision in Article 55 of the French Constitution. This provision was, in fact, first adopted by almost all the former French colonies during the process of decolonization in the early 1960s. Some of them, such as Gabon, have since dropped it from their subsequent constitutions. None of them have thought it necessary to go beyond the incorporation of treaties and embrace customary international law as well. This is unfortunate. For, as one commentator has observed, norms grounding international law and institutions in national constitutions are of more than symbolic value, although symbols are important on their own account.[55] Moreover, it has rightly been argued that:[56]

"These constitutional norms help delegitimize nonconforming conduct of states and enhance the visibility of, and respect for, international standards. They reinforce the state of legal certainty in the internal and international legal orders and advance the protection of individuals."

I do not share the scepticism of the Senegalese jurist Diaite who wrote, some twenty-five years ago, that "[in] the final analysis, the incorporation of certain principles of international law in African constitutions has scant legal value both on the internal and international plane".[57] The value attached to, and the reliance placed upon, international law, especially in the area of human rights and constitutional litigation, by both litigants and judges in the cases mentioned earlier in this discussion belies such a view. Indeed, it is heartening to note that international law has been invoked in courts even in those municipal legal systems in which it enjoys no constitutional affirmation.[58] It can only be hoped that other courts in the new constitutional democracies in Africa will, in time, also accord international law a role in the interpretative process. A constitutional democracy is nothing if it is not about the protection of peoples' fundamental rights and freedoms, and the role of international law in this scheme of protection ought to be self-evident. The challenge here falls principally upon the judiciary. But it also falls upon those involved in the teaching and dissemination of international law in the academy and elsewhere.

This challenge is, of course, not to be underestimated. It is also not new. Most ruling regimes and political elites in Africa have historically been suspicious and intolerant of any elements or organs which contest or constrain their hegemony over society. Such contestations or constraints may be implicit in the application of the "external" rules and regulations that international law imposes upon states and state officials, including political rulers. Or they may arise from the watchful and vigilant eye of an activist judiciary that takes seriously the protection of the individual's fundamental rights and freedoms and the application of the rule of law and the widely accepted values and norms of international law, especially international human rights law. The move by Parliament in Zimbabwe to amend the constitution by inserting a new provision, Section 111B(1), in 1993 was clearly aimed at preventing the courts from invoking norms of international law contained in a treaty which has not been specifically transformed into Zimbabwean law through legislative enactment. For a government which does not take kindly to any criticism of its human rights record, the kind of judicial activism demonstrated by the court in *A Juvenile* v *State* by importing "foreign" international human rights law as an aid to the interpretation and application of Zimbabwean law was an ominous development that could not be allowed to slide too far. The fairly progressive

Constitutions of Malawi, Namibia and, most especially, South Africa should never have to undergo such retrogressive amendments, at least as concerns the place and role of international law in the municipal legal systems of these countries.

In conclusion, one should emphasize two points. First, it is clear that the "newer" constitutions discussed here are products of the more liberal political environment evolving in some parts of Africa in the post-Cold War – or some might say post-communist – era. They are thus constitutions which seem to have benefited, overall, from an international consensus that is beginning to appreciate the importance of privileging international law and enshrining international human rights norms in domestic regimes more than ever before. As noted earlier, this heightened respect for international law and human rights would seem to be a shared characteristic in the new democracies in Southern Africa and Central-Eastern Europe. Second, it must be reiterated that the mere inclusion of provisions incorporating international law in national constitutions is not enough. To be sure, such a step represents only one aspect of a wider project. What is even more critical is the attitude and behaviour of the courts towards such a project: do municipal judges embrace international law as part of municipal law in actual judicial decisions? Beyond its mere mention in constitutional provisions, the incorporation of international law must be reflected in a practical sense in the executive, legislative and, most importantly, judicial decision-making in the domestic political community. This discussion has not examined any judicial decisions emanating from the relevant courts and tribunals in the countries mentioned above in any detail. This was not the principal aim of this chapter and, in any case, the constitutions under consideration have not been in existence long enough to have generated a respectable body of case law such as would enable us a more detailed investigation into the judicial approach to the incorporation of international law in the domestic systems of these countries. Such an enquiry must wait. However, it can at least be concluded with some measure of certainty that the emerging jurisprudence unmistakably suggests a readiness on the party of the judiciary to give real meaning to the interaction of international law and municipal law in these African countries.

Notes

1. The Constitution of the Republic of South Africa Act 108 of 1996 was drafted in terms of Chapter 5 of the interim Constitution of 1993. It was symbolically signed by President Nelson Mandela on 10 December 1996, International Human Rights

Day, at Sharpeville, scene of one of the most tragic massacres and human rights violations in South Africa's history. It entered into force on 4 February 1997.

2. See T. Maluwa, "International human rights norms and the South African interim Constitution 1993", *19 SAYIL 14* (1993/94).

3. G.M. Erasmus, "The Namibian Constitution and the Application of International Law", *15 SAYIL 81* (1989/90) at pp. 97–101.

4. *Ibid.* p. 93.

5. It is revealing that of the 52 constitutions examined in this survey, 40 are either wholly new constitutions or radically amended old constitutions which have been adopted in the period since 1990. All these constitutions reflect two underlying features: the inclusion of constitutional frameworks for multi-party political systems, and guarantees of fundamental rights and freedoms enshrined in justiciable Bills of Rights.

6. Municipal courts in a number of African countries have dealt with matters involving questions of international law. However, these decisions, some of which have been reported in the *International Law Reports* and similar publications, are not as such the focus of the present study. My enquiry here is specifically limited to addressing only two types of situations. First, where courts have to deal with cases in which a national constitution expressly incorporates international law into the municipal law of the country or where the constitution accords international law an interpretational role. Secondly, where, despite the absence of provisions in that regard, the courts have nevertheless accepted international law as part of the municipal law or as an aid to interpretation. This study is, therefore, only concerned with the procedural, and not the substantive, treatment of international law by municipal courts in Africa.

7. Discussions of these theories are to be found in almost all standard treatises on international law; see, for example, D.P. O'Connell, *International Law*, (2nd ed., 1970) pp. 38–79; I. Brownlie, *Principles of Public International Law*, (4th ed., 1990) pp. 32–56; see also, H. Lauterpacht, "International Law and Municipal Law", in E. Lauterpacht (Ed.), *International Law: Being the Collected Papers of Hersch Lauterpacht*, Vol. 1 (*The General Works*), (1970) p. 216; K.J. Partsch, "International Law and Municipal Law", in R. Bernhardt (Ed.), *Encyclopedia of Public International Law*, Vol. 10, (1991) pp. 238–257.

8. F. Jacobs, "Introduction", in F. Jacobs & S. Roberts (Eds.), *The Effects of Treaties in Domestic Law*, (1987) p. xxiv; J.G. Collier, "Is International Law really part of the law of England?", *38 ICLQ 924* (1989).

9. See Brownlie, *op. cit.* pp. 34–35 and the literature cited therein; J. Dugard, *International Law: A South African Perspective*, (1994) pp. 42–45; J.H. Jackson, "Status of Treaties in Domestic Legal Systems: A Policy Analysis", 86 *AJIL 310* (1992); Collier, *op. cit.* p. 935. See also Partsch, *op. cit.* pp. 240–241.

10 Jacobs, *op. cit.* p. xxvi.

11. For a comprehensive comparative survey of various approaches to this problem, see O'Connell, *op. cit.* pp. 56–79.

12. J. Fawcett, *The British Commonwealth in International Law*, (1963) *passim.*

13. M.S.C.A. Criminal Appeal No. 9 of 1992 (unreported).

14. *Ibid.* pp. 2–3. Thirty years earlier, the High Court of Uganda had followed a similar line, in a case concerning the status of a treaty, the Ankole Agreement of 1901, within the municipal legal scheme. It was held that "[unless] its provisions have been incorporated within the municipal law of Uganda those provisions do not confer rights or impose duties which are justiciable and therefore enforceable by the courts". See *Attorney-General* v *Katondwaki*, 51 I.L.R. 1 at p. 8.

15. W. Blackstone, *Commentaries on the Laws of England*, Book IV, Ch. 5, (7th ed., 1809) p. 67.

16. *Barbuit's Case in Chancery* (1735) Cas T Talbot 281 (15 ER 777).

17. [1974] 2 W.L.R. 593.

18. [1977] 1 Q.B. 529.

19. For a perceptive critique of these decisions, see Collier, *op. cit.* p. 931 *et seq.*

20. See the Ghanaian cases of *Lardan* v *Att.-Gen. & Others (No.1)*; *Lardan* v *Att.-Gen. & Others (No. 2)*, West Afr. L.R. (1958) at pp. 55 and 114; and *The State* v *Schumann*, 39 I.L.R. 433. See also the decision of the High Court of Uganda in *Uganda* v *Commissioner of Prisons, ex parte Matovu* [1966] EA 514,

21. 1978 (1) S.A. 893 (A) at 906B. The literature on the relationship between international law and South African municipal law in the pre-1993 Constitution era is fairly extensive. See, for example, J.W. Bridge, "The relationship between international law and the law of South Africa", *20 ICLQ 746* (1971); J. Dugard, "International law is part of our law", 88 *SALJ 13* (1971), and "The place of public international law in South African law", in C. Visser (Ed.), *Essays in Honour of Ellison Khan*, (1989) pp. 108–131; A.J. Sanders, "The applicability of customary international law in municipal law – South Africa's monist tradition", *40 THRHR 147* (1977), and "The applicability of customary international law in municipal

law – the Appeal Court has spoken", *XI CILSA 198* (1978); R.P. Schaffer, "The inter-relationship between public international law and the law of South Africa: an overview", *32 ICLQ 277* (1983); D. Devine, "Qualifications on the incorporation of international customary law into South African law", *1 Natal Univ LR* 58 (1973), and "What international customary law is part of South African law?", *13 SAYIL 119* (1987/88).

22. O'Connell, *op. cit.* p. 69. For a comprehensive discussion of Article 10 of the Italian Constitution of 1947, see A. Cassese, "Modern Constitutions and International Law", *192 Hague Recueil 331* (1985) at pp. 370–373; also same author's "*Lo Stato e la communita internazionale*", in G. Branca (Ed.), *Commentario della Constituzione*, (1975) p. 461 *et seq.* for a survey of the Italian case law relating to this provision.

23. C.H. Beck (Ed.), *Grundgesetzkommentar*, Vol. 2, (1983) p. 137 *et seq.*; A. Bleckmann, *Grundgesetz und Volkerrecht*, (1975). See also Cassese, "Modern Constitutions and International Law" *192 Hague Recueil* 331 (1985) at pp. 374–376, and the enormous literature cited in note 59 at p. 453.

24. O'Connell, *op. cit.* pp. 66–67.

25. See D. Carreau, *Droit International*, (1991) especially pp. 494–512; see also, N.Q. Dinh, "*La jurisprudence française actuelle et le contrôle de la conformité des lois aux traités*", *21* A.F.D.I. 859 (1975); L. Favoreu, "*Le conseil constitutionnel et le droit international*", *23* A.F.D.I. 95 (1977).

26. See J.D. de la Rochere, "France", in F. Jacobs and S. Roberts, *op. cit.* note 8 *supra*, pp. 39–61 at p. 48.

27. *Ibid.* pp. 58–59. See, for example, *Geoffrey et Delore* v *Compagnie d'assurances maritimes "La Bulgaria"* [Court of Appeal of Paris; judgment date: 20 April 1916], Sirey, *Recueil Générale* (1920), Pt. II, p. 17.

28. The English translations of the relevant provisions in the constitutions of the African States which have been reproduced in such collections as A. Blaustein and G. Flanz's *Constitutions of the Countries of the World* and C. Heyns's *Human Rights Law in Africa 1996*, (1996) differ in certain respects. Since the original French texts of these provisions are, in fact, a verbatim reproduction of Article 55 of the French Constitution, these differences in translation can only be attributed to the particular linguistic or stylistic choices of the translator concerned. I have here adopted the English translation used in the discussion by J.D. de la Rochere, cited in note 26 *supra*.

29. De la Rochere, *op. cit.* p. 42. See also Cassese, note 23 *supra*, pp. 406–408.

30. The full text of Article 11 states:

    "(1) International Law shall be an integral part of the Cape Verdian judicial system, as long as it is in force in the international legal system.

    (2) International Treaties and Agreements, validly approved and ratified, shall be in force in the Cape Verdian judicial system after their official publication, as long as they are in force in the international legal system.

    (3) Judicial acts emanating from competent offices of supranational organizations to which Cape Verde belongs shall take effect in internal law as soon as they have been established in respective legal conventions.

    (4) Rules and principles of International Law, validly approved and ratified internationally and internally, and in force, shall take precedence over all laws and regulations below the constitutional level".

    [English translation of original Portuguese text reproduced in Blaustein and Flanz, *op. cit.* note 28 *supra*, Vol. IV]

31. For my survey, I have mostly relied on the texts reproduced in Blaustein and Flanz's and Heyns's compilations cited in note 28 *supra*. Where necessary, I have checked the English translations supplied therein against the original French texts.

32. 39 I.L.R. 453 at p. 458 [Tribunal de Première Instance de Rabat; judgment date: 29 April 1964].

33. 89 L.L.R. 151 [Supreme Court of Gabon (Administrative Chamber); judgment date: 14 August 1970]. The treaties concerned here were the Franco-Gabonese bilateral treaty of 1960 and the Treaty establishing the Organisation Commune Africaine et Malgache (OCAM) of 1961. In a subsequent case, *L'Affaire Maugein*, the *Tribunal Administratif* held, in a judgment handed down on 17 January 1962, that:

    "Les dispositions conventionelles sont assimilable à des règles de droit interne dont le requérant est recevable à invoquer la violation devant la jurisdiction administrative".

    The Gabonese Constitution of 1994 subsequently dropped the provision granting treaties the status of binding internal law. However, it has been observed that despite the absence of an express constitutional provision in this regard, the Gabonese practice has been to accord international law primacy over internal law. J.B. Moussavou-Moussavou makes this observation but does not provide any specific reference to judicial or executive decisions evidencing this practice. See his, "L'état de l'application des accords dans la pratique gabonaise", p. 8; paper presented at the 9th Annual Conference of the African Society of International and Comparative Law, 2–6 August 1997, Abidjan, Côte d'Ivoire.

34. *Lansana & Others* v *R.* 70 I.L.R. 2; also [1970–1971] A.L.R. (Sierra Leone) p. 186.

35. Partsch, *op. cit.* p. 253. See also, for a similar discussion, P.C. Rao, *The Indian Constitution and International Law*, (1993) p. 53.

36. See, for example, U.O. Umozurike, *International Law and Colonialism in Africa*, (1979) *passim*; A.S. Osman, "The Attitude of Newly Independent States Towards International Law: the Need for Progressive Development", 49 *Acta Scandivavica Juris Gentium 15* (1979).

37. 1995 (6) BCLR 665 (CC).

38. *Ibid.* p. 686.

39. *Ibid.* pp. 687–688.

40. 1996 (8) BCLR 1015 (CC) at pp. 1031–1032.

41. R. Keightley, "Public International Law and the Final Constitution", *12 SAJHR 405* (1996) at p. 415.

42. 1994 (6) BCLR 1 (Botswana) [Appeal Court; judgment date 3 July 1992].

43. *Ibid.* at pp 29–30.

44. 1985 LRC (Const.) 699 (Botswana CA) at 714g.

45. 1990 (4) SA 151.

46. 1991 (3) SA 76 (NmS).

47. *Ibid.* at p. 88.

48. 87 I.L.R. 106 [High Court of Tanzania; judgment date: 22 February 1990]. However, this progressive approach may be contrasted with the view of the Court of Appeal of Mauritius in *Union of Campement Sites Owners & Others v Government of Mauritius*, 91 I.L.R 317. There, Acting Chief Justice Lallah held (at p. 330) that it was not for the courts of Mauritius to pronounce on the consistency of constitutional provisions (on equality and equal protection of the law) and the laws of Mauritius with the provisions of the International Covenant on Civil and Political Rights (to which Mauritius is a party) but, rather, that this was the function and responsibility of the UN Human Rights Committee.

49. E. Stein, "International Law in Internal Law: Toward Internationalization of Central-Eastern European Constitutions?", 88 *AJIL 427* (1994); T. Franck, "The Emerging Right to Democratic Governance", 86 *AJIL 47* (1992).

50. See Cassese, *op. cit.* note 23 *supra*, p. 351.

51. *Ibid.* p. 351.

52. Stein, *op. cit.* p. 429.

53. Dugard, *op. cit.* note 9 *supra*, p. 349.

54. Stein, *op. cit.* 447.

55. *Ibid.* p. 449.

56. *Ibid.*

57. I. Diaite, "*Les constitutions africaines et le droit international*", (1971–1972) *Annales Africaines*, p. 37. However, Diaite goes on to state that: "[Such sanctioning] has however an unquestionable political significance on the latter [i.e. international] plane. It not only meets a need for international prestige, but also takes care of one of the first questions which arises soon after the emergence of new states, namely the question as to what value the classical international law created before their independence should have for them. By including in the constitutions such fundamental principles as that concerning the submission of the state to international law and the priority of international treaties and agreements over internal law, African states clearly show that, although they challenge those rules and principles of international law which embody the injustices of the colonial past, they do not, however, reject the existing international legal order wholesale". (My translation).

58. See T. Maluwa, "International Law as an Aid to the Interpretation and Application of Law in Municipal Legal Systems in Africa", in D.H. van Zyl and B. Ajibola (Eds.), *The Judiciary in Africa*, (1998) pp. 47–63.

II

PRE-INDEPENDENCE TREATY OBLIGATIONS AND THE POST-COLONIAL STATE

3

THE NEWLY EMERGENT STATE AND THE DEVOLUTION OF PRE-INDEPENDENCE TREATIES

Introduction

Few areas of international law have generated as much interest, and controversy, from scholars and other legal commentators as that of State succession. Most modern writers commonly agree that State succession is an area of both great uncertainty and controversy. Furthermore, there would seem to be widespread agreement that this is partly due to the fact that the practice of States in this area of inter-State relations has been more equivocal than consistent; and that this divergence and lack of unanimity in State practice is largely responsible for the lack of settled legal rules in this area of international law. In the words of one leading scholar:[1]

> "[Much] of State practice is equivocal and could be explained on the basis of special agreement and various rules distinct from the category of State succession. Indeed, it is perfectly possible to take the view that not many settled legal rules have emerged as yet."

The equivocal nature of State practice referred to here is, perhaps, best demonstrated by the diametrically opposed approaches adopted by the Malagasy Republic and Upper Volta (as Burkina Faso then was) on the question of whether or not they were bound by pre-independence treaties entered into by the former colonial power, France. In a letter dated 6 February 1962, addressed to the Secretary General of the United Nations, it was stated, in part:[2]

> "[The] Malagasy Government considers that it ought to be in principle to acknowledge itself bound by the agreements and conventions entered into on [*sic*] its name by France before the Malagasy Republic became independent."

By contrast, in its letter dated 19 April 1962, also addressed to the U.N. Secretary General, Upper Volta expressed the categorical view that:[3]

> "Upper Volta, as a sovereign independent State, does not acknowledge itself bound by the agreements signed by France before the Republic of Upper Volta became independent."

The problem of State succession, and in particular the succession of newly independent States to pre-independence treaties, has been of particular relevance to the African continent during the last thirty years or so. Indeed, until the process of decolonization is fully and finally completed, the issue of State succession will continue to be of both theoretical and practical significance to the African legal scholar and politician alike. For it may be observed that State succession is generally regarded as arising when there is a definitive replacement of one State by another in respect of sovereignty over a given territory. Although such changes in sovereignty may be occasioned by such diverse political factors as the dismemberment of an existing State, annexation, cession, secession, and so on, the most common cause in recent times has been decolonization.

It is largely in the context of decolonization that the problem of State succession has historically arisen in Africa. From the legal point of view, one of the most important questions to have arisen out of such situations was whether the new State was bound by treaties entered into by its predecessor, the former colonial power. In fact, it may be argued that such an enquiry is really two-faceted: firstly, to what extent could the peculiar problems which arose out of the process of decolonization in Africa be adequately examined with the aid of the traditional devolution or non-devolution theories of classical international law in so far as succession to pre-independence treaties was concerned? And, secondly, what legal, or even philosophical, justification did the new African States advance for setting aside such treaties, where this, in fact, has been the preferred course of action?

But, of course, the relevance of this enquiry is not only one of retrospective or historical interest, nor is it limited to considerations of the decolonization process. For one thing, the term "decolonization" itself may be taken in a wide, non-classical sense to embrace the still unresolved problem of the Western Sahara. If, and when, the dispute regarding the independent Statehood of the

Sahrawi Arab Democratic Republic is finally resolved in favour of an independent State enjoying wider acceptance and recognition in the international community than is presently the case, the question of the devolution of treaties entered into, first, by Spain and, later, by Morocco in respect of the Western Sahara territory will have to be determined. Similar problems have no doubt been faced in the context of the recent emergence of Eritrea as an independent sovereign State: what has been the fate of pre-independence Ethiopian treaties over the new State? Secondly, at a different level, some commentators raised the issue of whether a post-apartheid, democratic government in South Africa would have to address the question of the continuing validity of certain treaties concluded by the previous minority racist regime. But here, the critical consideration, which the new government accepted without much equivocation, was that relating to the fundamental distinction between State succession stricto sensu and succession of governments.[4]

The contemporary relevance and pertinence of this debate can also be assessed from a different perspective: the manner in which the question of succession to the treaties and obligations of the ex-Soviet Union by the new independent States (the three Baltic States as well as the group of States now constituting the Commonwealth of Independent States) has been handled by the international community reveals an obvious preference, at least by the concerned major powers, such as the United States, for a political determination of the question of State succession rather than a logical adherence to the operation of the rules, such as they are, of international law regarding such matters. Indeed, it is quite conceivable that as legal scholars and commentators turn to analyze and examine the import of these recent events in the former Soviet Union, the weight of opinion will tend towards the conclusion that the manner in which the question of succession to pre-independence treaties has been handled here precisely proves the point: that the decolonization process and experience of the 1950s and 1960s did not lead to the establishment of a coherent body of rules and principles of international law governing State succession (or that the practice of States during this period left unresolved the apparent conflict between the existing devolution and non-devolution theories of nineteenth century international law) and, more ominously, that even those rules now embodied in the Vienna Convention on Succession of States in Respect of Treaties (1978) are liable to be disregarded, at the discretion of States, where power politics and expediency so dictate.[5]

But this study does not aim at examining all aspects of the problem of State succession in their detail; nor, indeed, is it a retrospective study of the practice of all African States in its generality; nor yet a prospective analysis of the various aspects of the current succession problem in the new independent

States which have emerged out of the previous Union of Soviet Socialist Republics. To do the former would be to follow a well-worn path which others have trodden with a depth and lucidity that may not be equalled or surpassed in a brief exposition such as this one. Besides, retrospective analyses of politico-legal events that occurred some thirty years or so ago, and are unlikely to repeat themselves in more or less similar fashion in the foreseeable future, often need to be justified in terms of relevance and pertinence, however rightly or wrongly such relevance and pertinence are perceived. Prospective studies, on the other hand, also run the risk of being characterized as mere academic discourses which may turn out to have no real bearing on the practical determination of future State policies and practice. Makonnen's excellent analysis of the problem of State succession and its application to Namibia, written in anticipation of the independence of Namibia and "in the event of succession of States in Namibia",[6] can now only be affirmed or disregarded by the actual practice of Namibia itself and other concerned States, following its accession to independence on 21 March 1990. Makonnen's general view was that as far as the succession of States in the event of the independence of Namibia was concerned, the most appropriate approach would be to apply the clean-slate doctrine. Makonnen came to this conclusion on the ground that all dealings by South Africa and other aliens concerning Namibia since October 1966 were illegal, and therefore invalid, as a result of the Advisory Opinion of the International Court of Justice (declaring the continuing South African occupation of the territory illegal) and certain relevant United Nations resolutions.[7]

This conclusion is quite correct, and has been vindicated by Article 145 of the Namibian Constitution.[8] Yet, from a practical point of view, it leaves open the problem of the legal status of treaties concluded by South Africa *before* 1966 – a matter upon which the constitution itself is rather vague – and the extent to which the theoretical expositions by Makonnen and other publicists on this issue have been taken into consideration in the formulation of policy by the new Namibian State.[9]

The present discussion will be limited to a retrospective examination of the legal position arising out of the succession of States in Malawi. And, in this regard, this chapter is concerned to demonstrate how, in a clear departure from the so-called traditional approaches to this question, the new State of Malawi elected to espouse the evolving "Nyerere Doctrine" as the guiding principle on these matters. The theoretical content of this doctrine and its practical application in the immediate post-independence treaty practice of Malawi will be assessed. Here it will be useful to pose two related questions: first, whether this practice reveals any particular thematic bases or *indicia* governing the choice of treaties to which the new State was prepared to succeed or become a party in the years following the attainment of its independence on 6 July 1964; second, whether, in fact, it is the case that the choice of such agreements has not been predicated upon any consistent thematic principle, but rather has proceeded on the basis of a haphazard pick and choose approach?

Malawi: A Post-Colonial Case Study

The choice of Malawi as the focus of this brief study has been based on three considerations. To begin with, Malawi represents a classic case of post-colonial State succession. For unlike some of its neighbours in the region, such as Namibia, Tanzania and Zimbabwe, its juridical and political evolution was subjugated to the colonial authority of only one power, Great Britain. The succession problem, therefore, has not been coloured by any changes of sovereignty over the territory in question prior to independence, as was the case in some of these other countries. Secondly, Malawi has never experienced any post-independence territorial dislocation. Thus, the succession policy put in place by the new State has never undergone any changes in order, for example, to accommodate new circumstances occasioned by changes in the personality of the State. Finally, and most importantly for the present writer, Malawi is one of the few States in Africa which, until fairly recently, produced and availed to the public at large an official record of its treaty relations with other States, in the form of the *Malawi Treaty Series*. Any international lawyer engaged in research on policy-related issues or seeking to examine some aspect of African State practice will testify to the difficulty – in some cases impossibility – of securing official documentation or other information from officialdom in Africa. The problem is often further compounded by the paucity of published official records and other information on such matters. In this regard, Malawi commended itself as a plausible case study in large part because of the existence of documented official information available to the writer.

The colonization of the Central African territories that came to be known as Nyasaland really goes back to 1883. On 1 October 1883 the British Government appointed a consul to look after British interest "[in] the territories of the African Kings and Chiefs of Central Africa adjacent to Lake Nyasa". But it was not until some eight years later, on 17 May 1891,[10] that Great Britain formally placed Nyasaland under its colonial wing. Except for the period between 1 August 1953 and 31 December 1963, when it became part of a federation of British dependent territories in Central Africa known as the Federation of Rhodesia and Nyasaland, Nyasaland was to remain a British protectorate until 6 July 1966.

It is a generally accepted view that the juridical evolution of most African States has been through a dialectical process. The first phase occurred in the pre-colonial era, during which time the indigenous societies constituted themselves into organized polities of one type or another, variously referred to in the literature as States, city-states, kingdoms or empires. The proper legal status of these entities in the international legal order of the time has been the subject of copious debate among both legal scholars and historians. The view that these so-called traditional African States had no status whatsoever in pre-colonial international law, and that they neither participated in nor contributed to the development of this law, has been forcefully challenged and rejected by some of these scholars.[11] Admittedly, the contribution to the development of international law by these entities was in many ways rather marginal, since the dominant view among the jurists of the sixteenth to the nineteenth centuries was that the existing African traditional States or kingdoms did not form part of European civilization or Christendom, and thus could not participate in the evolving regime of the law of nations. But, as one scholar has aptly pointed out:[12]

> "To say that Africans did not contribute actively or personally towards the development of the doctrine of the law of nations does not preclude the consideration that the indigenous polities within the continent [had] some knowledge of some law governing inter-State relations, which was strikingly similar to, if not identical with, the law governing inter-State relations in Europe. The latter's law came to be developed and christened, first, 'law of nations', and re-christened, later, 'international law'."

In any event, it may be argued that whatever stages of Statehood may have been attained by these indigenous African States and kingdoms, and however one may construe their relations with each other from the point of view of pre-colonial international law, their independent existence was altogether denied during the colonial era.[13] With the declaration of the various colonies and protectorates – the second phase of the juridical evolution of African States – the sovereignties of these constituent indigenous polities were subsumed into the wider territorial sovereignties of the colonial powers. Thus, the metropolitan powers assumed responsibility for the external or international relations of the colonized territories.

The second phase referred to above came to an end with the transformation of the colonized territories into independent States. This decolonization process has, of course, a longer history, but for the great majority of the new African States, such as Malawi, political independence only came in the early and mid-1960s in the wake of the well-known U.N. General Assembly

Resolution 1514 (XV) of 14 December 1960: Declaration on the Granting of Independence to Colonial Countries and Peoples.[14]

It is, as intimated above, in the context of the second and third phases of the juridical evolution of the modern African State that the issue of succession to treaties arises. More specifically, in the case of Malawi, two major questions may be posed: first, to what extent was the colonial power responsible for the foreign and treaty relations of the protectorate of Nyasaland prior to its independence? Or, to put the matter differently, were (all) treaties entered into by the United Kingdom necessarily applicable to Nyasaland? And, secondly, assuming that the previous question is answered in the affirmative, which of these treaties, if any, survived the emergence of the new, independent State of Malawi?

Colonial Treaty Obligations and Third Parties: Theory and Practice

The wholesale colonial partition of Africa that followed the Berlin Conference of 1884–1885[15] did not mean that the newly created colonial territories became vested with independent international legal personality. As has been pointed out above, the African colonies were not regarded as possessing the capacity to enter into treaty relations with foreign States or international organizations independently of the metropolitan powers. Conversely, the colonial power was regarded as possessing the sole authority and competence to conclude treaties for, and on behalf of, these territories.

To put the matter briefly, under British colonial practice, which of course bears the most immediate relevance to the present discussion, the presumption was generally that, unless otherwise provided, all British treaties were deemed to apply to all British territories and subjects. But this position did not forever remain the same with the older dominions (Australia, Canada, Ireland, New Zealand and South Africa) whose constitutional development was different from that of the newer States in the African-Asian block of the British Empire. Initially, the general rule expressed above applied equally to both the older dominions and new colonies. However, this practice was to change by the latter half of the nineteenth century: the dominions had gradually secured a measure of self-government from the United Kingdom and had begun to exercise some influence on the application of British treaties to their territories. By the time the first world war broke out, Australia, Canada and New Zealand had begun concluding, in particular, certain commercial and technical treaties in their own right. Equally, it had by this time also been recognized that not only did British treaties not devolve automatically upon these dominions, but that they could also withdraw from some of these commercial treaties at will. The dominions had thus become *de facto* international legal persons.[16] This was not to be the case with the British African colonies, all of whom acquired international status only after attaining their independence. Thus, the United Kingdom retained sole responsibility for the treaties and other foreign relations aspects of its colony of Nyasaland until the latter's independence on 6 July 1964.[17]

French colonial practice in this respect was initially similar to the British in that unless there was an express or implied limitation all French treaties were regarded as extending to the colonies. But the practice later evolved of inviting the overseas territories to participate in the conclusion of those treaties that would specifically affect them, and attaching to such treaties a territorial application clause. In its turn, this practice was by the beginning of the twentieth century replaced by the "*principe de la specialité legislative*", a principle that involved the exercise of locally promulgating a treaty before it could apply to a given territory, and this was later affirmed in two decisions by the *Cour de Cassation*.[18] However, it has been correctly noted that in actual practice, up to the independence of the French African colonies, Paris remained the sole authority with discretion to enter into international agreements, and that where the local authorities implemented these treaties by executive action, they did so upon direction from the metropolitan authority.[19]

By the time the new State of Malawi came into existence, the question of the succession of newly independent States to the treaties entered into by the predecessor State had long been the subject of scholarly debate among academic international lawyers. The major theories invoked and canvassed in this debate, as well as the practice of States in this area, can in fact be identified with certain chronological periods in the historical development of the doctrine of international law. A comprehensive account of this debate cannot be undertaken here; for the purposes of the present enquiry, only a broad statement of the main theoretical propositions will be sketched out.[20]

The two major theoretical standpoints that are relevant in this debate can be summarized thus: there is, on the one hand, the earlier theory of universal succession, particularly dominant in the nineteenth century, which likened the transfer of sovereignty to a transfer of property in a deceased's estate, and thus concluded that there existed a rule of absolute inheritance of rights and obligations flowing from engagements entered into by the predecessor State.[21] Although this universal succession theory only reached its apogee in the early nineteenth century, it is important to note that it had, in fact, first been imported into international law by the classical authorities: Grotius, Pufendorf and Vattel, among others.[22] On the other hand, this theory is to be contrasted with the non-devolution or negativist theory.

The non-devolution theory – also known as the "clean-slate" doctrine of State succession – is essentially a product of the late nineteenth century. This theory holds that a successor State acquires its territory with a "clean-slate", or *tabula rasa*, and is thus under no obligation to succeed to pre-independence treaties.[23]

Between these two divergent positions are to be found a number of varied propositions, in essence modifications upon the two major classical theories. It has been argued by some scholars, for example, that the universal succession theory must be distinguished from two other theories: the popular continuity theory and the organic substitution theory of continuity. Both these theories advocate a general transmissibility of rights and obligations, although they are thought to be based on different legal and philosophical rationales. Similarly, some authorities have advocated a distinction between two types of the clean slate theory: the classical doctrine as opposed to the socialist doctrine. But, as Makonnen has rightly observed, the socialist conception of the clean slate is, in essence, not at all different from the theory of *tabula rasa*.[24]

In any case, it is here argued that most of the evidence usually adduced in support of a separate socialist version of the clean slate theory tends to blur the distinction between State succession stricto sensu and the succession of governments. Thus, it is pointed out, by way of example, that neither the Soviet Union nor China claimed that there was a case of State succession as such after the socialist revolutions of 1917 and 1949 respectively; and, furthermore, it is also argued that opinion among socialist jurists as to whether these revolutions created new subjects of international law, or merely occasioned a change of government, has never been entirely unanimous.[25]

In spite of the uncertainties surrounding the debate regarding the devolution or non-devolution of pre-independence treaties upon newly emergent States, there would appear to be a certain degree of support for a number of propositions. For example, it may be observed that even those scholars who advocate the non-continuity or negativist theory have always, at the same time, also admitted certain exceptions to the rule of non-devolution, namely, that category of treaties known as "dispositive" treaties which affect territory, such as those guaranteeing rights of navigation, the use of ports, passage through certain territories, boundary treaties, and so on. This view, shared by the great majority of modern publicists,[26] was well illustrated in a statement explaining the attitude of the United Kingdom towards Finland's position regarding Russian treaties applicable to Finland prior to its independence:[27]

> "[In] the case of a new State being formed out of an old State there is no succession by the new State to the treaties of the old one, though the obligations of the old State in relation to such matters as navigation of

rivers, which are in the nature of servitudes, would normally pass to a new State. Consequently there are no treaties in existence between Finland and this country."

The phenomenon of independence presupposes the total destruction of the previous State identity and the creation of a new international legal person. The argument here is thus that the successor State does not derive its sovereignty from the predecessor State, but from international law and from its own statehood. In other words, there is not a transfer of one sovereignty, but a substitution of sovereignties by the extinction of one and the creation of another. The successor State is, therefore, regarded as possessing its own sovereignty because it has succeeded to the dignity of Statehood.[28]

In essence, therefore, the occurrence of independence means that the new State does not as such acquire its territory from the predecessor State as a "gift" but actually recaptures territory that had, in effect, been forcibly or unlawfully been acquired from the pre-colonial indigenous polity. Thus, the argument runs, the repossession of their sovereignty by the indigenes should not be fettered by any obligations to take over the encumbrances created by any agreements entered into by the departing colonial "usurper". It is interesting to note that it was to this clean-slate theory that the United States appealed upon obtaining independence from Great Britain to explain why the former colonies were not bound by treaties to which Britain was a party.[29]

The two doctrinal positions outlined above have not, however, been neatly reflected in the practice of newly emergent States, particularly in the practice of newly independent African States in the early 1960s. Thus, the International Law Association's Committee on State Succession was able to identify a number of trends in the approach of new States to the question of succession to treaties:[30]

"(a) The successor State assumes all responsibilities arising from treaties between the predecessor and third parties, as was the method adopted by Nigeria regarding treaty obligations assumed by Great Britain in respect of the former colony;

(b) The successor undertakes to maintain all treaties during a trial period while they are being studied. At the end of this period it announces which will be maintained while others lapse. This system was adopted by Malawi in 1964 [following the examples of Tanzania, Uganda, Kenya and Burundi];

(c) The successor announces its intention to abide by customary law, but seeks to avoid any general commitment in the treaty field and does not seek to renounce or ratify old treaties in any determined period of time. This was the method adopted by Zambia;

(d) A general declaration of succession to treaties is issued."

To this one could also, of course, add the other approach: the issuance of a general declaration renouncing all old treaties, as was done by Upper Volta. Some brief remarks about these purported trends would be in order.

The approach adopted by Nigeria, that of concluding a devolution or inheritance agreement with the predecessor State, represents an attempt to avoid the uncertainties surrounding the question of State succession. Such agreements seek to affirm the succession of the new State to particular or general treaties at the time of independence. [Other States, while not concluding devolution agreements, make declarations which have similar effect.] On its accession to independence on 1 October 1960, Nigeria followed the Ghanaian precedent and concluded a devolution agreement with the United Kingdom which partly provided as follows:[31]

"(i) All obligations and responsibilities of the Government of the United Kingdom, which arise from any valid international instrument are from 1 October 1960, assumed by the Government of the Federation of Nigeria in so far as such instruments may be held to have application to or in respect of the Federation of Nigeria.

(ii) The rights and benefits heretofore enjoyed by the Government of the United Kingdom in virtue of the application of any such international instrument to or in respect of the Federation of Nigeria are from 1 October 1960, enjoyed by the Government of the Federation of Nigeria."

All former British colonies in West Africa, with the exception of the Gambia, later concluded similar agreements. But these agreements leave a few questions unanswered. For instance, does the expression "valid international instrument" refer only to such a treaty as would bind a successor State under customary international law? If the question as to the validity of the international instrument is one that is left to be determined by customary law then, indeed, the devolution agreement itself achieves nothing. And, moreover, with regard to the wording "which arise from any valid international instrument" in clause (i), one may further wonder who is entitled to hold that the agreement in question is valid and has application over the successor State: the new State, the predecessor State, the other parties to the original treaty or an independent international tribunal? The problem with these devolution agreements is that they do not advance the position any further, so that an agreement between the United Kingdom and Nigeria that the latter should succeed to the former's treaties with third parties cannot affect such third parties since they are not parties to the devolution agreement itself. This is because the agreement is *res inter alios acta* and, by virtue of the maxim *pacta tertiis nec nocent nec prosunt*, can only be in force between the predecessor and successor States. Having said that, however, it must be pointed out that where a treaty is recognized as devolving upon the new State independently of the operation of the operation of any inheritance agreement, such an agreement, though not itself occasioning such devolution, may nevertheless serve a useful evidentiary function: that of declaring to other States the new State's willingness to maintain the legal relations entered into by the predecessor State – it therefore puts other parties on notice of the successor State's affirmative policy.[32]

The conduct and practice of the great majority of former French colonies in Africa was also generally in favour of regarding themselves as successors to pre-independence treaties, even while not signing devolution agreements with the former colonial power.[33] Accordingly, a number of these new States made unilateral declarations of a general character which were notified to other parties through the Secretary General of the United Nations and which had the unmistakable effect of accepting the principle of devolution. The declaration by the Malagasy Republic embodied in the letter cited at the outset of this discussion is only one such example.[34] Cameroon, Congo (Brazzaville), Cotê d'Ivoire and Niger, among others, also adopted this approach.[35] In this respect, it is instructive to note that although Upper Volta did, as was pointed out above, issue a declaration denouncing all pre-independence treaties entered into by France, it also submitted, at about the same time, the following notification to Switzerland (as depositary for the conventions for the protection of war victims, etc.):[36]

> "The four 1949 Geneva Conventions for the protection of war victims *apply by law* to the territory of the Republic of Upper Volta *in virtue of their ratification by France on 28 June 1951*."

Equally, Upper Volta acknowledged its succession to some thirteen ILO conventions also by virtue of their ratification by France. The conclusion to be drawn from this brief survey of African State practice appears to be that in practice there is nothing to distinguish those States which have concluded devolution agreements from those which have not done so. For even in the case of the latter, there would appear to be a general acceptance of the continued validity of treaties specifically applied to their territories before their attainment of independence. Furthermore, the recognition of this continuing validity does not appear to be solely predicated upon the distinction drawn earlier between personal (so-called non-heritable) and dispositive or real (so-called heritable) treaties. Two principles seem to have been recognized in this process. First, the recognition of the need for legal continuity, at least in the short term following the attainment of independence. In part, this was dictated by the feeling that the new State needed time to establish its own identity and policies without being unduly fettered by its colonial legacy, but without immediately prejudicing the rights and interests of third parties. The second principle implicit in this varied practice is that, ultimately, a new State has discretion whether or not to accept such pre-independence treaties.[37]

The second principle. with its accent on the discretion of the new state, is amply exemplified in the Malawian approach. This approach, termed the Nyerere Doctrine of State succession,[38] was itself an adoption of an earlier unilateral declaration made in 1961 by the then Prime Minister of newly independent Tanganyika to the Acting Secretary General of the United Nations. The relevant portion of the Declaration, made on 24 November 1964, may be quoted *in extenso* here:[39]

> "[As] regards bilateral treaties validly concluded by the Government of the United Kingdom or by the Government of the former Federation of Rhodesia and Nyasaland, on behalf of the former Nyasaland Protectorate, or validly applied or extended by either of the said Governments to the territory of the former Nyasaland Protectorate, the Government of Malawi is willing to continue to apply within its territory on a basis of reciprocity, the terms of all such treaties for a period of eighteen months from the date of independence (i.e. until 6 January 1966), unless abrogated or modified by earlier mutual consent. At the expiry of that period, the Government of Malawi will regard such of these treaties which could not by application of the rules of customary international law be regarded as otherwise surviving, as having terminated."

The Declaration went on to provide that with regard to multilateral treaties, the new government would review them individually and indicate to the depositary concerned what steps would be taken in relation to each such instrument, whether by way of confirmation of termination, confirmation of succession or accession. In essence this doctrine is really no more than a vague or general recognition that certain unspecified treaties do survive as a result of the application of rules of customary law, coupled with an offer of a grace period in which treaties remain in force on an interim basis without prejudice to the declarant's legal position with a requirement of reciprocity.

The Nyerere Doctrine was in time adopted by a considerable number of States, both in Africa and elsewhere, in similar situations, though with some variations (for example with respect to the duration of the grace period).[40] A quick examination of the various treaties actually accepted by the new State of Malawi after the passage of the eighteen-month trial period does not provide any justification for a categorical conclusion, one way or the other, regarding the *legal* nature of the type of treaty which new States following the Nyerere Doctrine do in fact regard as binding on them.

Concluding Observations: Devolution of Treaty obligations in the Post-Colonial Era

A list of the major bilateral treaties concluded by Great Britain, as the former colonial power, and succeeded to by Malawi is provided in the Appendix to this chapter. Only a few pertinent observations will be made here. First of all, it is argued that in order to get a proper picture regarding the import of Malawi's succession to these pre-independence treaties, attention should be directed, first and foremost, at the bilateral treaties. It is usually in the context of bilateral relations that a new State is better able to signify its willingness to take on legal obligations entered into by the predecessor State, since in such situations the position is not coloured a multiplicity of parties and legal relations. Here, it may be observed that, initially, all bilateral treaties entered into between the United Kingdom and other powers before Malawi's independence were adopted by the new State. Of these, thirty-two were subsequently extended by various Exchanges of Notes between Malawi and the other parties concerned beyond the dead-line which had been stipulated as marking the end of the grace period for the review of bilateral treaties under the Declaration submitted to the Secretary General of the United Nations, as was noted above.[41] Some of these Exchanges of Notes were effected as early as 7 April 1965, that is barely ten months after the attainment of independence: thus, for example, the extensions of the Treaty between the United Kingdom and the Kingdom of Norway relating to the Avoidance of Double Taxation of 2 May 1951, and the Treaty between the United Kingdom and Sweden for the Prevention of Fiscal Evasion with respect to Taxes on Income of 30 March 1949. Other treaties were, in effect, only extended after the passage of the 6 January 1967 dead-line itself. It is not altogether obvious why the new State marked out these treaties for priority treatment, given that problems of double taxation and tax avoidance were not likely to emerge in the scheme of bilateral relations between Malawi and these other States. Interestingly enough, the latest Exchange of Notes extending the application of a bilateral treaty beyond 6 January 1967 was only concluded on 7 June 1969: this treaty, between the

United Kingdom and the Kingdom of the Netherlands, was also concerned with the avoidance of double taxation and the prevention of fiscal evasion. This four-year gap in the adoption of treaties concerned with exactly the same matter would appear to suggest that there was nothing in the *nature* of the treaties themselves that commended them to either immediate adoption within a few months of Malawi's independence or the belated adoption effected almost five years after independence. Other treaties, also adopted by Malawi, relating to similar matters were those entered into by the United Kingdom, on the one hand, and, respectively, France, Switzerland and the United States, on the other hand.

Another category of treaties that seems to have been given prominence in this devolution process comprises those relating to the mutual surrender and extradition of fugitive criminals and offenders. Indeed, thirteen of the bilateral treaties succeeded to in this manner – representing just a little less than half of all such bilateral treaties – fall into this category. The other parties involved here are: Belgium, Bolivia, Germany, Greece, Iraq, Israel, Luxembourg, Monaco, the Netherlands, Portugal, San Marino, Switzerland and the United States. Here, again, the diversity of the parties concerned does not, of itself, provide any clue as to the extent of the bilateral relations enjoyed or anticipated by the new State and these other States at the time of succession to these treaties. The group includes the major European States, and the United States, with which Malawi proceeded to establish diplomatic relations almost immediately after independence, as well as those countries, such as Bolivia, Iraq and Peru, with whom Malawi has never initiated any diplomatic relations. It is probable that succession to these extradition treaties was predicated merely on the ground that they were, at the time of independence, in existence between these States and the United Kingdom, and had been extended to Nyasaland under the relevant territorial application clauses.

Two observations would be in order here: there has been a general tendency by almost all the new African States, the predecessor States and the third parties States concerned to maintain the application of extradition treaties on the basis of reciprocity. This position is thus not peculiar to Malawi.[42] Yet, traditionally it has also always been thought that extradition treaties represent a classic example of political or personal treaties – as opposed to dispositive or real treaties – and are thus non-heritable. Quite clearly, State practice has not always been consonant with theory in this particular regard.

Of the remaining treaties, two (concluded with Greece and Germany respectively) were concerned with visa abolition and consular affairs; four (concluded with Austria, Denmark, Germany and Greece respectively) related to legal proceedings in civil and commercial matters. The last category comprised three treaties concluded with Portugal: Treaty between the United

Kingdom and the Kingdom of Portugal Defining their Respective Spheres of Influence in Africa of 11 June 1891, Treaty between the United Kingdom and Portugal Relative to the Port of Beira and Connected Railways of 17 June 1950, and the Agreement between the Government of the United Kingdom and the Portuguese Government with Regard to the Nyasaland-Mozambique Frontier of 18 November 1954.

The three treaties with Portugal deserve special comment here. Unlike all the other treaties to which Malawi succeeded under the Nyerere Doctrine formula, these agreements can properly be described as dispositive or real treaties and thus, under the traditional theories of State succession, may be presumed to devolve upon a new State irrespective of that State's specific consent. As was noted earlier, boundary treaties, as a species of servitudes, are regarded as an exception even by those who advocate the clean-slate rule. The view expressed by Makonnen, that it is doubtful that this deviation [by African States in general] in practice is dictated by legal obligations in accordance with existing rules of State succession, cannot be readily accepted. Makonnen argues:[43]

> "[Politics] and various other factors were responsible for such positive attitudes and there is no evidence that they did so out of their sense of legal obligation to inherit the pre-existing colonial boundaries by virtue of the rules of State succession."

This comes close to denying the well-known principle of *uti possidetis*, adopted by the Organization of African Unity in July 1964 as the guiding principle for all its members on the question of succession to colonial boundary arrangements any legal validity and binding nature.[44] The present writer does not share this view; on the contrary, *uti possidetis* is one of the few principles of modern international law which the collective practice of African States can be said to have helped fashion. The fact that some African States have subsequently made (usually half-hearted) attempts at challenging the validity of some of these same boundaries does not detract from this conclusion. The occasional propensity by States (or individuals) towards law-breaking, or threats to that effect, is hardly a reason for denying the existence of a legal obligation on the matter concerned.

The pre-independence multilateral treaties to which Malawi succeeded upon independence is too numerous to be singled out for specific examination in this brief discussion. Suffice it to note that these range from the general multilateral treaties governing membership of international organizations, such as the U.N. and O.A.U. Charters, to treaties governing economic, scientific, technical and numerous other matters. Among these are the ILO Conventions, the four 1958

Geneva Conventions on the Law of the Sea, Intellectual Property Protection Conventions, the 1949 Geneva (War) Conventions, and those relating to education, health, transport and aerial navigation, postal and telecommunications and so on. Malawi acceded to some of these treaties within the context of joining pre-existing international organizations, and to others purely on the basis of a succession of States *stricto sensu*, in order to take over obligations and responsibilities entered into previously by the United Kingdom.[45]

It can only be noted, in concluding this brief retrospective consideration, that one underlying theme in all this is clearly that of sovereign discretion. The discretion of the new State here, and this is as true of Malawi as of most other newly-born States, seems to override all other considerations and purported legal theories. The manner in which States jealously guard their sovereign discretion in matters of State succession, particularly where the succession in question has been brought about through the process of independence, continues to manifest itself in the more recent cases alluded to at the beginning of this discussion.

Writing a little more than fifteen years ago, Greig echoed the views of earlier authorities by observing that "it is not easy to determine from these trends what stage the law has reached".[46] None of the recent instances of State practice in the area of succession to treaties in the intervening period have shed any further light on this aspect of international law. The international lawyer seeking a way out of this marshland is as likely as ever to be led into the centre of the miry bog itself.

Notes

1. I. Brownlie, *Principles of Public International Law*, (4th ed., 1990) p. 655.

2. See U.N. doc. A/CN.4/150 p. 31, para. 87.

3. See ILC Yrbk, 1962, Vol. II, p. 122.

4. The problem faced by post-apartheid South Africa has not been so much one of State succession as one of succession of governments. Most leading modern authorities agree that there exists a fundamental distinction between these two types of succession. (But see D.P. O'Connell, *State Succession in Municipal Law and International Law*, Vol. I, (1967) p. 5.) One of the questions mooted by some political commentators, but never pursued at all by the ANC-led government, was that concerning the moral obligation of a post-apartheid government to uphold those treaty obligations entered into by the previous National Party governments in furtherance of the perpetration of the crime of apartheid.

5. The Convention was concluded at Vienna on 23 August 1978 and is intended to govern the treaty relations of States in cases of State succession. It deals with cases of succession in respect of treaties by newly independent States, and with cases of succession arising from the transfer of territory from one State to another, or the uniting or separation of States. The Convention requires fifteen ratifications or accessions to enter into force; the process of ratification or accession has been so slow that in the first ten years of its existence, the Convention was able to attract only eight instruments of such ratification or accession: Dominica, Egypt, Ethiopia, Iraq, Morocco, Seychelles, Tunisia and Yugoslavia. See U.N. Press Release, 28 September 1988, L/T/4030.

6. Y. Makonnen, "Namibia: Its International Status and the Issues of State Succession", *3 Lesotho Law J 183* (1987) *passim.*

7. *Ibid.* pp. 203–210, especially at 209.

8. Article 145 provides as follows:

   "(1) Nothing contained in this Constitution shall be construed as imposing upon the Government of Namibia;

   (a) any obligations to any other State which would not otherwise have existed under international law;

   (b) any obligations to any person arising out of the acts or contracts of prior Administrations which would not otherwise have been recognized by international law as binding upon the Republic of Namibia.

   (2) Nothing contained in this Constitution shall be construed as recognizing in any way the validity of the Administration of Namibia by the Government of the Republic of South Africa or by the Administrator-General appointed by the Government of the Republic of South Africa to administer Namibia".

9. It is apparent that the post-independence Government of the Republic of Namibia has adopted a more cautious approach than pre-independence theoretical postulation and rhetoric would have suggested, in that for the time being there has not been a wholesale rejection of *all* treaties and other legal obligations entered into by the illegal South African regime *after* 1966. If nothing else, this might serve as a reminder that here, as in most other areas of international law, theory often has to give way to political expediency under the cover of pragmatism and realism.

10. Initially, the colonized territory was known as the British Central African Protectorate, but this was changed to Nyasaland on 6 July 1907. For a brief account of these developments, see J. Pike, *Malawi: A Political and Economic History*, (1968) p. 90 *et seq*.

11. See, for example, the various discussions in A.K. Mensah-Brown (Ed.), *African International Legal History*, (1975) *passim.*

12. A.K. Mensah-Brown, "Notes on International Law and Pre-Colonial Legal History of Modern Ghana", in Mensah-Brown, *ibid.* p. 107 at 109.

13. See in this regard, T.O. Elias, *Africa and the Development of International Law*, (2nd rev. ed., 1988) p. 21.

14. U.N. G. A. Resolution 1514 (XV) of 14 December 1960.

15. The Berlin Conference is generally described as laying the groundwork for the "scramble for Africa", although as a matter of historical fact the actual territorial partition of the continent had already been under way by the time the conference was convened on 14 November 1884. For the text of the General Act and Declaration of the Berlin Conference see 82 BFSP 55; see also M. de Courcel, *L'influence de la conférence de Berlin de 1885 sur le droit colonial*, (1935) *passim*. See also L.H. Gann and P. Fuigan (Eds.), *Colonialism in Africa 1870–1960*, Vol. I., (1969); Elias, *op. cit.* p. 18.

16. This situation was finally given legislative recognition in the 1931 Statute of Westminster which declared, in respect of Australia, Canada, New Zealand and South Africa, that no Act of the imperial Parliament could henceforth extend to the dominions without their own legislative consent. See, generally, J.E.S. Fawcett, *The British Commonwealth in International Law*, (1963).

17. As noted above, between 1 August 1953 and 31 December 1963, the Nyasaland Protectorate was part of the Federation of Rhodesia and Nyasaland. The Federation of Rhodesia and Nyasaland was not, of course, an independent State, nor did it attain dominion status along the lines of Australia, Canada, and so on. Nonetheless, it enjoyed limited constitutional powers to enter into certain types of agreements with other States. The Malawian Declaration of 24 November 1964 did acknowledge the binding nature and legal continuity of any treaties entered into by the Federation insofar as they were applicable to Nyasaland, at least for the duration of the grace period.

18. Dareste, 1913, B.175, cited by D.P. O'Connell, "Independence and Succession to Treaties", *38 BIYL 84* (1962) at 112.

19. F.C. Okoye, *International Law and the New African States*, (1971) p. 58.

20. Some of the leading scholarly works in this respect in the English language are: O'Connell, *State Succession in Municipal Law and International Law*, 2 Vols, (1967); see also same author's work cited in note 18 *supra*, and "Recent Problems of State Succession in Relation to New States", *130 Hague Recueil 95* (1970). Brownlie,

op. cit. note 1 pp. 654–675; O. Udokang, *Succession of New States to International Treaties*, (1972); R.W.G. De Muralt, *The Problem of Succession with Regard to Treaties*, (1954); K. Zemanek, "State Succession after Decolonization", *116 Hague Recueil 187* (1965); A.-U. Rehman, "Succession of Newly Independent States to Multilateral and Bilateral Treaties", *25 Indian J. Int. L. 67* (1985). As regards the position of African States in particular, see Okoye, *ibid.*; Y. Makonnen, *International Law and the New States of Africa*, (1983) *passim*; N.S. Rembe, "The Vienna Convention on State Succession in Respect of Treaties: An African Perspective on its Applicability and Limitation", *17 CILSA 131* (1984); see also the extensive literature cited by Brownlie, Makonnen and O'Connell, *ibid.*

21. On the classical origins of the theory, see H. Grotius, *De Jure Belli ac Pacis*, Bk. II, Ch. 9, 10 (1925); S. Pufendorf, *De Jure Naturae et Gentium*, Bk. II Ch. 9, s. 6 (1934); E. Vattel, *Le droit de Gens*, Bk. II, Ch. 12 (1916). (All the editions referred to here are the Carnegie Classics of International Law.)

22. See, for example, Makonnen, *op. cit.* note 20, pp. 132–133.

23. *Ibid.* pp. 132–136.

24. J.Z. Zourek, "Views of Eastern European Authors on State Succession", Working Paper No. 16, International Law Association, Committee on Succession of New States to Treaties and Certain Obligations of Their Predecessors; see also D.M. O'Connor, "Materials on Soviet Views of State Succession", American Society of International Law, Study Panel on State Succession, Working Paper No 2 (1968).

25. See, for example, Brownlie, *op. cit.* pp. 669–670; A.S. Hershey, *The Essentials of International Public Law and Organization*, (1965) pp. 173–175; J.L. Brierly, *Law of Nations*, (6th ed., 1963) p. 153; see also D.W. Greig, *International Law*, (2nd ed., 1976) pp. 15, 512 *et seq.*; O'Connell, *State Succession in Municipal Law and International Law*, Vol. II, (1967) pp. 12–23, 231 *et seq.*; A.D. McNair, *The Law of Treaties*, (1961) pp. 655–664.

26. See McNair, *ibid.* p. 605.

27. Greig, *op. cit.* p. 512.

28. In the discussion which follows in Chapter 4, I have termed this notion "the principle of independence". Notice in this regard the statement by McNair: "[Newly] independent states which do not result from a political dismemberment and cannot fairly be said to involve political continuity with any predecessor start life with a clean slate in the matters of treaty [obligations]". See McNair, *op. cit.*, at p. 601, with evidence of State practice at pp. 603–605. See also the

International Law Association's handbook, *The Effect of Independence on Treaties*, (1965) *passim*.

29. 384 UNTS (1961) p. 209; also Cmnd. No. 1214.

30. I.L.A., *Report of 52nd Conf.*, (1966), p. 557

31. The U.S. Consul General at Lagos (Emmerson) to the Secretary of State (Herter), Despatch No. 137, 8 September 1960. M.S. Dept. of State, file 641.45h9/9-860, cited in M. Whiteman, *ADIL*, Vol. II, p. 1000.

32. O'Connell, *op. cit.* note 25, p. 371; see also his *International Law*, Vol.I, (2nd ed., 1970) pp. 370–373. O'Connell's general view is that the practice of concluding devolution agreements has the advantage of enabling the new State to discontinue treaty relationships at its option, but the disadvantage of being a unilateral action; and that these devolution agreements are merely confirmatory of the continuity achieved by international law, since they purport to act as assignments only in respect of treaties which would not continue in force pursuant to international law. But see also the views of E. Lauterpacht, "State Succession and Agreements for the Inheritance of Treaties", 7 ICLQ 514 (1956); H.F. van Punhuys, "*La succession de l'Indonésie aux accords internationaux conclus par les Pays-Bas avant l'indépendence de l'Indonésie*", 2 *NILR* 67 (1957).

33. See similar view in Udokang, *op. cit.* note 20, p. 203.

34. See note 2 *supra*.

35. U.N. Doc. A/CN.4/150 p. 31, para. 87. Algeria, for rather obvious historical reasons, also issued a unilateral declaration denouncing pre-independence French treaties.

36. ILC Yrbk, 1962, Vol. II, p. 122.

37. Greig, *op. cit.* p. 514.

38. For a fuller discussion of this approach within the Tanzanian context, see E.E. Seaton and S.T.M. Maliti, *Tanzania Treaty Practice*, (1973) *passim*. In his excellent discussion of the subject, Makonnen characterizes the Nyerere Doctrine and its variants as together constituting "the Eastern African Optional Doctrine of State Succession"; see Makonnen, *op. cit.* note 20, pp. 197–259. See also same author's *The Nyerere Doctrine of State Succession and the New States of East Africa*, (1984) *passim*.

39. For text of the Declaration, see International Law Association, *The Effect of Independence on Treaties*, (1965) p. 388.

40. Among these States are Barbados, Botswana, Burundi, Guyana, Kenya, Lesotho, Malawi, Mauritius, Nauru, Rwanda, Swaziland, Uganda and Zambia.

41. The initial deadline of 6 January 1966 stipulated in the Declaration was subsequently postponed by a year, to 6 January 1967.

42. Makonnen, *op. cit.* note 20, p. 290.

43. *Ibid.* pp. 462–463.

44. The principle of *uti possidetis* was embodied, at least impliedly, in a resolution adopted by the first summit meeting of Heads of State and Government of the recently formed Organization of African Unity in Cairo, Egypt, in July 1964. It would appear that this decision, to "take Africa as it is" and renounce territorial claims, was prompted by the ardent desire on the part of the newly independent African States to "achieve African unity [and] not to introduce black imperialism". See O.A.U. Doc. AHG/RES. 17(I); see also *Proceedings of the Conference of Independent African States*, Addis Ababa, Vol. I, Sect. 2, Summit CIAS/GEN/INF/33 (30 May 1963) p. 2.

45. As far as succession to multilateral treaties is concerned, it is also important to note that there exist many similarities and parallels between declarations of succession and instruments of accession, acceptance or adhesion.

46. Greig, *op. cit.* p. 514. See also O'Connell, *International Law*, Vol. I, (2nd ed., 1970) at p. 371, where he observes: "The newly independent States have acted with such inconsistency that it is doubtful to what extent their 'practice' is significant in analyzing the present state of international law respecting treaty succession".

4

SUCCESSION TO TREATIES AND INTERNATIONAL FLUVIAL LAW IN AFRICA: THE NIGER TREATIES

Introduction

International fluvial law is one branch of international law that presents the student of international law with a seemingly irreconcilable paradox. On the one hand, judging from the scanty treatment often given to the issue in the standard treatises (and its almost complete absence from college syllabi), one could easily conclude that international fluvial law is only to be located on the periphery of international law; that it is a fringe subject, just as air law and space law were regarded only half a century ago. But, on the other hand, a more patient enquiry into the history and development of international law soon reveals that, in fact, international law has been concerned with the regulation of international watercourses (for example, lakes and rivers) for a long time, with individual pronouncements by publicists dating back to the writings of the so-called "fathers" of international law: Grotius, Pufendorf and Vattel. Viewed from this angle, then, international fluvial law, or the law of international watercourses, lies at the very core, rather than on the fringes, of the historical development of international law. Indeed, it is apt to observe that the history of the modern international organization, and thus the advent of the law of international institutions, dates back to the establishment of the various international commissions by European States in respect of some of the major international rivers in Europe between 1815 and 1866: the Rhine Commission (1815), the European Commission for the Danube (1856) and those dealing with the Elbe (1821), the Douro (1835), the Po (1849) and the Pruth (1866). In this regard, one may also mention the International Commission for the

Congo created under Articles 17–24 of the General Act of Berlin (1885) which, however, never became operational.[1] In fact, for the student of the history (and development) of international law in Africa, in particular, the General Act of Berlin is significant, *inter alia*, in this respect: it represented the first occasion whereby European formulated conventional rules of international law – for the Euro-centric international legal system of the time – were transplanted to a continent which had not, as yet, been in significant contact with international law whether as a participating subject or as an object of that system of law.[2] And these were the rules, embodied in Articles 13–33 of the Berlin Act, respecting the freedom of navigation for all nations along the Congo and Niger rivers. These rules form an aspect of what is now conceived as international fluvial law.

But all this is not to suggest that international fluvial law is of no more than historical interest; quite the contrary. The importance of the role that international watercourses have played in man's social and economic development over the centuries cannot be overemphasized. The earliest known civilizations originated around what are still some of the world's most important river systems; these rivers were essential not only for agriculture, but they also provided possible channels of communication, thereby facilitating both contact and trade among the early riparian communities. The interdependence of the modern world, coupled with the technological and industrial advances of the twentieth century, has increased and varied the uses of these watercourses. To the traditional uses of irrigation and navigation can now be added such diverse economic and industrial uses as fluvial mining, aquatic food production, manufacturing, timber floating, fishing, energy production and so on. The role that both national and international watercourses can play in the development of the developing nations, for example, is increasingly being recognized in national development policies and objectives. This is most evident in the movement towards integrated multilateral river basin development in some regions of the developing world, such as those relating to the Mekong River in Asia, and the Niger, Senegal and Gambia Rivers as well as Lake Chad in West Africa; and the Kagera Basin and the Zambezi River regimes in Eastern and Southern Africa respectively. These integrated river basin development projects have invariably been accompanied by the creation of specialized international riparian organizations. The role of international law and international lawyers in these activities cannot be doubted.

It is, perhaps, indicative of the importance attached to the regulation of international watercourses in actual modern State practice that the matter was recommended to the International Law Commission by the United Nations General Assembly in 1970. Paragraph one of General Assembly Resolution

2669 (XXV) of 8 December 1970 recommended that "the commission should take up the study of the law of the non-navigational uses of international watercourses, with a view to its progressive development and codification". This was included in the Commission's general work in 1971 under the proposed title of "The law of non-navigational uses of international watercourses". The Special Rapporteur presented his first report on the topic in the course of the commission's thirty-first session in 1979. The work of the Commission recently came to fruition with the adoption by the UN General Assembly of a Convention on the Non-Navigational Uses of International Watercourses.[3]

As regards the practice of modern African States, it must be pointed out that the development of international fluvial law, first initiated in 1885, has expanded in the post-colonial era. The post-1960 period has witnessed the conclusion of new international conventions by the new African States respecting the management and utilization of various international watercourses and drainage basins: the Niger, Senegal and Gambia Rivers and Lake Chad in West Africa and the Nile and the Zambezi in Southern Africa, to mention but a few. Except for the Nile, these treaty regimes have also been accompanied by the establishment of specialized international organizations embracing all the co-riparian or co-basin States concerned. A study of the various treaties and the international riparian organizations established thereunder clearly justifies the claim that the practice of African States in the last thirty-five years has achieved two things: first, the expansion of international fluvial law in general, from its originally Euro-centric base and its narrow concern with European rivers to a wider area embracing international watercourses in other parts of the world; and, secondly, the emergence of certain rules of international law which are peculiar enough to the African treaty regimes as to be suggestive of an original African contribution to the development of international fluvial law. Here, one discerns a shift in international legal theory from the "use-oriented" to a "resource-oriented" approach in the management and utilization of international watercourses.

The Niger regime presents the most instructive example of the practice of African States in this area of international law. Unlike the Congo, the Niger has been the subject of new post-colonial treaties which were concluded to replace the pre-independence conventions of 1885 and 1919 (the General Act of Berlin and the Convention of St. Germain-en-Laye, respectively). These new treaties are the Act Relating to Navigation and Economic Cooperation between States of the Niger Basin (1963) and the Agreement concerning the Niger River Commission and the Navigation and Transport on the River Niger (1964).[4] These agreements, usually referred to as the Niamey Treaties, were concluded following a series of consultations and conferences involving all the riparian States which were held in the Niger capital of Niamey from 1961 onwards. The 1963 Treaty laid down the principles of international law to be observed by the riparian States in their management and utilization of the watercourse, both in navigational and non-navigational matters. The latter accord established the intergovernmental organ charged with the multilateral regulation of the river – an international riparian organization modelled on the earlier European commissions referred to above.

Thus, it can be seen that the Niger has now been under an internationalized regime for more than three decades – longer than any other international watercourse on the African continent. For, although the Nile has also been the subject of treaty regulations for over a hundred years, no international riparian organization, similar to those set up for the Niger or the Senegal Rivers, has ever been established. Recent declarations of intent in this context by some of the Nile's riparian States have not, as yet, resulted in the creation of such an organization. So, for the international legal scholar interested in studying the evolution and development of international fluvial law in Africa over the past hundred years since its inception in the 1885 General Act of Berlin, the Niger regime easily commends itself as the most apt case-study. But this is not the aim of the present chapter.

The aim of this discussion is more limited. What is intended here is an examination of some of the pertinent questions that arose as a result of the accession to independent statehood of the various African States riparian to the Niger in 1960. More particularly, the problem being addressed here concerns the succession of the newly emergent African States to the pre-independence Niger treaties. Two questions may be posed. First, to what extent could the peculiar problems which have arisen from the process of decolonization in Africa be adequately examined with the aid of the traditional absolute devolution or non-devolution theories of international law, described in the preceding chapter, insofar as the pre-independence international fluvial conventions were concerned? Second, what was the proper legal or philosophical justification for denying or allowing the new States the right to set aside such conventions and to replace them with new post-independence accords – could such justifications be sought solely within the existing rules of international law? These questions may be regarded as forming only an aspect of the wider enquiry regarding the development of international fluvial law on the African continent and, in its turn, Africa's contribution to the evolution of this branch of international law.

The Pre-Independence Position

As has already been pointed out, the origin of international fluvial law in Africa lies in the provisions of the 1885 General Act of Berlin, a multilateral treaty concluded by some thirteen European powers along with the USA. A detailed discussion of this treaty is not intended here, nor will any attempt be made to examine the actual content of the regime of international fluvial law imported into Africa from "the principles of the Congress of Vienna" by the Berlin Act. Only a few points will be noted here.[5]

The first multilateral attempt to regulate the legal regime of international rivers in Europe can be found in Articles 108–116 of the Final Act of the 1815 Congress of Vienna.[6] These provisions were, more or less, concerned with the question of freedom of navigation for all nations, and were adopted in a number of subsequent European treaties, for example: the Act of Mainz (1815)[7], the Treaty of Paris (1856),[8] the Act of Navigation of the Danube (1857),[9] the Belgium-Netherlands Treaty (1863)[10] and the Act Relative to the Navigation of the Lower Danube adopted in 1865.[11] The principles embodied in the Final Act of Vienna were also incorporated in the identical treaties concluded in 1853 between France, Great Britain and the United States, on the one hand, and the Argentine confederation, on the other, in respect of the Parana and Uruguay Rivers.[12] By the time the Berlin Conference on Africa was convened in 1884, therefore, the principles enunciated in the Final Act of Vienna could be said to have entered into the domain of conventional international law.

The legal regime ushered onto the African continent by the General Act of Berlin was partially revised in 1890 at the Brussels Conference,[13] and was finally superseded by the regime established by the Convention of St. Germain-en-Laye in 1919.[14] No other international agreement was concluded by the European colonial powers regarding the regulation and utilization of the Congo and Niger watercourse systems prior to the independence of the African States which now exercise territorial sovereignty over them. However, it is important to point out here that the Congo and the Niger were not the only watercourses to be subjected to the evolving regime of international fluvial law in pre-independence Africa. Mention should also be made of the Nile regime.

The question of subjecting the Nile river to the principles of the Congress of Vienna was, of course, never discussed at the Berlin Conference. But the Nile has also been the subject of various international fluvial treaties, from the Protocol of 1891 between Great Britain and Italy[15] (then occupying part of the Sudan) to the Treaty of 1959 between Egypt and the Sudan.[16] Perhaps the most significant of these treaties is the Agreement of 7 May 1929 between the

United Kingdom and Egypt relating to the use of the waters of the River Nile for the purposes of irrigation.[17] This will be discussed later.

Revision and Abrogation of the General Act of Berlin in 1890 and 1919

As was noted above, the General Act of Berlin was amended by the 1890 General Act of Brussels and was subsequently abrogated by the Convention of St. Germain in 1919.

In fact, the Brussels amendment did not affect the regime of international navigation established in 1885, for it only related to the abolition of the customs immunity which had been instituted for the Congo basin under the Berlin Act. However, the First World War highlighted the inefficacy of the 1885 Act in a few areas, in particular the maintenance of the freedom of navigation during times of war. Moreover, it had by this time become quite clear that the Act had created a regime which was not compatible with the wishes of the future colonial powers in the Congo basin to exercise the full extent of their territorial sovereignty. Some of the provisions of the Berlin Act had fallen into neglect (for example, those relating to the international commission), while others had simply become irrelevant (for example, Articles 34 and 35, relating to formalities to be observed in the occupation of new territories on the African coast). Revision or total abrogation of the Act was therefore inevitable. The Convention of St. Germain adopted and affirmed certain aspects of the Berlin Act, while instituting certain limitations upon the provisions of that Act (for example, those relating to freedom of navigation and its beneficiaries). But Article 13 of the Convention expressly declared the abrogation of the General Act of Berlin and the General Act and Declaration of Brussels as between the parties to that convention. This legal fact was given judicial recognition by tile Permanent Court of International Justice in 1934 in the *Oscar Chinn* case (*Great Britain* v *Belgium*).[18]

In this case, the facts of which are not of immediate relevance here, the validity of the Convention of St. Germain as against the earlier treaties was not called into question by either party. On the contrary, it was on that Convention that both parties based their rights. Consequently, the Court saw no need to enquire into the validity of the 1919 treaty as against the Act of Berlin and the Act and Declaration of Brussels. It merely observed:[19]

> "The Convention of St. Germain was the successor, so far as the parties in the case are concerned and as regards the relations between them, of the Act of Berlin and the Act of Brussel."

On the other hand, the validity of the abrogation of the General Act of Berlin and the validity of the Convention repealing that Act was forcefully challenged by two of the dissenting judges. Judges van Eysinga and Schucking discussed this question in the context of Article 36 of the Berlin Act. This article, though not expressly providing for the manner of abrogation, stated:

> "The Signatory Powers of the present General Act reserve to themselves to introduce into it subsequently, and by common accord, such modifications and improvements as experience may show to be expedient."

Judge van Eysinga understood the "modifications" stipulated in this article to cover any purported abrogation, and thus concluded that abrogation of the Act by only some of the contracting parties (as was the case here) was precluded by the article. The learned judge therefore considered the Convention of St. Germain invalid and consequently concluded that the court ought to have approached the issue from the basis of the General Act of 1885 and the General Act and Declaration of Brussels.[20] Judge van Eysinga did not consider Article 38 of the Statute of the Court relevant in this matter. That article provided, *inter alia*:

> "The court shall apply international conventions, whether general or particular, establishing rules expressly recognised by contesting State."

Judge Schucking followed this reasoning, stating that this provision could not have been intended to mean that the court was bound to apply a convention which it knew to be invalid. Rather, he argued that the judge should only apply those rules which he recognizes as valid; in much the same way as the court cannot apply a convention which is contrary to good morals, so too it should not apply a convention invoked by the parties which is in reality invalid and without any legal effect. It was further contended that the fact that those parties which were signatories to the General Act but not to the Convention did not attack the validity of the latter did not prejudice the argument that in point of law the Convention was invalid. The judge concluded:[21]

> "The attitude of the tribunal should, in my opinion, be governed in such a case by considerations of international public policy, even when jurisdiction is conferred on the court by virtue of a Special Agreement."

The minority view never solicited much support from publicists, but an eminent commentator and scholar subsequently remarked:[22]

"Since not all of the Signatories of the General Act were also parties to the Convention, it was doubtful whether the latter was valid even between the parties which were signatories to both."

Verzjil thus had no doubt that the Court ruled in favour of the validity of the Convention for the sole reason that the litigants had presented it as the source of their reciprocal rights and obligations.

A few remarks may be made here. First, it could be said that the abrogation effected by Article 13 of the Convention should be viewed as being only of relative effect rather than as being valid *erga omnes*. As between parties who were signatories to the General Act but not the Convention, that Act remained the source of their respective rights and obligations. Such a position implied the dual effect of a juridical regime, an example of which was provided by the Geneva Conventions relating to the Red Cross: the coexistence of the Conventions of 1906[23] and 1929.[24] In any case, Article 13 of the Convention clearly intended only a relative effect of the purported abrogation. It is also important to recognize that Article 36 of the Berlin Act did not prescribe a power of veto, although it employed the words "by common accord". It simply signified that in case of revision, such revision would be unopposable to those who would not have subscribed to it. There is no reason why two parties who subscribed to and recognized such an amendment, and were both parties to the superseding treaty, should not be at liberty to invoke the latter agreement as between themselves. Confirmation that this was, indeed, the recognised rule of contemporary treaty law at the time of the *Oscar Chinn* trial may be sought in the provisions of two important instruments. First, Article 18 of the 1928 Havana Convention – regarded as an affirmation of the existing principles of treaty law – had provided that two or more States may agree that their relations are to be governed by rules other than those established in general conventions concluded by them with other States.[25] This issue was enunciated more clearly in Article 22(b) of the Draft Convention on the Law of Treaties prepared by the Harvard Research in International Law two years after the *Oscar Chinn* judgment.[26] This article provided:

"Two or more of the State parties to a treaty to which other States are parties may make a later treaty which will supersede the earlier treaty in their relations *inter se* only if this is not forbidden by the provisions of the earlier treaty and if the later treaty is not so inconsistent with the general purpose of the earlier treaty as to be likely to frustrate that purpose."

As has been argued above, it is wrong to construe Article 36 of the General Act of Berlin as having forbidden the conclusion of subsequent treaties by two or more of the signatories as regards their relations *inter se*. Nor can one claim that the Convention of St. Germain was so inconsistent with the *general* purpose of the General Act of Berlin as to have frustrated that purpose. It may thus be concluded that the decision by Belgium to base this action on the Convention of St. Germain and the acceptance by the court of that decision validly accorded with Article 38 of the Court's Statute.

Today, one may, perhaps, retrospectively reflect upon the problem of validity raised by the dissenting judges in the *Oscar Chinn* case in terms of the provisions of Article 30 of the Vienna Convention on the Law of Treaties (1969)[27] which would appear to support the view on the relative validity of the Convention of St. Germain. But, in any case, since it would seem that all States took on the new Convention without objection, the Permanent Court of International Justice was justified in seeing no reason for calling the validity of the convention into question: *error communis facit jus*.

So, it may be submitted that not only was the Convention of St. Germain a valid successor to both the General Act of Berlin and the General Act and Declaration of Brussels, but it also remained the immediate source of the international rights and obligations for the colonial powers which continued to exercise sovereignty over the colonial territories in which the two rivers were located. And, as has already been observed, since this convention was never superseded by any other treaty until the emergence of these colonies into independent States, it was this agreement which can be said to have devolved upon these newly born riparian States. Thus up to 1960, at least (when all the new riparian States gained independent statehood), the legal status of the Congo and the Niger continued to be that prescribed by the 1919 regime.

The Devolution of the Pre-Independence Niger Treaties upon the new Riparian States

The submission that has been made above, regarding the continued validity of the Convention of St. Germain right up to 1960, has not always been unanimously accepted by all legal commentators. Indeed, the underlying assumption in the *Oscar Chinn* judgment – that having superseded the earlier treaties the 1919 Convention was itself still in force at the time of the litigation in 1933 – has been challenged by some legal scholars. It has been contended that the convention in fact became a dead letter in 1929 since Article 15 had envisaged its revision after a period of ten years from the date of its entry into force.[28] The envisaged revision was never effected.

The *travaux préparatoires* reveal a clear division of opinion among the signatory States to the Convention of St. Germain in 1919. France and Belgium had proposed that in the absence of this revision the parties should consider themselves freed from the Treaty, while the opinion held by the United States and other Powers was that the Treaty was to continue in force in the absence of such revision.[29] The view here propounded is that where a treaty provides for an option to revise all or some of its provisions at a fixed date in the future without stating that the treaty shall cease to be in force should this option not be exercised, then the presumption ought to be that the treaty continues as a valid instrument, in the absence of the envisaged revision, after the expiry of that date. Consequently, the provision in Article 15 of the Convention of St. Germain cannot be read as suggesting that this treaty was to expire unless revised after a ten-year period. Rather, the intention of this provision was that the signatory States could meet at the end of that period to effect "such modifications as experience would have rendered necessary". Where no changes to the existing regime were considered necessary, as appears to have been the case here, the continued application of the convention was to be presumed. There have been precedents in the treaty practice of States to support this view. A relevant example from this era is the Treaty of Commerce between the United Kingdom and the former Kingdom of Korea of 26 November 1883.[30] Article XI of this treaty provided:

> "Ten years from the date on which this Treaty shall come into operation, either of the High Contracting Parties may, in giving one year's notice to the other, demand a revision of the Treaty or of the Tariff annexed thereto, with a view to the insertion therein, by mutual consent, of such modifications as experience shall prove to be desirable."

No revision of the treaty was ever undertaken, and yet it was still regarded as being in force after the expiry of the ten-year period stipulated in the provision above. Moreover, even after the annexation of Korea by Japan in 1910 the treaty survived for a while due to an undertaking given by Japan to Great Britain that it would "see to the execution of treaties actually existing between Korea and other Powers".[31]

Another example is afforded by the Definitive Statute of the Danube of 23 July 1921.[32] Article 42 stated as follows:

> "At the expiration of 5 years from the date of its coming into force, the present Statute may be revised if two-thirds of the signatory States so request and specify the stipulations which appear to them to require revision. This request shall be addressed to the Government of the French Republic, which

will summon, within six months, a conference in which all the States signatory of the present Convention shall be invited to take part."

As in the case of the Great Britain-Korea Treaty referred to above, the stipulated revision was never undertaken when the five-year period stipulated in Article 42 lapsed; and yet, none of the parties ever suggested that the treaty ceased to operate in the absence of this revision, at least up until the somewhat controversial "unilateral" abrogation occasioned by the 1948 Belgrade Convention, adopted by the Soviet Union and its allies but rejected by the Western Powers, including Great Britain, France, Italy, Belgium and Greece, who had been original signatories to the 1921 Treaty. On its part, for example, Great Britain had, throughout the period 1927 to 1940, continually recognized the treaty as an existing, valid instrument with only the observation, of course, that it was still "subject to revision on six months notice".[33] And similarly at the Belgrade Conference in 1948, Britain, Belgium, France, Greece, and Italy all upheld the uninterrupted validity of the Definitive Statute of the Danube of 1921 on the basis that it had neither been replaced nor modified in accordance with the requirements of Article 42 (as outlined above).[34] The Agreement of Sinaia of 1938[35] – which involved only three of the twelve signatories to the 1921 treaty and related to a modification of certain powers of the European Danube Commission – cannot be regarded as a valid revision under the provision of Article 42.

So, the view that, without revision, the Convention of St. Germain remained valid, as has been argued above, is not without precedent in the history of international law. And the evidence is that the signatories of the Convention themselves continued to rely on it as a valid treaty even in the absence of any revision after the expiry of the ten year period as stipulated in Article 15 of the Convention. It has already been pointed out that it was on the presumption and understanding that the Convention still validly governed their relations that both Great Britain and Belgium appeared before the Permanent Court of International Justice in the *Oscar Chinn* case in 1933. And, interestingly enough, it was only in 1934 that the United States ratified the Convention, and none of the other parties objected that the treaty, being ratified, had already ceased to be in force on account of its not having been revised ten years after its entry into force, namely in 1930. In this respect, it may be noted that as recently as 1977 the Convention of St. Germain was still regarded as one of the United States' "treaties in force", thereby implying its continuing validity, in spite of the absolute abrogation of that Convention in Article I of the 1963 Act of Niamey.[36] The problem here is that unlike Great Britain or France, the United States was never a predecessor State to any of the African States whose territory was affected by the Convention of St. Germain. Thus, whereas the United Kingdom and France ceased to be parties to the treaty, whether as a result of the process of State succession by, or devolution agreement with, the new African States, the United States remains an unaffected third party who, in theory at least, remains a party to the original treaty – a treaty which in practice can only be described as having fallen into desuetude. Indeed, it may be said that apart from the case just noted none of the parties to the Convention of St. Germain have invoked the continued validity of this treaty after the conclusion and entry into force of the Act of Niamey. This question is further examined later.

It is therefore the Convention of St. Germain which must be regarded as the only valid international legal instrument which could possibly devolve upon the newly born African States riparian to the Niger. The question of the devolution, or non-devolution, of this treaty upon these States belongs to the wider issue of the succession of States to international agreements. This discussion, as has been intimated above, does not aim at examining the question of State succession in its generality; rather, the focus of this enquiry is on those treaties relating to the regulation of international watercourses – international fluvial conventions.

The Colonial Position

The theory and practice relating to the extension and application of treaty obligations entered into by colonial powers to colonial territories were discussed in the preceding chapter. Thus, as was concluded in respect of the colonial territory of Nyasaland, Great Britain retained sole responsibility for treaties and other foreign relations aspects of its colony of Nigeria until the latter's independence on 1 October 1960. When the Convention of St. Germain was concluded on 19 November 1919, this colony had been in existence for some five years, born out of the amalgamation of the former Southern and Northern Nigerian Protectorates in 1914.[37] It can validly be concluded that having regard to the general rule under British practice the Convention of St. Germain was extended to this colony following its ratification by the British Government. Similarly, following French constitutional theory and practice, French overseas territories were bound by the Convention of St. Germain, along with the other Peace Treaties of 1919–1920, by virtue of its ratification by France. In the case of the Niger States, these colonies were Benin, the Ivory Coast, Mali, Niger, Guinea and Upper Volta (now Burkina Faso), all of whom were former members of the Federation of French West Africa, or *Afrique*

Occidentale Française (AOF), along with Chad which belonged to the other colonial entity, French Equatorial Africa, or *Afrique Equatorial Française* (AEF).

Cameroon underwent a very different political evolution from the eight other States. Formerly a German colony (from 12 July 1884), it was no longer such by the time the Convention of St. Germain was concluded. After the First World War the United Kingdom and France agreed upon an administrative partition of the colony, the two respective zones being established as British and French Mandates by the Council of the League of Nations in 1922. As to the question whether the Convention of St. Germain applied to this mandated territory one must give an affirmative reply. For the "B" class Mandate Agreements, in which category Cameroon was, provided that the mandatory power should apply to its mandated territories "any general international conventions applicable to its contiguous territory". The contiguous territory on the British side of the mandate was that of the colony of Nigeria, and on the French side that of the colonies of Oubangi-Chari (now the Central African Republic), Congo-Brazzaville and Gabon. And since it has already been concluded that the Convention of St. Germain must be deemed to have applied to these British and French colonies, so, too, on the basis of the said "B" class Mandate Agreements, must it be held to have extended over the Cameroon.

State Succession and the Devolution of the Convention of St. Germain

The various theoretical propositions relating State succession have already been outlined in the previous chapter. Here, the issue to be determined is if, as has just been concluded above, the Convention of St. Germain was still in force on the eve of the independence of the new States riparian to the Niger, did it continue to bind these States after their accession to independent statehood? Or did this treaty cease to be valid upon independence?

Although the majority of modern scholars of international law would seem to advocate the non-devolution theory, it cannot be said that the matter is now completely free of all controversy and uncertainty. Indeed, until the Vienna Convention on Succession of States in Respect of Treaties (1978) finally enters into force, there may not be any incontestably uniform view.[38] The contrasting views of O'Connell and Brownlie, two of the leading authorities of recent times, are illustrative of this divergence of opinion. While, in his various works on the subject, the former was generally in favour of devolution, Brownlie has argued that:[39]

> "[As] a matter of general principle a new State, ex hypothesi a non-party, cannot be bound by a treaty, and in addition other parties to a treaty are not bound to accept a new party, as it were, by operation of law."

And to this general rule of non-transmissibility Brownlie, in line with such earlier authorities as Hall, McNair, Oppenheim and Brierly,[40] gives a number of exceptions: treaties evidencing rules of general international law, treaties creating "objective regimes", and localized treaties as well as boundary treaties. In other words, the aforementioned theory of viewing "real" or "dispositive" treaties as qualifying the "clean slate" rule. It is to this view that the present writer subscribes. As regards the Convention of St. Germain, the question to be determined is whether it can be regarded as having belonged to the recognized exceptions so that it may be presumed to have automatically devolved upon the nine riparian States on their attainment of independence. In this regard, it may be noted that an examination of the practice of newly emergent States does reveal that the majority of these States have not only accepted automatic devolution of dispositive or localized treaties, but have in fact done so precisely because they view them as heritable treaties. In other words, State practice points to the existence of an *opinio juris* in this respect. It may be noted, too, that the 1978 Vienna Convention referred to above has also adopted this approach. Hence, Article 16 provides that:

> "A newly independent State is not bound to maintain in force, or to become a party to, any treaty by reason only of the fact that at the date of the succession of States the treaty was in force in respect of the territory to which the succession of States relates."

But it is also provided in Articles 11 and 12 of the Convention that the succession of States does not affect treaties relating to boundaries or to the use of any territory or restrictions upon its use whether for the benefit of any foreign State or group of States. And in this respect, treaties concerning water rights and navigation on rivers were regarded by the International Law Commission as belonging to the category of "treaties relating to the use of territory or restrictions upon its use".[41]

The fact that the principal objective of the Convention of St. Germain was the regulation of the freedom of navigation on the Niger (and the accompanying freedom of commerce in the area) is obvious from the provisions of the agreement itself and cannot be doubted. It was a navigation treaty. And, as has been noted, since the proposition that treaties relating to water rights and navigation on international rivers are regarded by the great majority of publicists, States and international tribunals (as can be seen from the *Aaland*

Islands case[42]) as an exception to the general rule of non-devolution, it may be validly concluded that the Convention of St. Germain did automatically devolve upon the new riparian States on their accession to independent statehood.

It may be recalled that some States have attempted to avoid the uncertainties surrounding the question of State succession by concluding what are known as devolution or inheritance agreements with the predecessor States. But the problems that arise from such agreements have also been noted. Take, for example, as regards the devolution agreement concluded between the United Kingdom and Nigeria, on the latter's accession to independence on 1 October 1960. Who was entitled to hold that the agreement in question was valid and has application over the successor State: the United Kingdom, the new State of Nigeria, the other parties to the original treaty or an independent tribunal? Was the fact that the *Oscar Chinn* judgment upheld the validity of the Convention of St. Germain, for example, conclusive for the purpose of the United Kingdom-Nigeria inheritance agreement? Following the line of argument canvassed in the discussion on the validity of these devolution agreements in the preceding chapter, it must be concluded that the devolution of the Convention of St. Germain upon Nigeria was not really dependent on the inheritance agreement of 1 October 1960 as might generally be assumed, but on the Convention's character as a dispositive treaty and thus as an exception to the general rule of non-succession.

The above submission is equally true of the other riparian States. In fact, none of them concluded any devolution agreements with France upon independence. One must recall here the unilateral abrogation by Upper Volta (as it then was) of all treaties concluded by France and purportedly applicable to it as a colony.[43] As for the other riparian States, they remained in theory committed to neither the principle of devolution nor that of non-devolution. However, it must be noted that in spite of the absence of any formal devolution arrangements, the conduct and practice of all the former French colonies in Africa has been to regard themselves as successors to France in respect of treaties specifically applied to them before the attainment of independence.

Thus, to state the matter briefly, in practice there is nothing to distinguish those States which have concluded devolution agreements from those which have not done so but which nonetheless generally acknowledge the continued validity of treaties specifically applied to them before the attainment of independence. It may thus be submitted that the Convention of St. Germain devolved upon all the new States riparian to the Niger whether or not they entered into formal inheritance agreements (Nigeria) or purportedly denounced all former colonial treaties (Upper Volta). This is so because of its nature as a dispositive treaty. And, as noted above, this category of treaties is regarded in international law as forming an exception to the general rule of non-transmissibility.

Having made the above submissions, the question may still be posed as to what concrete evidence of actual State conduct there is to show that the new riparian States did in fact consider this particular treaty as binding upon them. Was there, in other words, any evidence of the actual acceptance by the new African States of the continuing validity of the Convention of St. Germain during the period between their emergence as independent States and the abrogation of the convention in 1963?

To begin with, it must be recalled that with the sole exception of Guinea, which became independent in 1958, all the new African States riparian to the Niger attained independence in 1960. Thus, with one exception, all these States had had an independent statehood for only three years before the Convention of St. Germain was abrogated. Quite clearly, a time span of this nature is not long enough for a newly emergent State to manifest, by actual conduct, its acceptance of each and every treaty of the former parent State which may have devolved upon it. And, as is often the case, the question of whether or not a newly born State considers itself bound by any given treaty does not come up for consideration until a problem relating particularly to the given treaty has arisen. It has certainly never been the practice among newly born African States, as has already been pointed out, to singularly spell out which treaties are considered binding and which are not.

The negotiations leading to the conclusion of new treaties for the postindependence regulation of the Niger extended from 1960 to 1963. In fact, the first consultations in this respect were undertaken even before some of the future signatory States had achieved full international legal personality; that is, before full independence in August 1960. But, although it may be stated that none of the new States actually took steps to enforce the rights and to fulfil the obligations created by the Convention of St. Germain during the period 1960–1963, it cannot be doubted that, with the possible exception of Upper Volta, these States did consider themselves successors to this treaty. One major concern throughout the preliminary discussions preceding the conclusion of the Niamey Treaties was the need to revoke the Convention of St. Germain and to replace it with a new post-independence treaty. The argument that the Convention needed to be revoked by the new States implied, in itself, that these States did in fact consider the treaty as having remained valid until the time of their emergence as independent States and as having devolved upon them as successors to France and Great Britain.

In any case, so far as Nigeria was concerned, this conclusion would seem to follow automatically from the terms of the United Kingdom-Nigeria

Inheritance Agreement of 1 October 1960, discussed above. The view that the Convention of St. Germain had devolved upon the new States was never seriously contested by the plenipotentiaries and legal experts involved in the Niamey Conferences who, in the final analysis, were unanimous on the need to abrogate it *expressis verbis*.

The Convention of St. Germain as a Dispositive Treaty and the Source of an International Servitude

As pointed out above, the debate on heritable and non-heritable treaties has for a long time revolved around the distinction between personal and real treaties. Even the classical authorities viewed the problem in this light; thus, Vattel wrote:[44]

> "We must not confound those treaties or alliances which, since they impose the obligation of repeated acts on both sides, cannot remain in force except through the continued existence of the contracting powers, with those contracts by which a right is once and for all acquired, independent of any subsequent acts of either party. If, for example, a Nation has granted in perpetuity to a neighbouring prince, the right to fish in a river or to keep a garrison in one of its fortresses, the prince does not lose his rights even though the Nation from which he has received them should happen to be conquered by, or in any other way subjected to the control of, a foreign Power."

Thus the presumption was made that all personal treaties lapsed following a change of sovereignty such as arises in cases of independence, whereas real treaties continued to apply.

This traditional classification into "personal" and "real" treaties has come under criticism from modern authorities as being both misleading and insufficiently comprehensive. It has been pointed out, for instance, that the distinction between the two categories of treaties has not always been affirmed by historical analysis: continuity has not, apparently, been maintained in respect of supposedly real treaties even though there has occurred a general continuity of treaties of a clearly personal character throughout the same events. Indeed, in some cases it has not always been easy to define the difference between the two. An illustration of this is provided by the inconsistency of State practice regarding the effect of change of sovereignty upon extradition treaties, which were regarded by most authorities as personal treaties. This was the view taken by Denmark and the Netherlands, who claimed a non-devolution of their extradition treaties with the United

Kingdom upon the Irish Free State. Yet Hungary and Luxembourg held the opposite view. So, one can agree with Lester that if the classification of real and personal treaties breaks down when a single type of treaty is examined, the categories are obviously inadequate to unify broad groups of treaties of widely differing natures.[45] The other objection is that the notion of personal treaties is evidently irrelevant in modern times and should therefore be dispensed with in this debate. Personal treaties were relevant to the age when the "head of State" method was the normal way of entering contractual relationships with a sovereign State, with such treaties being terminated on the death of the particular monarch. The "head of State" method has lapsed and, consequently, the notion of personal treaties is no longer reflected in modern treaty practice.

In addition to the above objection, Okoye has made the correct observation that the earlier theoretical assumption of succession to dispositive treaties and non-succession to personal treaties took no account of the unique succession problems created by the evolution of the Afro-Asian States to an independent status.[46] For one thing, the practice of some of these States has been to succeed to the treaties of the parent State without drawing any distinction between personal and dispositive obligations. But, in spite of these criticisms, it remains relevant to examine the question of whether or not the Convention of St. Germain was a dispositive (or real) treaty for the following reason: although the notion of personal treaties has lapsed, even in the context of modern treaty practice one encounters those treaties which create "real" or "localized" obligations (those attaching to the territory) and those which do not. And State practice has indicated that the hard core of treaties which survive change of sovereignty – including change occasioned by accession to independence is the category of treaties which affect territory in essentially the same manner as executed conveyances, easements and servitudes affect personal estates in municipal law.

The term "dispositive", generally considered to have been invented by Westlake[47], is employed to designate a species of treaties which create real rights. Under such treaties, the territory concerned is impressed with a status which is both intended to be permanent and is independent of the personality of the State exercising sovereignty over it at the given time. The fundamental issue here is that the intention of the parties is presumed to be to establish a permanent relationship between their territories, a status which thus outlives those original parties to the treaty. The real rights thus created by a dispositive treaty are those which, in international law, attach to a territory and are in essence valid *erga omnes*.

The criterion for the category of dispositive treaties is evidently an elusive one. It could be said, however, that international lawyers generally consider these kinds of treaties as creating real rights attaching to the territory of a

State: treaties fixing frontiers, those relating to communication links such as navigation on rivers or canals, the use of rivers for irrigational purposes, the maintenance of river banks, or treaties regulating such matters as international railway connections or coastal fishing rights. A common feature of these treaties is that they can be likened to those covenants running with the land in English law. These treaties are thus more akin to conveyances than agreements and obviously involve the delimitation of sovereign competence within the impressed territory.

The view that treaties regulating matters of river navigation – or indeed other uses of international rivers – survive all changes of sovereignty and devolve upon newly established States has been advanced by the majority of legal scholars and does not appear to have been challenged. One can cite various instances of State practice as substantially validating this assertion in this respect. A good example of this practice in Africa is afforded by the devolution of the Nile river treaties. A brief discussion of the legal regime of the Nile is instructive, providing as it does a particularly apt analogy with the Niger regime.

Reference was made above to the Agreement of 7 May 1929 between the United Kingdom and Egypt. This treaty, reflecting four Commission reports undertaken in 1914, 1919, 1920 and 1925, stated that no works should be constructed on the Nile or its sources which might be under British administration, if these would prejudice the interests of Egypt, either in respect of the quantity of water arriving in Egypt or with respect to the date of its arrival. On the eve of its independence, the Sudan criticized this agreement on the grounds that it was too onerous, since it gave Egypt liberty to develop its resources, subject only to a sufficient flow of the river, while restricting the Sudan from doing likewise only with Egypt's consent. It was stated:[48]

> "[The] present Sudan Government considers that it was an unjust agreement because it limited the development of irrigation in the Sudan while leaving Egypt free to develop her irrigation as she pleased. [Sudan] does not dispute rights which have been established while her hands have been tied, but she claims that the time has now come to change the Nile Waters Agreement."

On his part, the British Foreign Secretary observed in a statement to Parliament on 26 November 1958:[49]

> "The 1929 Nile Waters Agreement was signed by [the] United Kingdom and [the] Kingdom of Egypt. I understand that the Government of the United Arab Republic recognizes its validity. For their part, Her Majesty's Government have continued to observe the Agreement in the territories for

which they are responsible. The first Government of independent Sudan declared that they did not regard themselves as bound by the Agreement."

What was apparent in the various pronouncements from the Sudanese Government was that Egypt's established legal rights in the Nile waters were not disputed at all. Rather, the argument was that economic and technical development since 1929 had rendered these provisions obsolescent. Sudan therefore formally repudiated the agreement in 1958 after a prolonged dispute and fruitless negotiations. But a new treaty was concluded the following year, substituting for the unilateral competence of Egypt pursuant to the 1929 agreement a system of technical and financial co-operation; the proportion to which each country had been entitled under the traditional regime was fixed and the disposal of the surplus was to be precisely regulated. In effect, therefore, the new treaty recognized Egypt's priority, to which the 1929 accord had given effect, but sought to limit it to the existing flow.

There can be no doubt that the rights created in favour of the Egyptian Government under the 1929 Treaty amounted to a grant of "real" rights. The treaty was thus a dispositive treaty – a fact which the Government of Sudan appeared fully to acknowledge. This is clear from the fact that Sudan did not at first seek an outright abrogation of the treaty, only its renegotiation in view of the changed economic and technical conditions and its own economic needs. Thus, Sudan was prepared to accept devolution of the treaty, albeit in an amended form.

In addition, it may also be noted that even the new Treaty of 1959 was itself essentially viewed as providing for "additional regulation of the Nile waters on the basis of [Egypt's] existing rights" – those being the rights created by the previous treaty. That this earlier treaty was actually abrogated is not so much a rejection of its character as a localized or dispositive treaty but rather an indication or reminder that in this, as in many other areas of international law, strict legal doctrine sometimes gives way to extra-legal considerations when political expediency so requires.

As regards the other upper riparian States it has been forcefully argued that they remain bound by the Nile Treaties.[50] But it must be pointed out that the Egyptian-Sudanese Treaty of 1959 did not seek to bind the other riparians, it being a bilateral treaty which, therefore, cannot bind third-party States. In fact, it may be noted that Ethiopia publicly expressed its immediate disapproval at not being invited to participate in the conclusion of the treaty.[51] With respect to the earlier treaty of 1929, the view of the British Foreign Secretary was that the British Government had continued to observe its obligations in the territories for which it was responsible, namely Kenya, Uganda and Tanganyika (as a Mandate Territory). Of these, Tanganyika did send a note to the Sudan stating that it did not consider itself bound by the 1929 treaty, not on the grounds of State succession, but on the ground that the agreement was obsolescent.[52] Yet neither Tanzania nor Uganda and Kenya have taken any action with respect to any of the Nile agreements which might be binding on them. In fact, in the case of Uganda, it may be pointed out that the construction of the Owen Falls Dam at Lake Victoria was the subject of a special agreement, intrinsic with that of 1929, between the United Kingdom and Egypt. Since Uganda is without doubt a successor to the former, it may well be held to be a successor to the latter as well. The other riparian States, Burundi, Rwanda and Democratic Republic of Congo, have not taken any action, one way or the other, with regard to the 1929 treaty.[53] The conclusion to be drawn from this is that in spite of their supposed disapproval, these States were at the time of their independence (and still remain) mindful of the dispositive character of the 1929 Anglo-Egyptian Treaty.

Similarly, one may also cite the case of the Agreement of 9 May 1906 between the United Kingdom and the Independent State of the Congo.[54] Article 3 of this treaty provided that:

> "The Government of the Independent State of the Congo undertakes not to construct, or allow to be constructed, any work on or near the Semliki or Isango River, which would diminish the volume of water entering Lake Albert, except in agreement with the Sudanese Government."

Article 6 of the Treaty conferred upon the trading vessels flying the Congolese or Belgian flags a similar right of navigation and trading on the Upper Nile as that given to British and Egyptian vessels subject, of course, to the due observance of Sudanese laws and regulations. This treaty has been recognized by the successor to the Congo Free State, Democratic Republic of Congo, as creating an international servitude and, consequently, no action has been taken, on its part, to abrogate the agreement.

Other classic cases of succession to international fluvial conventions are those relating to the navigation of the Mississippi and Mekong Rivers. As regards the former, it may briefly be noted that Article 7 of the Treaty of Paris (1763)[55] between Great Britain and France granted British subjects freedom of navigation on this river. After the transfer of Louisiana to Spain, immediately afterwards, the burden of this obligation was passed to the successor State. Following the end of the American War of Independence, a treaty was concluded between Great Britain and the United States on 3 September 1783[56] which stipulated that the navigation of the Mississippi "shall forever remain free and open to the subjects of Great Britain and the citizens of the United States".

When Spain later tried to restrict the freedom of American citizens to navigate the river, it was argued that the navigational rights previously enjoyed by the British must be regarded as having devolved upon the United States "because the grant of right made by His Britannic Majesty by Article VII of the Treaty of 1763 was intended to run with the soil, [it] was in other words an easement".[57] The issue was subsequently settled by the United States-Spain Treaty of 1795 which, though not expressly recognizing that rights had accrued to the United States under the Treaty of 1763, quite clearly constituted an important acknowledgement of them by Spain.[58]

The navigational regime of the Mekong River was regulated by a number of Franco-Siamese treaties, the first of which was the Boundary Treaty of 1867.[59] Other important treaties were concluded in 1893,[60] 1904,[61] and 1926.[62] Finally, the Convention of Pau of 1950[63] also guaranteed freedom of navigation to the nationals of all members of the French Union "without any infringement to the provisions of the Franco-Siamese Convention of 25 August 1926 or the annexes of any other texts in force in that matter". This was a clear recognition of the continued validity of the 1926 treaty, which had been concluded in the name of France and not that of Laos or Thailand. After the independence of the associated States of Indo-China in 1954, a new treaty was concluded; it regulated more completely the navigational rights of the three States *inter se* (that is, Laos, Cambodia and Vietnam) and, also, in an explanatory note preserved Thailand's rights under the 1926 treaty.[64]

Having regard to the foregoing discussion, it may be concluded that the devolution of the Convention of St. Germain may be considered in the context of the transmissibility of dispositive treaties. In fact, an example is afforded by the 1885 Berlin Act which this Convention supersedes, as already argued above.

King Leopold II's International Association of the Congo (which was a so-called unofficial participant at the Berlin Conference) had been granted recognition as a sovereign State – as the Congo Free State – by other colonial powers by the time the General Act of Berlin was signed on 26 February 1885. The so-called Congo Free State was ceded to Belgium by the International Association in November 1907, the Cession Treaty being adopted by the Belgian Chamber on 20 August 1908. The phantom State finally ceased to exist on 14 November 1908.

What is of significant interest here is that when the question of whether or not the General Act of Berlin was superseded by the Convention of St. Germain was considered in the *Oscar Chinn* case, both the majority judgment and the individual dissenting opinions proceeded on the assumption that the Berlin Act had in fact survived the change of sovereignty over the Congo Free

State. The possibility that this treaty may have been abrogated by the change of sovereignty was never considered.

The continued application of the General Act over the former territory of the Congo Free State was never doubted or contradicted by State practice between 1907 and 1919. Neither Belgium nor the other powers ever questioned the devolution of the 1885 agreement upon the former. The question here is whether the acknowledged survival of the General Act of Berlin after the transfer of sovereignty to Belgium affords any valid guide to the fate of the Convention of St. Germain with respect to the Congo and the Niger after the independence of the various States now exercising sovereignty over those two rivers. The view of one leading authority is that there is clearly some guidance to be obtained from the attitude taken after the 1907 transfer of sovereignty but a proviso is submitted that, since the new sovereign in 1907 was also a party to the 1885 agreement, it could be argued that the treaty survived by virtue of the transfer of sovereignty between its signatories.[65]

The other issue that arises in this debate is that of the effect of independence upon treaties creating international servitudes. The concept of a treaty independent of the personality of the sovereign has always been bound up with the notion of servitude. International servitudes have been defined as "those exceptional restrictions made by treaty on the territorial supremacy of a state by which a part or the whole of its territory is in a limited way made perpetually to serve a certain purpose or interest of another state".[66] So, the essence of an international servitude is that the right must belong to a State; it must be a permanent right; it must be one which makes the territory of a State serve the uses of another State, and it may be restrictive or permissive.

The notion of international servitudes has been attacked by various schools of writers. There are those who accord a State "absolute and indivisible" sovereignty and argue that a State cannot derogate from its sovereignty by an international contract.[67] It has also been argued that the analogy is a misleading importation, implying as it does too rigid an insistence on technical principles of civil law, and also importing the idea of adjacent territories in a dominant-servient relationship. And linguistic objection has even been made against the appropriateness of the term "servitude" itself.[68] These may be justifiable objections, but the rationale behind this notion is that in certain cases a State may depend for its livelihood on the co-operation of a neighbour, for instance, in the maintenance of a hydro-electric dam on a boundary river, or when a State's only contact with the coast may be by being permitted free navigation on a river passing through neighbouring territory. State practice would appear to disfavour the disruption of such regimes and to ensure their continuity in spite of changes in sovereignty over the territory in question. This may be said to hold true for the Convention of St. Germain insofar as it purportedly regulates the freedom of navigation – the right of access – in respect of all nations on the Niger and Congo Rivers.

One valid objection that may be raised is that the isolation of the notion of international servitudes from the category of dispositive treaties is somewhat elusive and questionable. Brownlie, in company with other writers who reject the existence of a special category of localized treaties, has rightly pointed to the considerable overlapping of the subject-matter between the two categories.[69] Admittedly, almost all the materials and examples usually cited in support of the existence of a category of dispositive treaties are also commonly adduced as evidence of an independent concept of international servitude, for example, treaties relating to international waterways, port rights, military bases and fishing rights. Accordingly it is the view here that these purportedly different categories of treaties must, in fact, be seen as belonging to the same category since, except for the case of the boundary treaty simpliciter, a dispositive treaty will normally imply the existence of servitude. However, whether one approaches the issue in this context, or continues to examine the Convention of St. Germain either as a dispositive treaty or as creating international servitude, the ultimate conclusion must still be that from the legal point of view, the 1919 treaty did devolve upon the newly independent States of the Niger (and also those of the Congo).

It is thus submitted that the Convention of St. Germain, under international law, remained binding upon the new States after their accession to independence. It has already been argued that although these States may not have manifested their acceptance of this treaty by actual conduct in the short period between their emergence as independent States and its abrogation in 1963 (in the case of the Niger States), the views expressed by these States' representatives in the deliberations preceding that abrogation (quite apart from Nigeria's explicit acceptance of the United Kingdom's former treaties which related to its territory) clearly suggest that the Convention of St. Germain was regarded as having devolved upon them. But it was also within the rights of these new riparians to abrogate the treaty and to replace it with a new one a right which arises from the acquisition and possession of independent sovereignty by any new-born State.

Article 1 of the Act of Niamey (1963): Abrogation of the Convention of St. Germain [70]

Article 1 of the Act of Niamey abrogates *expressis verbis* not only the Convention of St. Germain but also the General Act of Berlin and the General Act and Declaration of Brussels:

> "The General Act of Berlin of 26 February 1885, the General Act and Declaration of Brussels of 2 July 1890 and the Convention of St. Germain-en-Laye of 10 September 1919 are and remain abrogated as far as they concern the River Niger, its tributaries and sub-tributaries."

One thing that may be noted from the outset is the difference in the abrogation formula used here from that employed in the Convention of St. Germain. As was indicated above, Article 13 of that Convention abrogated the Berlin and Brussels Acts only so far as the parties to it were concerned – a relative abrogation. On the other hand, the Niamey formula, "as far as they concern the River Niger, its tributaries and sub-tributaries", clearly implies an absolute abrogation, so that parties to the earlier treaties are not permitted to claim the continuing validity of these treaties as against the 1963 Act of Niamey or, for that matter, the subsequent 1964 Agreement.

The question arises as to why it was deemed necessary to specifically stipulate the abrogation of the earlier instruments when, as has been pointed out, these had already been superseded by the Convention of St. Germain, insofar as France and Great Britain were concerned. It is obvious that underlying the exercise of concluding a new treaty for the Niger was the desire of the new States to make a complete break with those colonial pacts which were designed for Africa at a conference of largely European States without any African representation. The question of whether or not it was necessary to abrogate the earlier – already defunct – treaties did not pass without discussion at the Niamey Conferences and during the elaboration of the Niamey Act. Some delegates were of the opinion that they should proceed without any specific provision abrogating the former agreements since such abrogation ought to be taken for granted in view of the changed political circumstances – the operation of the doctrine of *rebus sic stantibus*. But the prevailing view was that in addition to the Convention of St. Germain, the two other treaties should be specifically mentioned so as not to leave any interested parties in any doubt whatsoever as to the status of those pacts and as to where the new States stood with regard to their binding effect. Thus, although in strict legal terms it would have sufficed to abrogate-the Convention of St. Germain only, it was felt that the matter should be expressed *ex abundanti cautela*, as one of the legal experts involved in the drafting of the treaty later aptly noted.[71] Hence, the overcautious provision in Article 1 of the Act of Niamey.

However, it is worth recalling here that in spite of this express abrogation the United States, as one of the original parties to the treaty, still continued to regard the Convention of St. Germain as one of its valid "treaties in force" long after the conclusion and entry into force of the Act of Niamey. This raises the following question: in a situation whereby new States succeed to a treaty (or treaties) of their predecessor State and subsequently abrogate that treaty, are third States at liberty to ignore such abrogation and continue to regard the validity of the treaty as unimpaired? The problem does not of course arise when all the old parties to the treaty have been replaced by new States who then agree to abrogate the treaty. But this is by no means the case with regard to the Convention of St. Germain; the new riparian States were successors to only two of the original parties to the 1919 Convention – Great Britain and France. In theory, therefore, it might be thought that the succession of these new African States to two of the original signatories – whether in consequence of inheritance agreements or as a result of the operation of the rules of international law – is a *res inter alios acta* as regards the other original parties. These States may thus be validly regarded as being unaffected by any purported abrogation of a multilateral treaty by the new successor States without their consent, So, even if such an abrogation is intended to be total and valid *erga omnes*, as is the case with Article 1 of the Act of Niamey, it may, in truth, be of relative legal effect only. Significantly, it was noted (around the time of the abrogation of the Convention of St. Germain by the new African States) that:[72]

> "It is one thing for the parent State and the so-called 'successor' State to agree as between themselves upon the devolution of certain treaty rights and obligations hitherto binding upon the parent; it is quite another for those two States to act in a manner which will effectively substitute the successor State for the parent in relation to a third State, either by entitling the third State to call upon the successor State to perform its obligations or by justifying the successor in making a similar claim upon the third State."

It is a logical result of this reasoning that American policy has been to continue to treat the Convention of St. Germain as an extant treaty so far as the United States is concerned.[73] However, it must be emphasized that perhaps all this is really of no more than theoretical significance. For it is inconceivable that the United States or, for that matter, any of the other original parties would actually invoke the operation of the treaty on the territories of the independent, sovereign African successor States, for whom the treaty is considered defunct. Indeed, apart from listing it as one of its treaties in force in the post-1963 period, there has never been any attempt by the United States to enforce or exercise any of the rights it acquired under the Convention of St. Germain – such as the right of free navigation – since its abrogation by Article 1 of the Act of Niamey. It is also significant that, according to the evidence available to the present writer, none of the other parties to the Convention of

St. Germain have continued to regard it as one of their "treaties in force" since its abrogation by the new African States in 1963. This would appear to indicate that in practice all interested parties have accepted the fact that the Convention is a dead letter which has been superseded by the Niamey accords. It is the contention here that any rights belonging to the former parties to the Convention of St. Germain under that treaty were validly extinguished by the Act of Niamey.

The right of the successor States to replace the Convention of St. Germain with a new treaty as between themselves cannot be doubted and is one that may be said to be inherent in their sovereignty. It cannot be argued, for example, that since there were third parties, such as the United States, unaffected by the succession, the new riparian States were not at liberty to abrogate the treaty without the consent of those third parties. Although this argument may, on the face of it, appear somewhat extreme, it is a valid and justifiable one in the particular situation under consideration. It is the view here that in a situation whereby a pre-independence treaty relates to a river running through the territories of newly born States (and not the territory of a third State such as the United States) and constituting an important part of their natural resources, the new States must be given the freedom to determine the utilization or exploitation of such a resource, including the right to set aside the pre-independence treaty and replace it with any new treaty regime deemed necessary for such exploitation. For to insist otherwise would be to deny the new States the right to make their own independent decisions regarding an important aspect of their existence as sovereign entities, namely the freedom to conduct their own treaty relations. But, as has already been intimated, this view may be valid only if confined to such treaties as the Convention of St. Germain, relating to rivers (or other watercourses) or other important aspects of the natural resources of a new State, and it is by no means suggested that this remains the case with respect to every treaty concluded before the emergence of the State(s) in question. The issue involved here may be termed the "principle of independence", that a new State ought not to be burdened with regimes to which it was not a party, since to demand otherwise would amount to a denial of the fundamental principle of sovereign equality and independence upon which the whole fabric of the modern international legal order is based. Intimately connected with this argument is the evolving concept of the "permanent sovereignty of States over their natural resources".[74] It was within the purview of this concept that the report prepared under the auspices of the United Nations' Secretary General on the administrative, economic and social aspects of integrated basin development in 1964 recommended that:[75]

"[The] United Nations encourage and assist in the creation of committees of interested parties, as a preliminary step to the establishment of permanent international commissions, by way of treaties, such as the US-Canadian Joint Commission."

In fact, this was also the content of paragraph 5 of Resolution 1803 (XVII) of the General Assembly adopted in 1962.[76] These recommendations are perfectly apt to the case of the newly independent States riparian to the Niger or, for that matter, any other river regimes. It is accordingly submitted that if it had been legally necessary for the new African States to override the objection of an existing party against the abrogation of the Convention of St. Germain and its replacement by a new, post-independence treaty, it is on the basis of the argument outlined above that these States would have founded their case and not on the operation of the doctrine of *rebus sic stantibus* as the plenipotentiaries and legal experts at the Niamey Conferences believed to be the case.

It is perfectly true that the doctrine of *rebus sic stantibus*, the essence of which is now incorporated in Article 62 of the Vienna Convention on the Law of Treaties (1969),[77] is an "interpretative technique" that has been used by a great number of newly emergent States to repudiate certain treaties on the ground that with a change of sovereignty, the basic foundation upon which the treaties rested has disappeared. In this regard it has been observed that:[78]

"One does not need a law of succession at all in order to arrive at the conclusion that most treaties do not devolve upon successor States, for this, clearly, is a conclusion yielded by the ordinary law of treaties that looks to the effective fulfilment of the parties' intentions – intentions ordinarily frustrated by a change of sovereignty."

However, an examination of the practice of newly emergent States also reveals that while change of sovereignty has been regarded as being sufficiently fundamental to justify a plea of *rebus sic stantibus* to terminate *personal* or *political* treaties, the same cannot be said of *real* or *dispositive* treaties. A new State cannot claim change of sovereignty as a pretext for disclaiming dispositive treaties, such as those relating to communication or river navigation. The present writer is thus in agreement with Piedelièvre, who wrote:[79]

"Le nouveau gouvernement devra éxcuter les conventions relatives à l'endiguement des rivières ou à la navigation fluviale."

An apt example is provided by Egypt, which never invoked *rebus sic stantibus* to try to terminate the Treaty of Constantinople of 1888 respecting Free

Navigation of the Suez Canal[80] as a successor State of the Ottoman Empire. So, it may be concluded that the new riparian States could not validly plead a case of *rebus sic stantibus* with respect to the Convention of St. Germain, which was undeniably a dispositive treaty. The invocation of this doctrine as the legal justification for the repudiation of the 1919 Convention at the Niamey Conference was, therefore, both legally irrelevant and misplaced.

Conclusion

A number of conclusions and observations have already been made in the preceding sections of the discussion. It is not the intention to repeat them all here but a number of points may be reiterated.

My principal aim in this chapter has been two-fold. Firstly, an attempt was made to answer the question whether, and to what extent, the peculiar problems thrown up by the process of decolonization among the former colonies riparian to the Niger and its tributaries could adequately be examined with the aid of the traditional theories of State succession in so far as the pre-independence international fluvial conventions relating to that river were concerned. Secondly, I sought to identify the proper basis for allowing the new riparian States the right to terminate these treaties and replace them with the new post-independence accords concluded at Niamey in 1963 and 1964. In this regard, it has been seen that such justification as there may be must be seen to lie beyond the existing traditional rules of customary international law; this justification, it has been argued, is based on the evolving notion of what the present writer has termed the "principle of independence".

It is now generally accepted that the major theoretical standpoints with regard to the question of State succession are represented by the absolute devolution and negativist non-devolution theories. But it has also been shown that, generally speaking, post-independence African State practice has not always neatly accorded with this theoretical distinction. And yet, this divergence between theory and practice notwithstanding, at least the following conclusion may firmly be drawn from the present study: the nine West African States riparian to the Niger and its tributaries did regard the pre-independence "Niger Treaties" – the General Act of Berlin (1885), the General Act and Declaration of Brussels (1890) and the Convention of St. Germain (1919) as dispositive treaties, or at least as possessing some dispositive characteristics. But, more specifically, it has been argued that the relevant treaty to be considered as having devolved upon the new riparian States was the Convention of St. Germain. The view that the earlier Acts of 1885 and 1890 had not been superseded by the 1919 Convention and that, therefore, they continued to apply to the Niger until their abrogation by Article 1 of the Act of Niamey in 1963 was legally misguided and irrelevant. Furthermore, as has just been noted in the previous section, it is equally wrong to invoke the doctrine of *rebus sic stantibus* as a ground for the termination of the Convention of St. Germain as both the plenipotentiaries at the Niamey Conference and some legal scholars appeared to suggest.[81] It is the view here that such legal justification for the abrogation of the Convention was, in any case, unnecessary. As argued above, the right of the new riparians to repudiate that treaty needs to be assessed with these legal facts in mind: that the signatories (to the Convention of St. Germain) who had exercised sovereignty over the Niger river area (Great Britain and France) had been completely replaced by new sovereign entities; and these new States were all in unanimous agreement about the need for a new treaty to govern their utilization of the Niger. This could not be done without first abrogating the pre-independence treaty which was, at the time, solely designed to benefit the metropolitan powers. Secondly, regard must also be taken of the fact that neither of the former parent States objected to the abrogation of the older treaty by their successors (who had themselves become, for a short while at least, parties to the treaty following their succession to the two parent States), nor did they contest their right to do so. And, of course, only by concluding new post-independence conventions could the new States draw up their own programme for the common integrated exploitation and management of the resources of the Niger basin, embodying the economic objectives and aspirations of new-born States.

Notes

1. For text of the treaty, see E. Hertslet, *Commercial Treaties*, Vol. 17, (1890) p. 62.

2. As to the forceful argument regarding the international legal personality of the pre-colonial "traditional" African States, see T.O. Elias, "African Law", in A. Larson *et al.* (Eds.), *Sovereignty Within the Law*, (1965) p. 220; see also, F.C. Okoye, *International Law and the New African States*, (1971) pp. 4–5; and C.H. Alexandrowicz, *The European-African Confrontation*, (1973) pp. 9–13.

3. See ILC Yrbk, 1971, Vol. II, Part 1, p. 350. The term "international watercourse", which was adopted by the International Law Commission, is thought preferable to "international river" by the majority of modern writers on the subject. The concept is one that includes the international river itself, its tributary streams and rivers, and lakes and canals constituting part of a system. See, for example,

Article II of the Helsinki Rules on "The Uses of the Waters of International Rivers", in I.L.A, *Rep. of 52nd conf.* (1966) p. 477 *et seq.*

4. The Act and the Agreement were signed on 26 October 1963 and 25 November 1964, respectively.

5. See T. Maluwa, "The Origins and Development of International Fluvial Law in Africa: A Study of the International Legal Regime of the Congo and Niger Rivers from 1885 to 1960", 29 NILR 368 (1982). See also M. Mubiala, *L'évolution de droit des cours d'eau internationaux à la lumière de l'expérience africaine, notamment dans le bassin du Congo/Zaire*, (1995) *passim*.

6. *2 BFSP 52.*

7. G.F. de Martens, *NRG*, Vol. 9, p. 252.

8. *Ibid.* Vol. 15, p. 770; see also, E. Israel (Ed.), *Major Treaties of Modern History 1648–1967*, Vol. 3, (1967) p. 147.

9 De Martens, *loc. cit.*, note 7, Vol. 16 part 2, p. 75.

10. *Ibid.* 2nd series, Vol. 1, p. 117.

11. *Ibid.* 2nd series, Vol. 1, p. 143.

12. *Ibid.* 2nd series, Vol. 19, p. 294.

13. For texts of the General Act and Declaration, see *82 BFSP 55.*

14. 8 LNTS 26.

15. *83 BFSP 19.*

16. See text in 64 *RGDIP* 878 (1960); also in *15 Rev. Egypt. de droit international 321* (1959).

17. 93 LNTS 43; also *160 BFSP 106*; Cmnd. 3050.

18. PCIJ Series A/B No. 63 (1934).

19. *Ibid.* p. 80.

20. *Ibid.* p. 135.

21. *Ibid.* p. 150.

22. J.H. Verzijl, *International Law in Historical Perspective*, Vol. I, (1968) pp. 79–80; see also the same author's *Jurisprudence of the World Court*, Vol. 1, (1965) p. 395 *et seq.*

23. 99 *BFSP* 968.

24. *130 BFSP 265.*

25. M.O. Hudson, *International Legislation*, Vol. IV, (1928–1929) p. 2378 at 2383.

26. 29 *AJIL* (1935) Supp., p. 657 at 661.

27. 8 ILM 679 (1969); see also, 63 *AJIL* (1969) p. 875

28. M. de Gourcel, *L'influence de la conférence de Berlin de 1885 sur le droit colonial* (1935) p. 354; R. Pinto, *"La préscription en droit international"*, *87 Hague Recueil 387* (1955) at p. 432. See also, "Congo Treaties in Disrepair", in *The Economist*, London, 25 June 1955.

29. De Gourcel, *op. cit.* note 28, pp. 329–330.

30. *74 BFSP* 86, also in E. Hertslet, A *Collection of Treaties and Conventions, etc.*, Vol 25, (1910) p. 880.

31. See D.P. O'Connell, *State Succession in Municipal Law and International Law*, Vol. II, (1967) p. 37; see also F.O. Conf. 371/877, 26687/988/10/12; G.P. Gooch and H.W. Temperley, *Documents (British) on the Origins of the War (1898–1914)*, Vol. VIII, (1926) p. 492.

32. *26 LNTS 173.*

33. *List of Commercial Treaties with Foreign Powers* (HMSO Publication, 1940) p. 55.

34. See S. Gorove, *Law and Politics of the Danube*, (1964) p. 130.

35. G.F. de Martens, *NRG*, 3rd series, Vol. 37, part 3, p. 741.

36. U.S. Dept. of State, *Treaties in Force*, (1977) p. 257.

37. See J.C. Anene, *The International Boundaries of Nigeria, 1885–1960*, (1970); see also B. Obichere, *West African States and European Expansion*, (1971).

38. This Convention still awaits the final (15th) instrument of ratification before it can enter into force and, like the Vienna Convention on the Law of Treaties (1969), it is not retroactive in effect. See *The Work of the International Law Commission*, UN Pub. Sales No. E.80.V.11. p. 299; also 17 ILM (1978) p. 1488.

39. Brownlie, *op. cit.* pp. 666–667; but see O'Connell, *op. cit.* note 31, *passim.*

40. W.E. Hall, *Treatise on International Law*, (1924) p. 115; McNair, *op. cit.* pp. 655–664; Brierly, *op. cit.* p. 153.

41. See commentary on Arts. 11 and 12 in ILC Yrbk, 1974, Vol. II, p. 183.

42. LNOJ Special Supp. No. 3 (1920) p. 3.

43. ILC Yrbk, 1962, Vol. II, p. 122.

44. E. Vattel, *Le droit des gens*, Bk. II, ch. 12, 178, (1916), (Carnegie Classics of International Law edition).

45. A.P. Lester, "State Succession to Treaties in the Commonwealth", *12 ICLQ 475* (1963) at pp. 496–497.

46. Okoye, *op. cit.* p. 52.

47. For this view see A.B. Keith, *The Theory of State Succession with Reference to English and Colonial Law*, (1907) p. 22. But J. Westlake also used the term "transitory" as a synonym for "dispositive": see his *International Law*, (1904) pp. 60–62.

48. *The Nile Waters Question* (Publication of the Sudanese Ministry of Irrigation and Hydroelectric Power, 1955) pp. 2–3.

49. 596 H.C. Deb. 5th ser., col, 342, 26 November 1958.

50. D. Bardonnet, *Annales Malgaches*, Vol. 1, (1964) p. 2.

51. *The Times*, London, 9 November 1969, p. 11.

52. See, O'Connell, *op. cit.* p. 247.

53. But these States were Belgian colonies, so that the question of the UK-Egypt Treaty devolving upon them does not even arise.

54. See C. Parry, *Consolidated Treaty Series*, Vol. 201, p. 182.

55. G.F. de Martens, *Recueil de Traites*, Vol. 1, p. 104.

56. W.M. Malloy, *Treaties, Conventions, International Acts (etc.) between the USA and other Powers, 1776–1909*, Vol. 1, (1910) p. 586.

57. H. Reid, *International Servitudes in Law and Practice*, (1932) p. 157.

58. For this view, see Reid, *ibid.* p. 158.

59. J. Basdevant, *Traités et conventions en vigueur entre la France et les Puissances étrangères*, Vol III, (1922) p. 352.

60. *Ibid.* p. 356.

61. *Ibid.* p. 357.

62. G.F. de Martens, *NRG*, 3rd series, Vol. 21, p. 460.

63. *La Documentation française: Notes et études documentaires*, (1951) no. 1425, p. 9; also in *18 Rev. Jur. et Pol. 185* (1964).

64. *Annuaire Français* (1962) p. 112. Text also available in Decree No.73-NG, 17 March 1955, Congo Bao Viet-Nam, 1955, p. 670 at 701.

65. O'Connell, *op. cit.* p. 308.

66. L.F. Oppenheim, *International Law*, Vol.1, (8th ed,. H. Lauterpacht, 1955) p. 356.

67. Among these critics are: A.D. McNair, "So-called State Servitudes", 6 *BYIL 111* (1925); Keith, *op. cit.*; G. Crusen, "Les servitudes internationales", 22 *Hague Recueil 31* (1928).

68. See, for example, O'Connell, *op. cit.* p. 19.

69. Brownlie, *op. cit.* p. 667; E.J. Castren, "La Succession d'Etats", *78 Hague Recueil 385* (1951).

70. It may be noted in passing that some writers on the subject are of the mistaken view that the abrogation of the Convention of St. Germain and the other pre-1963 treaties is contained in Art. 9 of the Act of Niamey. See, for example, F. Fisseha, "State Succession and the Legal Status of International rivers", in L. Caflisch and R. Zacklin (Eds.), *The Legal Regime of International Rivers and Lakes*, (1981) pp. 177–202 at p. 191 and pp. 175–200. These writers would appear to mistake Art. 9 of the *draft statute*, which originally contained the provision abrogating these treaties, for the actual Art. 9 finally adopted in the Act of Niamey on 26 October 1963. The present Art. 9 of the 1963 Act in fact concerns the registration of the treaty with the Secretary General of the United Nations in accordance with Art. 102 of the UN Charter.

71. See T.O. Elias, "The Berlin Treaty and the Niger River Commission", *57 AJIL 873* (1963) at 880.

72. Note by Stevenson, American Ambassador to the United Nations, to Secretary of State Rusk, A-1511, 20 March 1963, MS Dept. of State, file Pol, 4, cited by M.M. Whiteman, *Digest of International Law*, Vol. 2, (1963) pp. 1002–1003.

73. U.S. Dept. of State, *Treaties in Force*, (1977). See also previous issues of publication under reference since 1963.

74. Although this area of law is till both uncertain and controversial, the various United Nations resolutions on the matter can be said to provide a reasonable guide. The starting point is General Assembly Resolution 523 (VI) of 12 January 1952 which was followed by Resolution 626 (VII) of 21 December 1952. Later resolutions relating to this matter include Resolutions 1314 (XIII) of 12 December 1958 and 1515 (XV) of December 1960. See also resolution entitled

"Right to Exploit Freely Natural Wealth and Resources" (Resolution 626 (VII) of 14 December 1962).

75. E/C. 7/2/add.6.

76. See, for example, *Official Records of* ECOSOC, 52nd sess., Supp. No. 5 (E/5097 and corr. 1) para 20; also 54th sess., supp. No. 4 (E/5247) paras. 114, 129–137; and see further, 44th sess., supp. No. 3 (E/4177) part III. See also an early statement by the UN Secretary General to this end: *Survey of International Law*, Doc. A/CN.4/1/Rev 1 (UN Pub. Sales No. 1948. V.I.(1)) p. 34, para. 57.

77. 8 ILM 679 (1969).

78. D.P. O'Connell, "Independence and Problems of State Succession", in W.V. O'Brien (Ed.), *The New Nations in International Law and Diplomacy*, (1965) p. 14.

79. M. Piedelievre, *Précis de droit international public ou droit des Gens*, (1894) p. 165.

80. *79 BFSP 18*.

81. See Elias, *loc. cit.* note 71.

III

HUMAN RIGHTS

5

CONTEXTUALIZING DEMOCRACY AND HUMAN RIGHTS IN AFRICA

Introduction

The last few years have witnessed the adoption of new constitutions incorporating fully-fledged bills of rights, entrenching fundamental human rights, in a number of African countries. In Southern African, for example, Namibia, South Africa and Malawi provide the most recent examples. Of course the adoption of these bills of rights is not without precedent within the region. Botswana, the longest surviving constitutional democracy in Southern Africa, has had a bill of rights as part of its constitution since independence in 1966. However, the three constitutions referred to above merit special attention, at least to the international human rights lawyer, for two particular reasons.

First, all these constitutions seek to elevate certain specified legal rights to constitutional status through their entrenchment in a bill of rights. They have also adopted the notion of constitutional supremacy and, correspondingly, abandoned the doctrine of parliamentary sovereignty, which continues to be the guiding principle in the constitutions of most countries elsewhere. The significance of this for the protection of human rights in a constitutional democracy will be reiterated later. Second, all the three constitutions accord public international law, and in particular international human rights law, a constitutionally defined status within the respective municipal legal systems and an explicit role in the interpretative process. For lack of a more appropriate expression, one could describe these constitutions as "international human rights law-friendly".[1] But in a more general sense, these constitutional developments are also manifestations of the recent trajectories of democratic transition in contemporary Africa and elsewhere in the world. They provide evidence of the "heroic and wrenching stories of people determined to reclaim their freedom and dignity, their history and human rights, from the shackles of colonial and postcolonial tyranny".[2]

I start with these observations mainly to reiterate the rather obvious point that as we stand at the end of the twentieth century, virtually every State in the world has a constitution. Generally speaking, these constitutions set out the forms and institutions of government. They express or reflect a political-economic ideology, including the principles governing relations between the individual and society (as represented by the State). In the well-rehearsed language of constitutional lawyers and political scientists, legitimate constitutions must reflect respect for constitutionalism including, in particular, respect for the principle of the "rule of law" and individual human rights. Implied in this language is the assertion, captured in the quotation from Rosas cited above, that modern constitutional democratic governance presupposes respect for human rights and vice-versa. Indeed, the efforts that we observe all over the world today, especially in the newly emergent States rising from the ashes of the old Eastern Europe and the former Soviet Union, are generally directed at crafting new constitutional pacts that include commitment to the recognition and protection of individual human rights entrenched in a justiciable bill of rights. It is this path that was earlier followed by Namibia, and more recently adopted by South Africa and Malawi. As stated earlier, similar efforts have been under way in various other countries elsewhere on the African continent. The change in the political landscape that Africa has been undergoing over the last decade has been accompanied by marked changes, or in some cases attempted changes, in the constitutional landscape of the countries involved as new constitutions have been drawn up, or existing ones amended, to reflect changed political realities and on-going democratic struggles. The common theme running through all these changes has been the attempt to institute political pluralism and democratic rule in place of the single-party dictatorships and autocratic oligarchies that had become the political order of the day in all but a handful of African States. Allied to this is the project of building a political culture founded on a conception of human rights now taken for granted in the more established democracies.

One of the many questions that arise is whether the conceptual nexus between democracy and human rights implied in the foregoing remarks is really as self-evident as it is made out by most commentators. But our answer to this question may, in turn, depend on how we resolve other attendant conceptual queries: for example, how do we define democracy, and what are human rights? I do not propose to address these questions, and the many others that arise in this regard, in any detail.[3] My objective is much more limited. It is, first and foremost, to explore, in very broad terms, the idea of international human rights law. Second, to examine the relevance and significance of international human rights law to developing countries, especially in Africa, within the context of debates about democracy.

I acknowledge that the questions that arise are too complex to be given adequate and meaningful depth within the brief discussion I propose to undertake here. Different approaches to the question of the conceptual and practical nexus between democracy and human rights abound. A major school of thought comprises those human rights theorists and advocates in the West who simply and firmly proclaim that Western liberal democracy is the political regime that is consonant with human rights.[4] This conclusion seems to flow from the reasoning that wealth and openness are both necessary and sufficient conditions for liberal democracy,[5] and that this in turn promotes human rights.[6] This is opposed by the perspective advanced with equal firmness largely by scholars and commentators from Africa, Asia and other Third World nations. It is an argument that challenges the claim that Western liberal democracy is the best way to promote human rights. Advocates of this school rather seek to privilege alternative models of political management which also take cognisance of the need to safeguard the rights of all members of the society by focusing not on the *individual's* rights, as the Western liberal democratic model does, but on the rights of the *community* as a whole. Some see such possibilities in the Marxist or socialist tradition[7], or even in so-called African traditional systems of governance.[8]

Another issue that arises in relation to the human rights and democracy debate in Africa is the cultural argument. It is sometimes argued that human rights and democracy in Africa differ because its culture differs. This is an important and large question that requires a more focused treatment than would be possible in this brief essay. Such a treatment would have to address a number of related questions, among them: What is culture, and how does it fit into the African conception of human rights? Can we, in any case, generalize about African culture and an African view of human rights? In what ways would human rights specifically differ if this generalized African culture and African view were permitted? Is African culture merely a preserved heritage from the past which must have priority over present human rights claims, or is it, like all cultures, dynamic and changing, both internally and in response to external forces and influences, and perhaps susceptible to political manipulation? As has already been indicated above, the principal objective of this paper is much more limited, and the above questions are posed merely to indicate the complexity of the issues involved in this debate and not to provide a basis for detailed discussion and analysis here.[9]

International Human Rights Law: A Historical Note

Arguments for the international protection of human rights are based on the concept that every nation has an obligation to respect the human rights of its citizens, and that other nations and the international community have a right, and responsibility, to protest if this obligation is not met. International human rights law consists of the body of international rules, procedures, and institutions developed to implement this concept and to promote respect for human rights all over the world. Generally speaking, international law is primarily applicable to States and does not normally create rights directly enforceable by individuals in national courts. Therefore, international human rights law can in practice be made effective only if each nation makes these rules part of its own domestic legal system, for example through entrenchment in the national constitution.

Historically, concern for the protection of human rights found expression almost exclusively at the national or domestic level in accordance with varying notions of the limits of political power and authority at given times. In general, prevailing power structures resisted acceptance, beyond the purely metaphysical and philosophical, of the very notion of human rights, the dignity of the human person and the humanity of man and woman. Violations occurred and were wide-ranging, leading to popular upheavals. An early example was provided by the events that led to the granting of the *Magna Carta* in England (1215). More significant developments were to occur centuries later, culminating in the French Declaration of the Rights of Man and of the Citizen (1789) and the American Bill of Rights (1791). Although limited in scope and content, and aimed at specific social and political contexts, these events have influenced subsequent thinking and developments in many countries since.

At the international level, before the turn of this century, notions of human rights protection were no more than selective extensions of certain rights which powerful nations wanted their own nationals to enjoy elsewhere. Thus, for example, rights were protected in bilateral treaties (of commerce, etc.) not because of ethical, legal or moral considerations of a universal character, but due to the practical need to safeguard one's own national interests. Consequently, during this era, from an international legal standpoint, human rights questions were regarded as matters entirely falling within each nation's domestic jurisdiction and wholly inappropriate for regulation by international law. It was only after the First World War that the beginnings of universality emerged, although still limited in scope and content, due to a number of factors. Some of the critical factors were: the work of the antislavery movement; early concern for the treatment of the Jewish minority in Russia, and Armenians in the Turkish Empire; the establishment of the League of

Nations in 1919 (and the accompanying establishment of protection for minorities, international labour standards and the protection of workers, and provisions of the mandates system); and the creation of new States in Eastern Europe and the inclusion of provisions in the various peace treaties protecting minorities in these new States.[10]

In a real sense, modern international human rights law is a post-World War Two phenomenon. Its emergence in this era can be attributed to a number of factors, in particular the monstrous violations of human rights and the immense suffering witnessed during the Nazi holocaust and the belief that some of these violations might have been prevented or avoided if there had been a more effective system for the protection of human rights in the world. These considerations not only provided the driving force behind the formation of the United Nations but also the acknowledgement that the new organization should put the promotion of human rights and fundamental freedoms as one of the principal purposes of the organization. This concern is reflected in the organization's Charter (Articles 1(3), 4, and 55) and in the subsequent activities of the United Nations itself and its various specialized agencies. The conclusion of numerous international instruments and the adoption of declarations and resolutions on human rights, beginning with the United Nations' Universal Declaration of Human Rights (UDHR) in 1948 are evidence of this concern.[11] The subsequent expansion of the international community with the emergence of new States in Africa and Asia and the focus placed by these new States on specific questions of human rights, such as self-determination and racial discrimination, only served to universalize further the emerging consensus concerning the concept of human rights.[12]

International human rights law is thus a recently evolved branch of international law. Not surprisingly, the field is one in which relevant rules are still imprecise, fragmentary and, sometimes, overlapping. It is also a field in which institutions and procedures are still evolving. However, the basic concept of international human rights has become firmly established in international law and practice, and international human rights law is now recognized as a distinct branch of modern international law.

Sources and Content of International Human Rights Law

It was cautioned above that this discussion is not about human rights theory as such. If it were, it would be imperative to investigate certain conceptual assumptions and questions that arise with respect to the notion of human rights itself. The definition of human rights would be one line of enquiry. The identification of the sources of human rights would be another. Questions of this kind would involve both historical and philosophical considerations whose breadth and depth cannot usefully be covered in the limited context of this brief discussion. At the terrible risk of over-simplification, therefore, one may simply observe here that the sources of international human rights law are, broadly speaking, two-fold.

First and foremost, international human rights law exists principally as conventional international law. There is a whole host of international legal instruments (treaties, conventions or agreements and declarations of various types) which together provide the main source of international human rights law. These create direct obligations for States, either of a general character (for example, the United Nations Charter itself, the International Covenant on Civil and Political Rights (ICCPR), the International Covenant on Economic, Social and Cultural Rights (ICESCR)) or of a regional provenance (such as the African Charter on Human and Peoples' Rights (AFR), the European Convention on Human Rights (EHR) or the American Convention on Human Rights (AMR)).[13] Second, some aspects of international human rights law have their source in customary international law. In considering this source, a number of questions may arise, and these are questions that may generally be posed in relation to the nature of custom as a source of international law. Thus, one may ask, for example, whether the provisions of certain treaties may have crystallized into rules of customary international law such that they may be binding even on non-parties? Or, what other standards are regarded as acquiring such customary force, and what are the criteria for the recognition of such customary rules?[14] These questions need to be given some thought because it has been argued, for example, that some (or perhaps all) of the provisions of the Universal Declaration of Human Rights may have acquired the force of customary rules. Similar arguments may be made with respect to some of the universal conventions adopted under the auspices of the United Nations, for example the Convention on the Prevention and Punishment of the Crime of Genocide of 1948[15], or even mere declarations and resolutions of authoritative international bodies.[16]

As might be expected, the various universal and regional conventions have benefited from the shared historical experiences which have dominated the evolution of international human rights law over the last half century or so. The more recent instruments, in particular, have not only benefited from the earlier conventional regimes, but have built upon those conventions and broadened the content and scope of the protected rights even further. The following comparative list of some of the rights recognised in some of the leading international instruments mentioned above (with indications in abbreviated form of the relevant instrument and the relevant article of the instrument) is only meant as a rough demonstration of the scope of the protected human rights, especially in the broad area of civil and political rights. What needs to be noted here is that the inclusion of these and other rights in the "International Bill of Rights" as well as in the regional human rights conventions has influenced the drafting of some national bills of rights and the inclusion of these rights in such bills of rights. In some instances, even the phraseology employed in these instruments has been adopted almost verbatim in the relevant provisions of national constitutions. The rights protected under Chapter IV of the Constitution of Malawi of 1995 and Chapter 2 of the Constitution of South Africa of 1996 (incorporating the respective bills of rights), for example, must be seen in this light.

- *Right of peoples to self-determination*: ICCPR 1(1), ICESCR 1(1), AFR 20.
- *Right of peoples to dispose of its natural wealth and resources*: ICCPR 1(2), ICESCR 1(2), AFR 21.
- *Right to equality and non-discrimination*: UDHR 1, 2, & 7, ICCPR 2(1), 3 & 26, EHR 14, AMR 1(1) & 24, AFR 2 & 3.
- *Right to effective judicial remedies*: UDHR 8, ICCPR 2(3), EHR 6 & 13, AMR 25, AFR 7(1)(a) & 26.
- *Right to life*: UDHR 3, ICCPR 6, EHR 2, AMR 4, AFR 4.
- *Protection from torture or cruel, inhuman or degrading treatment or punishment*: UDHR 5, ICCPR 7 & 10, EHR 3, AMR 5(2) to (6), AFR 5.
- *Protection from servitude and forced labour*: UDHR 4, ICCPR 8, EHR 4, AMR 6, AFR 5.
- *Right to liberty and security of the person*: UDHR 3 & 9, ICCPR 9, EHR 5, AMR 7, AFR 6.
- *Protection from imprisonment for inability to fulfil a contractual obligation*: ICCPR 11, EHR Protocol 4, Art. 1, AMR 7(7).
- *Freedom of movement*: UDHR 13, ICCPR 12, EHR Protocol 4, Art. 2, AMR 22(1), to (5), AFR 12 (1) to (3).
- *Protection of aliens from arbitrary expulsion*: ICCPR 13, EHR Protocol 4, Art. 4 (restricted to collective expulsions), AMR 22(6) to (8), AFR 12 (4) & (5).
- *Fair and public hearing, presumption of innocence, procedural guarantees, protection from double jeopardy*: UDHR 10 & 11(1), ICCPR 14, EHR 5 & 6, AMR 8, AFR 7(1).

- *Non-retroactivity of offences and punishment*: UDHR 11(2), ICCPR 15, EHR 7, AMR 9, AFR 7(2).
- *Recognition as a person before the law*: UDHR 6, ICCPR 16, AMR 3, AFR 5.
- *Protection of right to property*: UDHR 17, EHR Protocol 1, Art. 1, AMR 21, AFR 14.
- *Protection of privacy, family, home, correspondence, honour and reputation*: UDHR 12, ICCPR 17 & 19(3)(A), EHR 8 & 10(2), AMR 10 & 14, AFR 18 & 27.
- *Freedom of thought, conscience, and religion*: UDHR 18, ICCPR 18, EHR 9, AMR 12, AFR 8.
- *Freedom of opinion and expression and of seeking, receiving and imparting information*: UDHR 19, ICCPR 19, EHR 10, AMR 13, AFR 9.
- *Freedom of assembly*: UDHR 20, ICCPR 21, EHR 11, AMR 15.
- *Freedom of association and to form and join trade unions*: UDHR 20, ICCPR 22, EHR 11, AMR 16, AFR 10.
- *Right to marry, equality of rights of spouses and protection of the family*: UDHR 16, ICCPR 3 & 23, EHR 12, AMR 17, AFR 18.
- *Rights of the child*: ICCPR 24, AMR 17(4) & (5), 18, 19 & 20. AFR 18(3).
- *Political rights and access to public office*: UDHR 21, ICCPR 25, EHR (First Protocol) 3, AMR 23, AFR 13.
- *Right of ethnic, religious or linguistic minorities with regard to culture, religion or language*: ICCPR 27.
- *Prohibition of war propaganda and protection from advocacy of racial or religious hatred*: ICCPR 20.
- *Limitations on derogation in emergencies*: ICCPR 4, EHR 15, AMR 27.

The human rights protected under Chapter IV of the Malawian Constitution are those relating to the following: life (s. 16); prohibition against acts of genocide (s. 17); personal liberty (s. 18); human dignity and personal freedoms (including prohibitions against torture, cruel, inhuman or degrading treatment, corporal punishment and non-consensual scientific or medical experimentation) (s. 19); equality (s. 20); privacy (s. 21); family and marriage (s. 22); rights of children (s. 23); rights of women (s. 24); education (s. 25); culture and language (s. 26); freedom from slavery, servitude and forced labour (s. 27); property (s. 28); economic activity (s. 29); development (s. 30); labour relations (s. 31); freedom of association (s. 32); freedom of conscience (s. 33); freedom of opinion (s. 34); freedom of expression (s. 35); freedom of the press (s. 36); access to information (s. 37); freedom of assembly (s. 38); freedom of movement and residence (s. 39); political rights (s. 40); access to justice and legal remedies (s. 41); rights of detained, arrested and accused persons (s. 42); and administrative justice (s. 43).

The South African Constitution provides for protection of the following rights: equality (s. 9); human dignity (s. 10); life (s. 11); freedom and security of the person (s. 12); slavery, servitude and forced labour (s 13); privacy (s. 14); freedom of religion, belief and opinion (s. 15); freedom of expression (s. 16); assembly, demonstration, picket and petition (s. 17); freedom of association (s. 18); political rights (s. 19); citizenship (s. 20); freedom of movement and residence (s. 21); freedom of trade, occupation and profession (s. 22); labour relations (s. 23); environment (s. 24); property (s. 25); housing (s. 26); health care, food, water and social security (s. 27); children's rights (s. 28); education (s. 29); language and culture (s. 30); rights of cultural, religious and linguistic communities (s. 31); access to information (s. 32); just administrative action (s. 33); access to courts (s. 34); and rights of arrested, detained and accused persons (s. 35).

It will be noticed that there is significant commonality between the rights stipulated in the Universal Declaration of Human Rights and the two International Covenants, on the one hand, and those enshrined in the Malawian and South African constitutions, on the other hand. The reliance placed upon the earlier human rights instruments by the constitution drafters in the two countries is self-evident and requires no further elaboration. It is a manifestation of the so-called cross-fertilization between the international and the municipal contexts of human rights protection which has emerged over the last three decades or so. This cross-fertilization has been particularly noticeable in the more recent constitution-making processes in some of the new democracies in Africa and the former communist regimes in Central and Eastern Europe. This discussion is, of course, concerned with the human rights and democracy debate in Africa. However, while the focus is limited to only one particular region of the developing world, it is hoped that the issues that are identified in this debate are of equal relevance and concern to other Third World, as well as Western, nations that share a common desire for a system of universal human rights.

Discourses on African Approaches to Human Rights

Human rights have been defined by some commentators as those rights held by all individuals merely by reason of their being human, without regard to status or position. These rights are not to be regarded as privileges granted by the State nor are they contingent upon any duties owed to it by the claimants or beneficiaries (of the rights) although they may depend on duties to other citizens. Rather, they are entitlements against the State.[17] On this view, the claim for the universality of human rights should be self-evident. For the claim for universal human rights is a recognition of the need for the protection of all individuals against the all-pervasive power of the modern State, and a recognition that this need is valid the world over, in developed and developing countries, in the rich North as well as in the poor South. This approach to human rights deliberately adopts what has been termed "a comprehensive perspective in which human rights underlie all human interactions [in] a wide, global context". According to Nagan:[18]

> "The core value honoured by human rights in the comprehensive perspective is the value of respect – the principle of mutual deference among human beings. This implies reciprocal deference to each other's freedom of choice to participate in and benefit from all the complex value processes in society. This requires a public order committed to the widest sharing and production of the greatest abundance of all values; it means the right not to be coerced and the reciprocal freedom of choice for all. This implies a contextual, problem-oriented, goal-guided, value-conditioned, dynamic conception of human rights."

The project of entrenching human rights in constitutional provisions, in bills of rights, represents an attempt to mark out the scope and limits of this principle of mutual deference on the political "power map" that is represented by the constitution. The argument for the universality of human rights has been advanced by commentators, such as Henkin, who suggest that we are in the age of rights, and that consensus exists on an "irreducible core of integrity and dignity" in which "human rights is the essential idea".[19]

The comprehensive perspective adopted here, of course, stands in opposition to the approach which postulates that there are few, if any, general human rights. The argument may be summarized as follows: even if many human rights are now accepted as universal aspirations or norms, their form, priority and scope of applicability will vary. In part, this is because some societies, mainly in Africa and Asia, place community in priority to the individual and proceed by consensus, not conflict.[20] It follows, so the argument goes, that the Western idea of human rights, which is driven by individualistic ethos, cannot be reconciled with the African or Asian conceptions of human rights, which are predicated on communitarian traditions. Thus, the logical conclusion adopted by the advocates of this approach is to reject the alleged universality of human rights.[21] The debate on universalism versus cultural relativism in human rights is a long-standing one, and the copious literature on the subject attests to this. Indeed, as Tay has observed:[22]

> "Culture haunts the search for a system of human rights that can truly be universal. Ever since Francisco de Vitoria's first consideration of the native-American Indians in "the new World", we have wondered if those who are not like us should be given rights and treated as human. In the modern development of human rights, cultural relativism was an early obstacle put forward by anthropologists: relativists argued that values were specific to a particular society and its culture and could not be said to be "universal" to all people. [Today], when we value cultural diversity, many recent works have considered human-rights perspectives in Islam, Hinduism, Confucianism, and other systems of religion and belief." [References omitted.]

The debate about universalism versus cultural relativism in human rights is beyond the intended scope of this essay. For the present discussion, it is enough merely to reiterate the observation that has been made by some commentators in this debate, namely that it would be a mistake simply to brush aside cultural issues in the interests of law reform and legal intervention for the sake of human rights. It has to be accepted that the effectiveness of the law itself, including human rights law, may, in large measure, ultimately depend upon the extent to which it is sensitive to cultural issues. Thus, human rights may be better respected when they coincide with the culture in which people believe and in which they live.[23] It is therefore important, as An-Na'im[24] has ably argued in his excellent work on this subject, to search for and identify cross-cultural values that serve this function. In this regard, it has also been argued that[25]:

> "[By] taking a dynamic view of culture as a series of ongoing internal and external debates, the role of cross-cultural dialogue in expanding cross-cultural understandings of human rights looks promising. [This] approach opens up opportunities for discourse by orienting us to the cultural and historical assumptions that inform human-rights debate."

It seems fair to say that sometimes what is lacking in the debates conducted by some Western scholars about human rights and democracy in Africa is an appreciation of this need for a cross-cultural dialogue and understanding. To say this is not to support those who seek to hide behind the cultural argument either to deny the very existence of human rights in African societies or to claim that only certain select rights should be accepted in such societies. The argument for cultural context may be a pretext for repression. For this reason, it important to be clear about what, in any case, is entailed in the cultural argument: what culture, and whose culture? For, as it has been argued, the problems in the cross-cultural approach soon "become apparent when we look beyond the culture that is recorded in history or 'museumized' ". Moreover, "when we see culture as a living thing, caught up in social and political forces, it becomes more difficult to posit any 'original' culture that supersedes or limits the search for truly universal human rights".[26] I endorse fully this cautionary observation, and would urge that this be borne in mind in the ongoing debates about human rights and democracy in Africa and in other communities elsewhere. Chanock's observations are relevant here. He writes:[27]

> "But the claim that 'rights' are cultural does not dispose of the question of the desirability of 'rights' being universal. There is little reason why the currently dominant versions of 'culture' in parts of Africa and Asia should remain unchanged and unchallenged, – they could as well be subjected to precisely the kind of cultural work that transformed a rhetoric of rights applicable only to property owning white men to one which eventually spread to encompass in form, and increasingly in practice, all persons regardless of wealth, gender, or colour."

A little later in the same work, he goes on to wonder just how much the current state of lack of rights in Africa has anything to do with cultures at all. He notes:[28]

> "Certainly the major abuses of political rights at the state level are the products of the political institutions bequeathed to Africa by the colonial powers; their weakness and failures to deal with the multi-ethnic states created by colonialism; and the powerlessness in relation to the goals of development because of the workings of the world economy. Why one should defend this state of affairs as culturally 'African' is not clear. On the other hand there are features of African 'cultures' which do not conform with the universalized version of rights rhetoric, particularly in relation to gender discrimination in property ownership and marriage. Should these be protected, on the grounds of cultural [inviolability]?"

Most commentators would join Chanock in responding to the above question with an unequivocal "no", and I am of that party.[29] To reiterate an earlier point: we must be mindful of the pitfalls inherent in the blind universalization of the rhetoric of human rights and democracy that does not take account of the cultural sensitivities of particular communities. However, we should also be careful not to allow the deployment of culture as a shield against legitimate demands for the recognition of what are, in essence, truly *universalizable* claims or rights that reside in our shared experiences as members of the common human family, irrespective of differences in cultural or geographical localities.

Now, it is commonly argued that human rights may be categorized three-fold: first generation (civil and political), second generation (economic, social and cultural) and third generation (collective or solidarity) rights. Not all human rights theorists agree on this categorization, or on what the priorities are among the various rights. Thus, for example, Cranston is one of the theorists who argue that human rights should be limited to civil and political rights and should not include economic or welfare rights.[30] Other theorists, such as Gewirth and Shue, include economic rights (encompassing the conditions for basic subsistence and survival) within their scheme of human rights.[31] A more comprehensive view of human rights is one that rather embraces both economic, social and cultural rights, on the one hand, and civil and political rights, on the other, and sees these different rights in relation to each other. In company with commentators such as Gould, I argue for the recognition of the inter-connectedness of all these rights.[32] In any case, the differentiation of these rights into the three-fold categories alluded to above unfortunately masks and underplays the necessary linkages between them.

Now, it has been claimed that African scholars or commentators interested in human rights do not at all question the need for the second or third generation rights, especially the rights to self-determination and development. Rather, the debate in Africa has generally been about the relevance of the first generation of human rights. Thus, it has been argued that even though democracy is now the stated goal of many African social movements, and is widely advocated as the means to autonomous internal development, the principle of a rights-based liberal democracy is not universally articulated. Howard summarizes the position as follows:[33]

> "Scholars writing on human rights in Africa presently fall into two camps, communitarian and liberal. Communitarians give ideological priority to the community (sometimes embodied in the state) over the individual. In their analysis of the need for human rights they stress group or collective, rather than individual rights-claims.
>
> In contrast to the communitarian approach, the liberal human rights literature on Africa reminds us of two absolutely necessary underpinnings of democratic practice, the rule of law and the elementary civil and political rights of all citizens as individuals. These aspects of democratic practice are

> necessary even in underdeveloped societies in which everyday social relations are largely regulated by tradition. The prime purpose of human rights everywhere is to protect the citizen against the state, as the individual's interests are always at risk of being undermined by political authority."

These two positions are, of course, wide generalizations. For the two respective camps also mask further divisions in themselves. On the one hand, communitarianism encompasses, *inter alia*, traditionalism and leftist collectivism or Marxist viewpoints. On the other hand, the liberal perspective may range from the classical Western European liberalism based on the Lockean conceptions of political democracy to the more integrative approaches inherent in social democracy. This is not the place to examine all these variants to the argument. The task of mapping out the detailed strands that underpin the various approaches to human rights in the developing world, especially in the African context will, for the moment, be left to others. I only propose to pick out two points for quick comments. First, I propose to offer some brief observations on communitarian and Marxist perspectives on human rights. Second, I will consider the argument that social democracy provides the most appropriate and relevant political framework for a meaningful recognition of human rights in constitutional schemes in developing countries in Africa.

Traditionalist and Marxist perspectives on human rights in Africa have one abiding common element: concern with the collectivity as opposed to the individual, and hence the submergence of the individual in the community. Ake's viewpoint is that:[34]

> "[Abstract] legal rights attributed to individuals will not make much sense for most of our people, neither will they be relevant to their consciousness and living conditions. It is necessary to extend the idea of human rights to include collective human rights for corporate social groups such as the family, the lineage, the ethnic group. Our people still think largely in terms of collective rights and express their commitment to it constantly in their behaviour."

According to this approach, therefore, the civil and political rights as traditionally defined in Western human rights discourses, and incorporated in the major international human rights instruments referred to above, are quite irrelevant. Human dignity, which underlies the concept of human rights, is protected by means other than individualistic, atomically disintegrative methods. Thus, it is argued, the approach in the industrialized democracies of Western Europe and North America, which requires the legalistic concept of rights to mediate in the atomistic model of their social organization, is not appropriate for the developing world, or at least the African society.[35]

For somewhat different reasons, the more radical Marxist approaches also lead us to a rejection of the near-exclusive emphasis placed by Western liberal human rights advocates on civil and political rights. By adopting international political economy perspectives, combined with a realistic assessment of internal class, communal and political factors, the advocates of these approaches locate the causes of human rights abuses, and the analysis of the human rights problematic, in a different context: the role of imperialism. And the starting point here is simply that "no meaningful conditions of life can be achieved on the [African] continent, even at the individual level, as long as the continent remains under imperialist influence", and that "[the] African concept of human rights will make sense only in the collective context of people's rights or group rights as against individual rights [especially] in terms of ensuring [the] right to development".[36]

The view being advanced here carries with it the implicit warning that since the modernist conceptions of human rights are Western-inspired, they are part of the larger baggage of neo-colonialism and imperialism. Furthermore, they are essentially a bourgeois artifact and a reflection of the bourgeois experience. Our espousal of this conception of human rights ought, therefore, to be tempered with great circumspection. Both the traditionalist and Marxist approaches thus emphasize the role of solidarity rights in the African conception of human rights in order to critique the relevance of the Western liberal conception of human rights. Perhaps the most sustained attack against this conception has come from Shivji. His fairly recent work, *The Concept of Human Rights in Africa*, represents an eloquent advocacy of the Marxist/collectivist, anti-individualist approach to human rights. Shivji argues that:[37]

> "The prevailing human rights discourse [on Africa] is fundamentally within the idealist philosophical world outlook. It is abstracted from social history and thereby arrives at conclusions which make human rights both eternal in historical time and universal in social space."

And, after critiquing the dominant discourse, Shivji posits an argument for the revolutionizing of the human rights framework:[38]

> "[It] is clear that human rights-talk should be historically situated and socially specific. For the African perspective this ought to be done frankly without being apologetic. Any debate conducted on the level of moral absolutes or universal humanity is not only fruitless but ideologically subversive of the interests of the African masses."

Shivji does not believe in universal, equal and individual rights, but rather recognizes only "peoples' rights", and even these are, in the final analysis, compressed into two principal rights: the right to self-determination, and the right to organize.[39] Underlying all this is the old argument, that human rights are irrelevant to very poor people; that, to paraphrase the famous speech by former Tanzanian president Julius Nyerere, for the subsistence farmer unsuccessfully trying to scratch a living from the soil, freedoms to vote and speak are meaningless.[40]

Of course, nobody can quarrel with the proposition that the imperialist domination of Africa, from colonial to neo-colonial forms, constitutes the point of departure for understanding the condition of the African masses. Nor can one dispute that a proper appreciation of the structural inequality endemic to the existing international system and inherent within the post-colonial State in the developing world is central to any analysis of the human rights problem in Africa. To this extent, there is no doubt that the Marxist perspective adopted by Shivji and other commentators raises questions that must be given serious thought in any attempted critique of the dominant human rights discourse in the developing world, and especially in Africa. But, of course, these questions, and the analysis itself, are not as such new. The questions that earlier commentators such as Ake posed still remain with us: Does a starving person care about being tortured and brutalized? Does she or he care about voting? Does she care about suing her torturers? Or does such a person care only about the next meal? Are these choices even available to such a person?[41] In brief, are individual civil and political rights as relevant to the masses of subsistence farmers, street hawkers, office cleaners, and so on and so forth, in the poor regions of the world as are their economic and social rights? Or, are the second and third generation rights all that matters in the developing countries, as some advocates of the traditionalist/collectivist or Marxist approaches seem to suggest?

It is of course true to say that, generally speaking, human rights scholarship in Africa has presented a dichotomy between the communal basis of African societies and the notion of individual rights predominant in Western liberal thought. But this is only a loose generalization. There is a multiplicity of approaches to human rights theorizing even among African scholars, as El-Obaid's and Appiagyei-Atua's recent work ably demonstrates.[42] Besides, one should bear in mind the apt observation by the Ghanaian philosopher, Gyekye, that:[43]

> "[The] African social order is, strictly speaking, neither purely communitarian nor purely individualistic. But the concept of communalism in African social

thought is often misunderstood, as is the place of the individual in the communal social order."

Relying in part on Gyekye's schema and analysis of the African social order, El-Obaid and Appiagyei-Atua have provided a powerful and informed critique of some of the recent African human rights scholarship in their study, which seeks a rethinking of the human rights debate in Africa. They conclude:[44]

> "[While] a communitarian concept of human rights has existed in African communities, the exercise of rights is primarily based on the individual. Economic, social and cultural rights are best promoted and protected by focusing first on the individual. An organic connection exists between communal and individual rights as well as between modern rights and rights in the African traditional society." [References omitted.]

It is easy to see, if one adopts this perspective, that an integrated conception of human rights avoids the sterile debate about the dichotomous paradigm of "communitarianism versus individualism". It also allows us to see the interconnection between civil and political rights, on the one hand, and economic and social rights, on the other. African States and governments do not have to choose either one category of rights or the other. Both can be promoted and respected within the same human rights scheme. The specific conditions for their implementation and fulfilment may differ from one context to another, but they must be regarded as part of an integral human rights protection regime. The inclusion of both categories of human rights in the bill of rights of the new South African Constitution is an affirmation of this approach.

Democracy and Rights

The claim that democracy and human rights not only presuppose each other but are also genuinely intertwined requires qualification. It certainly should not be supposed that the two concepts are synonymous; rather, it is important to recognize that there may be tensions between majority decision-making and certain specific human rights.[45] And, depending on our own definitions of the two concepts, it is possible to view human rights both as a limitation upon democracy or as an inherent component of democracy.

An appeal to human rights can be regarded as a limitation on democracy especially in contexts in which arguments about human rights are underpinned by an appeal to the principle of the rule of law. Such an equation is often easily made among exponents of so-called liberal democracy. Observe the following statement by Howard:[46]

> "Liberalism [promotes] individual human rights regardless of the individual's wealth or status. The citizen is not required to be a member of a group in order to have rights.
>
> [The] classic civil and political rights [protect] citizens against unjust categorization into rightless social groups excluded from the collectivity. The rule of law demands that all individuals be treated equally and afforded the protection of the entire range of human rights, regardless of their class membership."

The priority accorded to the rule of law in this scheme of a so-called liberal conception of human rights is all too obvious. In Western Europe, at least, the rule of law preceded civil and political rights. Once assured of both justice and the right to political participation, the citizens (more properly, organized workers) were able to claim the economic and social rights that are now taken for granted in the modern (European) welfare state.

But, as most constitutional lawyers and political scientists (including, especially, the more "progressive" African scholars) would now agree, the rule of law (and all the implications that flow from that notion) must be understood in its proper context. No one can disagree with Mamdani that as originally formulated in Western political thought, the notion of the rule of law was designed "to set parameters on popular sovereignty" by formulating the rights of the minority in opposition to the majority.[47] As has been demonstrated in constitutional debates in most Third World countries, and more recently in South Africa, arguments for the rule of law (and a justiciable bill of rights) can be used as a tool by the privileged minority as a legal umbrella to protect their privilege, all in the name of safe-guarding human rights![48] In the final analysis therefore, it is important to bear in mind that the rule of law is meaningless without a political culture that promotes and values human rights for all. The claim that human rights and the rule of law provide for just treatment of all individuals regardless of social status or class membership cannot be regarded as a self-evident truth.[49]

My argument is that human rights are part of the essential substructural aspect of democracy in any modern society. The conception of democracy one has in mind here is the "integrative democracy" model which appeals to an ideal of equal membership in a political community. According to Dyzenhaus, such a conception of democracy has three constitutive principles. First, the principle of participation, which guarantees each individual a role which allows her or him to participate in or make a difference to the character of political decisions. Second, the principle of equal stake, under which every individual is treated as an equal under any collective decisions so as to count as a full member of the political community. Third, the principle of independence, which allows each member of the political community to see moral and ethical decisions as their responsibility rather than the responsibility of the collective unit.[50] But none of these principles can work in a context of gross economic and social inequality. And economic and social inequality is a form of political inequality, since it disables individuals from making use of the means given to them to participate in politics. Dyzenhaus's integrative model seeks its basis in a collectivist, communitarian conception that aims to create and preserve equal concern and respect for individuals. This leads him to conclude that:[51]

> "Its emphasis on the individual is distinctly liberal [and] democrats might be surprised to discover they have been liberals all along. But equally liberals will be surprised to discover that they are democrats of an egalitarian, even socialist, cast."

If one accepts this conclusion, it becomes clear, then, that Howard's assertion, that the collectivist perspective that focuses either on the nation or the people, at the expense of the rule of law and individual civil and political rights, necessarily contains the seeds of undemocratic repression, must be rejected as a *non sequitur*.[52] This need not always be the case. In any event, some of the more recent discourse on democracy suggests that even Western democratic movements are increasingly organizing around struggles for civil and community rights, economic empowerment, environmental protection, and so on – that is to say, on issues that take the debate beyond the narrow concern with the rule of law and elementary civil and political rights.[53]

The notion of democracy does not, of course, lend itself to easy definition, and this is not the place to attempt an analysis of the complex arguments about what democracy is and what it is not. That said, however, it is possible to point at some basic assumptions that are commonly accepted in this debate. First, that the system of governance in question must be based on the principle of popular sovereignty and respect for the will of the people if it is to be deserving of the description "democratic". Such a state of affairs requires adherence to certain prerequisite processes: periodic elections which are free and fair and thus provide an opportunity for public contestation between different actors and claimants in the political arena; a guaranteed environment for free discussion and decision-making, ensuring an unimpeded exchange of political ideas; and, as was implicitly indicated above, the existence of a political community comprising of the (adult) members of the society in question in which the operative principle is that of equality (in the sense in which Dyzenhaus, following Dworkin[54], defines the notion). Secondly, the procedural processes described above must be supplemented by certain minimum substantive requirements regarding the contents or nature of decisions. A democratic system of governance is one that aims at producing the best substantive decisions by, for example, facilitating decisions which will distribute material and other resources in an equal and just way.[55] Underlying this substantive requirement is the principle of mutual deference among human beings which was alluded to earlier.

Conclusion

Now, it should be fairly obvious that the conception of democracy briefly sketched out above is one which cannot be satisfied purely by an appeal limited to respect for the traditional civil and political rights of the individual. To be sure, there are mandatory requirements for the procedural element of democracy: free speech, freedom of association, the right to vote, and so on. Moreover, these are features which characterize the most basic form of democracy and enhance the idea of political equality. But this is not enough. Substantive equality, in the sense of economic and social equality, can only flourish if the other types of rights that aim at securing an equal and just distribution of resources – the second and third generation rights – are also guaranteed. It is precisely in this regard that the case for the relevance of economic, social and cultural rights, as well as solidarity rights, to the debate about democracy and constitutionalism can be made. In this limited sense, therefore, democracy and human rights become intertwined, like the proverbial Siamese twins, for one cannot be fully secured without the other.

The conclusion reached above needs to be coupled with a brief caveat, however. It has been cautioned that the current attempts to promote democracy in Africa by focusing only on the holding of multi-party elections can be seen as a confusion of form with content. One commentator has aptly described this thinking thus:[56]

> "Human rights are recognized as an essential aspect of democracy. Democracy is represented by one of its manifestations, multi-party elections. Multi-party elections are then thought to automatically imply both democracy and human rights, so that if a country holds such elections, it will be fulfilling all of its human rights obligations."

This is clearly not the sense in which the relationship between democracy and human rights ought to be viewed, and one can only reiterate the point made earlier, that to say that the two are intertwined is not to say that they are synonymous. The integrative conception of democracy referred to earlier is one that places emphasis on the need to go beyond form (the procedural process of periodic elections) and, instead, to focus on content (by identifying and pursuing the substantive goals of the practice of democratic governance itself). The recognition of, and respect for, human rights in all their generational contexts ought to be a continuous, living aspect of this practice.

No particular constitutional model has been suggested in this discussion, for no two constitutions are or should be the same. Each constitution must reflect the particular society for which it has been designed: its history, economy, traditions, culture and political ideology, among other factors. As Cover has written, "[no] set of legal institutions or prescriptions exists apart from the narratives that locate it and give it meaning. For every constitution there is an epic, for each decalogue a scripture".[57] Similarly, no specific form of democracy can be suggested as the most appropriate for every society. However, it is argued that the variant of liberalism generally styled "social democracy" represents an approach which, at least, places emphasis on the satisfaction of certain social objectives as a defining characteristic of democracy itself: the provision of social and economic goods and security are regarded as an inherent aspect of respect for the individual. This, in turn, means that equal recognition must be placed on economic and social rights as on civil and political rights.

It follows that the answer to the question posed in the preceding section of this discussion is, categorically, that all the three generations of human rights are of equal relevance and significance to all human beings. They are even more relevant to societies in the developing world, given the long history of political, economic, cultural and other forms of domination and exploitation that they have had, and continue, to endure. Thus, to echo the words of the preamble to the African Charter on Human and Peoples' Rights, civil and political rights cannot be disassociated from economic, social and cultural rights, and the satisfaction of the latter is a guarantee for the enjoyment of the former.[58] The entrenchment of these rights in national constitutions is, in political and legal terms, the most visible way of affirming their respect and recognition by the State. Such entrenchment ensures, in a formal if not substantive sense, that the rights so protected have constitutional supremacy and are thus largely immunized from the ordinary political process. The supremacy accorded to all the three categories of human rights in the Namibian, South African and Malawian constitutions, to name only the specific examples that the discussion started off with, are testimony to the fact that human rights are regarded as being particularly central to the new democratic culture which these respective constitutional arrangements seek to consolidate. The same can be said of other constitutional projects in the new democracies elsewhere in the developing world.

Notes

1. For some of the discussions on the role of international law, including in particular international human rights law, in the constitutions under reference see: G. Erasmus, "The Namibian Constitution and the Application of International Law" *15 SAYIL 81* (1989/90); J. Dugard, "The role of international law in interpreting the bill of rights", *10 SAJHR 208* (1994); see also same author's *International Law: A South African Perspective*, (1994) pp. 339–346; D. Devine, "The relationship between international law and municipal law in the light of the interim constitution for South Africa 1993", *44 ICLQ 1* (1995); see also T. Maluwa, "International Human Rights Norms and the South African Interim Constitution 1993", *19 SAYIL 14* (1993/94); and "The Role of International Law in the Protection of Human Rights under the Malawian Constitution of 1995", *3 African Yrbk Int'l L 53* (1995).

2. P.T. Zeleza, *Manufacturing African Studies and Crises*, (1997) p. 406.

3. The literature on democracy and human rights is so extensive that not even a brief indication of all the relevant discussions can be rendered here. See F. Bealy, *Democracy in the Contemporary State*, (1988) *passim*; J. Schumpeter, "Capitalism, Socialism and Democracy", in P. Green, *Democracy*, (1993) pp. 83–92.; also C.B. McPherson, "Democratic Theory", in Green, *ibid*. p. 153 *et seq*.; D. Dyzenhaus, "Democracy, Rights and the Law", 7 SAJHR 24 (1991); D. Harris, "Returning 'Social' to Democracy", in G. Duncan (Ed.), *Democratic Theory and Practice*, (1993) pp. 218–234; C. Gould, *Rethinking Democracy*, (1988). On the human rights debate, particularly in the African context, see C. Ake, "The African Context of Human Rights", *34 Africa Today* 5 (1987); see also discussions on the same theme by other contributors in the same issue of the publication under reference; W. Nagan, "African Human Rights Process: A Contextual Policy-Oriented Approach", *21 Southwestern Univ. L. Rev 63* (1992); Z. Motala, "Human Rights in Africa: A Cultural, Ideological, and Legal Examination", *12 Hastings Int'l & Comp L Rev 373* (1989); I. Shivji, *The Concept of Human Rights in Africa*, (1989) *passim*; see also J.A.M. Cobbah, "African values and the human rights debate: an African Perspective", 9 *Human Rights Q 309* (1987); R. Howard, *Human Rights in Commonwealth Africa*, (1986); O.C. Eze, *Human Rights in Africa: Some Selected Problems*, (1984); M. Mutua, "The Banjul Charter and the African cultural fingerprint: an evaluation of the language of duties", *35 Virginia J Int'l L 340* (1995).

4. See, for example, R. Howard & J. Donnelly, "Human Dignity, Human Rights, and Political Regimes", 80 *Am. Pol. Sc. Rev. 801* (1986).

5. S. Huntingdon, *The Third Wave: Democratization in the Late 20th Century*, (1991).

6. Howard & Donnelly, *op. cit.* note 4 *supra*; see also R. Scalapino, "Democratizing Dragons: South Korea and Taiwan", *4 J. Democracy 70* (1993).

7. See, for example, Shivji, *op. cit.* note 3 *supra*.

8. Cobbah, *op. cit.* note 3 *supra*. See also C.C. Mojekwu, "International Human Rights: The African Perspective", in J.L. Nelson & V.M. Green (Eds.), *International Human Rights: Contemporary Issues*, (1980); A. Lagesse, "Human Rights in African Political Culture", in K.W. Thompson (Ed.), *The Moral Imperatives of Human Rights: A World Survey*, (1980); L. Morasinghe, "Traditional Conceptions of Human Rights in Africa", in C.E. Welch & R.I. Meltzer (Eds.), *Human Rights and Development in Africa*, (1984).

9. S.S.C. Tay discusses some of these questions in relation to similar debates about the "Asian" view of human rights in his "Human Rights, Culture, and the Singapore Way", *41 McGill L.J. 743* (1996). See also A.A. An-Na'im, "Conclusion", in A.A. An-Na'im (Ed.), *Human Rights in Cross-Cultural Perspectives: A Quest for Consensus*, (1992) p. 427.

10. See, generally, I. Szabo, "Historical Foundations of Human Rights and Subsequent Developments", in K. Vasak (Ed.), *The International Dimension of Human Rights*, 2 Vols., (1982); E. Pagels, "The Roots and Origins of Human Rights", in A.H. Henkin (Ed.), *Human Dignity: The Internationalization of Human Rights*, (1979).

11. The Universal Declaration of Human Rights was adopted as General Assembly Resolution 217A (III) by 48 votes to none with eight abstentions. Its impact on the subsequent development of human rights cannot be doubted, and it has been invoked by courts in several national jurisdictions, including, for example, the United States in, among other cases, *Filartiga* v *Pena-Irala* 630 F 2d 876 (2d Cir 1980); *Fernandez* v *Wilkinson* 505 F Supp 787 (D Kan 1980).

12. The crystallization of this consensus among African States was evidenced, in institutional terms at least, by the adoption in 1981 of the African Charter on Human and Peoples' Rights under the auspices of the Organization of African Unity. See text in 21 ILM 58 (1982).

13. Some conventions may not seem to be directly aimed at governing human rights issues but are, in fact, part of this human rights regime: for example, the various refugee conventions (the 1951 UN Convention Relating to the Status of Refugees; the 1969 OAU Convention Governing the Specific Aspects of Refugee Problems in Africa, and so on).

14. Cf. the International Court of Justice's criteria stipulated in the *Asylum* case, 1950 ICJ Rep. 266; *North Sea Continental Shelf* cases, 1969 ICJ Rep. 3 at 44; see also the

Court's pronouncements in the *Military and Paramilitary Activities In and Against Nicaragua* case, 1986 ICJ Rep. 14 *passim*. The generally accepted view is that the practice in question must meet with a *general* rather than *universal* acceptance (in addition to the requirement of *opinio juris*, the accompanying psychological disposition).

15. 78 UNTS 277.

16. Thus, for example, U.N. General Assembly Resolution 1514 (XV) of 14 December 1960, the Declaration on the Granting of Independence to Colonial Territories and Peoples, which subsequently evolved into the right of self-determination, now almost universally recognized as a fundamental right under modern international law. The right is now also specifically recognized in some conventions, for example in the International Covenant on Civil and Political Rights (Art. 1(1)), the International Covenant on Economic, Social and Cultural Rights (Art. 1(1)) and the African Charter on Human and Peoples' Rights (Art. 20).

17. See Howard, *op. cit.* note 3 *supra*, p. 16.

18. Nagan, *op. cit.* note 3 *supra*, p. 77.

19. L. Henkin, *The Age of Rights*, (1990) p. 193.

20. See, for example, discussion by Tay, *op. cit.* note 9 *supra*; see also Cobbah, *op. cit.* note 3 *supra*.

21. See, for example, R. Pannikar, "Is the Notion of Human Rights a Western Concept?", *120 Diogenes 75* (1982) at p. 84; see also, generally, Shivji, *op. cit.* note 3 *supra*.

22. Tay, *op. cit.* note 9 *supra*, p. 749.

23. Tay, *ibid.* pp. 777–778. See also T. Nhlapo, "International Protection of Human Rights and the Family: African variations on a common theme", *3 Int'l J Law & Family 1* (1989).

24. An-Na'im, *op. cit.* note 9 *supra*.

25. See K.L. Savell, "Wrestling with Contradictions: Human Rights and Traditional Practices Affecting Women", *41 McGill L.J. 781* (1996) at p. 786.

26. Tay, *op. cit.* note 9 *supra*, p. 788.

27. M. Chanock, "Justice and Rights in Context", p. 7; paper presented at the Workshop on Cultural Transformations in Africa, African Studies Centre, University of Cape Town, 11–13 March 1997. (Copy on file with the writer.)

28. *Ibid.*

29. See T. Maluwa, "Changing Power Relations between Men and Women in Southern Africa: Some Recent Legal Developments"; paper presented at the Workshop on Transformations of Power and Culture in Africa, Center for Afroamerican and African Studies, University of Michigan, Ann Arbor, 11–20 November 1996.

30. See, generally, M. Cranston, *What Are Human Rights?*, (1973), and "Human Rights, Real and Supposed", in R.R. Raphael (Ed.), *Political Theory and the Rights of Man*, (1967).

31. A. Gewirth, "The Basis and Content of Human Rights", in J. Pennock & J. Chapman (Eds.), *Human Rights*, (1981); H. Shue, *Basic Rights*, (1980).

32. Gould, *op. cit.* note 3 *supra*, p. 191.

33. R. Howard, "Communitarianism and Liberalism in the Debates on Human Rights in Africa", *11 J Contemp. Afr. Studies 1* (1992) p. 2.

34. Ake, *op. cit.* note 3 *supra*, p. 5.

35. *Ibid.* p. 10.

36. See M. Anikpo. "Human Rights and Self-Reliance in Africa", in G.W. Shepherd, & M.O. Anikpo, *Emerging Human Rights: the African Political Economy Context*, (1990) p. 214.

37. Shivji, *op. cit.* note 3 *supra*, p. 43.

38. *Ibid.* p. 69.

39. *Ibid.* p. 72, where he argues: "[It] is clear that throughout there has been no such thing as 'integrated' rights. Rather there have been certain rights which have occupied the central place and attention. In the heyday of [the] bourgeois era, for instance, the right to property was central. In that sense it took priority over other rights including life and liberty. In the present African conjuncture, it is submitted that the *central* rights are the 'right to self-determination' and the 'right to organize' ".

40. See, generally, the discussion by O.C. Eze, "Human Rights Issues and Violations: the African Experience", in Shepherd & Anikpo, *op. cit.* pp. 87–106. See J. Nyerere, "Stability and Change in Africa" reproduced in *2 Africa Contemporary Record* (1969–1970) C30–31, where he asks: "What freedom has our subsistence farmer? He scratches a bare living from the soil provided the rains do not fail; his children work at his side without schooling, medical care, or even good feeding.

Certainly he has freedom to vote and speak as he wishes. But these freedoms are much less real to him than his freedom to be exploited. Only as his poverty is reduced will his existing political freedom become properly meaningful and his right to human dignity become a fact of human dignity."

41. Nagan, *op. cit.* note 3 *supra*, p. 85.

42. E.A. El-Obaid & K. Appiagyei-Atua, "Human Rights in Africa – A New Perspective on Linking the Past to the Present", *41 McGill L.J. 819* (1996).

43. K. Gyekye, *An Essay on African Philosophical Thought: The Akan Conceptual Scheme*, (1987) p. 154.

44. El-Obaid & Appiagyei-Atua, *op. cit.* note 42 *supra*, p. 853.

45. A. Rosas, "Democracy and Human Rights", in A. Rosas & J. Helgesen (Eds.), *Human Rights in a Changing East/West Perspective*, (1990) p. 17.

46. Howard, *op. cit.* note 30 *supra*, p. 7.

47. M. Mamdani, "Social Bases of Constitutionalism in Africa", *28 J Mod. African Studies 361* (1990) at p. 373.

48. See, for example, the discussion by A. Sachs, "Towards a Bill of Rights in a Democratic South Africa", 6 *SAJHR 1* (1990).

49. Howard, *op. cit.* note 30 *supra*, p. 7. For a general Marxist critique of the rule of law see, for example, N. Poulantzas, *State, Power and Socialism*, (1978); S. Picciotto, "The theory of the state, class struggle and the rule of law", in B. Fine *et al.* (Eds.), *Capitalism and the Rule of Law*, (1979). The general line of attack followed in these discussions can be summarized thus: first, that the various forms of political freedom and the legal equality of citizens which are supposedly secured by the rule of law are indeed the product of the Western liberal, capitalist order but that their functions are different from those that the liberal theory emphasizes, and that they are essentially ideological constructs to project ideas of freedom and equality in order to hide the exploitation that is carried on in the economy since economic resources are unequally distributed. Furthermore, it is argued by Picciotto, for example, that the democratic rights and freedoms projected by the principle are spurious and the rule of law ought to be exposed for the myth it is. See also Y. Ghai, "The Rule of Law, Legitimacy and Governance", *14 I.J. Soc. Law 179* (1986) at pp. 181–184.

50. See Dyzenhaus, *op. cit.* note 3 *supra*, pp. 35–36.

51. *Ibid.* p. 49.

52. Howard, *op. cit.* note 30 *supra*, p. 9. On the whole, Howard's discussion is singularly disparaging and dismissive of anything other than the liberal perspective and seems to be obsessed with the idea that appeals to "popular democracy" in Africa could be but the thin end of the dangerous wedge of "underdeveloped fascism" in Africa. Yet, the evidence for this is sketchy and speculative, and the connection she attempts to draw between the two is neither ideologically nor intellectually convincing. Observe the following proposition (on p. 9), for example: "The connections between populist democracy and fascism are strong. Strong popular movements and support underpin some fascist governments, such as that of Peron in Argentina as well as of Hitler and Mussolini. [If] populist democracy is not to result in a new form of underdeveloped fascism in Africa, then liberal human rights measures must be implemented". There must be more articulate explanations for the emergence of fascism in Africa (or elsewhere for that matter) than this. Popular democracy might be one of the defining characteristics of fascism but is not, of itself, the reason for fascism.

53. See Zeleza, *op. cit.* note 2 *supra*, p. 7.

54. By his own admission, Dyzenhaus relies for his discussion on Ronald Dworkin's "What is Equality? Part 4: Political Equality", *22 Univ. of San Francisco L Rev 1* (1987); "Equality, Democracy, and Constitution: We the People in Court", *28 Alberta L Rev 325* (1990); "What is Equality? Part 3: The Place of Liberty", *73 Iowa L Rev 1* (1987).

55. Dyzenhaus, *op. cit.* note 3 *supra*, p. 29.

56. Howard, *op. cit.* note 30 *supra*, p. 12.

57. R. Cover, "Nomos and the Narrative", *97 Harvard L. Rev 4* (1983) p. 19.

58. Para 7; see note 12 *supra*.

6

PROTECTING HUMAN RIGHTS IN THE CONSTITUTION: THE CASE OF MALAWI

Introduction

The new Constitution of the Republic of Malawi[1] (hereafter "the 1995 Constitution") was signed into law by the President of Malawi on 17 May 1995, exactly one year after the country's first post-independence democratic elections held on 17 May 1994. In fact, the 1995 Constitution is a slightly amended version of a constitution which was first enacted by the Malawian Parliament on 16 May 1994. The adoption of the earlier constitution itself followed the national referendum of 17 June 1993 which had confirmed that a substantial proportion of voters in Malawi were in favour of a change to political pluralism in the country.[2] The constitution adopted in 1994 was thus, in both conception and substance, the product of negotiations involving a number of political parties and pressure groups brought together under the aegis of the National Consultative Council, and was initially intended to apply provisionally for a period of twelve months, during which it could be amended or repealed, in terms of section 212, by the new democratically elected Parliament which came into being following the elections already referred to above.[3] It was therefore meant to provide the basis for an interim constitutional order, much along the lines of the interim Constitution of South Africa of 1993. It had also been envisaged that during this period of provisional application it would provide the focus for a national debate by various segments of Malawian society on the search for the most acceptable system of democratic governance for the country.

Accordingly, a national constitutional conference involving a wide spectrum of participants was convened in the Malawian capital, Lilongwe, in February 1995 to consider various proposals and submissions on the constitution received from members of the public, political parties, non-governmental organizations, interest groups, and so on, in the preceding twelve-month provisional period. A special session of Parliament was subsequently convened to consider the recommendations which emanated from this conference. It was during this session that a number of amendments were effected to the original (i.e. 1994) constitution through the Constitution (Amendment) Act No. 6 of 1995. The amended constitution was then formally re-enacted as the Constitution of the Republic of Malawi 1995 through the Republic of Malawi (Constitution) Act No. 7 of 1995. The new Constitution came into force definitively on 18 May 1995.[4]

One area in which there is a remarkable similarity between the recent constitutional developments in Malawi and those in South Africa is in the structure and content of the bills of rights enshrined in their respective constitutions.[5] The two constitutions are significant in at least two specific senses. First, in elevating certain specified legal rights to constitutional status, through the embodiment of these rights in an entrenched bill of rights. Second, in their adoption of the doctrine of constitutional supremacy, on the one hand; and, on the other hand, in their abandonment of the doctrine of parliamentary sovereignty, which had always been the root of the previous constitutional orders in both countries.[6]

In providing for a bill of rights in Chapter IV (entitled "Human Rights"), the Malawian Constitution follows not only the recent example provided by the adoption of a similar bill of rights in the South African Constitution, but also that of the Constitution of Namibia of 1990. Among the more common characteristics shared by the three constitutions is the status accorded to public international law in the municipal legal orders; and, in the case of South Africa, the explicit reference to the role of international human rights law, in particular, in the interpretative process.[7]

The principal aim of this chapter is to explore the role and relevance of international law in the interpretation and protection of the fundamental rights and freedoms enshrined in the new Constitution of Malawi. I intend, therefore, to examine the relationship between international law and municipal law in Malawi before and after the new Constitution. In doing so, I will attempt to place the new constitutional provisions in their proper historical and temporal perspectives by comparing them not only with the previously applicable common law rules, but also with the position adopted by other countries in the Southern African sub-region especially insofar as the protection of human rights is concerned. It will be shown that even although some of these countries have not accorded international law any explicit role in their constitutional schemes, they have nevertheless developed a constitutional jurisprudence which takes account of the relevant norms of public international law in the interpretation of constitutionally protected rights.

In brief, then, this discussion is aims at exploring the relevance of international human rights law in judicial-decision making under the new constitutional dispensation in Malawi. What approach or approaches are the courts likely to adopt as and when direct their minds to the protection of the human rights guaranteed in Chapter IV of the 1995 Constitution? More directly, the question that arises for consideration is: what role should international law play in the domestic protection and enhancement of human rights? What is implied in this question is the need to look at the way in which human rights are protected at the international level through the rules and mechanisms provided by international law, and to see how they impact upon the protection of such rights in the municipal legal sphere, especially through their recognition and enforcement by the domestic courts.[8] In fact, this question has already been addressed in the discussion in the previous chapter. It was also noted in that discussion that there now exists a core of internationally recognized human rights which States are increasingly incorporating in their national constitutions through entrenchment in Bills of Rights. It may only be recalled here that the Malawian Constitution now protects the following rights: life (s. 16); prohibition against acts of genocide (s. 17); personal liberty (s. 18); human dignity and personal freedoms (including prohibitions against torture, cruel, inhuman or degrading treatment, corporal punishment and non-consensual scientific or medical experimentation) (s. 19); equality (s. 20); privacy (s. 21); family and marriage (s. 22); rights of children (s. 23); rights of women (s. 24); education (s. 25); culture and language (s. 26); freedom from slavery, servitude and forced labour (s. 27); property (s. 28); economic activity (s. 29); development (s. 30); labour relations (s. 31); freedom of association (s. 32); freedom of conscience (s. 33); freedom of opinion (s. 34); freedom of expression (s. 35); freedom of the press (s. 36); access to information (s. 37); freedom of assembly (s. 38); freedom of movement and residence (s. 39); political rights (s. 40); access to justice and legal remedies (s. 41); rights of detained, arrested and accused persons (s. 42); and administrative justice (s. 43).

International Law and Municipal Law in Malawi

In order to place international human rights in their proper context, one needs to examine the relationship between international law and municipal law in Malawi. This can only be a very general – and brief – comment, and one that does not purport to address the multiple issues that arise in the debates regarding the inter-relationship between these two systems of law. However, even such a brief discussion may help to articulate the role of the relevant aspects of international human rights law (both customary and conventional) in the domestic protection of human rights in the Malawian municipal legal sphere. The major propositions regarding the relationship between international law and municipal law are reflected in the opposing theories commonly known as the monist and dualist theories, discussed in Chapter 2 above.

In any event, it is apt to recall the observation made earlier that most scholars are of the view that the two theories alluded to above are of relevance only in the specific context of customary international law. For it is accepted, at least in the English common law tradition, that all these arguments are beside the point where statutes and treaties are concerned. The position is that whether a given rule of international law is part of the municipal law of the State in question or not, where a matter is governed by a statute and the words of the statute are clear, or the meaning thereof can be construed clearly, the municipal courts must apply such a statute even if its application results in the contravention of an acknowledged rule of international law. Similarly, an obligation contained in a treaty does not form part of the municipal law, and may not be enforced by the municipal courts as such, unless it has been incorporated into municipal law by means of legislation.[9]

The Pre-1995 Constitution Period

To date, international law has played very little part in the advancement and protection of human rights by Malawian courts. Malawi achieved independence from Great Britain on 6 July 1964 under a "Lancaster House" type of constitution which, in theory, allowed political pluralism and incorporated a fully-fledged bill of rights under which the traditional fundamental rights and freedoms recognized under English constitutional law were secured. But in the short period between the attainment of independence and the adoption of a new constitution on 6 July 1966 (hereafter "the 1966 Constitution")[10], the legal and political landscape in the country had quickly been transformed into an autocratic one-party regime under an effective all-powerful ruler in the person of Dr. Hastings Banda. This dramatic change was accompanied by a virtual abrogation of the fundamental rights of citizens from the constitutional and legal order; the fully-fledged bill of rights of the 1964 Constitution was repealed, and in its place a statement of "Fundamental Principles" of government declared, *inter alia*, in Section 2(1) of the 1966 Constitution that:

> "(iii) The Government and the people of Malawi shall continue to recognise the sanctity of the personal liberties enshrined in the United Nations' Universal Declaration of Human Rights, and adherence to the Law of Nations; [and]
>
> (iv) No person should be deprived of his property without payment of fair compensation, and only where the public interest so requires."

But, as Ng'ong'ola[11] has aptly noted, these were no more than tepid acknowledgements of fundamental human rights, and were in any case subsequently visited with the clarification that:[12]

> "Nothing contained in or done under the authority of any law shall be held to be inconsistent with or in contravention of [the fundamental principles of government] to the extent that the law in question is reasonable and required in the interest of defence, public safety, public order or the national economy."

This, then, was the extent of any mention of, or reference to, international law (or the law of nations) and human rights norms in the 1966 Constitution. As a member of the United Nations, and thereby a party to the United Nations Charter, Malawi has always been obliged, in accordance with Articles 55 and 56, to promote "universal respect for, and observance of human rights and fundamental freedoms for all without distinction to race, sex, language or religion". However, neither these provisions, nor the entire United Nations Charter, have ever been incorporated into the municipal law of Malawi. And, moreover, Dr. Banda's Malawi Congress Party government was never prepared to ratify or accede to any of the major international human rights instruments which comprise the corpus of international human rights law. Thus, until recently,[13] Malawi never became a party to some of the most critical international instruments in the area of human rights, such as the International Covenant on Civil and Political Rights, the Convention against Torture and Other Cruel, Inhuman or Degrading Treatment or Punishment, and so on. Consequently, none of these treaties could ever become part of the law of Malawi through the process of legislative incorporation through which, as has been pointed out above, a treaty could be given effect as a source of rights and duties in the domestic legal sphere; nor were any of the treaties which Malawi did, in fact, ratify ever transformed into municipal law through such a process.

Given all this, the question that may still be posed is whether a case could be made for the relevance of international law, and especially international human rights law, in the pre-1995 constitutional order in Malawi? Could, or did, the courts in Malawi ever attempt to invoke the rules and principles of international human rights law in other ways? In essence, these questions require a two-stage enquiry: first, what was the status of rules of customary international law, including of course human rights law, in the municipal legal scheme? Second, what rules of conventional international law, arising from the various human rights treaties, could be said to have been binding on Malawi, and within Malawi, through their crystallization into customary rules, for example? In brief, what was the treatment of customary rules and treaties relating to human rights before the municipal courts in Malawi?

In contrast with, say, the experience in other countries in the Southern African region, especially South Africa, the courts in Malawi have never been seized with the opportunity to examine and pronounce upon the question of whether or not international law is part of Malawian law. The exception in this regard was provided by the fairly recent case of *Chakufwa Chihana* v *The Republic*[14]. Mr. Chakufwa Tom Chihana, at the time one of the two vice-presidents in the new democratic Malawi, had been charged in the High Court of Malawi with importation and possession of seditious materials contrary to section 51 of the Penal Code and was subsequently convicted and sentenced to two years imprisonment on 14 December 1992. He appealed to the Supreme Court of Appeal against both conviction and sentence. In this case, the appellant raised a number of arguments bearing on the question of the relevance of international law in interpreting and protecting human rights in the domestic legal regime; but, with due respect, the court missed the opportunity to address the question in any depth.

The starting point in *Chihana* was that one of the principles upon which the Government of Malawi was founded was the "commitment to the continuation of human rights", and that these human rights were derived from the United Nations Universal Declaration of Human Rights. The appellant argued that the personal liberties enshrined in the Universal Declaration were embodied and incorporated in the 1966 Constitution and formed part of Malawian law by virtue of section 2(1)(iii); and that the fact that they had not been listed in full in that subsection did not negate their being part of Malawian law.

Thus, in advancing the argument that the State had violated the appellant's fundamental rights and liberties in various respects – right to liberty and security of person; freedom of opinion, expression and association; right to legal representation; right to equality and non-discrimination – great reliance was placed on the relevant provisions of the Universal Declaration. Furthermore, it was argued that these rights are echoed and reiterated in the African Charter on Human and Peoples' Rights, to which Malawi was already a party at the time of the hearing. The upshot of the appellant's argument was thus that his conviction in the lower court was contrary not only to the domestic law of Malawi, but also to Malawi's obligations under international law. The appellate court had no difficulty in accepting the binding nature and status of the Universal Declaration as part of the law of Malawi (in terms of section 2(1)(iii) of the 1966 Constitution).[15]

As has just been noted, the argument advanced in the *Chihana* case, that the provisions of the Universal Declaration of Human Rights were part of the law of Malawi, was predicated on the explicit reference contained in section 2(1)(iii) of the 1966 Constitution. But this constitutional provision was itself a rather curious attempt at a legislative incorporation of international law into the municipal legal order; the wording was certainly not without ambiguity, for it provided that "the people of Malawi shall continue to recognise [the liberties enshrined in] the Declaration", instead of committing the State itself to recognizing and protecting these rights and liberties with respect to its citizens. On the face of it, the language employed here does not suggest a categorical commitment on the part of the State to respect the rights of citizens in the usual vertical scheme of constitutional rights protection. Similarly, a constitutional statement to the effect that "the people of Malawi shall continue to adhere to the law of nations" cannot, of itself, be interpreted as an unequivocal incorporation of international law as part of the municipal law. Section 2(1)(iii) of the 1966 Constitution could have benefited from clearer and more categorical language.

A different line of argumentation would, in fact, have achieved the same result: this would be to say that either the whole, or parts of, the Universal Declaration had acquired the status of customary international law; and thus that since Malawi's position was in line with the judicial practice followed in the United Kingdom and other Commonwealth countries, it could be concluded that these rules of customary law were applicable as part of Malawian law. It would then have been possible to conclude that it was open to the courts in Malawi to apply those norms of international human rights law enshrined in the Universal Declaration (and in other instruments) that had acquired the status of custom, unless they were in conflict with legislation. The case for the recognition of the Universal Declaration as customary international law has been made by the overwhelming majority of international legal scholars and commentators and does not require repetition here.[16] But the real theoretical misconception in the appellant's argument in *Chihana* lay in the interpretation placed upon the African Charter on Human and Peoples' Rights as part of Malawian municipal law. Malawi ratified the African Charter on 17 November 1989 and subsequently deposited the instrument of ratification on 23 February 1990; by article 65 of the Charter, the provisions thereof became binding on Malawi three months after the date of deposit of the instrument of ratification.

Now, the term "ratification" is said to have two meanings. In the first place it refers to the international process in terms of which a treaty requiring ratification in addition to signature to bring it into force on the *international* plane is confirmed by the necessary State authority, usually (but by no means always) the executive. Secondly, it refers to the internal procedure by which the legislature approves the treaty and thereby incorporates it into *municipal* law.[17] The former is called *international* ratification, while the latter is termed *constitutional* ratification. Now, article 65 of the African Charter on Human and Peoples' Rights referred to above provides that:

> "For each of the States that will ratify or adhere to the present Charter after its coming into force, the Charter shall take effect three months after the date of the deposit by that State of its instrument of ratification."

It cannot be doubted that article 65 concerns the binding effect of ratification upon the ratifying State *in its relations with other State parties*; in other words, the binding status of the treaty upon the State from the point of view of international law, rather than the effect of the treaty as a source of the rights and duties of individuals, the subjects of the State, within the domestic legal sphere. The arguments presented in the *Chihana* case failed to draw this distinction; in fact the view was being expressed that the Charter could be relied upon as a source of Malawian municipal law by reason only of its ratification by Malawi. This was clearly mistaken, since it was the *international* rather than the *constitutional* ratification, in the sense explained above, that was at issue. Banda CJ's pronouncement regarding the African Charter on Human and Peoples' Rights, and his rejection of the appellant's argument on this issue, was brief but correct in point of law. He stated that:[18]

> "This Charter, in our view, must be placed on a different plane from the UN Universal Declaration of Human Rights. Whereas the latter is part of the law of Malawi the African Charter is not. Malawi may well be a signatory to the Charter but until Malawi takes legislative measures to adopt it, the Charter is not part of the municipal law of Malawi and we doubt whether in the absence of any local statute incorporating its provisions the Charter would be enforceable in our Courts."

Some brief remarks about the status of treaties as sources of municipal law may be made here. Under the previous constitutional order in Malawi, the power to enter into treaties belonged to the executive, as is the case in the United Kingdom and most other countries. Similarly, ratification of treaties was an executive act, and not the legislature's responsibility. Since the legislature played no part in the treaty-making process itself, in most cases treaties did not become part of the municipal law without some act of legislative transformation. That said, however, it is imperative to recognize that even a treaty not incorporated into municipal law may be considered by a municipal court in certain circumstances; thus, for example, a municipal court may have recourse to an unincorporated treaty in order to interpret an ambiguous statute; or an unincorporated treaty may be taken into consideration in challenging the validity of delegated legislation on grounds of unreasonableness; or where the unincorporated treaty provides evidence of a rule of customary international law. In the last instance, the treaty would be applied as a customary rule, but not as a treaty, and this would apply with equal force both to treaties to which the State in question is a party and those to which it is not.[19] It is argued here that in the absence of any act of incorporation, the African Charter on Human and Peoples' Rights could not be considered to be part of the municipal law in Malawi, even though it was binding upon Malawi on the international plane. In the circumstances, it could only operate as a source of legal rights and obligations which could be directly invoked by a municipal court if the provisions in question provided evidence of customary international law. Since the provisions under consideration (relating to freedom of expression, opinion, association, and so on) were merely an echo of similarly worded provisions in the Universal Declaration of Human Rights, again, in the final analysis, the argument rests on the status of the latter instrument as customary international law.

As noted earlier, the court missed an opportunity to pronounce upon these important questions regarding the relationship between international law and Malawian law, in general; nor was the question of the relevance of international human rights norms addressed with any seriousness. The failure by the Malawian courts to make use of the rare opportunity afforded to them to apply international human rights norms can be ascribed mainly to the lack of awareness of the importance attached to international human rights norms in other jurisdictions, and a certain hostility to the international human rights movement. This antipathy was obviously borne out of the long years of isolation and paranoia which characterized the autocratic rule of Dr. Banda's regime. It required the new dispensation ushered in by the new constitutional order now enshrined in the 1995 Constitution to change this position.

The Position under the 1995 Constitution

Whatever doubts or uncertainties may have attended the previous constitutional order, the question regarding the place of international law in Malawian law is now governed by the 1995 Constitution. This Constitution, unlike the previous ones of 1964 and 1966, expressly recognizes international law and the role it plays in Malawian municipal law. A brief account of the present position may be given; first, in relation to customary international law, and then the status of treaties.

(i) Custom

The relevant provision in this regard is section 211(3) which declares, in apparently clear and unequivocal language, that:

> "Customary international law, unless inconsistent with this Constitution or an Act of Parliament, shall have continued application."

A number of quick observations may be made here. To begin with, section 211(3) is meant to be a constitutional confirmation of the previous (common law) position, namely that customary international law has always been part of Malawian municipal law, even if there has never been any clear judicial pronouncement on the matter. However, it is submitted here that section 211(3) suffers from a certain degree of inelegant drafting. As it stands, the phrase "shall have continued application" could be interpreted as suggesting that it is only that customary international law *already in existence* at a particular point in time (at the commencement of the Constitution, for example?) which is contemplated here. But this would be to "freeze" the content of customary international law to that which stood at a "fixed" date, precisely the opposite of what was intended. Would it not have been preferable to cast the provision in more categorical terms, by simply stating that customary international law "shall form part of the law of Malawi", or words to that effect? This is the form in which similar constitutional provisions elsewhere have been couched. It is instructive to compare this wording with the corresponding provision in the South African Constitution, for example. Section 231(3) of the latter reads:

> "The rules of customary international law binding on the Republic, shall, unless inconsistent with this Constitution or an Act of Parliament, form part of the law of the Republic."

Two further observations may be made in respect of this issue. First, it is to be noted that section 211(3) does not distinguish between different types of customary international law; all types, whether universal, general, regional, local or particular, are incorporated. This could be contrasted with section 144 of the Namibian Constitution which incorporates only *general* rules of international law, or the South African provision which presupposes certain types or categories of customary international law which may not be binding on the Republic of South Africa. The Malawian approach is preferable (subject to the suggestion that has just been made above regarding the scope for improvement in the wording of section 211(3)), since it ensures the incorporation of customary international law in its totality, thus rendering the Malawian Constitution even more "customary international law-friendly" than its Namibian or South African counterparts. The second general observation to be made with regard to this provision is simply that customary international law has now been accorded a high constitutional profile in Malawian law, given that the Constitution itself is, according to section 5, the supreme law of the Republic.

The upshot of the above observations regarding section 211(3) is that where a particular international human rights norm is regarded as having matured into a rule of customary international law, such a rule must be applied by the domestic courts as part of the municipal law of the country. Again, as under the previous position, if there is any ambiguity as to whether or not there is a conflict between the rule of customary international law and a statutory provision, an attempt should be made to reconcile the two before declaring the customary rule invalid, since there is a presumption of statutory interpretation that the legislature does not intend to violate international law.

(ii) Treaties

The role of treaties in Malawian law has also been radically changed by the new Constitution. As was noted above, previously a treaty entered into by the executive had no effect domestically, and could thus not be enforced in the domestic courts, unless it had been incorporated into Malawian municipal law through the legislative process. The matter is now governed by section 211(1) and (2). But, as will shortly be argued, the current formulation is not without problems.

The present position may be summarized as follows: first of all, section 89(1)(f) authorizes the President "to negotiate, sign, enter into and accede to international agreements or to delegate such power to ministers, ambassadors and high commissioners". This clearly accords the treaty-making power to the executive branch of government, in line with common practice elsewhere; and, in carrying out this executive function, the President shall be assisted by the cabinet. For, according to section 96(1)(f), one of the duties and functions of members of the cabinet is "to assist the President in determining what international agreements are to be concluded or acceded to and to inform Parliament thereon". The question that comes to mind immediately is one relating to the role of Parliament under the new constitutional scheme. Does the Constitution now require ratification of treaties by the legislature (as opposed to ratification by the executive, as under the old regime) before they can become binding on the Republic externally, that is in its relations with other States? It is pertinent to pose this question because, on the face of it, there is nothing in the Constitution (including sections 66 and 70, which provide for the powers and functions of the National Assembly and the Senate, respectively) which explicitly suggests that Parliament must ratify (or approve) treaties for them to become binding on the international plane. And, yet, the wording of the provision in section 211(1) seems to imply such a requirement, or at least that Parliament is empowered to ratify international agreements. This provision states:

> "Any international agreement ratified by an Act of Parliament shall form part of the law of the Republic if so provided for in the Act of Parliament ratifying the agreement."

Now, it is important to recall that there are, broadly speaking, three main constitutional regimes governing the treaty-making power and implementation of treaty obligations in municipal law. First, the British system, which empowers the executive to sign and ratify a treaty, but requires the legislature to incorporate the treaty into municipal law if it provides for the creation of rights and duties for individuals. Second, the American system, in which the treaty-making power is shared by the executive and one house (the Senate) of the bicameral legislature; under this arrangement, a treaty entered into by the President and approved by the Senate shall have domestic effect without legislation, unless the treaty concerns matters that require legislation adopted by both houses of Congress. Finally, the system favoured by most States with bicameral legislatures, which vests the treaty-making power in the executive and both houses of the legislature; under this system, international obligations affecting the rights and duties of individuals are translated into domestic law by statute or by approval of both houses of the legislature.[20]

It is submitted that the wording employed in section 211(1) is somewhat vague and confusing, especially when read with section 89(1)(f). The inclusion of "enter into" and "accede" in the latter provision would appear to indicate that Parliament does not have to ratify or approve treaties for them to be binding upon Malawi externally. For it may be argued that since an international agreement is entered into when it becomes binding, and since the power "to enter into international agreements" is, under section 89(1)(f), accorded to the President without any requirement for prior approval by Parliament, it would be redundant to suggest that subsequent ratification (or approval) by Parliament is necessary for the international agreement to become binding on Malawi vis-à-vis other parties. Similarly, treaty practice suggests that once a State accedes to an international agreement (in accordance with the constitutionally prescribed procedures) the binding effect, on the international plane, of the agreement acceded to cannot be made dependent upon subsequent ratification or approval by the national legislature. It would thus seem that the employment of the term "ratification" in section 211(1) is not wholly appropriate, given the implications of section 89(1)(f) as discussed above.

In fact, it seems that the apparent ambiguity in section 211(1) arises from the failure on the part of the framers of the provision to distinguish between the two senses of ratification discussed above: *constitutional* and *international* ratification. It is perhaps instructive here to compare this provision with the corresponding provisions in the South African interim Constitution of 1993 (from which the constitution-makers in Malawi partly drew inspiration and guidance). Section 231 of the latter had provided, in part:

> "(2) Parliament shall, subject to this Constitution, be competent to agree to the ratification of or accession to an international agreement negotiated and signed in terms of section 82(1)(i).
>
> (3) Where Parliament agrees to the ratification of or accession to an international agreement under subsection (2), such international agreement shall be binding on the Republic and shall form part of the law of the Republic, provided Parliament expressly so provides and such agreement is not inconsistent with this Constitution."

It is significant to note in this regard that section 82(1)(i) of the South African interim Constitution only granted the President power to "negotiate and sign international agreements", but not to "enter into" or "accede to" such agreements. It is therefore clear that in the South African constitutional context, under the interim Constitution, a treaty could only be binding on South Africa internationally once it had been ratified by Parliament (i.e. *international* ratification); or, in the case of accession, if Parliament had agreed to the accession to such agreement.

It has been suggested that perhaps the difficulty with section 211(1) arises from the fact that in the earlier stages of the constitutional negotiations and the drafting of the new Constitution, the original intention had been to include a provision empowering Parliament to approve treaties. But, it is reported, the National Consultative Council subsequently decided that the

President should be able to enter into treaties without approval from Parliament, and the original provision concerning Parliament was thus removed. In the process, it would seem that section 211 was not amended in parallel to make the position clear and consistent with section 89(1)(f).[21] There is need to clear up the present ambiguity surrounding the use of the term "ratification".

A final point regarding the role of treaties under the new constitutional arrangements relates to section 211(2); this provision presents a radically different, and in a sense clearer, approach from the corresponding provisions in the South African interim Constitution. One of the criticisms levelled against section 231 of the South African interim Constitution was that it created a differentiated regime, at the *municipal* level, between treaties entered into before and after the 1993 Constitution; for although treaties entered into before 27 April 1994 (when the interim Constitution came into effect) remained in force at the international level, they did not form part of municipal law unless they had been incorporated by legislation (under the "old" constitutional regime); treaties entered into thereafter, and which had been ratified by Parliament under section 231(3), on the other hand, would form part of South African law without any need for a further specific act of legislative incorporation, at least in the view of some commentators.[22] Section 211(2) of the Malawian Constitution avoids creating such a dichotomy by simply providing that international agreements entered into before the commencement of the new Constitution (18 May 1995) and binding on the Republic of Malawi shall form part of Malawian law, unless Parliament subsequently provides otherwise or the agreement otherwise lapses. The advantage of this provision is that it not only affirms continuity in Malawi's treaty relations with other parties, but also imports into Malawi's constitutional scheme the presumption of incorporation into the municipal law of all existing treaties to which Malawi is a party. Otherwise Parliament would have to engage in the painstaking, and perhaps cumbersome, exercise of sifting out and singularly incorporating all pre-existing treaties into Malawian law through individual legislative acts. This is particularly significant in relation to those treaties which have a bearing on the interpretation and protection of the rights enshrined in Chapter IV. The only criticism one would direct at this provision is that the phrase "or the agreement otherwise lapses" is tautological, given the previous words "binding on the Republic"; quite obviously, a lapsed agreement ceases to be binding on the Republic.

In all this, what needs to be reiterated is that the arguments for parliamentary or legislative approval to give internal effect to treaties are predicated on the need to ensure democratic control of the nation's conduct of its foreign relations, as well as to ensure the proper application of the constitutional doctrine of separation of powers which is thought to be indispensable to democratic governance and the rule of law. The argument here is that without such a requirement, the executive authority could, by entering into a treaty, alter the municipal law without the democratic participation of the legislature. Such an argument is bound to have a particular currency and relevance in Malawi, as also in South Africa, entering as they are into a newly discovered culture of democratic governance based on real constitutional legitimacy and the rule of law.

Conclusion

As noted above, Malawi is presently a party only to a few human rights treaties. It may be argued that the incorporation of a bill of rights in the 1995 Constitution provides clear evidence of Malawi's new-found commitment to the protection of human rights and lays the foundation for the country's accession to the various other international human rights conventions referred to above. Moreover, it is fairly obvious that, as is the case with both the Namibian and the South African bills of rights, Chapter IV of the 1995 Constitution shows the clear influence of international human rights conventions; some of its provisions were modelled on those of the International Covenant on Civil and Political Rights. It is also apt to observe that the provisions of Chapter IV are sufficiently similar to those of the major international and regional conventions, in particular the European Convention on Human Rights, to ensure that the jurisprudence of the United Nations Human Rights Committee and thc European Court of Human Rights will guide the Malawian judiciary on these matters. In this regard, attention ought to be brought to section 11(2), which provides that:

"In interpreting the provisions of this Constitution a court of law shall –

(a) promote the values which underlie an open and democratic society;

(b) take full account of the provisions of Chapter III and Chapter IV; and

(c) where applicable, have regard to current norms of public international law and comparable foreign case law."

Two general propositions may be made in relation to section 11(2). First, although it is true to say that Malawi is not a party to most of the major human rights conventions, it cannot now be said that international human rights norms are of no relevance to Malawian law. Moreover, it must be reiterated that, notwithstanding the lack of any judicial pronouncement in this respect, customary international law has always been part of Malawian law, except where it is inconsistent with legislation. This proposition is in line with the approach of the English courts which have always provided obvious precedential guidance for the Malawian courts. Consequently, even where a human rights treaty has not been ratified or acceded to, nor expressly declared to be part of Malawian law, under section 211(1), it would be permissible to apply the relevant provisions of such a treaty if it can be shown that such provisions have passed into the corpus of customary international law or provide evidence of a customary rule. As was noted above, certain provisions originating from various conventions are now generally recognized as rules of customary international law, and have been accepted as such by municipal courts in various countries: prohibitions on torture, cruel, inhuman and degrading treatment or punishment; non-discrimination; the right not to be deprived of one's liberty unlawfully and arbitrarily, and so on; in doing so, a Malawian court would be applying these rules of customary international law in the same way as it would apply rules of the common law.[23]

One way of looking at section 11(2) is to say that it is merely a statement of principles of interpretation which have been recognized by many courts; and that the reference to public international law and comparable foreign case law hardly required articulation in the Constitution, since it is inevitable that the courts will be significantly influenced by the manner in which courts in other countries have interpreted rights similar to those enshrined in Chapter IV. In fact, it is apposite to note here that under section 11(2), recourse to both "norms of public international law" and "foreign case law" is couched in mandatory terms, since the operative words which govern the entire subsection provide that a "court of law *shall*...".

It is submitted that section 11(2) strengthens the role of international law in the interpretive process since it requires the courts to apply international law where it is applicable. Almost every provision in the new Malawian bill of rights has some corresponding provision in one international human rights convention or another, or is governed by general principles of international law; thus, it would be difficult to conceive of any situations in which public international law would not be applicable under section 11(2). And since the reference in section 11(2) is to "public international law" in the broad sense of the term, it may be concluded that in interpreting Chapter IV Malawian courts are therefore required to have regard to international law contained in general treaties[24], custom, general principles of law, the writings of publicists and the decisions of international and municipal courts. In brief, recourse will be had to all the sources of international law enumerated in article 38(1) of the Statute of the International Court of Justice.

The new Constitution provides Malawian courts with an opportunity to develop a constitutional jurisprudence in which international law and comparative law will play a major part. In fact, as was observed in Chapter 2 above, there is already an emerging jurisprudence, within the Southern African sub-continent, which the courts in the new constitutional democracies, such as Malawi, can look to.[25] It can only be hoped that when the occasion arises Malawian courts will also follow this emerging regional jurisprudence, as well as other equally relevant jurisprudence from other parts of the world. A proper understanding of this human rights jurisprudence, as well as international human rights law in general, is a prerequisite for the development of a human rights culture which is indispensable to the existence of a viable system of human rights protection within the municipal legal sphere. Without this, the fundamental rights enumerated in Chapter IV, the bill of rights, of the new Constitution of Malawi will have no real practical meaning for the people they aim to protect.

Notes

1. Republic of Malawi (Constitution) Act No. 7 of 1995. The Constitution came into force on 18 May 1995.

2. According to statistics quoted in *The Monitor*, Blantyre, 18 June 1993, 62.2 per cent of voters voted in favour of political pluralism, 34.5 per cent opted for retention of the one-party system, and 2.3 per cent of the votes were spoiled ballots or declared null and void. For a discussion of some of the legal aspects relating to the referendum, see C. Ng'ong'ola, "The Malawi Referendum of June 1993: Some Pertinent Legal Issues", paper presented at the First Regional Conference on Law, Politics and Multiparty Democracy in East Africa, 17–23 October 1993, Dar-es-Salaam, Tanzania.

3. Thus, section 212 provides, in part, as follows:

   "212.(1) This Constitution shall provisionally come into force on 18th May 1994, being the appointed day, and shall provisionally apply as the Constitution of the Republic of Malawi for a period of not less than and not more than twelve months from that date (in this section referred to as the 'period of provisional application').

   (2) During this period of provisional application Parliament may amend or repeal this Constitution in accordance with this section subject only to section 196".

4. The Constitution (Amendment) Act of 1995 has effected amendments to some nineteen provisions and repealed one provision altogether (section 64). Among the most significant, and contentious, of these amendments is that relating to section 210; the amendment provides that the Senate shall not be established before the end of May 1999. This means that the principle of bicameralism, thought by most commentators to be one of the most fundamental principles that underpin modern democratic constitutions, will not be implemented for the life-span of the present government. The repeal of section 64 will naturally entail a renumbering of some provisions when the consolidated version of the Constitution incorporating all the amendments is produced. At the time of writing (July 1998) this had not been done yet. In any case, none of the provisions referred to in this discussion has been affected by these amendments.

5. See Chapter IV of the Malawian Constitution and Chapter 2 of the South African Constitution of 1996, respectively.

6. Thus, section 5 of the Malawian Constitution provides as follows:

   "Any act of government or any law that is inconsistent with the provisions of this Constitution shall, to the extent of such inconsistency, be invalid".

7. See the discussion in Chapter 2 and 5 *supra*.

8. For similar discussions relating to the South African interim Constitution of 1993, see, for example, J. Dugard, "The Role of International Law in Interpreting the Bill of Rights", 10 SAJHR 208 (1994); also same author's *International Law: A South African Perspective*, (1994), pp. 36–57, 339–346; T. Maluwa, "International Human Rights Norms and the Interim Constitution of South Africa", *19 SAYIL 14* (1993/94).

9. See the discussion of these theories in Chapter 2 above and the literature cited therein.

10. The adoption of a new constitution in 1966 also ushered in a new constitutional development which saw Malawi declared a "republic". Under the 1966 Constitution, Dr. Banda ceased to be Prime Minister and, instead, assumed the office of President and Head of State. This constitution also provided the first occasion for the formal declaration of the one-party State (s. 4) and the consecration of Dr. Banda as the "supreme executive authority of the Republic". See, generally, discussion by Ng'ong'ola, *op. cit.* pp. 3–7.

11. *Ibid.* p. 4.

12. Section 2(2) of the Republic of Malawi Constitution (1966), as amended by Act No. 6 of 1968.

13. In the period 1992–1994, partly in response to both international and local criticism and pressure, Malawi finally became a party, through either ratification or accession, to a number of international human rights treaties, including the major U.N. instruments. As at 30 June 1994 Malawi was a party to the following U.N. treaties: International Covenant on Economic, Social and Cultural Rights; International Covenant on Civil and Political Rights; Convention on the Rights of the Child; Convention on the Elimination of All forms of Discrimination against Women; Convention on the Political Rights of Women: Convention on the Nationality of Married Women; Slavery Convention of 1926 (as amended); Supplementary Convention on the Abolition of Slavery, the Slave Trade, and Institutions and Practices Similar to Slavery; Convention for the Suppression of the Traffic in Persons and of the Exploitation of the Prostitution of Others; Convention Relating to the Status of Refugees; and Protocol Relating to the Status of Refugees. See United Nations, *Human Rights: International Instruments (Chart of Ratifications)*, (New York and Geneva, 1994), (ST/HR/4/Rev.10), U.N. Pub. Sales No. E.87 XIV.2.

14. M.S.C.A. Criminal Appeal No. 9 of 1992 (unreported). (Copy of judgment on file with the writer. All page references henceforth are to this copy).

15. Accordingly, Banda CJ observed: "We accept that the UN Universal Declaration of Human Rights is part of the law of Malawi and that the freedoms which that Declaration guarantees must be respected and can be enforced in these Courts. [This] Court must be the protector of the fundamental Human Rights which are part of our law. However, that right to freedom of speech or expression may be subject to restrictions and limitation: while Section 2(1)(iii) of the Constitution recognizes the sanctify of the personal liberties enshrined in the [Declaration], Section 2(2) of the Constitution accepts that reasonable restrictions and limitations will be imposed on those liberties". See *ibid.* p. 2.

16. R.B. Lillich, "Civil Rights", in T. Meron (Ed.), *Human Rights in International Law: Legal and Policy Issues*, (1984) pp. 115–170, at pp. 116–117; J. Humphrey, "The International Bill of Rights: Scope and Implementation", *17 Wlm. & Mary L. Rev 527* (1976) at p. 529. Some commentators adopt a more cautious view, namely that only some of the provisions in the Universal Declaration may be said to have crystallized into general customary international law; see, for example, Dugard, *op. cit.* note 18 *supra*, p. 205. The suggestion by M. McDougal, H. Lasswell & L. Chen in their *Human Rights and World Public Order*, (1980) at p. 64, that the Universal Declaration has "the attributes of *jus cogens*" is one that has not been universally accepted. I share the view that this proposition goes too far, if it is intended to imply that all the rights enumerated in it have this character.

17. Dugard, *International Law: A South African Perspective*, (1994) pp. 342–342.

18. Note 14 *supra*, pp. 2–3.

19. See discussion by Dugard, *op. cit.* note 17 *supra*, pp. 53–55.

20. See Dugard, *ibid.* pp. 344–355; see also S.A. Riesenfeld, "The Doctrine of Self-Executing Treaties and *U.S. v Postal*: Win at any Price?" *74 AJIL 892* (1980) at p. 898.

21. I am indebted to John Barker, at the time a research scholar at Cambridge University, for supplying me with the texts of the original drafts of section 211 together with experts' comments on the drafts. This section of my discussion partly draws from his own critical insight and comments on the provision under discussion.

22. According to this view, all that was required under section 231 of the South African Interim Constitution was a Parliamentary resolution accompanying the ratification of the treaty in question. See Dugard, *op. cit.* note 17 *supra*, at p. 343; but see D.J. Devine, "The Relationship between International Law and Municipal Law in the light of the Interim South African Constitution 1993", *44 ICLQ 1* (1995) at p. 15 for a different interpretation, namely that an Act of Parliament would be required to translate even post-27 April 1994 treaties into municipal law.

23. Some of the potential problems that may be envisaged here concern the possibility of conflict between a rule of customary international law and a rule of the common law. In the South African context, it has been argued that the *dictum* by Nicholas J in *Liebowitz & Others v Schwartz & Others*, 1974 (2) SA 661 (T) at 662A, suggests that in such a situation, the court has the same kind of choice that it has when it is faced with a conflict between two common law rules, and it is thus not a foregone conclusion that common law rules must always prevail over customary international law; see Dugard, *ibid.* p. 47.

24. The argument here runs as follows: the use of the term "public international law" without qualification in section 11(2)(c) suggests that Malawian courts will now be required to consult all the sources of international law recognized by article 38(1) of the Statute of the International Court of Justice; consequently, although a Malawian court would normally only be obliged to apply bilateral treaties to which Malawi is a party, under section 11(2)(c) it is, in fact, required to consider all relevant general or multilateral treaties, whether Malawi is a party to the treaty in question or not.

25. See the discussion under "International Law and Constitutional Interpretation: A Southern African Perspective", in Chapter 2.

IV

REFUGEE RIGHTS

7

THE REFUGEE PROBLEM IN POST-APARTHEID SOUTHERN AFRICA

Introduction

Refugee statistics are notorious for their imprecision and fluidity. The endless cycles of violence, military conflict and civil strife have ensured that as one refugee population in one part of the world is repatriated to the country of origin, integrated in the host country or resettled in third countries, new communities of refugees and displaced persons are generated elsewhere. At the beginning of 1997, it was estimated that there were over 13 million refugees and asylum-seekers and almost 5 million internally displaced persons in the world. Of these, about 4.3 million refugees and almost 2 million internally displaced persons were to be found on the African continent.[1] The refugee problem is not, of course, new to Africa. Some studies have shown that refugee movements and population displacement in Africa have a longer history than is usually imagined to be the case; in fact, a history that goes back to pre-colonial times.[2] However, although it is important for discourses on the African refugee problem to take account of this historical perspective, it is not proposed to embark upon any discussion of the history of refugee movements here. This discussion has a more specific objective. I aim to limit myself to an examination of the problem of refugees in its present conjuncture and its significance to peace and security in Southern Africa.

The phenomenal increase in the number of African refugees over the last thirty years bears testimony to the magnitude of the problem: from 400,000 in 1964 to the current levels mentioned above. As thousands upon thousands of refugees have been successfully repatriated to their countries of origin following the apparent resolution of long running political conflicts in some parts of the continent, yet more thousands, indeed millions, have been forced into flight as a result of new crises elsewhere in other parts of Africa. Southern Africa has had its share of these experiences. Thus, for example, the repatriation of about 1.6 million Mozambican refugees from neighbouring countries in the two-year period from 1992 to 1994 was followed by a significant rise in the number of new refugees in the region, especially those fleeing from the recent (1994) genocide and carnage in Rwanda. South Africa, until recently a major source of refugees scattered in countries all over the region and beyond, now finds itself in the paradoxical position of having to deal with seemingly massive flows of refugees crossing into its territory. In examining this problem in the context of regional peace and security, one of the principal questions that may be posed concerns its impact on national policy-making processes. To what extent, for example, has the problem influenced policy-makers, both at the national and regional levels, in the areas of peace and security? Or, to put the question differently, in what respects, if at all, should the refugee problem feature in foreign policy formulation? But, before attending to this question, and the many others that arise, a few remarks about the concepts of peace and security would be in order.

As is widely recognized, one of the primary roles of the State is to provide peace and security for its citizens within the national territorial boundaries as well as to ensure their protection against threats from outside. It is also generally argued that in order to perform this function effectively the State, on the one hand, needs to command a critical mass of institutional capabilities to regulate societal relations and provide the standard public goods of which peace and security are primary; and, on the other hand, it requires widespread mass support and loyalty from the citizenry.[3] Although definitions of national security in the conventional literature are often said to be nebulous, ambiguous and value-loaded, they all, at least, seem to be agreed on one underlying characteristic: threat perceptions. For a long time, the standard assumption, at least within the post-World War II "realist" conceptualization of national security issues, was that such threats arose externally, from outside the State's borders, and were quantifiable only in military-strategic terms.[4] But a reformulation of this concept can be discerned in some of the more recent writings: essentially the argument that with changing actors in world politics come changing goals. National security has become more complicated as threats shift from the military (that is, threats to territorial integrity) to the economic and ecological. Consequently, the range of issues that fall under national security considerations now has also been broadened to include the protection of the national economy, ideology, the environment, drugs, and so on. Clearly, some of these newly defined threats to national security cannot, as such, be characterized as emanating from an "external enemy" in the traditional sense.[5]

Another factor which needs to be added to this changing catalogue of threats to peace and security is the refugee problem. Of course, this is not as such a wholly recent phenomenon; by the end of the 1980s, the refugee problem had become a permanent element in international relations all over the world. Quite aside from the enormous increase in the numbers of refugees and forced migrations, other considerations have been of particular relevance in recent discussions of the problem, for example the serious constraints in the international system itself, which have tended substantially to limit the possibilities of successful settlement of these refugee problems. Thus, the relevance of the question which this paper seeks to address, namely the significance of the refugee problem in the search for peace and security between nations in Southern Africa, is pertinent to other regions of the world as well. However, it is important to note from the outset of this discussion that although there has been a proliferation of refugee studies in recent years there is, surprisingly, very little systematic research and discussion of the political and strategic factors that both cause refugee problems and determine the policy responses of States to these problems; nor has the question of how refugee problems are linked to security, peace and foreign policy considerations been examined in great detail.[6] It is instructive to note that the refugee problem does not feature at all in discussions of the sources of insecurity in Africa in the otherwise excellent studies by, for example, Rugumamu and Nyinguro.[7] The latter merely observes, without further elaboration, that:[8]

> "Suppression of human rights in developing countries, especially in Africa, has more often than not led to civil strife. For instance, the refugee problem which is today a critical security issue in Africa, is in part the result of the non-observance of human rights, equality, freedom and justice by most governments in Africa."

Nyinguro then proceeds to discuss what he regards as the five broad sources of insecurity in Africa: (a) inadequate political systems; (b) economic underdevelopment; (c) inter-state conflicts; (d) external intervention; and (e) environmental degradation. Now, is the refugee problem to be regarded simply as a consequence and manifestation of the lack of peace and security among nations or is it, in fact, one of the root causes of insecurity in the international system? Or is it both a source and a consequence of insecurity?

Refugees, Peace and Security: Anatomy of the Problem

In his fairly recent study on refugee movements and international security, Loescher aptly observes that the enormous changes and instability generated by the end of the Cold War have triggered new mass movements of people across the globe.[9] In a real sense, the end of the Cold War was itself precipitated by the exodus of refugees from East to West Germany which increased dramatically in 1989 and immediately led to the collapse of the Berlin Wall towards the end of that year. Subsequent developments in Europe, especially in parts of the former Yugoslavia and the former Soviet Union, have only led to increased disintegration of previously stable territorial entities. The result has been not merely increased threats to the integrity and peaceful co-existence of long settled communities, but also massive dislocation of such communities and the creation of more and more refugees. The recognition by the United Nations High Commissioner for Refugees (UNHCR) of the existence of "internal refugees" in the Chechnya region of Russia, in the wake of the recently ended military conflict between Chechen separatists and the Russian army, is merely confirmation of this phenomenon. Africa has not been spared this tragedy. Civil war, genocide and mass displacement of peoples in some parts of the continent – the Horn of Africa (Somalia and Sudan), East Africa (Rwanda), West Africa (Liberia) and Southern Africa (Angola) continue to undermine the peace and security of all States concerned.

The conclusion of the liberation struggle in Southern Africa, which culminated in the demise of the apartheid regime in South Africa and its replacement by a democratically elected government on 10 May 1994, has not brought to an end the refugee exoduses that the region has been experiencing for the better part of the last three decades. On the contrary, mass movements of people from within and without the region have continued. Thus, to focus for the moment on the refugee presence in present-day South Africa, for example, the older wave of Mozambican and, to a lesser extent, Angolan refugees continues to be joined by new arrivals from as far afield as Rwanda, Somalia and Zaire. These refugee movements in Southern Africa, as in other parts of the world, have commanded the attention of high-level policy-makers not only for humanitarian reasons and because of the increasing numbers involved, but also because of the consequences that such movements have for national stability, international security and the emerging new world order.[10] Thus, as indicated above, an understanding of the nature of the refugee problem – the root causes as well as the strategic consequences – must form part of the research agenda for scholars of peace and security in Southern Africa. Such an agenda might include such questions as: how is the refugee problem linked to the security and foreign policy considerations of States in the region? How have refugees affected, and in their turn been affected by, international politics in the region, both in the pre- and post-apartheid eras? Do refugees, for example, feature in the foreign policy considerations of Southern African States in the manner in which they feature in post-Cold War foreign policy formulation in the United States and in Europe?[11] Thus, there is need to understand the refugee problem in the wider context of both State formation and social transformation processes.

In his discussions, Loescher has attempted to demonstrate that it is no longer sufficient to discuss the subject of refugees within a narrow national context or as a strictly humanitarian problem requiring humanitarian solutions. He notes how refugees already figure prominently on the post-Cold War political and security agendas, at least in the West. To take one example: the disintegration, civil war and redrawing of boundaries in the former Yugoslavia, and the accompanying explosion of long repressed ethnic tensions in the region, are now generating refugee flows and population movements which have seriously threatened international peace and security over the last couple of years or so.[12] No major European security or foreign policy initiatives or institutions can be designed without taking into account the implications of the various political confrontations between majority and minority groups, and the pogroms and persecutions currently taking place not only in the former Yugoslavia, but in post-communist Eastern Europe generally.

Moreover, it has been noted that refugee movements can also both exacerbate and influence relations between States in many ways. First, the exploitation of refugees for military and strategic reasons – refugees have been used instrumentally as "freedom fighters" to wage wars of national liberation in all continents in the last half-century. Refugee populations have often been regarded by national liberation movements as recruiting ground, and international humanitarian assistance given to such refugee groups has on occasion been used to sustain the liberation effort. This phenomenon has not been altogether absent in the various liberation wars and other types of conflict fought over the last three decades in Africa.[13] Secondly, the presence of refugees on a particular State's territory can exacerbate domestic political tensions which may, in the long run, impact upon inter-State relations at a regional or international level. As was recently experienced in Malawi during the Mozambican refugee crisis, the presence of massive numbers of refugees entails obvious economic burdens on the host State; this in turn can create feelings of resentment and suspicion, as the refugee population increasingly, and often wrongly, gets to be blamed for the economic difficulties that may arise within the domestic population.[14] This problem is already being played out on an even greater scale, and with stronger feelings, in the current South African debates about the presence of refugees and so-called economic migrants. Poverty, unemployment, scarcity of resources, and even crime and disease, are suddenly attributed to the presence of these refugees and other foreigners. In extreme conditions, such developments may also be accompanied by social and cultural tensions and threats to a country's communal identity and cultural cohesion. The nationalist backlash arising from such situations cannot be ignored by policy-makers designing not only domestic (immigration) but also foreign and security policies of the country. As has just been noted above, the refugee problem (and the related problem of illegal immigrants) is already assuming a highly emotional tenor in the public debates in South Africa. To what extent will the problem direct and determine South Africa's bilateral and regional relations with its neighbours and other African countries in the foreseeable future? In what respects should the problem be regarded as an integral component of the search for peace and security in the Southern African region as a whole? As intimated above, this last question lies at the core of the principal aims of this discussion.

Issues for Preliminary Consideration

In examining the question of refugees in the scheme of bilateral and multilateral relations in Southern Africa, a number of preliminary questions need to be examined. The major lines of inquiry may be summarized as follows. First, who are refugees, and how can we distinguish that population from other displaced groups? Is a purely legalistic approach to these definitional questions helpful in our analysis? Second, the traditional epistemology regarding refugees leads to the individualization of "refugeehood": "the refugee problem is then seen as one of individual persons, thus masking their distribution into classes, class fractions, social categories, social strata", and so on.[15] How can we recast these traditional notions, and would such a recasting necessarily give us a better insight into the refugee problem and its implications for peace and security? Third, is the implicit distinction so often assumed by most commentators (and in the relevant international legal instruments) between *political* and *economic* refugees tenable, or does this merely give rise to false notions and analogies? Fourth, what is the relevance of the notion of State sovereignty in debates about refugees, given that the traditional definition of a refugee is predicated on the need to "cross an international boundary", and thus assumes that "refugeehood" can only arise in the context of inter-State relations?[16] And, finally, is the notion of citizenship, or the relationship between the State and its members, of any import here, or is the State a "class neutral" entity owing and guaranteeing equal protection and assistance to all its members, citizens and non-citizens alike? The relevance of this last question lies in the fact that, by definition, refugees are not regarded as citizens of the host or receiving State, but as non-citizens whose presence is dependent on that State's readiness to grant them asylum within its territory.

On the whole, it is important to acknowledge that the refugee question has implications for other types of discourse arising around the notions of peace and security, for example: the amalgamation and transmutation of cultural identities; images of representation and the production of discourse around gender, class and ethnicity; the emergence of "partial" and marginalized communities within host countries; and so on.

The Concept of a "Refugee": The Question of Definition and Approach

The recent debates in South Africa have only managed to reveal the need to define and clarify the concept of a "refugee". Lately, there has been a clamour, bordering on hysterical xenophobia, among certain sections of the media and the general public to characterize whole groups of foreigners as either illegal immigrants or economic migrants not deserving of the status of refugees. Discussions conducted in the South African print and electronic media leave no doubt that there a growing apprehension that the country is being overwhelmed by increasingly huge numbers of refugees and illegal immigrants, especially from neighbouring African countries. Unfortunately, these debates, such as they are, do not seem to distinguish between the two categories and there has been a tendency to collapse the two into one and the same thing, and to label everybody as essentially an "illegal alien". There is no doubt that there is a huge problem concerning illegal immigration into South Africa; equally, there is no doubt that there is a lot of exaggeration about the actual extent of the refugee presence in the country. There are no reliable statistics, partly because not all refugees (or people who legally qualify for refugee status) are officially known to the UNHCR or the relevant government agencies. It has been reported that as at the end of February 1995, there were 95,000 Mozambican refugees awaiting repatriation from South Africa; and, further, that of the 2,485 applications for refugee status and asylum lodged in the previous year only 357 were accepted, 293 were rejected outright, while the rest were pending further consideration.[17] Thus it can be seen that, on the face of it, the magnitude of the refugee problem in South Africa is not as huge as is has been made out to be; at any rate, it is not as critical as the situation that, say, a smaller and poorer country like Malawi had to deal with, until fairly recently, at the height of the Mozambican refugee influx. There is clearly a serious problem of illegal immigration and the public outcry over this issue is no doubt justified, but even here informed policy debate is hampered by the lack of reliable information and statistics. The government's own official estimates put the number of illegal immigrants at between 2 and 8 million – a somewhat unhelpfully wide and vague margin!

The term "refugee", as traditionally defined, has a specific legal connotation. The United Nations Convention Relating to the Status of Refugees of 1951 defines a refugee as a person who is outside the country of his/her nationality (or place of last habitual residence, in the case of a stateless person) due to a well-founded fear of persecution on account of race, religion, nationality, membership of a particular social group or political opinion or owing to such fear is unwilling to avail himself or herself of the protection of that country.[18] Thus defined, refugeehood depends on two prerequisites: first, the existence of a fear of individual or personal persecution for the reasons stipulated in the definition; second, the need for the person in question to leave his or her country of origin and cross the national border into another country. Without satisfying the latter requirement, the person only remains an "internally displaced person". In theory, internally displaced persons cannot avail themselves of the legal protection afforded by the international refugee legal regime and are therefore, on the face of it, not the concern of international refugee law. Yet, as Helton[19] has rightly observed, increasingly the practice has been for the UNHCR, at the request of the Secretary General and the General Assembly of the United Nations, to extend its mandate to such people under a "good offices" jurisdiction. The most recent example of this was the extension of such a mandate to care for the "internal refugees" displaced in the conflict in Russia's Chechnya region.

As most commentators have noted, the concept of a "refugee" can be traced to classical times, to ancient Greece and Rome, but in its modern conception we need only go as far back as the inter-war, League of Nations, era.[20] The 1951 Convention definition has generally provided the conceptual parameters within which the problem of refugees has been discussed in both academic and policy-making circles. Now, this definition has elicited copious criticism. In the first place, it has repeatedly been pointed out that since the recognition of refugeehood is predicated on the need to cross national boundaries, it leaves out internally displaced people.[21] Secondly, the granting of asylum and refugee status on the basis of a "well-founded fear" of personal persecution has been criticized as rather nebulous.[22] Finally, it is thought that this definition implies the problematic distinction between those fleeing political persecution (so-called political refugees or refugees *stricto sensu*) and those fleeing economic and other life-threatening conditions (so-called economic migrants or economic refugees).[23]

This is not, of course, the place to trace the entire history of the evolution of the concept; it is enough merely to note that in their modern forms, the definitions of the concepts of "refugee" and "asylum" were motivated by the Russian Revolution of 1917 and the tragic experience of displaced persons during the two World Wars. The result was that most early international instruments on human rights and refugees relied on European conditions as the context within which to promulgate definitions of persecution and standards of universal rights. In essence, most criticisms of the 1951 Convention definition are directed at the major epistemological principle which is thought to inform the concept of a "refugee" and on which most liberal discussions are based. Ibeanu identifies this as the subjectivist idealistic outlook which leads to the individualization of refugeehood. He argues that:[24]

> "The problematic underlying this is that of the subject. Consequently, the refugee problem is seen as one of individual persons, thus masking their distribution into classes, class fractions, social categories and social strata. The problem is seen as that between the individual subject and the state in which the 'normal' bond between them is severed as manifested in persecution or denial of basic needs. This is why the determination of refugee status, consequent upon these definitions, requires an individual proof of persecution. The subject of the enquiry then becomes the individual human being [rather] than social forces and their interaction."

Quite clearly, the definitions given in the 1951 Convention and, earlier, in the Statute of the Office of the United Nations High Commissioner for Refugees were quickly rendered obsolete by the subsequent realities of the Third World. The restrictive nature of these definitions, elaborated in the special circumstances of post-war Europe to address specific historical, social and political contexts, was ill-suited to respond to the unique problems posed by refugee movements and forced migrations in other parts of the world, especially in the post-1960 period. It was for these reasons that subsequent regional instruments adopted broader definitions of the term "refugee", in recognition of the wider social reality which lies at the root of refugee movements in the modern world.[25] Thus, Article 1 of the OAU Convention Governing the Specific Aspects of Refugee Problems in Africa[26], adopted on 10 September 1969, incorporated the earlier definitions and added that:

> "The term 'refugee' shall also apply to every person who, owing to external aggression, occupation, foreign domination or events seriously disturbing public order in either part or the whole of his country of origin or nationality, is compelled to leave his place of habitual residence in order to seek refuge in another place outside his country of origin or nationality."

A detailed exposition of the history of the OAU Convention and the various considerations underlying the adoption of the broadened definition cannot be undertaken here. Many commentators have rightly noted that the overriding consideration was the need to respond to the African reality at the time: the reality of armed conflict which was so pervasive on the continent (arising both from the on-going anti-colonial struggles and internal civil wars within newly independent States) and was largely responsible for the flight of massive numbers of refugees. Thus, Arboleda has stated:[27]

> "The new terminology responded to the obvious humanitarian concerns and sought to provide a practical solution to the problem of determining refugee status; the massive migrations occurring at the time made individual determinations quite impractical. Unlike developed countries, where the existence of refugee determination procedures allowing case by case determination is assumed, the absence of decision-making infrastructures in Africa demanded not only a humanitarian but also a pragmatic approach. In responding to the real and urgent African needs, the drafters of the new definition gave secondary consideration to the strict legal meaning of its terminology and case law."

As I have commented elsewhere,[28] the definition contained in Article 1 of the OAU Convention broke new ground in international law by recasting the traditional definition of a refugee in embracing, as it does, an additional category of persons as refugees, i.e. all those persons who are compelled to leave their country of origin in order to escape violence, regardless of whether they are in fact personally in danger of political persecution. However, it has been suggested that one of the problems with the OAU Convention's definition is that it employed terms which had not yet acquired widely agreed or settled meanings in international law at the time: "external aggression", "occupation", and "foreign domination".[29] But, of course, "aggression" is now a term that has a specific technical meaning in international law, at least since 1974, following the adoption of the "Resolution on the Definition of Aggression" by the UN General Assembly (Res. 3314 (XXIX)). And it is safe to assume that the terms "occupation" and "foreign domination" here were principally intended to address, in particular, the continuing problem of colonial occupation and domination on the continent. It is precisely for this reason that we find that in the refugee policy and practice of African States, presumptive recognition was granted to freedom fighters engaged in struggles against colonial or racist minority governments as bona fide refugees. The relevance of this interpretation in the context of the liberation struggles in Southern Africa cannot be overemphasized.[30]

In this discussion I follow the approach of various other students of refugees and forced migration in adopting the broadened definition. The term "refugee" as used here thus refers to any person who has been uprooted from his or her habitual physical and social environment because of persecution or violence or any of the other circumstances stipulated in the OAU Convention regardless of whether such a person has left his or her country of origin or whether he or she is recognized as a refugee by the host State or by the UNHCR.[31] This approach is more reflective of the reality of the Southern African refugee problem.

Political Refugees and Economic Migrants: What's in a Name?

Reference has already been made to the distinction thought to be implicit in the 1951 Convention, and generally accepted by most commentators, between political refugees and economic refugees or "migrants". It is argued that this distinction must be approached with the greatest circumspection. First of all, it is quite obvious that those who insist on this distinction often resort to it as an opportunistic device to mask their political biases in accepting or rejecting refugees from one particular country or another. Thus, although it was clear that quite a good number of the East Germans and other nationalities from Eastern Europe who continued to stream across into West Germany just before the Berlin Wall came down were motivated by the desire to live in the more affluent West, no Western European government ever openly described any of them as economic migrants in search of better economic and employment opportunities outside their own countries of origin. Margaret Thatcher, the then British Prime Minister, for example, loudly hailed them as political refugees and heroes of the anti-communist struggle while, at the same time, essentially dismissing the great majority of refugees seeking asylum in the country from the African continent and other Third World countries as economic migrants.

The point, as Loescher argues, is really this: refugee policy can be used to deny refugee status to nationals of a friendly State, and will often imply foreign policy support for the sending government; correspondingly, the decision to bestow formal refugee status on citizens of a particular State usually implies condemnation of the sending government for persecuting its citizens.[32] This double-faced approach has been consistently evident in American refugee policy: for example, the readiness with which Cubans have been accepted (at least until recently) as genuine political refugees fleeing an oppressive communist regime, while Haitians fleeing even more odious and repressive regimes under Papa and Baby Doc Duvalier, and more recently under General Raoul Cedras's military junta, were automatically turned away as economic migrants. The denial by the United States government of refugee status to Haitians has always been motivated by the fear of being flooded by migrants from one of the poorest countries in the world. In cases such as this, the attempt to draw a distinction between genuine political refugees and economic migrants is both arbitrary and dishonest. It is a distinction based on a deliberately narrow interpretation of the term "persecution". Paradoxically, some African countries have tended to adopt this narrow interpretation in their approaches to the refugee crises on the continent. It would appear this is also the approach now being adopted by some commentators and policy-makers in South Africa.

The second problem here arises from the ambiguities inherent in the refugee definition itself. As is indicated in the UNHCR's *Handbook on Procedures and Criteria for Determining Refugee Status* (para. 51), "persecution" is ordinarily considered to include a threat to an individual's life or freedom. Now, if one adopts the restrictive "basic-rights approach", one would be inclined to conclude that the core sense of persecution consists in the denial of, or threats to, a person's basic individual rights, traditionally understood to mean civil and political rights. But a wider definition of persecution ought to embrace threats to other kinds of basic rights as well – economic and social rights or entitlements, such as the right to work or to earn a living, to education, to found a family and so on. Where one is deprived of such rights by the government or its agents on the basis of one's race, religion, nationality, membership of a particular social group or political opinion, one ought equally to be regarded as a victim of persecution which may well justify flight to another country. I would thus follow Dowty in concluding that "so-called economic migrants are often responding as much to political repression as to material deprivation".[33] Ibeanu is certainly right in arguing that:[34]

> "Persecution is political in the sense that it involves State power. But State power is the more or less organized power of a dominant class, power bloc or hegemonic fraction in its relations with other classes and fractions. These relations are not exclusively political but also economic and ideological [Thus], for instance, the migration of Bakolori peasants to Niger Republic because their land has been taken away by capitalist farmers in Nigeria is no less political than the migration of Iraq Kurds to Turkey because of attacks by the Iraqi army."

I would argue that the attempt to separate the notions of "political refugee" and "economic refugee" is apt to lead us into false analogies, especially in the African context, unless we have a proper understanding of the notion of "persecution" itself. Is it legitimate to dismiss as mere economic migrants those

Mozambicans who were compelled to cross the border into South Africa in search of a more viable means of earning a living principally due to the fact that the economic resources and infrastructure in their own country were devastated in the long-running civil war which was so ruthlessly executed by the RENAMO movement and actively, if secretly, supported by the former South African regime? Equally, is it legitimate to label all such people as "illegal aliens" without a proper inquiry into the causes and political circumstances of their flight?

Of course, there will always be people, within Southern African countries and elsewhere, who can legitimately be considered to be illegal immigrants. Every country has a sovereign right to determine the legal procedures and immigration requirements that must be satisfied for non-nationals seeking entry into that country. And no country would allow every illegal immigrant to escape that designation simply by claiming refugee status. Indeed, in the words of Arboleda and Hoy:[35]

> "Whether we like it or not, it is not to be expected that States will enter into an agreement that would eliminate their right to determine whom they admit within their borders."

But it ought to be borne in mind that refugee movements in Africa, including especially Southern Africa, have mostly involved large numbers of people crossing the border en masse. It may be argued that the question of individual eligibility for refugee protection becomes largely theoretical and of little relevance when a great mass of people crosses a frontier, often suddenly and within a matter of days. The reality of mass displacement and large-scale border crossings in Africa is such that inevitably the people involved in these crossings will not have satisfied the required immigration formalities, particularly in view of the fact that such crossings are not effected at properly policed immigration or border posts. The right approach to be adopted by the receiving State in such cases is to protect such people against automatic expulsion by allowing them the protection afforded by the well-known principle of *non-refoulement*, subject to the condition that they report to a competent officer (immigration, police, border or security officer) within a designated time-period of such "illegal" entry. Such an approach would ensure that ultimately genuine refugees will be identified and separated from illegal immigrants stricto sensu. In the current South African situation, for example, the reliance upon the ordinary immigration law (in the form of the Aliens Control Act of 1991) in dealing with the refugee problem is wholly unsatisfactory. In the absence of proper refugee legislation and a willingness to address the question of refugee determination objectively, the bureaucratic tendency will continue to be one of labelling all potential refugees as illegal immigrants.[36]

Refugeehood and Citizenship

Writing exactly a decade ago, Shacknove observed that refugeehood results when the "normal, minimal bonds of trust, loyalty, protection and assistance" between a citizen and the State is severed.[37] Implicit in this statement is the suggestion that the State is a "class neutral" entity owing equal protection and assistance to all its citizens; this is an idea opposed by those, such as Ibeanu and Ake, who argue that the State is never "class neutral" since it arises in the first place from class domination and exists in the context of the class struggle.[38] The State may formally guarantee equal protection to all its citizens, but in reality this is never always the case. Rather, it is argued that there exist forms of structural violence in the State which not only belie the idea of equal protection of citizens, but also forms the deep-seated basis of the refugee problem. Thus, the causes of refugee flights lie in indirect forms of violence exerted through channels that are not immediately visible as violence. These indirect forms may involve such social conditions as exploitation, domination, repression and discrimination.[39] Furthermore, it has been suggested that:[40]

> "Refugees are people (distributed into classes, fractions, categories, strata) under siege; whether this siege is expressed objectively in wars and physical torture or structurally in exploitation and domination is irrelevant. Fleeing is only the extreme manifestation of siege mentality."

A person may thus qualitatively be regarded as a refugee even if he or she has not fled his or her country of origin for another country. On this account, the crossing of an international boundary should therefore not be the defining characteristic of refugeehood. The major implication of this approach is that refugeehood and displacement are aspects of the same process of social disintegration: refugees represent the most extreme form of displacement, because their condition involves a physical dislocation from the territorial bounds of their original social formation called the State. But it is only the narrow legalistic approach which compels us to insist that a person can only be a refugee if the dislocation from his or her social formation involves the crossing of an international boundary. From an anthropological perspective, the condition of refugeehood may exist even as a person is dislocated only within the territorial bounds of his or her own social formation, without formally relinquishing the bonds of citizenship, as long as such dislocation is the result of persecution (broadly defined to include the existence of conditions of exploitation, poverty, repression and other forms of structural violence).[41] Structurally, the problem of refugees and displaced people is the same and the two categories ought to be regarded as requiring the same legal protection. At any rate, this would appear to be the case in Africa where, until fairly recently, the population of internally displaced people far outnumbered that of refugees properly so called.[42]

Strategic Roots of Refugee Movements

There are a number of issues that fall to be considered when examining the strategic roots of refugee movements. But in the context of the declared underlying themes of this study – regional peace and security – only two particular issues need to be singled out in the present discussion: first, the exploitation of refugees as a foreign policy tool of the sending State (or State of origin); and, secondly, refugees as a foreign policy tool of the host (receiving) State.

Refugee Movements as a Foreign Policy Tool of Sending States

Refugee-generating States have been known to use forced migrations as a foreign policy tool for a variety of objectives. One objective, for example, might be to project their economic and political influence (including territorial control or extension of sovereignty); another objective would be to try and effect changes in the policies and politics of other States, and compel a neighbouring State to provide recognition, aid, credit or other advantage in return for stemming or regularizing the refugee flow.[43] Thus, classical colonialism involved in part deliberate population shifts by the colonizing powers in order to impress their authority and sovereignty over the colonized territory. In modern times, in Africa, a clear example of a State using population movements as a tool for claiming and asserting control over territory has been provided by the "popular marches" organized by Morocco over the disputed territory of the Western Sahara. In essence, these have been deliberate attempts to populate the territory in order to tip the balance of demographic advantage in its favour. On a different level, the much publicized flight of 16,000 Ethiopian Jews ("Falashas") from Ethiopia to Israel in 1991 was reported to have been facilitated by the payment by the Israeli government of $2,000 for each refugee[44]. This was intended to extract both foreign policy advantage and financial benefit. Exploitation of refugees in this blatant manner has not occurred in Southern Africa.

Refugee Movements as a Foreign Policy Tool of Receiving States

It has been suggested that often States' responses to refugees have been based more on political, ethnic and ideological sympathies and considerations of national and international security than on humanitarian concerns alone. In other words, receiving States may also exploit mass refugee movements for their own foreign and security policies. One of the more obvious examples advanced by commentators is the United States, which has always placed political and strategic importance in its responses to refugee crises and in devising its refugee admissions policy. For example, *inter alia*, policy has been dictated by the United State's concern to minimize the destabilizing effect of large refugee populations in areas of the world deemed vital for its national security (with regard to the admission of Indochinese refugees – the so-called boat people – from South East Asia); or as a symbolic statement about the bankruptcy of communism and the triumph of free-market capitalism (Cuban and Eastern European refugees); or out of a sense of national obligation following past military and political involvement in the country from which refugees are now fleeing (Indochinese refugees); and as a consequence of political commitment rooted in previous colonial or imperialist ties (the admission of Filipino exiles during the Marcos dictatorship).[45] The last consideration, of course, played a very important part in the decision by the British government to accept thousands of Asian refugees from Uganda in the early 1970s.

Receiving States may also regard refugees as a means of bolstering their domestic power base, national self-confidence or dominant ethnic community. It is no secret that for decades Israel viewed the influx of Jews from the Soviet Union as a demographic boost to the Jewish population in the State. In Southern Africa, a loose analogy is provided by the immigration policies of the former apartheid regime in South Africa which, over the four decades in which it was in power, deliberately encouraged immigration from Europe in order to boost the white proportion of the population. Not an insignificant number of such white immigrants were people who characterized themselves as "refugees" from the former communist regimes of Eastern and Central Europe.[46]

Thus, strategic, historical, cultural and ethnic factors all play a part in the foreign policy and security calculations of both sending and receiving States in refugee matters. Equally important are, of course, ideological and political reasons. The history of refugee movements in modern Africa reveals that during the independence struggles, countries that had already gained their political freedom sought to encourage anti-colonial struggles in other countries, first, by accepting refugees and, second, by providing them with the necessary material, diplomatic and political support to organize themselves into effective national liberation movements. Often, this kind of consideration also involved the provision of support for guerrilla operations across international borders through the refugee camps. This is nowhere better illustrated than in Southern Africa. The international consensus that emerged in the early 1960s against the policy of apartheid and the widespread support for the various national liberation movements fighting against the white minority governments and settler colonial regimes in Angola, Mozambique, Namibia, Rhodesia and South Africa were critical factors in the determination of refugee policies of the host States in the region. The thousands upon thousands of refugees that went into exile from these countries were received by the host States without the need to determine individually whether they qualified as refugees according to the criteria laid down in the 1951 UN Refugee Convention.

The Dynamics of Refugee-Creation in Southern Africa

It has been argued that most studies on refugees have tended to view refugee-creation in Africa as resulting from ancient un-solvable inter-tribal or inter-ethnic conflicts, rather than as a reflection of the underlying issues of State formation and class conflict. One common feature of these studies is that they generally focus on the micro (psychological, familial or individual) consequences, with little or no attention being paid to the macro (for example, social class, political, regional and global) causes. Causes and effects are rarely ever linked, nor are the structural implications of refugee flows always considered. Only isolated studies have attempted to integrate sociological analyses with a political economy perspective (in other words, employing a macro-level approach) to understand the refugee crisis in Africa.[47]

In employing the macro-level approach, we are urged to adopt a perspective which considers the importance of inter-group conflict at the sub-national, national, regional and global levels; conflicts which reflect the underlying competition and struggles by one group/country to control others' political, economic and social existence. In all this, one issue which should not be lost sight of is the need to recognize that Africa's peripheral nation-states emerged from the colonial experience balkanized, with weak social, economic and political institutions and dependent on the core metropolitan (i.e. colonial) powers. It is also important to recall that colonial policies often deliberately initiated or reinforced the tendency for the educated, powerful ruling classes to be dominated by a specific ethnic group or tribe. Thus, post-colonial class conflict and State-sponsored repression may be seen as explicable consequences of intense local and international pressures to consolidate State power rapidly in response to inherited underdevelopment. It is submitted that this class conflict has often turned out to be the precursor to the creation of refugees, and must be examined as such.[48]

As has already been stated above, the definition of a refugee embodied in the OAU Convention is an acknowledgment that the causes of refugee flight in Africa are complex and multi-dimensional. Fear of persecution for reasons of race, ethnicity, religion, or political opinion is only one of many reasons people have been forced to leave their countries of origin or normal places of residence. But, furthermore, as Rogge has noted:[49]

> "Military conflicts, first between independence movements and colonial authorities, and later between warring factions in post-independence power struggles or inter-ethnic conflicts, have been responsible for so much of the continent's displacements. Secessionist struggles and conflicts arising from irredentist territorial claims, legacies of colonial partition of Africa which bore little relation to regional or ethnic entities, have further added to the masses of involuntary migrants."

Other factors that may be identified in this catalogue of causes of refugee flight or displacement are: environmental factors, especially drought; economic deprivation and outright economic oppression and exploitation; and the various localized ethnic, religious and other non-ideological conflicts which, following the arrival of the so-called new world order, have replaced the regional conflicts previously fuelled by Cold War rivalries.[50] Most, if not all, of these factors have, at one point or another, been relevant determinants in the history of displacement and refugee movements in the Southern African sub-continent over the last three decades or so. Even today, the great majority of refugees in the region continue to be as much a product of war, famine, environmental degradation and impoverishment as of persecution. In Southern Africa as elsewhere, these refugee movements have generated a mixture of humanitarian concern for the thousands of people forced into exile, and fear of the potential disruption of the social, economic and political stability of the host States posed by the new arrivals. It has been observed that the largest and most dramatic population movements have occurred in the developing world. This means that the great majority of refugees seek shelter in the world's poorest States. And yet, as has been observed:[51]

"Africa, which hosts a large proportion of the world's refugees, is in the total grip of a structural economic crisis, manifested in a drastic decline of per capita income, low or negative rates of economic growth, a collapsing social and physical infrastructure, high rates of population increase. [In] 1988, among the 20 African countries classified by the UN as critically affected by famine, 13 were hosting a substantial number of refugees."

Among the poor and, at times, famine-stricken countries that have had to support large refugee populations in recent years in the Southern African region are Malawi, Tanzania and Zambia. The pressures that large numbers of refugees place upon already poor economies and grossly inadequate infrastructures require no elaboration.

Until recently, most commentators were agreed that the internal and external policies of apartheid South Africa were responsible for the threat to peace and security in the region. Moreover, the view was also generally held that Pretoria's deliberate policy of destabilization of its black-ruled independent neighbours and its illegal occupation of Namibia were at the core of population displacement and refugee-creation in Southern Africa. These accounts are too well known to require detailed repetition in this study. To revisit, in comprehensive detail, the argument that the system of apartheid has been the single most important factor in refugee-creation in Southern Africa would be to belabour a well-known point.[52] It will suffice here merely to reiterate that the problem of refugees and other displaced persons in Southern Africa was situated in the context of the struggle for domination among specific social forces in the region. At the nodal point of this struggle were South Africa's apartheid policies and the philosophy of racial domination and superiority. The role of South Africa's regional destabilization policies in the refugee problem needs to be understood in the context of the "low intensity conflict" strategy which was increasingly employed by South Africa and its supporters against States that were adopting, or thought to be adopting, alternative development strategies and perspectives on the liberation struggle.[53] However, it is also important to reflect on the continuing post-apartheid effects of this strategy on refugee-creation and population displacement in the region.

Aside from the above considerations, it may be said that other, more specific, factors that played, and have continued to play, a role in displacement and refugee-creation are: first, the internal difficulties inherent in nation-building and social transformation, for example in Angola, Mozambique and, for a brief while, Zimbabwe. Secondly, the long drawn out ideological and ethno-political conflicts (civil wars) following the attainment of independence in these countries. In both Angola and Mozambique, massive flows resulted from the revolutionary changes in the political, economic and social systems of those countries. Thirdly, bipolarity and superpower conflict which characterized the 1980s and was imported into the political arena provided by the developing countries, including some in Southern Africa: bipolar support in terms of weaponry, military and economic assistance. All these factors led to massive internal upheavals and conflict. But, furthermore, the refugee experience in Southern Africa shows that refugee flows can also be the result of attempts by a dominant group trying to marginalize or eject minorities; or a government trying to impose cultural or political homogeneity in the form of a new national identity (as happened in Malawi during the earlier period of Dr. Hastings Banda's rule); or the ruling regime imposing an alternative ideology in place of nationalism in order to unite diverse peoples for the purposes of nation-building. Another relevant point for consideration is Loescher's argument, namely that although East-West conflict was a factor in the past, the underlying dynamic of many Third World conflicts has been competition for political power among fiercely rival ethnic groups. He thus suggests, *inter alia*, that "although the Angolan civil war was largely perceived as an East-West proxy conflict, it was fundamentally a competition for political power between the Ovimbundu of Southern Angola, who form the political base for UNITA, and the Mbundu-led coalition that held power in Luanda".[54] This is a plausible explanation, and perhaps the example of the brief post-independence conflict in Zimbabwe between the Ndebele-dominated ZAPU party and the Shona-dominated ZANU-PF government in the early 1980s may also be seen in a similar light. The observation has already been made in this study that these ethno-political considerations are quite common in the literature and discourses on the African refugee-problem. However, one should caution against the temptation to view these struggles in these seemingly straight-forward ethnic perspectives. Not every refugee problem in Africa can be explained in terms of inter-ethnic competition for political domination. And even the extreme example afforded by the Hutu-Tutsi conflict and the resultant genocide and refugee problem in Rwanda needs to be understood within the larger historical context of colonialism and imperialist manipulation.

Finally, it may be noted that at least one other explanatory factor rooted in the international political economy perspective has been advanced in the debate, namely the international character of class struggles and their link with population displacement. With regard to the earlier Mozambican refugee flows into South Africa, for example, it has been argued:[55]

> "At another level, South Africa's economic stranglehold on the other countries of the region, usually backed by external forces, represents another dimension of the class struggle. The virtual dependence of Mozambique on South Africa [makes] it possible for the pursuit of the economic interests of

the dominant classes in South Africa to generate population displacement in Mozambique. [This fact] points to an aspect of the whole problem of displacement which students of international relations seldom recognize: the fact that the pursuit of the interests of the ruling classes of one State could generate displacement in another independent State."

The need to take account of this perspective when examining the current refugee problem in Southern Africa, particularly as it affects South Africa, is implicitly acknowledged by the few policy-makers and political leaders in South Africa who advocate a rearrangement of regional economic relations, within the framework of the existing regional integration groupings, as a way of stemming the tide of refugees and illegal immigrants from the poorer neighbouring economies. In brief, a regional "Marshall Plan" or "reconstruction and development programme" is required to meet the refugee problem in the overall context of addressing the region's development needs.[56]

Strategic Consequences and Security Implications

Generally speaking, refugee movements can both create and exacerbate conflict between the sending and the receiving States, and perhaps even challenge the integrity of both States. Moreover, refugees and other migrants will often be perceived by both the sending and the receiving States as a threat to national stability and security. Obviously, where the receiving State is only too ready to welcome the refugees (as was generally the case with regard to the reception given to South African refugees fleeing from apartheid rule), there can be no problem. As noted earlier, the arrival of refugees in the country may even be perceived as strengthening the host State's power base or its moral and political authority over that of the sending State. On the other hand, where the refugees pose a threat to the security or economic and social fabric of the receiving State, this will lead to tension and conflict.

Unwanted migrants and refugees may cause tension not only at the bilateral or regional level between the States involved but, more worryingly, intercommunal tension within the receiving State. A number of factors may be at play here: antagonistic ethnic, cultural, religious and linguistic forces within the host population; endangerment to the host country's social and economic stability and security, especially where the presence of large numbers of refugees begins to translate into competition for scarce jobs, economic resources and social security services and entitlements; political and diplomatic problems which would arise if refugees began to use the host country as a base to launch campaigns against what may be perceived by the host State as a friendly country. In brief, refugee flows and mass migrations can be both a political embarrassment to the States concerned and a destabilizing factor in international relations. The acceptance or rejection of refugees not only has a political symbolism to the sending and receiving States, but also operates as a powerful foreign policy determinant on both sides.

Refugees, who are mostly victims of domestic political conflict in their countries of origin, can also be a source of international conflict. As the history of refugee movements within Southern Africa has amply demonstrated, offering sanctuary and support to refugees, especially those who may be involved in political and/or military campaigns against the sending State, frequently incurs military retaliation and draws asylum countries into turmoil. Freedom fighters may mingle with refugee populations, using the refugee camps as a cover, or for medical relief and food, or even recruitment. As apartheid South Africa and Ian Smith's Rhodesia clearly showed, refugee (and resettlement) camps became legitimate targets for retaliatory or so-called pre-emptive military strikes in the neighbouring host countries.

What, then, are the implications of the refugee problem for peace and security in Southern Africa at this juncture? At the macro-level, in countries affected by the problem (both countries of origin and receiving States), there is first and foremost the undermining of productive capacities and the disintegration of national economies; in particular, the link between rural and urban sectors, resulting in the loss of economic infrastructure and problems of reconstruction.[57] This has several dimensions to it, including, from an international relations point of view, increased difficulties and strains on regional cooperation and integration initiatives. In turn, these difficulties and strains are bound to retard progress towards peace and security. Furthermore, in the Southern African context, the implications of the refugee problem for the quest for peace and security must be located within the following processes. In the first place, there is the question of the polarization of the region into a rich-minority and a poor-majority, a process organically related to problems of exploitation, poverty, inequality, discrimination and underdevelopment. Second, the continuing political conflicts and the militarization of social life in some of the Southern African States, despite recent advances and developments in democratization and political pluralism in the region. Finally, the role of political exclusivity, factionalism and competition within ruling groups; and the corresponding denial of the right of people to control their social and bio-physical environments, which entails a corresponding prevalence of external intervention in national and regional problems, as well as the denial of the enjoyment of a genuine right of nationalities to self-determination. All these implications need to be factored into domestic and foreign policy formulation by all States in the region insofar as such policies have a bearing on the refugee problem.

Conclusion

It has been argued by a number of observers that an approach which aims at providing refugees and displaced persons merely with humanitarian assistance and relief is not enough. Furthermore, it is commonly argued that the durable solutions to refugee crises are repatriation, third country resettlement or local integration in a country of first asylum. For internally displaced persons they are basically the same: return to home areas, resettlement in other parts of the country, or integration into their area of displacement.[58] However, it may be counter-argued that these so-called durable solutions cannot work effectively unless the overall international political and security context in which the refugee problem arises is also effectively considered. Which of these solutions, if any, would be the most viable in dealing, for example, with the Congolese (former Zairean), Liberian and Rwandan refugees who have crossed a number of countries across the sub-continent to seek refuge in South Africa?

Changing global political and economic conditions are challenging deeply held beliefs, definitions and concepts – as well as laws and policies – in almost all regions of the world, including Southern Africa. The need for, and the development of, any new approach to the problem of refugees and population displacement will be strongly influenced by the ways in which the international community re-defines its existing assumptions and perspectives about the nature of persecution, the character of the State or ruling regimes, the applicability of human rights doctrine over national interests, and so on. It is hoped that the present study will stimulate a particular kind of debate: as rapidly changing political and economic conditions in the world force dramatic shifts in the causes of forced migration, there is need for a sustained discussion among those who devise and implement the decisions addressing these causes and social scientists (including legal scholars and human rights advocates) who have studied them in a broad context.[59] Here, at least three interwoven primary themes provide a context for further investigation of the changing causes of forced migration and the region's response to them. First, the response of the major regional powers to the democratic changes and the realignment of political alliances in the region and their implications for individual governments' foreign policy-making: how do States respond to the continuing refugee crisis in post-apartheid Southern Africa while trying to manage fundamental political and social changes in their domestic arenas? Second, current attempts to either expand or limit the role of human rights issues in refugee and asylum situations: how do responses predicated more on immigration enforcement rather than on enlightened human rights approaches impact on the quest for peace and security in the relations between States in the region? Can countries which are neither parties to any international refugee instruments nor have devised appropriate domestic refugee legislation manage the refugee crisis adequately and effectively? Finally, the increasing complexities in the social, political and economic origins of refugees and asylum-seekers, and the reversal in the direction of refugee flows; the role-reversal, in the case of South Africa, from a refugee-generating to a refugee-hosting country. Is the previous personal, familial and group experience which some of the present-day political leaders and policy-makers underwent during their own stay as refugees in neighbouring countries impacting in any meaningful way upon the search for solutions to the refugee problem that South Africa, in particular, now faces?

With regard to the last point, it only needs to be reiterated that growing concern for environmental degradation and the complete collapse of capacities for economic survival has added new complexities to the causes of forced migration. Both these conditions challenge the application of existing concepts of persecution and, therefore, the ability of existing regional and international refugee regimes to respond adequately. They also create a fundamental strategic shift: is this not the time to argue for a full extension of a human rights doctrine to include social and economic rights in defining persecution, and bury the controversial notions of "economic refugees" (or "economic migrants") now so redolent in the public imagination, especially in South Africa?

At bottom, the refugee problem in Southern Africa, as elsewhere, must be seen as part of the struggle against the State's violation of the human rights of certain classes, groups and individuals. The class struggle manifests itself in the denial of the rights of nationalities and States either to participate in or control the running of their own affairs as they see fit. The resolution of the refugee problem in Southern Africa lies in the intensification of the struggle for democracy and human rights. Since for a long time the apartheid policies of South Africa provided the focal point for understanding the dynamics of refugee-creation and displacement in the region, the overthrow of the apartheid system, and the earlier decolonization of Namibia, represented only the short-term resolution of the problem. In the long run, the more complex struggle against underdevelopment, poverty, ignorance, hunger, disease, and so on, must be fought as part of the larger struggle for democracy, social justice and equality. As long as the siege on democracy continues, the region cannot hope to be truly peaceful and secure. Without peace and security, the refugee problem will continue to bedevil relations between States in the region, both at the bilateral and multilateral levels. It is for this reason that there will be a continuing need to impose upon the body politic of the region such structures as are necessary to ensure the existence of viable autonomous, self-sustaining political and economic entities which can satisfy the varied needs of the citizenry and eradicate the factors which compel nationals to flee their countries of origin in order to seek succour in foreign lands. Only thus can peace and security in the region be assured for all the region's nations and peoples.

The refugee problem in Southern Africa (and elsewhere in the world) cannot be solved in the foreseeable future. On current evidence, there can be no hope for a quick and permanent resolution of the multi-faceted causes of refugee flows and population displacement identified in this study. However, I propose to end this discussion with some brief suggestions as to what ought to be done as part of the process of identifying long-term strategies in addressing the problem.

First, the refugee problem requires a concerted regional approach involving all concerned States. In particular it is a problem that must find its way onto the agenda of the Southern African Development Community (SADC) sooner rather than later. For, as has been argued above, it is a problem that has immense political, economic and diplomatic implications for the on-going initiatives and projects in regional cooperation and integration. The tensions arising from South Africa's treatment of the relatively small number of unwanted refugees and thousands, perhaps millions, of so-called economic migrants and illegal aliens from its neighbours can only damage the fledgling bilateral and regional relations between the States in the region, and ultimately the whole effort to secure lasting peace and security. Some of these countries remember only too well how, until fairly recently, their own territories provided refuge to thousands and thousands of exiled South African patriots, and how their people and governments steadfastly supported the struggle for the liberation of South Africa in the face of great difficulties. But this is not, in itself, reason enough to require South Africa to accommodate the ever growing masses of bona fide refugees and illegal immigrants streaming across its borders unchecked. A coordinated effort to examine and root out the causes of these continuing refugee and migration flows is the only way to go.

In addition, it is also suggested here that there is need to strengthen the existing international (UNHCR) as well as regional (OAU's Bureau for Refugees) machinery in order to enable individual States and the region as a whole to be better equipped to handle future refugee crises.[60] For example, the forecasting of refugee flows, to the extent that it has occurred at all, has relied primarily on *ad hoc* guesses. Individuals and organizations close to refugee situations have speculated about likely developments. What is required is the development of mechanisms that would allow for long-term strategic forecasting of refugee flows and forced migrations. It is revealing that despite some early warning signals, the massive explosion of refugee flows from Rwanda in 1994 seemed to have caught the country's neighbours and the international community off-guard. The strengthening of these long-term forecasting mechanisms also requires that States and the relevant international and regional organizations put in place structures that will allow them to deal with mass exodus emergencies adequately. Malawi's experience of dealing with the massive flows of Mozambican refugees ought to provide an invaluable lesson in this regard. At the height of the influx during the first half of 1988, refugees were entering Malawi at a rate well in excess of 20,000 per month, and during just one 24-hour period in June 1988 more than 13,000 refugees crossed into Malawi's eastern district of Mulanje.[61]

In the final analysis, of course, one can only reiterate that the best guarantee of peace and security in Southern Africa lies in the resolve of governments to tackle the immense problems of underdevelopment, poverty and exploitation in a manner that also ensures respect for democracy and human rights. For, when all is said and done, it must be accepted that the refugee problem is, in fact, merely a tragic symptom and manifestation of the failure of States, governments and ruling regimes to treat their citizens in a manner that accords with their inalienable human rights and human dignity. It may be noted, for example, that one of the most laudable, but little discussed, achievements in Southern Africa in the period 1993–1995 was the voluntary repatriation of about 1.6 million Mozambican refugees referred to at the outset of this discussion. This was reportedly one of the most successful refugee repatriation exercises in peacetime in recent years. Quite obviously, this could not have been possible without the resolution of the conflict between RENAMO and the Mozambican government and the accompanying political changes which resulted in the holding of the country's first democratic elections since independence some twenty years ago. Thus, although democratization and respect for human rights may not guarantee an end to all conflicts and refugee movements, they certainly do provide, if not the way forward, at least the most viable starting point towards a distant but desirable destination.

Notes

1. These statistics are based on information contained in UNHCR, *The State of the World's Refugees 1997–1998*, (1997) pp. 286–289.

2. For a brief historical perspective on the African refugee problem, see G. Kibreab, *African Refugees: Reflections on the African Refugee Problem*, (1985) pp. 11–20.

3. S. Rugumamu, *Post-Cold War Peace and Security Prospects in Southern Africa*, SAPES Occasional Paper Series No. 5, (1993) p. 1.

4. For classic realist approaches see, for example, H. Morgenthau and K. Thompson, *Principles and Problems of International Relations*, (1956); H. Morgenthau, *Politics Among Nations*, (4th ed., 1966); K.N. Waltz, *Theory of International Relations*, (1979).

5. A brief discussion of these conceptual issues in relation to peace and security in Southern Africa may be found in Rugumamu, *op. cit.* note 3 *supra*; see also P. Nyinguro, "Peace and Security in Post-Cold War Africa: Safeguarding the Future", *African J Pol Economy 119* (1993); M. Walt's "The Renaissance of Security Studies", *35 International Studies Q 211* (1991) presents the argument that the recent changes in the world political order make realism, and in particular realist scholars, relevant to the practice of international relations; but see the critique by E. Kolodzief, "Renaissance in Security Studies? Caveat Lector!", *36 International Studies Q 421* (1992); and R.N. Lebow, "The long peace, the end of the cold war, and the failure of realism", *48 International Org. 249* (1994).

6. However, among the few studies on the subject the pioneering work of Gil Loescher stands out; see, especially his *Refugee Movements and International Security*, Adelphi Papers, No. 268, (1992). The discussion in this chapter adopts, in part, the conceptual framework developed in the work under reference. See also same author's "Introduction", in G. Loescher & L. Monahan, *Refugees and International Relations*, (1989) pp. 1–33; L. Gordenker's *Refugees in International Politics* focuses on the international community's ability to ease the plight of refugees and is not, as such, a security and foreign policy oriented study.

7. See works cited in note 5 *supra*.

8. Nyinguro, *op. cit.* p. 122.

9. Loescher, Refugee Movements and International Security, (1992) p. 3.

10. *Ibid.*

11. See, for example, C. Keely & L. Wrigley (Eds.), *Immigration and US Foreign Policy*, (1990); P. Koehn, *Refugees from Revolution: US Policy and Third World Migration*, (1991); M. Weiner, "On International Migration and International Relations", *2 Population and Development Rev 441* (1985); also G. Loescher, "The European Community and Refugees", *65 International Affairs 617* (1989); C. Mitchell,

"International Migration, International Relations and Foreign Policy", 23 *International Migration Rev* 682 (1989).

12. Loescher, *op. cit.* note 9 *supra*, p. 4. (All subsequent references to Loescher are to this work).

13. Article 3 of the OAU Convention Governing the Specific Aspects of Refugee Problems in Africa enjoins parties not to allow refugees to use their respective territories as a launching pad for armed attacks or any subversive activities against any member States of the OAU. However, it is well known that in the Horn of Africa, for example, until recently some States intervened repeatedly in the affairs of their neighbours by supporting different groups of rebels or guerilla fighters even where such rebels had entered the host country under the pretext of being refugees. Thus, at various times, Sudan assisted guerrillas fighting in northern Ethiopia, and Ethiopia, in turn, backed the Sudan People's Liberation Army in southern Sudan. Similarly, Somalia supported the activities of groups fighting against the Ethiopian government, while Ethiopia supported Somali insurgents, and so on.

14. See T. Maluwa, "The Legal Regime for the Protection of Refugees in Malawi", in G.C.Z. Mhone (Ed.), *Malawi at the Crossroads: The Post-Colonial Political Economy*, (1992) p. 349 at 359–361.

15. O. Ibeanu, "Apartheid, Destabilization and Displacement: The Dynamics of the Refugee Crisis in Southern Africa", *3 J Refugee Studies 47* (1990) p.49.

16. A.C, Helton, "What is Refugee Protection?", IJRL (Special Issue, 1990) p. 119 at 120. for an extensive discussion of the definition of a refugee, see G. Goodwin-Gill, *The Refugee in International Law*, (2nd ed., 1996) pp. 3–31. But see D. Warner, "We Are All Refugees", *4 IJRL 365* (1992), for a sociologically-oriented analysis of the definition which advances the case for a narrowing of the differentiation between refugees and non-refugees. See also the excellent discussion by A. Shacknove, "Who Is a Refugee?", 95 *Ethics 274* (1985).

17. This is based in part on information provided by the UNHCR Office, Johannesburg, South Africa (March 1995).

18. See Article 1(2); for text of the Convention see 189 UNTS 150.

19. Helton, *op. cit.* p. 119.

20. A fuller discussion of the development of this notion is to be found in G. Goodwin-Gill, *op. cit.* note 16 *supra*. See also A. Grahl-Madsen, *The Status of Refugees in International Law*, Vol. 1, (1966) chap. 1; S. Sinha, *Asylum and International Law*, (1971); E. Arboleda & I. Hoy, "The Convention Refugee

Definition in the West: Disharmony of Interpretation and Application", 5 *IJRL* 66 (1993) pp. 68–71. For a classical perspective see R. Gorman, "Poets, Playwrights, and the Politics of Exile and Asylum in Ancient Greece and Rome", 6 *IJRL 402* (1994).

21. See, generally, Shacknove, *op. cit.* p. 119.

22. Gordenker *op. cit. passim.*

23. A. Dowty, *Closed Borders: The Contemporary Assault on Freedom of Movement* (1987); E. Ferris, "Overview: Refugees and World Politics", in E. Ferris (Ed.), *Refugees and World Politics*, (1985).

24. Ibeanu, *op. cit.* p. 49. (References omitted).

25. See discussion by E. Arboleda, "Refugee Definition in Africa and Latin America: The Lessons of Pragmatism", *3 IJRL 185* (1991).

26. OAU Doc. CM/267 Rev.1; text in 1001 UNTS 45.

27. Arboleda, *op. cit.* p. 195.

28. See T. Maluwa, "Human Rights and Refugees in Southern Africa: Some Perceptives on Recent Legislative Developments in Malawi", *53 ZaöRV* 88 (1993) at 105; see also R. Hofmann, "Refugee Law in Africa", *39 Law and State 79* (1989) at 83, 87–88; M. Rwelamira, "The 1969 OAU Convention Governing the Specific Aspects of Refugee Problems", *1 IJRL 557* (1989) at 558; Shacknove, *op. cit.* pp. 275–276.

29. Arboleda, *op. cit.* pp. 195–196.

30. The prohibitions in Article 2 of the OAU Convention referred to in note 13 *supra* apply only in respect of member States of the OAU; since the former colonial and racist minority regimes in Southern Africa (the Portuguese colonies of Angola and Mozambique, and Rhodesia and South Africa respectively) were not members of the OAU, Article 3 did not apply to any armed attacks or other activities carried on by refugees from these territories in the context of the national liberation wars.

31. Loescher, *op. cit.* p. 8. See also discussion by R. Plender, "The Legal Basis of International Jurisdiction to Act with Regard to the Internally Displaced", 6 *IJRL 345* (1994).

32. Loescher, *ibid.* p. 37.

33. Dowty, *op. cit.* p. 183; see also, Helton, *op. cit. passim.*

34. Ibeanu, *op. cit.* p. 50.

35. Arboleda & Hoy, *op. cit.* p. 89.

36. The problem is not new; writing almost twenty years ago, one commentator argued that South African immigration law, which is intended to cope with individuals, could not deal adequately with large refugee problems; see J.A. Faris, "The Angolan Refugees and South Africa", *2 SAYIL 176* (1976) at 185: "The problem of the refugee is totally unrelated to immigration law and to the law relating to ordinary aliens. [To] classify the refugee as an ordinary alien evades the problem. Immigration law is intended to cope with the admission of individuals and not a mass influx [of people]". A similar argument was made ten years later by C.M. Murray, "Mozambican Refugees: South Africa's Problem", *2 SAJHR 154* (1986) at 163.

37. Shacknove, *op. cit.* pp. 277–281.

38. Ibeanu, *op. cit.* p. 51; C. Ake, "The future of the State in Africa", 6 *Int'l Pol Sci Rev* (1985) *passim*.

39. O. Nnoli, "Revolutionary Violence, Development, Equality and Justice in South Africa", *34 Africa Today 37* (1987).

40. Ibeanu, *op. cit.* p. 51.

41. See, generally, R. Mazur, "The Political Economy of Refugee Creation in Southern Africa: Micro and Macro Issues in Sociological Perspective", *2 J Refugee Studies 441* (1989); also same author's "Refugees in Africa: The Role of Sociological Analysis and Praxis", *36 Current Sociology 43* (1988).

42. At the beginning of 1995, there were reported to be about 6.8 million refugees and almost twice as many internally displaced persons in Africa. See UNHCR, *The State of the World's Refugees*, (1995) *passim*. It should be pointed out that estimates of the total number of refugees tend to vary between different sources; one major difficulty is that the figures usually quoted in the official reports or publications only include such persons as are "of concern to the UNHCR" or have been registered as such. In Africa, the problem is often compounded by the fact that quite a lot of refugees tend to flee across largely unpoliced frontiers and may not always all report to the officially designated reception centres.

43. Loescher, *op. cit.* p. 31.

44. *The Independent*, London, 31 May 1991.

45. Loescher, *op. cit.* pp. 34–35.

46. In this regard, one commentator recently noted: "In the sixties and seventies, white immigrants were welcomed with open arms. In 1965 no fewer than 38,337

were welcomed in the country. Their 'qualification' was that they were white. [Workers] were lured with travel and housing subsidies. All the Aliens Control Act required of them was that they should assimilate with the white population of South Africa. Most of these whites [were] recruited in Eastern Europe. [In] 1993, the Ministry of Home Affairs spent money assisting in the resettlement of 9,824 white immigrants". See L. Mosia, "Economic Integration in Southern Africa – Peace and Security in South Africa", p. 24; paper presented at the SAPES Trust-SARIPS Annual Colluquium, 24–30 September 1994, Harare, Zimbabwe.

47. Mazur, "The Political Economy of Refugee-Creation in Southern Africa" *op. cit.* note 41 *supra*, pp. 442–447.

48. Mazur, *ibid.* p. 445.

49. J. Rogge, "The Challenges of Changing Dimensions among the South's Refugees: Illustrations from Somalia", *5 IJRL 12* (1993) at p. 18. For a more extended discussion of the root causes of the African refugee crisis see, generally, G. Kibreab, *op. cit.* note 2.

50. Rogge, *ibid.*

51. Loescher, *op. cit.* p. 12.

52. See, for example, the studies by Faris, Ibeanu, Mazur, and Murray cited *supra.*

53. See Mazur, *op. cit.* p. 445; also Ibeanu, *op. cit.* especially p. 56 *et seq.*

54. Loescher, *op. cit.* p. 31.

55. Ibeanu, *op. cit.* p. 61.

56. In a discussion programme ("Top Level") aired on one of South Africa's national television channels (CCV) on 12 February 1995 Mr. Aziz Pahad, the South African Deputy Foreign Minister, admitted that what was required in response to the refugee problem in South Africa was the adoption of a "holistic approach" which would address the economic and development problems of the Southern African region as a whole in an effort to identify and remedy the causes of the refugee crisis in consultation with all concerned countries.

57. Mazur, *op. cit.* p. 445.

58. Rogge, *op. cit.* p. 25.

59. See discussion by R.L. Bach, "Human Rights, Refugees and North-South Relations", paper presented at the Meeting of the International Research and Advisory Panel, Refugee Studies Programme, 2–6 January 1991, Oxford, United Kingdom.

60. Cf. H-W. Kerll, "New Dimensions of the Global Refugee Problem and the Need for a Comprehensive Human Rights and Development-Oriented Refugee Policy", *IJRL* (Special Issue, 1990) p. 237 at 247–250; on the OAU regional machinery see J. Oloka-Onyango, "The Place and Role of the OAU Bureau for Refugees in the African Refugee Crisis", 6 *IJRL 34* (1994) *passim*.

61. See, generally, L. Long, L. Cecsarini & J. Martin, *The Local Impact of Mozambican Refugees in Malawi* (1990); unpublished study undertaken for the United States Embassy and USAID-Malawi, Lilongwe, Malawi.

8

REFUGEES, LAW AND POLITICS: THE EVOLUTION OF REFUGEE POLICY IN MALAWI

Introduction

The refugee problem which the tiny Southern African State of Malawi had to deal with in the late 1980s presented something of a paradox. At one point, estimates of the refugee population in the country put the numbers at between 800,000 and 1,000,000. This represented at least 10% of the country's entire population, at the time estimated at about 8 million. In fact, this ranked Malawi within the top five countries in the world with the highest proportions of refugees per total (*de jure*) population.[1] Yet, until the recent mass influx of Mozambicans into the country, which started in earnest in the mid-1980s, the refugee problem in Malawi had been largely ignored by most of the international community, and only barely acknowledged by the national authorities. Scholarly studies on the subject have been equally limited, if not altogether lacking.[2]

In fact, Malawi's experience as a host country for refugees goes farther back in time than the mid-1980s. For it is a matter of historical record that during the long period running from the 1960s to the early 1980s, Malawi did provide, albeit in a limited and highly selective way, transit facilities to members of some of the national liberation movements that were then engaged in prosecuting their respective wars of national liberation in the Southern African sub-continent, in particular in Mozambique and Rhodesia. A number of individuals from these countries did seek, and were granted, refuge in Malawi. This was so despite Malawi's own generally accommodating, and at times overtly friendly, attitude towards the colonial and minority regimes which these national liberation movements were fighting against.[3] In this regard, it has been observed that Malawi had, right from an early stage, opted for integration as the main guiding principle in its management of the evolving refugee problem, in preference to the other so-called classical or durable solutions to refugee problems, namely voluntary repatriation and third country resettlement. Moreover, it has been argued that the choice of integration seems to have been predicated upon "the African notion of brotherhood", coupled with the traditionally "humanitarian nature" of Malawians.[4] The nature and extent of this humanitarianism is left rather vague and undefined. But, in any case, it may be argued that the integration solution assumes, *inter alia*, the existence of generous asylum and naturalization policies in the country of asylum. A more considered examination of Malawi's actual practice does not appear to justify this assumption. For, as Hedges has observed, Malawi's attitude towards Mozambican refugees, for example, or at any rate towards those that were identified as FRELIMO supporters and sympathizers, was quite often less than humanitarian:[5]

> "[In 1966] the attitude of the Malawian Government towards Mozambican refugees and Frelimo hardened considerably. Malawi warned Frelimo that any individual or group indicated by the Portuguese secret services, which had a considerable penetration in the country, would be returned to the Mozambican authorities."

There is evidence to suggest that not an inconsiderable number of refugees from Rhodesia and South Africa were subjected to similar treatment, particularly from the late 1960s till the mid-1970s. Yet, the idea that Malawi's treatment of the large number of Mozambican refugees on its soil was merely a reflection and confirmation of an age-old humanitarian approach rooted in the nation's tradition and culture is one that recurs in the limited discussions hitherto presented on this subject.[6] Indeed, there are those commentators who went so far as to suggest that Malawi's obligations towards the Mozambican and other refugees are founded upon the inherent humanitarian nature of African peoples and nations, and need not be couched in terms of actual positivistic legal obligations. Observe, for example, the following categorical statement by Machika:[7]

> "By being a member of the [United Nations], Malawi has obliged itself to comply with the principles of the Organization. One of the basic principles of the Organization is that human life will be assured by governments. The refugee is usually a person who runs away from a country because of danger to his life, for whatever causes. The situation in Mozambique poses danger to the lives of many people. These people have,

> through the Universal Declaration of Human Rights, been given the 'right' to seek and enjoy in other countries asylum. Hence their presence in Malawi. The Government of Malawi is not, of course, legally bound to admit them but then humanity demands that they be accorded a refugee status."

All these commentators seem to be agreed on the essential conclusion that, at least until Malawi acceded to the UN Convention relating to the Status of Refugees of 28 July 1951 and the Protocol relating to the Status of Refugees of 31 January 1967 on 10 December 1987, it was only bound by humanitarian considerations in its treatment of refugees, and this only in an *ad hoc* fashion;[8] and that, technically, Malawi was "not bound to accord to the refugees the treatment that should be accorded to them under the convention".[9] Indeed, it was alleged as recently as mid-1988 that "there was not, and still is not, a law on refugees in Malawi".[10] As has just been intimated above, this would, *inter alia*, imply that the regulation of refugees was, for the greater part of the last three decades during which Malawi has existed as an independent State, more or less determined by sheer political and humanitarian expediency, and not much else, in the absence of any binding legal regime for the protection of refugees in this regard.

It will be argued in this chapter that this view is both simplistic and wrong. A proper examination of the historical development of the legal regime governing the protection of refugees in Malawi ought to address the matter from two angles: municipal law and international law. Thus, it may well be correct to argue that there was, until recently, no refugee law in existence in Malawi, if in so doing one limits one's considerations solely to the municipal legislative sphere. But the question becomes more complex and problematic when it is cast differently: could Malawi, as a State, be regarded as bound by certain rules and principles of international law, in its relations with refugees located within or seeking entry into its territory, in the absence of any municipal legislation in that regard and before its specific acceptance or adoption of the relevant international legal instruments embodying such rules and principles? And, in point of fact, what considerations can be said to have informed Malawi's policy, if such existed, towards refugees in the period preceding the adoption of these legal instruments? These questions are particularly pertinent here, given that the legislative and policy developments in Malawi at the end of the 1980s actually followed, rather than preceded, the massive refugee problem created by the influx of refugees from Mozambique as already mentioned above. I propose to address this question before proceeding to examine the legislative and policy developments under consideration.

The Legal Regime for the Protection of Refugees in Malawi, 1964 to 1988

The arguments advanced by all the commentators quoted or referred to above all relate to the legal regime as it existed in Malawi prior to the country's accession to the three relevant international refugee instruments on 10 December 1987. The international legal instruments concerned here are: the UN Convention relating to the Status of Refugees of 28 July 1951; the Protocol relating to the Status of Refugees of 31 January 1967; and the OAU Convention governing the Specific Aspects of Refugee Problems in Africa of 10 September 1969.[11] According to the instruments of accession, the Protocol entered into force for Malawi on the date of deposit of the instrument, that is on 10 December 1987, while the Convention was due to enter into force on 9 March 1988, the ninetieth day following the deposit of the instrument. Malawi also ratified the OAU Convention on the same date as it notified the United Nations Secretary General of its accession to the UN instruments.[12] Elementary treaty construction and interpretation would suggest that Malawi's position with regard to the protection of refugees is now governed by these international conventions. This is the case at least from the international legal perspective.

But, of course, it is important to bear in mind that the legal regime relating to the protection of refugees is always founded upon two systems: on the one hand, one must bear in mind the rights and obligations laid down by both customary and conventional norms of international law; on the other hand, it is also imperative to examine the issue in the light of the provisions of any relevant domestic legislation in force in the State under consideration. There was no legislation specifically bearing on the status of refugees in Malawi until the somewhat belated enactment of the Refugee Act of 1989. This raises the interesting question whether, indeed, in these circumstances one is entitled to conclude that there was no refugee law in Malawi, binding upon that country in its relations with the refugee community, prior to the entry into force of the various instruments under reference?[13]

Malawi's Succession to Pre-Independence International Refugee Conventions

Upon its accession to independence on 6 July 1964, Malawi adopted the so-called Nyerere doctrine of State succession. This doctrine is embodied in a unilateral declaration made in 1961 by the Government of Tanganyika (as it then was) to the Acting Secretary General of the United Nations in the following terms:[14]

> "[As] regards bilateral treaties validly concluded by the Government of the United Kingdom on behalf of the territory of Tanganyika, or validly applied or extended by the former to the territory of the latter, the Government of Tanganyika is willing to continue to apply within its territory on a basis of reciprocity, the terms of all such treaties for a period of two years from the date of independence [unless] abrogated or modified earlier by mutual consent. At the expiry of that period, the Government of Tanganyika will regard such of these treaties which could not by the application of rules of customary international law be regarded as otherwise surviving, as having terminated."

The declaration went on to provide that with regard to multilateral treaties, the new government would review each of them individually and indicate to the depositary concerned what steps would be taken in relation to each such instrument, whether by way of confirmation of termination, confirmation of succession or accession. In essence this doctrine is really no more than a vague or general recognition that certain unspecified treaties do survive as a result of the application of rules of customary law, coupled with an offer of a grace period in which treaties remain in force on an interim basis without prejudice to the declarant's legal position and with a requirement of reciprocity.[15] As was noted in the discussion in Chapter 3 above, Malawi, in company with a number of other newly independent African States, followed the Tanganyikan approach and thus issued a unilateral declaration modelled more or less verbatim on the declaration quoted above.

Now, it is interesting to note that, until the recent accession alluded to above, no action was ever taken, one way or the other, regarding the refugee treaties to which the United Kingdom, the former colonial power, was in fact a party. The only related multilateral treaty to which the new State acceded is the Protocol relating to a certain case of Statelessness of 12 April 1930.[16] Why did the new nation prefer to accede to a treaty on statelessness but not to those agreements concerning the protection of refugees?

The application of the 1930 Protocol had been extended to the Protectorate of Nyasaland, Malawi's colonial designation, by virtue of its ratification by the United Kingdom, in accordance with the provision in the treaty governing its extended application to the signatories' colonial territories.[17] Equally, the 1951 Convention had also been deemed applicable to the territory of the Federation of Rhodesia and Nyasaland in accordance with the provision in Article 40 of the Convention, as from 11 July 1960, again by virtue of the fact that the colonial authority was a party to the treaty.[18] Even more interesting, the earlier 1933 Convention relating to the International Status of Refugees became operative in Nyasaland, through the territorial application clause, on 30 May 1940.[19] But, of course, since the latter agreement was itself superseded by subsequent treaties and has since ceased to be applicable as between Great Britain and the other original signatories, logically the question of whether or not it devolved upon Malawi at independence does not arise. What must be noted here, however, is that the 1930 Protocol on Statelessness was not the only international agreement of its kind to have been extended in application by the former colonial power to the territory of the Nyasaland Protectorate during the colonial period and before the emergence of the new State of Malawi. From this it can only be concluded that the decision by the new State to succeed to the one but not the other treaties was the result of a deliberate policy not to take on any treaty obligations previously assumed by the colonial authorities regarding the protection of refugees. This was consistent with the Nyerere doctrine since, in a sense, under that doctrine States reserve to themselves the right to determine which existing treaty obligations to assume or not; but even here, it is also recognized that there are certain exceptions to this rejection, for this is what the doctrine is really all about, of an absolute, wholesale and permanent transmissibility of pre-independence treaties: treaties evidencing rules of general international law, treaties creating "objective regimes", localized treaties as well as boundary treaties.[20] Can it be argued, for example, that treaties relating to the status and protection of refugees fall within these recognized exceptions, for example as treaties evidencing rules of general international law, in which case the unilateral declarations remain irrelevant?

In fact, in what is most probably the only case of its kind, the Judicial Committee of the Privy Council in the United Kingdom, at the time the highest court of appeal for most of the former British colonies, did not approach the issue from the angle suggested above. On the contrary, and this is quite instructive, in *Molefi* v *Principal Legal Adviser*, a case referred to the Privy Council from the Lesotho High Court and involving, in part, considerations of the effect of the Nyerere doctrine-type declaration on the continuing validity of the 1951 UN Convention relating to the Status of Refugees, Lesotho's declaration was treated by the Privy Council rather as an accession to the convention.[21] As in the case of Nyasaland, the United Kingdom had, by notification addressed to the UN Secretary General, extended the application of the convention to the territory of Basutoland, as from 9 February 1961. The new sovereign State of Lesotho came into being on 4 October 1966. On 22 March 1967, the Prime Minister, Chief Leabua Jonathan, addressed a letter to the UN Secretary General incorporating a declaration, also modelled on the Tanganyikan one, relating to both bilateral and multilateral treaties.

To begin with, the Privy Council rejected the argument put forward by the respondent, that the letter was a mere statement of policy not having the effect of succession to, or confirmation of, treaties binding on Basutoland. Rather, the bench expressed the view that:[22]

> "In agreement with Maisels JA their Lordships consider that, so far as concerns multilateral treaties, the reasonable meaning of the letter is that they are to continue in existence and binding on Lesotho until such time as decisions could be made in regard to them and about which of them should be [terminated]. The Prime Minister's letter was, therefore, a declaration that pending individual [examination] of these multilateral treaties which had resulted in treaty relations between the country formerly known as Basutoland and other States, Lesotho would adhere to those treaties. The [1951 UN] convention was one of them."

On the other hand, the appellant had argued, *inter alia*, that in fact Lesotho became a party to the convention as a result of the operation of principles of international law relating to succession (quite apart, so it would seem from this line of argumentation, from any considerations of the effect of the declaration embodied in the Prime Minister's letter of 22 March 1922). The Privy Council rejected this argument, finding it:[23]

> "[Unnecessary] to consider the various views which have been held by international lawyers as to the circumstances under which there may be succession to treaties or conventions by a new State."

Quite clearly, therefore, the Privy Council preferred to approach the question of succession to the convention purely within the context of the declaration by the new State itself regarding its position on the continuity of such pre-independence treaties. But it would also seem that their Lordships' opinion was informed by the recognition of the need for legal continuity in the relations of States in the international order, particularly where the emergence of new States is involved.[24] This approach, and the conclusion ultimately arrived at, would, presumably, hold good with regard to the Malawian declaration as it did in respect of the Lesotho case. Whether or not the International Court of Justice, or any other international tribunal for that matter, would adopt this approach can only be a matter for conjecture.

The question of succession in the *Molefi* case could also have been approached from a different perspective: that a multilateral treaty of this nature may arguably be regarded as evidencing rules of international law; thus, in the absence of a clear and specific rejection of such a treaty a presumption in favour of accession ought to be made.

The Principle of *Non-Refoulement* as *Jus Cogens*

The problem encountered here is not unknown in international law. In part, the issue has to do with the question whether or not all or some aspects of the law relating to refugees, as embodied in the international refugee conventions alluded to above, have now acquired the status of *jus cogens* such as to be binding upon States non-parties to these conventions? If so, what are these principles?

Current scholarly opinion in the area of international refugee law seems to suggest at least two candidates for the status of *jus cogens*: the principle of *non-refoulement* and the right of (or to) asylum. A brief discussion of the former would be in order here, since it is quite pertinent to any consideration of the problem of mass influx of refugees from one country into another.[25]

Most commentators appear to be in agreement that evidence relating to the meaning and scope of *non-refoulement* in its conventional sense amply supports the conclusion that today the principle of *non-refoulement* forms part of general international law, and is thus to be regarded as a general binding norm. Thus, in the words of Goodwin-Gill:[26]

> "There is substantial, if not conclusive, authority that the principle is binding on all States, independently of specific assent. [No] formal or informal opposition to the principle of *non-refoulement* is to be found, and where objection has been made on occasion to protection and assistance activities of UNHCR, it has been founded on a challenge to the status as refugees of the individuals involved."

Indeed, the learned writer, in company with others, goes on to assert that certain grey areas exist in the formulation of *non-refoulement* hardly confirms its lack of status in international law.[27] For, as Brierly once aptly observed, "the principles of international law are not susceptible of precise formulation...[the rules are] constantly changing and modelling themselves on the ever-changing needs of international life".[28] This is nowhere more true than in the area of refugee law.

The principle has been too widely discussed in the copious literature on the subject to need any detailed examination here.[29] But its basic tenet may be reiterated: in broad terms, the principle stands for the proposition that no refugee should be returned to any country where he or she is likely to face persecution or danger to life or freedom.[30] *Refoulement* itself has been described as a term of art, covering, in particular, summary reconduction to the frontier of those discovered to have entered illegally and summary dismissal of those without valid papers.[31] The practice of *refoulement* was quite common in Europe until the beginning of the nineteenth century, and only prior undertakings in bilateral treaties could justify any attempt to challenge its application. Thus, it was not until 1933 that the principle of *non-refoulement* was imported into an international treaty, namely the Convention concerning the International Status of Refugees of 28 October 1933, already mentioned above.[32] For Article 3 of this agreement enjoined the contracting parties not to remove resident refugees or keep them from their territory by application of such measures as expulsions or non-admittance at the frontier, unless dictated by national security or public order; they also undertook not to deny entry to (or "*refoule*") refugees at the frontiers of their countries of origin. However, even this belatedly laudable effort never took root, as the convention was ratified by only eight States, half of which either entered strong reservations or outright objection against the putative principle.[33] The full expression of the principle was only eventually embodied in the more widely embracing UN Convention relating to the Status of Refugees of 1951, already referred to above. Article 33(1) provides:

> "No Contracting State shall expel or return ('refouler') a refugee in any manner whatsoever to the frontiers of territories where his life or freedom would be threatened on account of his race, religion, nationality, membership of a particular social group or political opinion."

What is interesting in this brief historical survey is that it should have taken the international community, and legal scholars, so long to accept the idea of an unfettered principle of *non-refoulement*. For, had not Vattel, one of the acclaimed "fathers" of modern international law, already recognized and argued for the acceptance of the right of a refugee to an abode somewhere on the face of the earth, even if this right be an imperfect one with regard to any particular country, some two centuries or so ago?[34]

Today, little would be gained from an analysis aimed at tracing the acceptance or rejection of the principle, or indeed its historical evolution. The great majority of leading publicists agree that the principle is now a settled principle of customary international law, and not merely a principle in *statu nascendi* or simply an expression *de lege ferenda*; it is, indeed, widely acknowledged as providing the very foundation of refugee law.[35] One line of argumentation is thus that although the principle is conventional in origin, it has now crystallized into a customary rule. In this regard, it may be observed that even the conventional character of the principle reveals interesting aspects. First, although Article 33(2) of the 1951 UN Convention provides some exceptions under which the principle enunciated in Article 33(1) may be obviated, the Conference of Plenipotentiaries quite clearly attached so much importance to the principle that they devised Article 42(1), which in turn enumerates Article 33 as one of those provisions in respect of which reservations may not be made. Second, the principle has been repeated in two regional instruments: Article 22(8) of the 1969 American Convention on Human Rights and Article II(3) of the OAU Convention governing the Specific Aspects of Refugee Problems in Africa, also of 1969; neither of these provisions allows for qualification or exceptions. While there is no European instrument directly prohibiting *refoulement*, Article 3 of the European Convention on Human Rights has been construed as also covering such a prohibition.[36] And, it may also be noted, the UN Declaration on Territorial Asylum of 1967 affirms this international conventional acceptance of the principle by providing in its Article 3(1) that a refugee within the terms of Article 1(1) of the Declaration shall not be subjected to such measures as "rejection at the frontier or, if he has already entered the country in which he seeks asylum, expulsion or compulsory return to any country where he may be subjected to persecution".[37] Exceptions can only be made in the interests of national security or for the sake of safeguarding the population, as in the case of a mass influx of persons.

Conventional as well as individual State practice since at least 1951 would thus appear to have firmly anchored the principle as a basic tenet of international refugee law. Both the Executive Committee of the High Commissioner's Programme (1977) and the Arusha Conference on the Situation of Refugees in Africa (1979) unequivocally re-affirmed the fundamental need for the observance of the principle.[38] Moreover, it has also been asserted that State practice in cases of mass influx also offers some support for the view that *non-refoulement* applies both to the individual refugee with a well-founded fear of persecution, and to the frequently large groups of persons who do not in fact enjoy the protection of the government of their country of origin.[39] The masses of Mozambicans who have crossed the frontier into Malawi since mid-1987 belong to this category.

In view of all this, it is not surprising that a number of scholars and other legal experts have, in recent times, argued that the principle of *non-refoulement* has now acquired the status of a peremptory norm of international law, or *jus cogens*.[40] This is a conclusion with which the present writer is in full agreement. It is, therefore, arguable that even before the accession and ratification on 10 December 1987 of the 1951 UN and 1969 OAU Conventions, respectively, Malawi, like other members of the international community, was already bound by at least this one cardinal principle of international refugee law, *non-refoulement.*

On this account, therefore, it would seem quite mistaken to conclude that either there was no refugee law in, or binding upon, Malawi prior to the ratification and accession to the various international instruments, or that the binding effect of (or at least some of) the provisions of these treaties depended upon Malawi's specific consent. If any part of international refugee law can be regarded as having crystallized into general customary law at all, then it is most probably the rule relating to *non-refoulement* that can legitimately be cast in the character of a *jus cogens*, which is thus valid *erga omnes*. It is the view here that Article 33(1) of the 1951 UN Convention and Article II(3) of the 1969 OAU Convention must be regarded as being of a fundamentally norm-creating nature.

The conclusion reached here, that Malawi was in any case bound by the principle of *non-refoulement* even in the absence of specific consent is one that other commentators have not been too ready to accept. Thus, Mponda has observed:[41]

> "[During] this period, the [Malawi] Government applied refugee law without having formally accepted that law as embodied in the relevant conventions. This is not a curious position or one peculiar to Malawi."

This is an interesting observation, but perhaps it merely begs the question: why do States, in certain instances, apply even those rules of conventional international law to which they have not yet formally acceded, and what inferences can be drawn from the fact that States do sometimes so behave?[42]

It is submitted here that the more correct view, in the light of the various opinions briefly surveyed above, is to regard the principle of *non-refoulement* as a peremptory norm of international law whose binding effect is not dependent upon specific consent by the particular State concerned. The more pertinent question which this enquiry ought to address, therefore, should rather be: given this view what, then, was the content of Malawi's obligation in this regard; and how, in the face of the mass influx of refugees from Mozambique, was this obligation met, and continues to be met, in practice?

The Application of the Principle of *Non-Refoulement* in Situations of Large-Scale Influx: Malawi's Approach

Thus, it can be seen that Malawi's accommodation of the massive influx of refugees from Mozambique need not be explained away in terms of the so-called "humane nature of the African race".[43] Debates as to whether or not Africans or, more specifically, Malawians are by nature humane and thus more receptive to refugees and other aliens probably miss the point. In any event, African peoples have had their share of inter-communal, ethnic or tribal wars over the ages. Moreover, modern versions of such wars, combined with despotic and brutal undemocratic rule in most parts of the continent, continue to be the major cause of the refugee problem all over Africa. How is one to reconcile all this with the claims about the *inherent* humanitarian nature of Africans which commends itself to a ready accommodation and integration of "refugees from across the border"?[44]

Malawi, like other States in Africa and elsewhere, exists as part of the modern international community and its obligations towards that community must be sought within the legal order which governs all other members of the community. While a nation's humane character may go towards explaining its place and behaviour in the normative order which governs the international community, it is argued here that a more fruitful line of enquiry would be one directed at the nation's acceptance, or rejection, of the legal order in which it is required to operate as an incidence of its membership of that community. What has been Malawi's attitude towards the evolving international refugee law over the last quarter-century or so of its existence? And what has been its approach, in point of fact, to the refugee phenomenon occasioned by the mass influxes from Mozambique over the last four years or so?

As was noted earlier above, Malawi did not accede to any of the relevant refugee conventions at independence in 1964, nor did it participate in the conclusion, as an original signatory, of the 1967 Protocol subsequently. Yet, it is interesting to note that Malawi did take part, as one of the forty-one original signatories, in the conclusion of the OAU Convention two years later. Of course, mere participation in the deliberative conference(s) leading up to the conclusion of a multilateral treaty without any subsequent ratification or other act of adoption of the treaty does not of itself signify an intention to be bound by such a treaty. And, save in the exceptional cases of the so-called law-making treaties, the unratified treaty remains outside the legislative schema of the State concerned, unless, as has been argued in this discussion, the treaty in fact embodies peremptory norms of international law or rules enjoying the status of *jus cogens*.

In any case, Malawi's accession to the 1951 UN Convention and the 1967 Protocol was soon followed by the conclusion of an agreement between Malawi and the UNHCR concerning the establishment of a UNHCR Branch Office in the country[45] and, a year later, the enactment of the Refugee Act.[46] The agreement and the legislation entered into force on 28 April 1988 and 8 May 1989 respectively. It is generally believed that both these developments were prompted by the belated realization that the growing refugee problem in the country could no longer be managed and contained on an *ad hoc* basis without a properly defined legislative framework. Thus, in a sense, these developments may be characterized as the legislative equivalent of "slamming the stable door after the horse has bolted": for more than two decades, Malawi had not made any visible effort to draw up a refugee-related legislative policy agenda, and appeared to be doing so now only as a reaction to an already existing problem. And partly, too, in response to the external pressures engendered by the growing international sympathy towards the plight of Mozambican refugees seeking refuge *en masse* in neighbouring countries such as Malawi, South Africa, Swaziland and Zimbabwe. This is in stark contrast with the approach adopted by other African States in the region, which had placed refugees on their political and legislative agendas almost immediately following the attainment of their independence.[47]

Part of the explanation for Malawi's hesitation in formulating a well-defined refugee policy during the first quarter-century of its existence as an independent State lies in the paradoxes and opportunistic ambivalence that has always underlain its regional politics. Reference was earlier made to the fact that during the early 1960s, Malawi did not only provide transit facilities to various members of some of the national liberation movements operating in the Southern African sub-region, but it also granted refuge to certain individuals from some of the colonized or oppressed communities concerned, particularly those from Mozambique and Rhodesia. Yet, at the same time, Malawi's support and sympathy for these national liberation movements was always selective and, from certain perspectives, questionable; on the contrary, Malawi's open collaboration with the Mozambican and Rhodesian colonial authorities during this period is widely acknowledged by students of the region's politics and history, as well as other commentators generally.[48] To date, Malawi's role in what was characterized as the "low intensity conflict" which is responsible for the creation of refugees in Mozambique and elsewhere in Southern Africa remains a matter for speculation and debate. But, again, at least one point seems to be widely accepted: that initially, at least, Malawi did contribute, to a lesser or greater extent, to the creation of the Mozambican refugee influx by colluding with the Mozambique National Resistance (MNR) rebels whose destabilization of the socio-economic infrastructure of Mozambican society lies at the centre of this entire problem. Thus, it would seem that Malawi's complicity was intimately linked to South Africa's destabilization schemes – the so-called total strategy – in the region. Fauvet, Metz and Morna are among the many commentators who have chronicled Malawi's alleged role in this process. Fairly recently, Mazur has observed thus:[49]

"The largest numbers of Mozambicans are in Malawi and South Africa; numerous MNR bases were operational in Malawi in 1985 and 1986 before the grand entrance into Mozambique in late 1986. The relative neglect of Mozambican refugees by Malawian authorities, particularly in the early stages before international opinion forced greater material aid in late 1987, is continued evidence of Malawian complicity in South Africa's schemes. Though unclear whether the MNR currently maintains training bases in Malawi, at the very least they appear to have 'no great problems' transitting through Malawi."

Elsewhere, the same writer has claimed that in South Africa, and possibly in Malawi, refugees "are sometimes initially screened to identify those who may be recruited into the MNR".[50] These suspicions were never totally dispelled by the establishment of a Joint Security Commission between the Malawian and Mozambican Governments, nor the conclusion of the tripartite repatriation commission between Malawi, Mozambique and the UNHCR.[51] Thus, quite clearly, it may be argued that in essence, the subsequent legislative and policy developments in Malawi revealed a deliberate attempt to reconcile the tensions and contradictions which had hitherto informed the country's position in relation to the recognition, treatment and protection of refugees, and its whole role in the continuing drama surrounding the liberation and decolonization of the sub-continent. Has this attempt succeeded, at least as judged from Malawi's management of the Mozambican refugee crisis?

It has to be recognized that situations of large-scale influx of refugees pose problems and characteristics which are different from those encountered in individual or small group cases. Even where the potential asylum State is willing to accept such large numbers of asylum seekers, the mere presence in the country of hundreds of thousands, or in Malawi's case almost a million, refugees or asylum-seekers is bound to present serious socio-economic, political and even cultural difficulties. To begin with, the very process of determining refugee status in such cases presents peculiar problems. Employment, access to land and business opportunities may not be adequately available. Economic self-sufficiency is almost out of the question for the great majority, if not all, of such refugees. More immediately, the large-scale influx poses major problems of accommodation, food and health. All these problems can, in turn, endanger public order, national security, and international peace and security. These are only some of the major problems that any country formulating policy and legislation to cope with large-scale influxes of refugees has to address.

The Malawian Government's official position was described as aiming to address precisely the kind of problems enumerated above. Thus, an official policy statement has made the categorical claim that:[52]

> "Malawi's hospitality extends long before Mozambique was independent from Portugal. Since then there have been many Mozambicans in Malawi who sought refuge including freedom fighters. Since 1982, as a result of internal civil strife in Mozambique, small numbers of displaced persons, mainly from Zambezi and Tete Provinces, have been seeking refuge with their relatives in Nsanje, Chikwawa, Mulanje, Mwanza, Mangochi, Zomba, Ntcheu, Dedza and Lilongwe Districts of Malawi. The Government and the people of Malawi welcomed and assisted these people without external assistance. The nationals provided land, food and domestic utensils and the Government made available all its services without discrimination."

A few quick observations may be made here. First, it will be noted that the terminology employed here is that of "displaced persons" rather than that of "refugees". Now, this is not the place to engage in a detailed discussion of the epistemological principle underlying the concept of "refugeehood". However, it may be noted that there are certain conceptual and policy implications arising out of the distinction between refugeehood and displacement. It is not without significance that when occasion arose to refer to refugees either in the municipal context or at international fora, Malawi consistently applied the term "displaced" persons.[53] Second, the statement quoted above makes reference to the fact that these "displaced" persons have sought refuge "with their relatives". This betrays both a conscious political sentiment and a geo-political reality. It is trite that one painful legacy of colonialism and the demarcation of colonial boundaries is that ethnic groups, perhaps even families, have ended up falling under different State (territorial) jurisdictions. The result is that, in quite a number of cases, people of the same ethnic grouping have found themselves straddling the opposite sides of the same international boundary. Expansionist and hegemonic governments and politicians in Africa have sometimes used this as an excuse to advance claims for the re-drawing of the "arbitrary" colonial boundaries and for the due expansion of the inherited colonial State to include all kith and kin now located on the "wrong" side of the border. Long before the emergence of the present Mozambican refugee problem, Dr. Hastings Banda, the late Malawian President, had made claims for Malawi's so-called historic titles to the very provinces in Mozambique from which today's refugees are drawn. The attempt by the Malawian authorities to regard the Mozambicans as seeking refuge with their relatives rather than with the State as such may be seen in this light.

And perhaps, too, the overstretched claims about limitless Malawian hospitality and the African spirit of brotherhood referred to earlier ought to be examined in this context.[54] The problem here is that such arguments might be used as an insidious weapon to deny the refugees recognition of their right to organize themselves and assert their separate political identity while in the country of asylum (by insisting on the fiction that they are part and parcel of the national or social formation in the country of asylum). Indeed, their very entitlement to legal protection as refugees, and all the rights that flow from recognition of that status, could be jeopardized by such an approach. Some of the consequent problems have been identified by a number of writers. Thus, Mazur observed:[55]

> "In Malawi, refugees are prohibited from farming, working, or selling handicrafts because of pressures on available land and fears that they may flood the local market."

Morna also reported about Mozambican refugees who, in an effort to achieve a measure of self-sufficiency, would sneak across the border back into Mozambique during the daytime to cultivate their fields.[56]

We must now revert to the more specific question regarding the application of the principle of *non-refoulement* in the context of the Mozambican influx situation. The content and juridical status of the principle itself have already been discussed above. It remains here simply to reiterate that the question of individual eligibility for protection becomes largely theoretical and of little relevance when a great mass of people cross a frontier, often suddenly and in a matter of days. In such cases, mass or group determination can, and ought to be, made. The Refugee Act of Malawi specifically provides for this procedure. Thus, Section 7(3) states:

> "The Minister may, by notice published in the *Gazette*, direct that, with respect to any group of foreign nationals specified in the notice, seeking refugee status in Malawi, the Committee shall apply such group determination procedure as may be prescribed."

This is a commendable provision which does not appear in some of the earlier national legislation on refugees in other African countries.[57] It is, of course, a provision specifically tailored to meet the special circumstances in which the Malawian legislation was conceived. The only problem which may arise here is to decide when the situation which created the refugee influx is over and, therefore, when to change to individual status determination. This is particularly the case where large-scale arrivals continue while some of the parties involved begin to perceive the emergency as having come to an end.

On an official level, Malawi's preferred solution was that of the voluntary repatriation of the Mozambicans as and when conditions permit.[58]

The principle of *non-refoulement* is incorporated in Section 10 of the Act. This provision stipulates that a person shall not be expelled or returned to the borders of a country where his life or freedom will be threatened on account of his race, religion, nationality or membership of a particular social group or political opinion; or external aggression, occupation, foreign domination or events seriously disturbing the public order in either part or the whole of that country. Thus, the Act embraces both the classical approach to the principle of *non-refoulement*, as reflected in Article 33 of the 1951 UN Convention relating to the Status of Refugees, and the wider conception of that principle as embodied in Articles I(2) and II(3) of the 1969 OAU Convention governing the Specific Aspects of Refugee Problems in Africa. Section 10(2) is more specific in this regard:

> "A person claiming to be a refugee shall be permitted to enter and remain in Malawi for such period as the Committee may require to process his application for refugee status."

Section 10(4) deals with persons who enter Malawi illegally for the purposes of seeking asylum. Such persons are fully protected against expulsion or *refoulement*, the only condition being that they must report to a competent officer (immigration, police, border or security officer) within twenty-four hours of such entry or "such longer period as the competent officer may consider acceptable in the circumstances". By comparison with similar legislation from other countries, even this provision is not as onerous as it might at first sight seem.[59] The provision can only have been designed to meet the realities of mass displacement and large-scale border crossing: in the nature of things, the great majority of such refugees will have entered the country without satisfying the required immigration formalities, particularly in view of the fact that such border crossings will not, in any case, have been effected at properly policed immigration or border posts. This is the reality that attends the continuing Mozambican refugee influx into Malawi.

It can, therefore, be seen that Section 10 of the Malawi Refugee Act represents an explicit and faithful incorporation of the principle of *non-refoulement* in all its ramifications. Needless to say here, that this legislation has been purposefully based more upon the OAU Convention than the UN Convention for the simple reason that it is the former instrument, with its more widely embracing definition of the term "refugee", which is more directly relevant to mass influx situations. Thus, the definition adopted in Section 2(1) of the Act is almost verbatim that contained in Article I(1) and (2) of the

OAU Convention. The actual practice and procedures which the Malawian authorities employed for the determination of refugee status and the application of the principle of *non-refoulement* with respect to the Mozambican refugees thus appear to have been within the scope of the widely accepted rules of conventional international law, as reflected in the various instruments discussed here.

Conclusion

The main objective of this chapter has been to examine the evolution of the recent policy and legislative developments concerning the protection of refugees in Malawi. More specifically, the preceding discussion has been directed at examining Malawi's response to the phenomenal refugee problem occasioned by the mass influx of about one million Mozambicans over a relatively short span of time. The argument here has been three-fold. First, an attempt has been made to locate the existence of a legal obligation (or obligations), within the purview of international law, binding upon Malawi with regard to its treatment and protection of refugees even prior to its accession to the various international legal instruments in question. Second, in terms of the historical perspective, it has been observed, in passing, that a proper account of the political economy of refugee-creation in Mozambique must include Malawi's alleged role in the South African-backed "low intensity conflict" or destabilization strategy which was largely responsible for the plight of the Mozambican refugees and *deslocados*, to borrow Mazur's terminology,[60] now seeking sanctuary in Malawi. In this regard, Malawi was viewed by some observers not only as a factor in the creation of the refugee problem, but also as a victim of that problem, given the immense burdens and responsibilities it had to bear as a host State. Finally, the argument has also addressed the present legal position ushered in by Malawi's accession to the international refugee conventions and the enactment of its own municipal legislation, as well as the effect of these legislative developments.

The argument that there exist within the broader area of international refugee law certain rules of *jus cogens* which are binding erga omnes and, therefore, not dependent upon specific consent by individual States is not, of course, universally accepted by all international lawyers. But it is a proposition that has been gaining more and more wide-spread support in recent times, at least insofar as the principle of *non-refoulement* is concerned. In this light, it would thus appear mistaken to insist that Malawi's obligations as regards the recognition and acceptance of that principle and all that it implies only arose with its belated accession to the refugee conventions discussed above. Of course, the reality of international refugee law today, as in many other areas of international law in general, is that even rules which claim the status of *jus cogens* are often subordinated to the wider claims of the principle of territorial sovereignty and the "absolute" right of States to choose whether or not to admit aliens, including refugees and asylum-seekers, into their territories.[61] It is doubtful whether such claims to unfettered and absolute sovereignty would still find a place in a world presently dominated by increasing demands upon States to respect the human and fundamental rights of not only their own nationals, but also those of the nationals of other States as well. Refugee rights, including the right to asylum and *non-refoulement*, ought surely to be recognized as a legitimate part of this rights-talk and global political agenda.

Other issues have only been partially mooted, and not fully addressed, in this discussion. There is, for example, the question of the historical processes that have determined the formulation of refugee policy in Malawi; a proper examination of this issue could not have been undertaken with any depth of analysis and justice in a discussion that was more specifically aimed at examining only the recent or present developments regarding a particular refugee phenomenon. A fuller historical evaluation of the evolution of Malawi's refugee policy over the last thirty years remains to be undertaken. Among other things, such an enquiry would, perhaps, reveal whether, indeed, there was ever a conscious attempt at formulating a clear, deliberate policy in this regard during the period under consideration; or whether the often contradictory and ambiguous attitudes adopted by the Malawian Government towards refugees was simply one aspect of its rather ambivalent position regarding the wider issues of decolonization, liberation and racism in Southern Africa?

Whatever answers are given to these and other questions, at least one thing is clear: the post-1988 legal regime for the protection of refugees in Malawi represents a significant advance upon the various other regimes established earlier in other African countries. Admittedly, some of the reservations entered by Malawi to some of the provisions of the 1951 Convention may at first sight appear to detract from its commitment to respect fully the rights and status of refugees on its territory.[62] Yet, it can also be argued that none of these reservations touch upon the fundamental elements of refugee law embodied in the various international instruments: the right of asylum and *non-refoulement*. As has been argued above, the principle of *non-refoulement*, which has an especial relevance in the context of mass influxes, is now firmly enshrined in Section 10 of the Refugee Act of 1989. The significance of the importation of such an important principle of international law into Malawi's municipal legislation cannot be overemphasized.

Notes

1. Estimates of the total number of Mozambican refugees in Malawi tended to vary between different source. According to the information made available by the UNHCR Branch Office in Lilongwe, Malawi, the total population of Mozambican refugees was 891,186 as at 31 October 1990. Subsequent unofficial estimates put the total number of refugees at slightly over one million as at 30 September 1991.

2. A number of commentators have, in fact, addressed the recent refugee crisis in Malawi, but most of this work largely consists of unpublished reports or conference papers. See R. Mponda, "Some Perceptions on the Development of Refugee Law in Malawi", and K. Mhone, "Malawi's Humanitarian Approach to Refugees", unpublished papers presented at the Legal Protection Seminar held in Liwonde, Malawi, 17–20 May 1988. See also M. Machika, "The Status of Refugees in Malawi", unpublished seminar paper, (University of Malawi, Zomba, 1988). M. Cisternino, *Report on the Situation of Mozambican Refugees in Malawi up to 12 June 1987*, (Comboni Missionaries, Rome, 1987), unpublished; K. Wilson *et al.*, *Food Provisioning Amongst Mozambican Refugees in Malawi: a study of aid, livelihood and development*, (Refugee Studies Programme/World Food programme, 1989). The following studies also deal, in part, with the Malawian dimension of the Mozambican refugee problem: R. Mazur, "The Political Economy of Refugee Creation in Southern Africa: Micro and Macro issues in Sociological Perspective", *2 Journal of Refugee Studies 441* (1989); J. Nunes, and K. Wilson, "Repatriation to Mozambique: Current Processes and Future Dilemmas", paper presented at the UNRISD Symposium on Social and Economic Aspects of Mass Voluntary Return from one African country to another, Harare, Zimbabwe, 12–14 March 1991.

3. Unlike most other independent African States, from the mid-1960s to the mid-1970s when FRELIMO (and, to a limited extent, other organizations such as COREMO) was engaged in its war of national liberation, Malawi maintained a quasi-diplomatic presence in the Portuguese colony and, from September 1967, full diplomatic relations with the colonial power, Portugal, following the accreditation to Lisbon of Mr. Timon S. Mangwazu as a non-resident ambassador based in London. Similarly, Malawi continued to maintain low-key inter-governmental and trade links with Rhodesia even while Dr. Hastings Banda, the Malawian President, was repeatedly affirming his partial support for U.N. mandatory sanctions against the U.D.I. regime. In the due course of time, on 8 July 1969, Dr. Banda openly announced that Malawi would cooperate with Rhodesia "within certain limits". See *Banda, H.K.: Press Conference*, (Dept of Info., Transcript, Blantyre, 8 July 1969), quoted in P. Short, *Banda*, (1974) pp. 310, 345 n. 21. For a general historical account

of Malawi-Mozambique relations during this period and of Malawi's diplomatic and political role in the Mozambican liberation struggle and its early attitude towards Mozambican refugees see D. Hedges, "Notes on Malawi-Mozambique Relations, 1961–1987", *J. of Southern African Studies 617* (1989). It should be cautioned, however, that this account largely reflects the Mozambican point of view.

4. See Mponda, *op. cit.* note 2, p. 6.

5. Hedges, *op. cit.* note 3, p. 630.

6. See, for example, Mhone, *op. cit.* note 2, p. 1.

7. Machika, *op. cit.* note 2, p. 6.

8. See, for example, Mponda, *op. cit.* p. 5.

9. Machika, *op. cit.* pp. 66–67. Machika's view is based, in part, on the interpretation that, as it then stood, under Article 9 of the Agreement between the Government of Malawi and the UNHCR relating to the establishment of a Branch Office in Malawi of 28 April 1988, the Government of Malawi "denounced the 1951 UN Convention Relating to the Status of Refugees under Article 40 thereof". This interpretation of the provision in question was occasioned by a drafting error which resulted in a conjugation of two clauses that had originally been intended to remain separate. The error was readily acknowledged, on the Malawian side, in a *Procès-verbal* of Rectification dated 31 May 1988, and a proposed amendment to the provision was agreed upon by the UNHCR in a *Note* dated 16 September 1988. Both the *Procès-verbal* and the *Note* now form an integral part of the Agreement of 28 April 1988. It is now clearly understood that the purported denunciation of the UN Convention was erroneous and that Malawi regards itself as a party to that instrument subject to certain reservations as communicated along with its instrument of accession. (Malawi has entered reservations in respect of Articles 7, 13, 15, 17, 19, 22, 24, 26 and 34).

10. Mponda, *op. cit.* p. 15. In fairness to Mponda, it may be noted that he does point out that this assertion should be understood in a qualified sense because, in his view, the practice of the Malawian legal system, in the application and perception of the relationship between municipal law and international law, is divergent, and not yet settled. He goes on to argue: "On this count, it is therefore arguable [that] the relevant refugee instruments became part of Malawi law by virtue of the country's subscription thereto". But even here, Mponda adopts a cautious, indeed hesitant, position, as opposed to the categorical conclusion adopted by the present writer in this discussion, at least as far as the question of the incorporation of customary rules of international law into the municipal legal system is concerned.

In fact, on this point at east, the issue is not as divergent and unsettled as Mponda argues, for Article 2(1)(iii) of the Constitution of Malawi of 1996 (then in force) explicitly stipulated that the Government and the people of Malawi "shall continue to recognize [adherence] to the Law of Nations" as one of the principles upon which the sovereign Republic of Malawi is founded.

11. For the full texts of these treaties, see respectively; 189 UNTS 137; 606 UNTS 267; and OAU Doc. CM/267/Rev.1 (reproduced in I. Brownlie, *Basic Documents on African Affairs*, (1971) p. 18 *et seq.*).

12. Mponda, *op. cit.* p. 25 n. 30, reports that internally the formal decision to accede to the various refugee instruments was taken by the relevant Malawian Government authorities on 2 August 1987; the instruments of accession were signed by the President on 4 November 1987 and deposited with the UN Secretary General on 10 December 1987. He further notes that the Secretary General issued his Depositary Notification on 29 January 1988 (Ref. C.N.316.1987.TREATIES 02/4), and that the 1951 Convention entered into force for Malawi on 10 December 1988, exactly a year after the deposit of the instruments of accession. In the view of the present writer, this date of entry into force is rather difficult to reconcile with Article 43(2) of the Convention itself which provides that for each State ratifying or acceding to the Convention after the deposit of the sixth instrument of ratification or accession [i.e. after the Convention had already come into force], the Convention shall enter into force on the ninetieth day following the date of deposit by such State of its instrument of ratification or accession.

13. The Refugee Act (Act No. 3 of 1989) was passed by Parliament on 3 April 1989 and became operative on 8 May 1989. One of the fundamental questions which arises here is whether it could be argued, for example, that there are certain principles of customary international law relating to refugees which may be regarded as having been transformed into the municipal legal system of Malawi as part of the law of the land.

14. Reproduced in ILC Yrbk., 1974, Vol II, Part 1, p. 63.

15. This approach has been adopted by a number of States in similar situations, though with some variations (for example with respect to the duration of the grace period). Among these are Barbados, Botswana, Burundi, Guyana, Kenya, Lesotho, Malawi, Mauritius, Nauru, Rwanda, Swaziland, Uganda and Zambia. See discussion in Chapter 3 *supra*.

16. See text in 179 LNTS 115. Malawi's accession became effective on 9 October 1967; see 600 UNTS 415.

17. For a brief survey of British colonial practice regarding the application of its treaties to its colonies, see the discussion in Chapter 3; see also, generally, J.E.S. Fawcett, *The British Commonwealth in International Law*, (1963).

18. The Federation of Rhodesia and Nyasaland, which had been created on 1 August 1953, ceased to exist on 31 December 1963. Another angle to the question of whether or not this convention survived the change of sovereignty occasioned by the birth of the new State of Malawi is to ask whether it had, in fact, survived the changes brought about by the demise of the federal State and the emergence of the three States which had constituted the federation: Malawi, Zambia and Southern Rhodesia (Zimbabwe).

19. See 159 LNTS 199. This Convention, concluded on 28 October 1933, was applicable to Russian, Armenian and assimilated refugees, as defined by the Arrangements of 12 May 1926, and 28 June 1928.

20. Among the leading publicists who subscribe to this view are: W.E. Hall, *Treatise on International Law*, (1924) p. 115; A.D. McNair, *The Law of Treaties*, (1961) p. 655–664; I. Brownlie, *Principles of Public International Law*, (4th ed., 1990) pp. 669–673.

21. [1970] 3 All ER 724.

22. *Ibid.* p. 730; *per* Lord Morris.

23. *Ibid.* p. 728.

24. *Ibid.* p. 730, where it was observed: "The point is made that although the Kingdom of Lesotho has emerged into full independence, yet it is clearly desirable to maintain legal continuity between Lesotho and the various countries with which Basutoland has enjoyed treaty relations. The 'declarations which followed were made accordingly'. They were made with the desirability of legal continuity in mind".

25. I have elsewhere discussed the concept of asylum and advanced an argument for a reconsideration of the content and scope of the concept itself as traditionally understood in contemporary international law. See T. Maluwa, "The Concept of Asylum and the Protection of Refugees in Botswana: Some Legal and Political Aspects", *2 Int'l J. Ref. L. 587* (1990).

26. G.S. Goodwin-Gill, *The Refugee in International Law*, (2nd ed., 1996) pp. 167–168.

27. *Ibid.* p. 170.

28. J.L. Brierly, *The Basis of Obligation in International Law*, (Eds. H. Lauterpacht and H. Waldock, 1958) p. 74.

29. For comprehensive accounts of the principle of *non-refoulement*, see Goodwin-Gill, *op. cit.* note 26, Chap. 4; see also G. Stenberg, *Non-Expulsion and Non-Refoulement*, (1989) *passim*, and the extensive literature cited therein.

30. See Goodwin-Gill, *ibid.* p. 117; A. Grahl-Madsen, *The Status of Refugees In International Law*, Vol. II, (1972) p. 93.

31. Goodwin-Gill, *ibid.*

32. See note 19 *supra.*

33. In fact, three of them, by reservations and declarations, emphasized their intention of sovereign competence in the matter of expulsion, while the United Kingdom expressly objected to the principle of non-rejection at the frontier. See in this regard Goodwin-Gill, *op. cit.* p. 118.

34. E. Vattel, *Le droit des gens ou principes de la loi naturelle*, (1758), Bk. 2, Pt. 117; And, as Hathaway has aptly noted: "[The] founding fathers of public international law viewed asylum as a natural right of the individual and a duty of the State. They believed that in pursuance of an international humanitarian duty, States which granted asylum were acting on behalf other *civitas maxima* or the community of States. Today we translate the idea of universal society into the humanitarian duty of international protection of refugees, and the right of the individual to seek international protection". See J.C. Hathaway, "A Reconsideration of the Underlying Premise of Refugee Law", *31 Harvard Int'l LJ 129* (1990) at 130 n. 1.

35. In addition to the works by Goodwin-Gill and Stenberg cited in note 29 *supra*, see also A. Grahl-Madsen, *Territorial Asylum*, (1980) *passim*, and "Refugees and Refugee Law in a World of Transition", *19 AWR Bulletin* 96 (1981); see also same author's "International Refugee Law Today and Tomorrow" *20 Archiv des Volkerrechts 439* (1982). But for the view that the principle is still only in statu nascendi, see W. Kalin, *Das Prinzip des Non-Refoulement*, (1982) p. 72.

36. Thus, as far back as 1965 the Parliamentary Assembly of the Council of Europe adopted Recommendation 434 ("Concerning the Granting of the Right of Asylum to European Refugees") which states, *inter alia*: "[Considering] Art. 3 of the Convention for the Protection of Human Rights and Fundamental Freedoms which, by prohibiting inhuman treatment, binds contracting parties not to return refugees to a country where their life or freedom would be threatened..."; for analyses of the practice under the European Convention see F. Jacobs, *The European Convention on Human Rights*, (1975); D. Nance, "The individual right to asylum under Article 3 of the European Convention on Human Rights", in D. Levy *et al.* (Eds.), *Transnational Legal Problems of Refugees*,

(1982) p. 477; T. Einarsen, "The European Convention on Human Rights and the Notion of an Implied Right to de facto Asylum", *2 Int'l J. Ref. L. 361* (1990).

37. GA Res. 2312 (XXII) of 14 December 1967.

38. See Conclusion No. 6(XXVIII) (*Non-Refoulement*), para. 9; see, generally, Report of the 28th Session of the Executive Committee: UN Doc. A/AC.96/546. For a summarized report of the Arusha Conference, see UN. Doc. A/AC.96/INF.158; see p. 9 for recommendation regarding the principle of *non-refoulement*.

39. See, for example, Report of the Meeting of the Expert Group on Temporary Refuge in Situations of Large-Scale Influx, Geneva, 21–24 April 1981, reprinted in *20 AWR Bulletin 241* (1982), especially para. 40(ii).

40. See G. Fourlanos, *Sovereignty and the Ingress of Aliens*, (1986) p. 147 *et seq*.

41. Mponda, *op. cit.* p. 8.

42. The short answer to this question is simply that notwithstanding occasional denials to that effect, States do, in fact, generally acknowledge that there exist some rules and principles of international law whose binding nature and effect is not dependent upon specific consent by the individual States concerned. This is a matter that has been debated over and over again by international legal scholars over the years; see, for example, Brierly, *op. cit.* note 28 *supra*. The recent attempts by some writers and commentators to question the existence of such rules, or even to deny the notion of *jus cogens* altogether, are most unlikely ever to gain majority support among international lawyers, for as Frowein has rightly noted: "The notion of *jus cogens* became essential for the understanding of international law at a time when it was again realized that the individual and arbitrary agreement of States could not be the highest value in the international community, and that the goal of preserving peace and protecting peoples and individuals presupposed the recognition of some basic values". The view that there is a close connection between *jus cogens* and the recognition of a "public order of the international community" has not lost currency; on the contrary, recent calls for the strengthening of this order go towards re-affirming the need for a recognition of the notion of *jus cogens*. See J.A. Frowein, "Jus Cogens", in R. Bernhardt (Ed.), *Encyclopedia of Pub. Int'l L.*, Instalment 7, (1984) p. 327 at 330; see also L.A. Alexidze, "The Legal Nature of *Jus Cogens* in Contemporary International Law", *172 Hague Recueil 219* (1981); H. Mosler, *The International Society as a Legal Community*, (Rev. ed. 1980) p. 19.

43. See Mhone, *op. cit.* pp. 1, 6.

44. The myth regarding the traditional "humane nature", "openness" or "hospitality" of the African race pervades some of the literature on refugees, and is sometimes used to support the argument that African refugees must be resettled and taken care of within the African continent instead of being encouraged and enabled to relocate to Europe and North America. Hathaway, *op. cit.* note 34, appears to embrace this view. Thus, on p. 176 he argues: "The regional arrangements that exist today in Africa and Latin America demonstrate a comparable degree of generosity premised on mutuality of interest and cultural compatibility". See also E.R. Mbaya, *La Communauté Internationale et les mouvements des populations en Afrique*, (1985) p. 14. Of late, this myth has been strongly challenged and dismissed by some scholars and practitioners of refugee law as being, at best, premised on certain naive and largely unproven cultural assumptions. See, for example, G. Kibreab, *African Refugees: Reflections on the African Refugee Problem*, (1985). More recently, even the UNHCR itself has questioned these assumptions: UNHCR, "Africa: Host States under pressure", *48 Refugees 18* (1987).

45. See note 9 *supra*. But, of course, the lack of any formal presence and representation for the UNHCR did not mean a total denial of access by the relevant international relief or aid agencies, including the UNHCR itself, to the refugee community, particularly after the on-set of the Mozambican influx.

46. See note 13 *supra*.

47. Among the earlier statutory enactments in the region are: the Refugees (Control) Act of Tanzania of 1966; the Refugees (Recognition and Control) Act of Botswana of 1967; the Refugees (Control) Act of Zambia of 1970; The Refugee (Control) Order of Swaziland of 1978; and the Refugees Act of Zimbabwe of 1983.

48. See, for example, Hedges, *op. cit.* note 3. See also C. McMaster, *Malawi: Foreign Policy and Development*, (1974); R. Henderson, "Relations of Neighbourliness – Malawi and Portugal, 1964–1974", *15 Journal of Modern African Studies 429* (1977).

49. Mazur, *op. cit.* note 2, p. 461. See also P. Fauvet, "Malawi Aiding Rebels", in *The Guardian*, London, 23 July 1988; S. Metz, "The Mozambique National Resistance and South African Foreign Policy", 85 *African Affairs 491* (1986) at 498; C. Morna, "Malawi: Shouldering the Refugee Burden", *33 Africa Report 51* (1988).

50. *Ibid.* p. 456.

51. The first meeting of the Joint Security Commission was held in the Mozambican town of Nampula on 4 December 1986, and was followed by a working session in the Malawian capital of Lilongwe on 11–12 December. The leader of the Malawian delegation, Mr. John Tembo, is reported to have told the working

session: "The objective of the Malawian Government is to achieve peace, the maximum cooperation, harmony and determination to eliminate the armed bandits and all forms of destabilization existing in Mozambique"; see *Noticias*, Maputo, 14 December 1986; quoted in Hedges, *op. cit.* p. 642.

52. Malawi Government policy statement entitled: *Government Interventions On The Refugee Programmes*, presented to the Legal Protection Seminar held in Liwonde, Malawi, 17–20 May 1988; see p. 1 para. 1.

53. The question of definition is central to any discourse on refugees and forced migration, partly because the determination of refugee status and the implications of that status depend on the definitional parameters one chooses to adopt; see, for example, the discussion by O. Ibeanu, "Apartheid, Destabilization and Displacement: The Dynamics of the Refugee Crisis in Southern Africa", *3 Journal of Refugee Studies 46* (1990) at pp. 48–53. It has been noted that in the Malawi context, a distinction seems to be drawn between refugees stricto sensu, namely those persons confined to camps, and displaced persons, being either that group of individuals who leave their country of origin and integrate themselves into the local population or those who come for brief spells and return to their country of origin thereafter. It has further been noted that this distinction was made by the Malawian delegation during talks held with the United Nations High Commissioner for Refugees and his delegation on 23 April 1988 in Lilongwe, Malawi. Malawi is also said to have pointed out to the UNHCR that the term "displaced persons" was used for "its humane appeal rather than aversion to the term 'refugee'". See, in this regard, Mponda, *op. cit.* p. 21 n. 14. It can only be pointed out here that this is clearly not the sense in which the distinction between the two terms is normally understood in refugee studies.

54. It is acknowledged that one should be careful not to read a hidden agenda into these types of statements, but this interpretation does not appear to be as implausible and simplistic as it might at first seem when set within the wider historical framework in which Malawi-Mozambique relations, and Malawi's overall regional policy, have evolved over the past three and half decades. Moreover, a relevant historical factor not to be overlooked here is that trans-boundary migration and population movements involving people from Mozambique across the southern part of Malawi are not a recent, twentieth century, phenomenon. Traditionally, it suited the ruling authorities in the various Maravi "states" to incorporate such foreigners into the local body politic, partly as a way of consolidating their own political power and territorial jurisdiction. On this, see R.B. Boeder, *Silent Majority: A History of the Lomwe in Malawi*, (1984) *passim*;

55. Mazur, *op. cit.* p. 459.

56. Morna, *op. cit.* p. 58.

57. Thus, for example, the Refugees (Recognition and Control) Act of Botswana does not provide for group determination procedures despite the fact that Botswana was one of the first countries in the region to experience a mass refugee influx (mainly from South Africa) though not of the same scale and magnitude as the later influx into Malawi. By contrast, Zimbabwe's Refugees Act gives the Minister power to declare any class of persons refugees, provided such a declaration is published in the *Gazette* "and in such other manner as he considers will best ensure that it is brought to the attention of authorized officers and persons to whom it relates" (Section 3(2) and (3)).

58. See Mazur, *op. cit.* p. 460. But some estimates put the figures as high as 300,000 to 350,000. Such figures were at the time generally viewed as being too high and may not adequately have taken into account the number of persons who moved back and forth across the Malawi-Mozambique border on a regular basis. See Nunes and Wilson, *op. cit.* note 2 pp. 8–9.

59. Thus, while the machinery provided for under Sections 7, 8 and 13 of the Zimbabwe Refugees Act affords refugees and asylum-seekers protection against *refoulement* even where their initial entry was illegal, as is the case under the Malawian legislation, by contrast the Refugees (Recognition and Control) Act of Botswana does not contain any explicit provision in this regard, and Sections 5 and 6 of this Act cannot be said to have incorporated the principle of *non-refoulement* in its true sense.

60. Mazur, *op. cit.* p. 445.

61. This so-called absolute right has been challenged by some writers. See, for example, J. Nafziger, "The general admission of aliens under international law", *77 AJIL 804* (1983).

62. See note 9 *supra*. The general tenor of Malawi's reservations to Article 7, 13, 15, 19, 22 and 24 of the Convention is simply that it considers these provisions merely as recommendations and not legally binding obligations; in relation to articles 17 (wage-earning employment) and 34 (naturalization), the essence of the reservation is that Malawi does not consider itself bound to grant refugees any more favourable facilities or treatment than are granted, in accordance with the relevant laws and regulations, to aliens generally. Reservations of this nature are not uncommon among States parties to the Convention, and in some cases the limitations contained in such reservations have actually been embodied in the relevant municipal legislation.

V

TERRITORY, SOVEREIGNTY AND DISPUTE SETTLEMENT

9

THE PEACEFUL SETTLEMENT OF INTERNATIONAL DISPUTES IN POST-COLONIAL AFRICA: THE FIRST TWO DECADES

Introduction

The settlement of international disputes by peaceful means has been described as one of the principles basic to the whole structure of international society. Indeed, it has been contended that this principle is the natural corollary of the prohibition of the use of force in the settlement of international disputes enshrined in Article 2(4) of the UN Charter.[1] The principle is embodied in Article 2(3) of the Charter, which states: "All Members shall settle their international disputes by peaceful means in such a manner that international peace and security, and justice, are not endangered". The universality of this basic principle of international law is attested to by its adoption in various regional arrangements and treaty regimes. Thus, Article III of the Organization of African Unity Charter, for example, partly provides as follows:

> "The Member States, in pursuit of the purposes stated in Article II, solemnly affirm and declare their adherence to the following principles: [...]
>
> 4. [Peaceful] settlement of disputes by negotiation, mediation, conciliation or arbitration."

Furthermore, Article XIX provides:

> "Member States pledge to settle all disputes among themselves by peaceful means and, to this end decide to establish a Commission of Mediation,

> Conciliation and Arbitration, the composition of which and conditions of service shall be defined by a separate Protocol to be approved by the Assembly of Heads of State and Government. Said Protocol shall be regarded as forming an integral part of the present Charter."

In fact, it may be noted in this regard that, as is the case with the United Nations, the Organisation of African Unity ("the OAU") has defined dispute settlement as one of its major institutional objectives.[2] As is clear from the provision quoted above, the specific issue of dispute settlement was intended to be the responsibility of a specialized organ, the Commission of Mediation, Conciliation and Arbitration. The Protocol defining the constitution and powers of the Commission was concluded in Cairo, Egypt, on 21 July 1964.[3] Member States of the OAU are urged to resort to any one of three alternative modes of dispute settlement: mediation, conciliation and arbitration. But it is equally clear from Articles XIII(2), XIV and XX of the Protocol that the aim was not to establish a system of compulsory jurisdiction, but rather one that is dependent upon the consent of the parties.

Among African States, the principle of the peaceful settlement of international disputes has also, occasionally, been adopted at a different, more particularized level: namely, through the practice of including in treaties a provision enjoining the signatories to resolve all their disputes arising from the interpretation and application of such treaties by peaceful means. This has been the case, for example, with multilateral treaties establishing regional international organizations or similar alliances. The earliest example of such a provision can be seen in Article 7 of the Act Relating to Navigation and Economic Co-operation between the States of the Niger Basin concluded at Niamey, Niger, on 26 October 1963. This article states:

> "Any dispute that may arise between the riparian States regarding the interpretation or application of the present Act shall be amicably settled by direct agreement between them or through the Inter-Governmental Organisation referred to in Articles 5 and 6 above.
>
> Failing such settlement, the dispute shall be decided by arbitration, in particular by the Commission of Mediation, Conciliation and Arbitration of the Organisation of African Unity, or by judicial settlement by the International Court of Justice."

It is apt to observe here that there is implied in Article 7 of the Act of Niamey a distinction between two types of peaceful settlement of international disputes: settlement by legal means as opposed to settlement by *political* means.

This distinction has been emphasized by a number of scholars. Bowett, for example, has observed:[4]

> "[Yet] settlement of disputes by *peaceful* means is not the same as settlement by *legal* means. Realistically, we have to accept that the vast majority of disputes will be settled by political rather than by legal means." [Author's emphasis.]

Article 33(1) of the UN Charter lists the various methods of peaceful settlement as "negotiation, inquiry, mediation, conciliation, arbitration, judicial settlement, resort to regional agencies or arrangements, or other peaceful means". This list is not exhaustive, nor are the various methods ranked in any order of priority. However, two of these – arbitration and judicial settlement – may be said to represent what is generally understood as settlement by legal means, while the rest can be ranked together as denoting settlement by political means. But this is not to suggest a rigid and categorical differentiation between the two techniques of settlement; quite the contrary. For, as it has been observed, even settlement by political means often has to take into consideration the legal interests and rights of the disputants. Thus, Mosler states:[5]

> "No one questions the impossibility of drawing a satisfactory logical distinction between legal and political disputes or, more specifically, between disputes which may appropriately be decided by a court and those which require a political solution possibly by the decision of an international organ. [Even] delicate political matters which may directly affect world peace can still in theory be regulated entirely by treaties or general international law."

Indeed, as is sometimes the case, the parties themselves may invoke legal arguments even when pursuing what they regard as essentially a political settlement of their dispute. This has certainly been the case in some of those situations in which the peaceful settlement of disputes between African States has been attempted.[6]

The Principle of Peaceful Settlement

That the principle of the peaceful settlement of international disputes has been recognized and accepted as a binding principle of international law by African States cannot be doubted. At least that is the theoretical position.

The question that arises, however, is: to what extent has this theoretical acceptance been borne out by the actual practice of African States?

This question arises partly because, it may be observed, the charge has been made by some legal commentators that African States have paid only lip service to this basic principle of international law; that over the first quarter-century or so of their existence as independent States, African States have showed little inclination to resort to legal techniques for the settlement of their disputes. In fact, this is an observation that has been made not only with regard to the "new" African States, but also those belonging to the Asian bloc. In this regard, the view has often been advanced that it is lack of confidence in the international judicial system which has accounted for the relatively little use made of the International Court of Justice, and of arbitration, by the "new" African and Asian States. It has further been suggested that this lack of confidence derives from the European origins, and bias, of many of the rules of international law employed by such international judicial forums as the International Court of Justice, and the distrust of colonialism and neo-colonialism.7

These are very plausible explanations. No one can seriously doubt the loss of confidence, and mistrust, generated by the *South West Africa/Namibia* judgment of 1966 on the part of African States with respect to the whole question of international judicial settlement by the International Court. In fact some commentators, such as Falk,[8] have gone further and attributed great importance to the effects of the 1966 decision on the attitudes of Third World States in general. And, similarly, Gross has written of the "profound" and "widespread" dissatisfaction with that decision, which was expressed in criticism of the composition of the International Court of Justice and its insensitivity to anti-colonial and anti-apartheid sentiments as expressed in the various resolutions and declarations of the UN General Assembly.[9]

The question that arises, however, is whether, and to what extent, the issue of confidence has played any role in the attitudes of African States to the settlement of international disputes by political means. The question, indeed, is whether the issue of confidence pervades the whole process of dispute settlement in both its legal and political senses, or whether it is one whose relevance is to be limited only to considerations of settlement by legal techniques. Or has the issue of confidence, perhaps, been given a somewhat exaggerated account as an explanation for the apparent lack of interest shown by African (and Asian) States in the settlement of disputes by peaceful means? The scepticism is fairly apparent in Bowett's observations:[10]

> "[It] is difficult to subscribe to the view that a particular group of States is justified, for special reasons, in having less confidence than other States.

> For, to take the example of the Afro-Asian States, how does one account for the apparent upsurge of confidence that has brought Libya and Tunisia before the Court, or Libya and Malta? Or the relatively little use made by the African States of their own machinery, the Commission on [*sic*] Conciliation, Mediation and Arbitration, established by the OAU in 1964?"

Apropos of the apparent upsurge of confidence referred to here, it may also be noted that much more recently other African States referred their boundary disputes to the World Court for consideration under the new procedure for chambers of the Court, as well as under the normal procedure requiring the full sitting of the bench.[11]

But it is the second question posed by Bowett in the observation quoted above that this chapter seeks to address, that is: the relatively little use made by the African States of their own machinery, the Commission of Conciliation, Mediation and Arbitration. In fact one may, with all due respect, correct the learned author's observation and point out that the Commission has *never* been used by any African States for the settlement of their disputes. The issue is, therefore, not about the "relatively little use" but rather the *non*-use of the Commission.

One principal reason for looking at this issue is that, as it may be recalled, Article III(4) of the Organisation of African Unity Charter enjoins the member States to observe the principle of the peaceful settlement of disputes by negotiation, mediation, conciliation and arbitration. But, to reiterate the question already posed above in this regard, to what extent have these States manifested, in actual practice, their adherence to this principle of international law? This chapter attempts to answer this question by examining some of the pertinent aspects of African State practice in this area of international law in the first two decades of the existence of the OAU (1963 to 1983).

Most of the literature that has appeared on the attitudes of new States to international law in general, and to the peaceful settlement of international disputes in particular, has tended to be rather descriptive of what this attitude could or ought to be rather than of what it is in fact.[12] In the specific case of African States, some of the earlier literature tended to lean more towards expressions of academic optimism regarding their espousal of the lofty principles of international co-operation, peaceful settlement of disputes and African unity than towards empirical analyses of the actual attitudes of these States, based on an examination of their practice.[13]

The Commission of Mediation, Conciliation and Arbitration

Reference has already been made to the creation of the Commission of Mediation, Conciliation and Arbitration as one of the four principal organs of the OAU under Article XIX of the Charter (the other institutions being the Assembly of Heads of State and Government, the Council of Ministers, and the General Secretariat).

The adoption of the Protocol of the Commission of Mediation, Conciliation and Arbitration, which defined the composition and conditions of service of the Commission's members as well as the procedures for settling disputes, by the first ordinary session of the Assembly of Heads of State and Government in July 1964 was generally received with much optimistic approval. It was regarded as an expression, by the new African States, of their respect for, and adherence to, the ideal of international law and, in particular, the principle of peaceful settlement of international disputes. As Emperor Haile Selassie of Ethiopia was to comment later:[14]

> "[There] is nothing closer to our hearts than the task with which the Commission is entrusted, that is, the peaceful settlement of disputes. It is a task of great significance, for, without the conditions of security and peace, none of the objectives and aspirations enshrined in the Charter can be realised."

Similarly, the Secretary-General of the OAU went on to observe, during the first formal meeting of the Commission in 1968, that the functioning of the Commission was the *sine qua non* for the realization of all the aims and objectives pursued by African governments in order to achieve unity, progress and rehabilitation in every field. From the outset, it was emphasised that the Commission did not seek to establish compulsory jurisdiction, nor did it regard itself or, for that matter, the OAU, as possessing the right to impose sanctions on recalcitrant States. But the hope was nevertheless expressed, with equal emphasis, that the Commission would be able to generate enough confidence to make States willing to submit themselves to its jurisdiction, and thereby increase respect for the principle of peaceful settlement of disputes embodied in the OAU Charter.[15]

The subsequent history of the Commission during the first two decades of its existence has shown that these hopes and expressions of optimism were almost totally misplaced. Under the Cairo Protocol of 1964, the OAU's Assembly of Heads of State and Government was empowered to appoint 21 members who would constitute the Commission.[16] This was duly done at the OAU's second ordinary session in Accra, Ghana, in October 1965, but not until two years later was the Commission able to hold its first meeting. During this meeting, held in Addis Ababa from 11 to 15 December 1967, the Commission adopted its rules of procedure and its budget.[17]

That the Commission would be dogged by failure and a general lack of interest and widespread cynicism from the great majority of the OAU's member States themselves was evident almost from the outset. Of the 21 members elected to serve on the Commission, only 12 were able to attend its first meeting; some absentees had been arbitrarily and forcibly prevented by their governments from taking up their places on the Commission, while others simply did not communicate their acceptance or otherwise of the appointments. Indeed, it would appear that in some cases, certain States simply informed the Secretary-General of the OAU that their nationals who had been elected to serve on the Commission were no longer available and should be replaced.[18] Subsequent attempts by the Secretary-General to solicit more detailed explanations from the States concerned met with no response from most of them. This state of affairs continued until 1970.

The seventh ordinary summit of the Assembly of Heads of State and Government, held at the OAU's headquarters in Addis Ababa in 1970, was invited to examine various proposals aimed at reviving the moribund Commission. It was pointedly noted, for example, that during the entire five-year period in which the Commission had been struggling to translate its theoretical existence into reality, a number of disputes among various African States had been resolved, not through the mediation efforts of the Commission but through those of various African heads of State and *ad hoc* committees set up by the Assembly of Heads of State and Government. The proposal was made, therefore, that perhaps the key to the eventual success of the Commission lay in reconstituting it as an *ad hoc* body, with new members, conducting its business in the territories of those States involved in a dispute if and when called upon to do so.

These proposals were adopted by the Assembly of Heads of State and Government, and the Commission was duly reconstituted as an *ad hoc* body composed of part-time members rather than full-time functionaries with their own secretariat based at the OAU's headquarters in Addis Ababa. It is important to note in this regard, however, that one proposed amendment which the Assembly of Heads of State and Government felt unable to adopt was that relating to the functions of the Commission themselves. It had been suggested by the Secretary General, as early as 1968, that the functions of the Commission might be enlarged to enable it to act as an advisory body on legal questions arising out of the implementation and application of the Charter. The idea here was really that the Commission should exercise an *advisory* function similar to that exercised by the International Court of Justice. This idea never gained any support, whether among States or from legal scholars as such.

But even the reconstituted Commission did not fare any better than the previous body. Not a single dispute was referred to it during the subsequent years; and, in 1977, the Assembly of Heads of State and Government decided to reopen the issue of restructuring the Commission. Thus, a resolution which was adopted at the OAU's 14th ordinary session directed the Secretary-General:[19]

> "[To] reconsider, as a matter of urgency, the procedures contained in the Protocol of the Commission of Mediation, Conciliation and Arbitration, and submit recommendations for their modification to enable the Commission to react more promptly to crises whenever they explode anywhere in Africa and then submit a report to the thirty-first ordinary session of the Council of Ministers on all desirable improvements to be made on the Protocol."

One interesting development that came out of the 14th summit meeting was the formation of an "*ad hoc* committee on inter-African disputes". Unlike the various other *ad hoc* good-offices committees established over the previous years to deal with particular disputes, this committee was meant to be more or less permanent, with a standing mandate to function for as long as the Commission was unable to carry out its functions.[20] To date, the Commission has not carried out any of the functions stipulated in the Protocol. Further proposals to amend the Protocol (including the proposal by a committee of legal experts in 1979 to the effect that the decisions of the Commission should be regarded merely as recommendations to the Assembly of Heads of State and Government, who would then consider them and take up their implementation with the heads of State of the countries involved in the dispute) have not changed the position. It is quite clear, therefore, that the history of the Commission of Mediation, Conciliation and Arbitration has been nothing but a lesson in abject inactivity and irrelevance, at least as far as the *practice* of peaceful settlement of international disputes is concerned.

The Practice Adopted by States

In the two decades from 1963 to 1983, there were about 50 major disputes among African States which required, or were at least submitted to, third-party mediation or conflict resolution. Of these mediation efforts, only 30 could be said to have originated from the OAU. None of these, however, had anything to do with the Commission of Mediation, Conciliation and Arbitration.

A number of factors characterise these disputes. First, apart from the two referred to the International Court of Justice,[21] all the disputes have involved settlement by political or diplomatic means (that is to say, mediation, conciliation or negotiation) rather than settlement by legal means, namely judicial settlement or arbitration. The most notable exception here relates to the dispute regarding the distribution of the assets of the defunct East African Community (involving Kenya, Uganda and Tanzania) which was, by common consent, submitted to arbitration.[22]

Second, as has already been alluded to above, none of the States involved in the various disputes ever invoked the Commission of Mediation, Conciliation and Arbitration in the resolution of such disputes. Exclusive emphasis has been placed on either *ad hoc* mediation committees (or commissions) or good offices, usually under the aegis of a head of State. As intimated earlier, some commentators have wondered why African States have found it easier to repose their confidence, trust and so on in such *ad hoc* committees but not in the standing Commission, even when such *ad hoc* committees are also a product of the OAU's machinery and diplomacy.

The third characteristic of these disputes is that almost all those arising during the period under review belong to the categories of territorial disputes or disputes involving jurisdiction and/or control over persons and property. Within these categories, one may identify different types of case: border disputes, allegations of subversion by one State against another, civil wars raging in one State but allegedly instigated or supported by another State or by elements within that other State, and so on.

Ad hoc Commissions and Solitary Diplomacy

While echoing the observation that as long as the Commission of Mediation, Conciliation and Arbitration is incapable of coming into being *ad hoc* commissions are, and will continue to be, the organs used for conflict resolution, Kouassi has gone on to observe that these organs:[23]

> "[Utilise] classical procedures for the peaceful settlement of international disputes. These extend from the solitary diplomacy of the 'peace pilgrims' to the resources of conciliation, mediation, inquiry, consultation, even arbitration."

Kouassi is of the view that the essence of solitary diplomacy – referred to above as mediation under the aegis of a head of State – is that the intervention of certain African heads of State acts as a mechanism for dissuasion, inhibition, or pacification. In other words, that while this type of diplomatic exercise may not in itself provide a definitive resolution of the conflict, it nevertheless serves the effective purpose of preparing for the institution of a commission for the peaceful settlement of the dispute in question.

Kouassi's position here would appear to be somewhat over-generalized and exaggerated. The effectiveness of this method of conflict resolution is rather modest. Success was recorded by Emperor Haile Selassie and President Modibo Keita of Mali in the Morocco-Algeria conflict of 1963; by President Abboud of Sudan in the Ethiopia-Somalia dispute of 1964; by President Mobutu Sese Seko of Zaire in the Rwanda-Burundi dispute of 1966. Similarly, the mediation efforts of President Eyadema of Togo resolved a border dispute between Mali and Burkina Faso in 1974 and, subsequently in 1978, led to a reconciliation between Ivory Coast, Guinea and Senegal. These are only some of the major examples of successful mediation efforts. But, equally, one can also catalogue a number of examples on the negative side: the failure recorded by President Julius Nyerere in respect of the Kenya-Somalia frontier dispute (1965); by President Kaunda in his efforts to resolve differences between Somalia, Kenya and Ethiopia (1967); by President Gaddafi in the Tanzania-Uganda war (1979) and, more particularly, by the various heads of State who have attempted, both severally and collectively, to reconcile the warring factions within Chad (an internal dispute) and the related territorial dispute between Chad and Libya (an inter-State dispute) over the years.[24]

But even assuming that such solitary diplomacy does play an important function of moderating and reducing tension between parties pending a more definitive settlement by a wider commission, the question remains as to how far such *ad hoc* commissions, utilizing the classical procedures referred to earlier, have succeeded in providing permanent solutions to the numerous inter-State disputes that have arisen among African States. As indicated earlier, such classical procedures are usually conciliation and mediation. Some authorities regard "negotiation" as an additional category, while yet others particularize "consultation and inquiry".[25] My view is that the latter two are not so much separate categories of dispute settlement as preliminary stages to settlement either by mediation, conciliation or, indeed, arbitration. This is not to deny that the institutions of consultation and enquiry are, in their operational senses, of great importance and frequent components of dispute settlement.

In any event, the only notable attempt at employing a commission of consultation and enquiry in the context of dispute settlement arose in the wake of the Nigerian civil war. But then, as a number of scholars have already observed,[26] it is most doubtful whether the ill-fated OAU Commission that was set up in November 1967 (some six months after the commencement of hostilities) could be considered as a procedure for peaceful settlement of disputes at all, since its alignment with one of the parties to the conflict was barely disguised.

Conciliation

Conciliation has been attempted on more occasions but, again, with rather unsatisfactory results. Conciliation has been defined as:[27]

> "[A] method for the settlement of international disputes of any nature according to which a commission set up by the [parties] proceeds to the impartial examination of the dispute and attempts to define the terms of a settlement susceptible of being accepted by them, or of affording the parties, with a view to its settlement, such aid as they may have requested."

Two important points must be noted regarding this process. First, unlike arbitration or judicial settlement, conciliation does not aim at imposing a binding solution on the parties, merely one that may be accepted as a basis for the settlement of the dispute. Second, unlike a mere consultation or an enquiry, the *raison d'être* of conciliation is not simply to shed light on the dispute, but actually to conciliate (or reconcile) the disputant States in the real sense of the word. For these reasons, it is suggested that the key to a successful conciliation is that the States concerned must retain control over the dispute, to avoid the possibility of producing a result that would then be rejected out of hand by the parties.[28]

Two of the earliest, and most important, instances of conciliation commissions involving African States were created in 1964 and 1966 respectively. The former, comprising Cameroon, Ethiopia, Guinea, Somalia, Nigeria, Egypt, Tunisia, Kenya and Upper Volta (as Burkina Faso was then known) was established to look into the Congo conflict. The 1966 commission, comprising Kenya, Sierra Leone and Zaire, was charged with the task of reconciling Ghana and Guinea over certain disputes arising from the overthrow of President Nkrumah's government in Ghana. Neither commission succeeded. It would appear that one of the possible explanations for the failure of these conciliation missions was the highly political – as opposed to legal – elements that characterized the disputes in question. For I am in full agreement with Merrills who, after a brief but instructive survey of conciliation practices, has aptly observed that conciliation has proved most useful for disputes where the main issues are legal, but the parties desire an equitable compromise.[29] Purely political disputes appear not to be susceptible to the conciliation processes – at least conciliation in its restrictive, operational sense as a formal technique for the settlement of disputes.

There is another important factor which most modern writers on this subject have quite correctly identified: the continuing, some would say growing, popularity of conciliation as a technique of third-party settlement of disputes. Quite apart from the retention of conciliation in bilateral treaty practice over the past half-century, there is also its continued incorporation into some of the major multilateral treaties of modern times. The Vienna Convention on the Law of Treaties (1969) and the UN Convention on the Law of the Sea (1982) are only some of the more recent examples. But to what extent have African nations been part of this trend?

The available evidence suggests that no African treaty, whether bilateral or multilateral, contains any provisions incorporating the kind of conciliation procedures provided for in the treaties referred to above. Of course, as was indicated earlier in respect of Article 7 of the Act of Niamey of 1963, there are those treaties which do contain provisions enjoining the signatories to resolve all their disputes arising from the interpretation or application of such treaties by peaceful means. But a proper examination of these provisions shows that they aim at either settlement by direct negotiations between the parties, or mediation or arbitral settlement by an organ or a tribunal stipulated under the treaty, and not at conciliation procedures as such. An early example of this type of provision is Article 56 of the Economic Community of West African States Treaty of 28 May 1975:

> "Any dispute that may arise among member States regarding the interpretation or application of this Treaty shall be amicably settled by direct agreement. In the event of failure to settle such disputes, the matter may be referred to the Tribunal of the Community by a party to such disputes and decisions of the Tribunal shall be final."

This provision was more recently incorporated, almost verbatim, into the Treaty for the Establishment of the Preferential Trade Area for Eastern and Southern African States of 21 December 1981.[30]

Mediation

Among the classical procedures for the peaceful settlement of disputes, mediation has clearly been the most frequently tried formula among African States over the past quarter-century. The question is whether the practical achievements or consequences of these mediation efforts give us a clear indication, one way or the other, of the actual operation of the principle of peaceful settlement of international disputes among these States, quite aside from the theoretical espousal of this principle alluded to earlier. Mediation is generally regarded as an extension of negotiations, except that here a third party – an international organisation, a State or an individual – is brought in to play a direct and more decisive role. The functions of such a mediator may be simply to provide good offices and facilitate the reduction of tension or hostilities between the disputants; but a mediator may also be required to effect a more substantive examination of the dispute and advance his own proposals for a solution.[31]

The key to a successful mediation is, of course, consent: not only is availability of a mediator a prerequisite, but the parties to the dispute must also consent to the particular mediator or mediators. These issues are so obvious that they tend to be overlooked by most commentators on this issue. Take the question repeatedly posed by some scholars: why is it that African States have not utilized the mediation and arbitral machinery which they themselves set up back in 1964, namely the Commission of Mediation, Conciliation and Arbitration? The point that is overlooked here is that since, in fact, the Commission has never been actually constituted as envisaged under the Cairo Protocol, as was shown in the brief historical account above, the question of States taking their disputes to *that* Commission does not logically arise. For, in a real sense, there are no agreed mediators to take the disputes to, hence States' recourse to *ad hoc* mediation commissions, sometimes still under the aegis of the OAU, at other times independently of it. The correct question to ask, in my view, is not why African States have made no use of their own Commission of Mediation, Conciliation and Arbitration, but why they have never been able to go beyond the theoretical provisions in the OAU Charter and the Protocol to ensure the actual materialization of the envisaged Commission. Why has the Commission failed where the various *ad hoc* mediation committees referred to earlier seem to succeed?

The Issues of Confidence and Control

The picture is somewhat mixed, combining as it does what are essentially political considerations on the one hand, and legal considerations on the other. To begin with, it is quite evident that the Commission was unable to become operational during the first few years of its "existence" largely due to a certain lack of the requisite political goodwill from some of the very States which had agitated for its creation back in 1964.[32] Moreover, there was the perennial problem of budgetary contributions which has plagued the OAU for the greater part of its existence. As the Secretary-General noted in his report to the Council of Ministers as recently as July 1978 – some 14 years after the conclusion of the Cairo Protocol – the Commission had not been provided with funds even for its inaugural meeting to establish its rules of procedure.[33] The combined effect of these political and financial problems was the emergence of a functional paralysis almost from the outset.

From the legal point of view, there was an even more fundamental problem, which could be characterised as an inherent unworkability in the very idea of d commission of mediation, conciliation, and so on, as conceived under the OAU's arrangements.

During the tenth ordinary session of the Council of Ministers in Addis Ababa in February 1968, Kenya and other States warned that it was not necessary to have a permanent bureau for the Commission since almost all countries with disputes to be settled preferred to have eminent personalities in whom they had confidence to handle their disputes.[34] Attempts to use this line of argument to block the approval of the Commission's budget did not altogether succeed. All the same, these sentiments embodied a crucial legal issue that should not be overlooked here: the issue of confidence.

Jenks, among others, has suggested that the crucial factor in persuading States to accept legal techniques of settlement is confidence. He argues: "The essence of the question is confidence; confidence in the stability and adequacy of the law, and confidence in the integrity and predictability of the courts and tribunals administering the law".[35] It is also significant that in his address to its first formal meeting, in 1968, the Commission's President expressed the hope that its members would be able to establish enough confidence to make the OAU's member States willing to submit themselves to the jurisdiction of the Commission.[36]

It would seem that closely related to this issue of confidence is the question of control: the claim that one of the deterrents to resorting to settlement by legal means is the feeling States have that, by doing so, they lose control of the case. Bowett has put the matter quite succinctly:[37]

> "[Whilst] specific reasons change from State to State, the basic reason for avoiding legal settlement is simply that States prefer to retain control over the settlement process, so as to ensure either that any settlement is acceptable to them or, if that cannot be achieved, that no settlement is reached."

Bowett goes on to conclude that with political techniques States retain such control, whereas with legal techniques States evidently lose control. It is submitted here that the issues of confidence and control of the settlement process provide the key to much that is seemingly puzzling in the attitude of African States toward the settlement of disputes, in general, and the Commission of Conciliation, Mediation and Arbitration in particular.

The inherent unworkability of the Commission of Mediation, Conciliation and Arbitration alluded to earlier on arises from the following considerations: first of all, although it is true that according to Article XIV of the Protocol the Commission can exercise jurisdiction over disputes only with the consent of the parties involved, it must be emphasised, however, that once such consent has been granted, the right of the parties to retain and exercise control over the settlement process becomes rather limited. It will be observed that under the Protocol, the right of the parties to chose the mediators, members of the conciliation board or arbitrators is clearly restricted. It is true that in the first two cases the appointments by the President of the Commission have to be consented to by the parties to the dispute, and that in the case of arbitration the parties themselves actually have the right to choose one arbitrator each. But in all these instances, all the appointments can be only from among those persons already serving on the Commission. In other words, the Protocol does not provide for the possibility of parties to a dispute choosing anybody from *outside* the Commission, even if they agreed to it.

It is this very ability to exercise unfettered control over the choice of negotiators, conciliators or mediators that lies at the heart of what the various authorities have termed the "right to retain and exercise control over the settlement process". And, as has been noted above, this characteristic marks out the essential difference between settlement of disputes by political or diplomatic means and settlement by legal means. This is not to deny that parties to a dispute submitted to settlement by legal means – arbitration and judicial settlement – may, and often do, enjoy some measure of control over the settlement process. But, then, a judicial tribunal, whether an arbitral tribunal or a standing court, cannot be subjected to unfettered control by the disputant States if it is to operate as an independent judicial body, applying the law in an impartial and objective manner. There must needs be limits to the control the parties can enjoy in such situations, limits which are not pertinent where the parties are merely seeking a political solution or accommodation for their dispute instead of a judicial settlement *stricto sensu.*

Thus, while it might appear as if the parties to an arbitration are granted unrestricted control over the settlement process under Articles XXVII and XXIX of the Protocol, clearly the principle of *jus cogens* and non-derogation from peremptory norms would operate to deny them the right to agree on any rules whatsoever to govern their dispute; nor, it may be added, are the parties at liberty to agree on procedural rules that may, in fact, impinge upon the arbitrators' judicial function and, indeed, independence.

Having regard to the above considerations, it would not be unreasonable to conclude that the structure of the Commission and the settlement machinery provided for in the Protocol are not such as would permit the parties an unfettered right to retain control over the settlement process. This, in its turn, means that the confidence needed to make the OAU's member States willing to submit themselves to its jurisdiction can never be established. I believe that it is precisely this issue of confidence which would provide an adequate explanation as to why these States have preferred to submit their disputes to *ad hoc* committees, over which they have a considerable degree of control, instead of submitting to the jurisdiction of the Commission. It would be quite wrong to suggest, as some authorities appear to have done that the issue of confidence is not an adequate and valid explanation for the generally unenthusiastic attitude of some States towards the settlement of international disputes. This explanation becomes even more valid when one turns to consider the preference of these African States for political or diplomatic settlement over legal settlement. For it is an established fact that the *ad hoc* committees, whether appointed under the aegis of the OAU or not, have always varied from good offices to mediation, negotiation and conciliation, but never embraced arbitral or judicial settlement. In this regard it is doubtful whether the handful of disputes which have been submitted to judicial settlement – between Tunisia and Libya, Burkina Faso and Mali and, more recently, Cameroon and Nigeria, and Namibia and Botswana – before the International Court of Justice[38] – can be regarded as such an upsurge of confidence as might signal a significant change in the general attitude of African States towards the peaceful settlement of international disputes.

Conclusion

The principle of settlement of disputes by peaceful means still remains to be translated from the largely theoretical desideratum that it presently is into a real aspect of African State practice. The evidence relating to the readiness and willingness of African States to submit their disputes to third-party conflict resolution and management leaves a lot to be desired. And even in the limited area of political or diplomatic settlement, the overriding function of the various *ad hoc* commissions of mediation and conciliation has been merely to act as "tension reducers" rather than to prescribe definitive solutions to the disputes in question. Small wonder, therefore, that there have been instances of a recurrence of disputes in certain situations in which previous mediation efforts in respect of the same disputes had recorded apparent success. The most instructive example here is that of the Burkina Faso-Mali boundary dispute: although it had, apparently, been resolved politically through Togolese President Eyadema's mediation back in 1974, as was indicated earlier, it is only the recent ruling by the chamber of the International Court of Justice that appears to have provided an acceptable legal solution to the dispute. In general, the *ad hoc* commissions have tended to avoid pronouncing on the international legal rights and wrongs of the disputants or, still less, to apportion *culpa* in all such disputes. This is to be expected since, as has been pointed out in this article, the whole essence of settlement by political means is that the parties seek to achieve an equitable compromise and not necessarily a legal solution that properly ascribes the parties' respective legal rights and obligations.

The claim that the Organization of African Unity, in pursuance of the so-called "try OAU first" principle, assumed primary responsibility for certain complex and seemingly insoluble problems, and that it indeed established undisputed jurisdiction as a body of first instance over inter-State disputes during the first two decades of independence, must surely be regarded as an extravagant exaggeration of the real position.[39] On the contrary, it must be admitted that, if anything, the enthusiasm which States did display regarding the acceptance of the jurisdiction of the OAU over their disputes in the first decade (1963–1973) slackened quite significantly during the second decade of the OAU's existence, and even more so during the first half of the third decade. Having regard to these continuing trends in the practice of African States it is difficult to subscribe to the claims of undisputed jurisdiction accorded to the OAU. But, equally, I do not share the view, mooted by some earlier commentators,[40] that the solution to the problems raised here lies in the transformation of the Commission into a Court of Conciliation, Mediation and Arbitration or the creation of a special international court for African States.[41] The past and present trends in the attitudes and practice of African States regarding the settlement of international disputes by *legal* means do not suggest that such a court would succeed where the Commission of Conciliation, Mediation and Arbitration has failed. The creation of the "Mechanism for Conflict Prevention, Management and Resolution" within the OAU by the Assembly of Heads of State and Government on 29 June 1993 in Cairo, Egypt, signified a new and deliberate attempt to institutionalize the *political* means of dispute settlement in preference to *legal* mechanisms.[42] It also signified a recognition by the OAU itself of its failure to operationalize and implement the Protocol establishing the Commission on Mediation, Conciliation and Arbitration adopted by the Assembly of Heads of State and Government, also in Cairo, some thirty years earlier. An assessment of the success or failure of this new mechanism requires a separate study from the present discussion.

Creation of ad hoc commission / committee	*Parties to the mediation*	*Charge/task*	*Results (Task achieved: yes/no; dispute contained; conflict management)*
Oct. 1963. Bamako*	Ethiopia, Mali	Morocco-Algeria cease-fire	Yes
CM2. Nov. 1963 Dar-es-Salaam	Ethiopia, Mali, Ivory Coast, Nigeria, Senegal, Sudan, Tanzania	Reconcile Morocco-Algeria on border conflict	Conflict management
Feb. 1963 Khartoum*	Sudan	Ethiopia-Somalia cease-fire	Yes
CM3, Sept. 1964 Addis Ababa	Cameroon, Ethiopia, Egypt, Guinea, Ghana, Kenya, Nigeria, Somalia, Burkina Faso, Tunisia	Reconcile Zaire and Rebels. Normalize Zaire-Congo-Burundi relations	Decision favourable to Zaire
CM5, June 1965 Lagos	Gabon, Ethiopia, Mali, Nigeria, Tunisia	Reconcile Ivory Coast, Niger and Ghana	Yes
CM5, Oct. 1965 Accra	Tanzania	Reconcile Somalia and Kenya	No
CM7, Nov. 1966 Addis Ababa	Kenya, Sierra, Leone, Zaire	Reconcile Guinea and Ghana, free Guineans in Ghana	Conflict management
AHG3, Nov. 1966 Addis Ababa	Egypt, Ethiopia, Liberia	Free Guinean hostages	Yes
AHG3, Nov. 1966 Addis Ababa	Egypt, Ethiopia, Liberia, Mali, Tanzania	Reconcile Guinea and Ghana	Yes
AHG3, Nov. 1966 Addis Ababa	Zaire	Reconcile Rwanda and Burundi	Yes
AHG4, Sept. 1967 Kinshasa	Cameroon, Ethiopia, Ghana, Liberia, Nigeria, Zaire	Enquiry and consult Nigeria on Biafra	No

AHG4, Sept. 1967 Kinshasa	Zambia	Reconcile Somalia, Kenya and Ethiopia	Conflict management
1963–1969*	Senegal, Tunisia, Guinea, Algeria	Reconcile Morocco and Mauritania	Yes
AHG8, June 1971 Addis Ababa	Algeria, Cameroon, Ethiopia, Niger, Liberia, Mali, Mauritania, Somalia, Assembly of Heads of State and Government	Reconcile Guinea and Senegal	Yes
Sept. 1972*		Reconcile Uganda and Tanzania	Yes
AHG10, May 1973 Addis Ababa	Guinea, Liberia, Mali, Nigeria, Senegal	Reconcile Ethiopia and Somalia	No
1975	Guinea, Niger, Senegal, Togo	Reconcile Mali and Burkina Faso	Yes
AHG13, July 1976 Pt Louis	Burundi, Ethiopia, Rwanda, Sudan, Zambia, Zaire, Cameroon, Lesotho, Liberia, Mauritius, Nigeria, Senegal, Sudan, Tanzania	Reconcile Ethiopia and Somalia	No
July 1977*	Algeria	End Egypt-Libya war	Yes
AHG14, July 1977 Libreville	Algeria, Gabon, Mozambique, Nigeria, Cameroon, Senegal	Reconcile Chad and Libya	No
AHG14, July 1977 Libreville	Sudan, Central African Republic, Gabon, Gambia, Madagascar, Nigeria, Togo, Tunisia, Zambia, Zaire	Reconcile Tanzania and Uganda	No
AHG14, July 1977 Libreville	Sudan, Central African Republic, Gabon, Gambia, Madagascar, Nigeria, Togo, Tunisia, Zambia, Zaire	Reconcile Tanzania and Uganda	No
AHG14, July 1977 Libreville	Angola, Guinea, Libya, Mozambique, Niger, Nigeria, Zambia	Enquiry into attack on Benin	Reported

AHG14, July 1977	Algeria, Cameroon, Gabon, Nigeria, Sierra Leone, Senegal, Togo, Zaire, Zambia	Reconcile Ethiopia and Sudan	Yes
AHG15, July 1978 Khartoum	Guinea, Ivory Coast, Mali, Nigeria, Sudan, Tanzania; later, Sierra Leone, Nigeria	Resolve Saharan dispute; later implement recommendations	No
AHG15, July 1978 Khartoum	Tanzania, Zaire	Reconcile Burundi and Rwanda	Yes
1978*	Liberia, Togo	Reconcile Ivory Coast, Guinea Senegal	Yes
AHG15, July 1978 Khartoum	Cameroon, Nigeria, Rwanda, Sudan	Supervise Zaire-Angola reconciliation	Yes
Feb. 1979*	Libya	Mediate Uganda-Tanzania war	No
AHG16, July 1979 Monrovia	Ivory Coast, Liberia	Reconcile Gabon and Benin	Yes
CM34, Feb. 1980 Addis Ababa	Liberia	Reconcile Tunisia and Libya	Yes
AHG19, June 1983 Addis Ababa	Benin, Cameroon, Congo, Guinea, Libya, Niger, Nigeria, Central African Republic, Sudan, Togo, Ethiopia	Reconcile Chad factions and Chad and Libya	No

Notes:
*Established without the assistance of OAU.
CM = Established by Council of Ministers of OAU.
AHG = Established by Assembly of Heads of State and Government of OAU.

Source:
This compilation is based, in part, on information available in *African Research Bulletin*, *Keesing's Contemporary Archives*, and El-Ayouty and Zartman (Eds.), *The OAU After Twenty Years* (Praeger Publishers, New York, 1984).

Notes

1. See D.W. Bowett, "Contemporary Developments in Legal Techniques in the Settlement of Disputes", *183 Hague Recueil 177* (1983).

2. See Arts. II(1)(e) and III(4) of the OAU Charter.

3. Text in 3 I.L.M. 1116 (1963).

4. Bowett, *op. cit.* p. 177.

5. H. Mosler, *The International Society as a Legal Community*, (1980) pp. 282–283.

6. A classic example was the Leté Island dispute between Benin and Niger. Legal arguments were invoked by both parties throughout the duration of the dispute (1960–1965) although what was sought and achieved – partly through direct negotiations between the disputants and partly through the mediation of the *Conseil de l'Entente* – was not a legal settlement as such but a political settlement.

7. See, for example, Bowett, *op. cit.* p. 180; see also J.K. Gamble and Fischer, *The International Court of Justice*, (1976) pp. 24–25 and the literature cited therein; I. Shihata, "The Attitude of the New States Toward International Law", *19 Int' Org. 203* (1965); R.P. Anand, "Attitude of the 'New' Asian-African Countries Toward the International Court of Justice", *4 Int. Studies 119* (1962); M. Mushkat, "The African Approach to Some Basic Problems of Modern International Law", *7 Ind. J Int'l L 335* (1967); H. Fox, "The Settlement of Disputes by Peaceful Means and the Observance of International Law: African Attitudes", in *International Relations* (1968) (the David Davies Memorial Institute of International Studies), Vol. 3, No. 6. See also Y. Makonnen, *International Law and the New States of Africa*, (1983) pp. 85–97.

8. Quoted by Gamble and Fischer, *ibid.* at p. 25. It is also instructive to note the statement by Ghana to the ninth session of the Asian-African Legal Consultative Committee in New Delhi: the statement probably reflected the views of the rest of independent Africa:

   "The decision of the International Court of Justice which, in effect, has given legal sanctity and blessing to the claims of [South Africa] must constitute a serious affront to the legal conscience of the world community and shake the very basis of decency in international life. It is the unspeakable irony of our time that an institution of the order of the International Court of Justice, forged out of contemporary norms and principles, should be used to frustrate and stultify the implementation and furtherance of these ideals".

   See Asian-African Legal Consultative Committee, *Report of Ninth Session, New Delhi, 18–29 December 1967* (Secretariat of the Committee, New Delhi), p. 85.

9. L. Gross, "The International Court of Justice: Considerations of requirements for Enhancing its Role in the International Legal Order", 56 *AJIL 256* (1971), at p. 267. See also, generally, "The International Court of Justice and the United Nations", *120 Hague Recueil 313* (1967); L.C. Green, "The UN, S.W. Africa and the World", *7 Ind. J. Int. L. 491* (1976).

10. Bowett, *op. cit.* note 1 *supra*, at p. 180.

11. *Frontier Dispute* (*Burkina Faso* v *Mali*): judgment of the chamber delivered on 22 December 1986; see [1986] I.C.J. Rep. 554. At the time of writing, two cases involving boundary disputes between four African States (*Botswana* v *Namibia*, and *Cameroon* v *Nigeria*) are pending before the World Court.

12. See, for example, Shihata, *op. cit.* p. 203; J. Brierly, *The Law of Nations*, (1963), p. 43; see also the literature cited in note 7 *supra*.

13. See, for example, the overly optimistic sentiments expressed by B. Andemichael and D. Nicol, "The OAU: Primacy in Seeking African Solutions within the UN Charter", in El-Ayouty and I. Zartman (Eds.), *The OAU After Twenty Years*, (1984) pp. 101 *et seq*. For some of the earlier perspectives on the role of the OAU in dispute settlement, see B. Andemichael, *Peaceful Settlement among African States: Roles of the United Nations and the Organisation of African Unity*, (1972), UNITAR Study, PS No. 5; B.D. Meyers, "Intra-regional Conflict Management by the OAU", 28 Int. Org. 345 (1974); Morjane, "*L'Organisation de l'Unité Africaine et le règlement pacifique des différends africaines*", *31 Rev. Egypt. de droit internationale 17* (1975). For more recent views see Adeniran, "Pacific Settlement Among African States: The Role of African Unity", *2 Conflict Quarterly* 8 (1981); M. Wolfers, "The Organisation of African Unity as Mediator", in S. Touval and I. Zartman (Eds.), *International Mediation in Theory and Practice*, (1985), pp. 175 *et seq*.

14. Quoted in C.O. Amate, *Inside the OAU: Pan-Africanism in Practice*, (1986) p. 158.

15. *Ibid.*

16. Art. II(1) of the Protocol.

17. The Assembly of Heads of State and Government had appointed Mr. Justice M.A. Odesanya (Nigeria), Dr. W.C. Daniels (Ghana) and Dr. A.R. N'Gandzadi (Congo) as President and Vice-Presidents respectively. However, efforts by the Secretary General of the OAU to convene a meeting of these and other members of the Commission remained wholly futile until the fourth Ordinary Session of the OAU Assembly of Heads of State and Government in Kinshasa, Zaire, in September 1967 when the Assembly mandated the Secretary General to proceed

with the inaugural meeting of the Commission irrespective of how many Commissioners were able to attend. For details, see 5 *Africa Research Bulletin 1924* (1967).

18. See, generally, *Review of Activities*, 1963–1968, General Secretariat, OAU Off. Doc. (1968, Addis Ababa); see also Amate, *op. cit.* p. 160.

19. AHG Res. 109 (XIV), December 1977.

20. The committee consisted of seven States: Gabon, Madagascar, Nigeria, Togo, Tunisia, Zaire and Zambia, with Nigeria acting as chairman. In addition, three States would be co-opted on to the committee from the region most immediately affected by each dispute. This committee never became any more operational than the Commission itself.

21. The two cases referred to here are the *Continental Shelf* (*Tunisia* v *Libya*) case [1982] I.C.J. Rep. 18, and *Frontier Dispute* (*Burkina Faso* v *Mali*) [1986] I.C.J. Rep. 554. The *South West Africa/Namibia* cases are not included here since the commencement of the proceedings fell outside the period under review and, in any case, involved issues going far beyond the narrower definition of "inter-African" disputes. Similarly, the *Continental Shelf* (*Libya* v *Malta*) case [1985] I.C.J. Rep. 13 has not been taken into account since the other party to the dispute was a non-African State.

22. Following the collapse of the East African Community in June 1977, Dr. Victor Umbricht, a Swiss national, was appointed in 1978, at the suggestion of the World Bank, to mediate on issues relating to the Community's finances; see 28 *Keesings' Cont. Arch. 31497* (1982).

23. Kouassi, "The OAU and International Law", in El-Ayouty and Zartman, *op. cit.* note 13 *supra*, at pp. 45, 49.

24. See table appended at the end of this chapter for a summary of the major disputes between African States from 1963 to 1983.

25. For an excellent but concise account of the various methods of international dispute settlement, see J.G. Merrills, *International Dispute Settlement*, (2nd ed., 1991). See also Pechota, *Complementary Structures of Third-Party Settlement in International Disputes*, (1991), UNITAR Study PS No. 3; Randolph, *Third Party Settlement of Disputes in Theory and Practice*, (1973); W. Jenks, *The Prospects of International Adjudication*, (1964); H. Waldock (Ed.), *International Deputes: The Legal Aspects*, (1972); M. Lachs, "Some Reflections on the Settlement of International Disputes", 68 *Proc. Am. Soc. Int. L 323* (1974).

26. See, for example, Kouassi, *op. cit.* pp. 50–55; See also Achuku, "Peaceful Settlement of Disputes: Unresolved Problem for the OAU (A case study of the Nigeria-Biafra Conflict)", *24 Africa Today 39* (1977); Y. Tandon, "The Organization of African unity", *Round Table* (April 1972), p. 223.

27. Art. 1 of the Regulations on the Procedure of International Conciliation adopted by the Institut de droit international in 1961; see *49 Annuaire de l'Inst. 385* (1961). In his classic monograph, Cot has defined conciliation as: "[Intervention] in the settlement of an international dispute by a body having no political authority of its own, but enjoying the confidence of the parties to the dispute and entrusted with the task of investigating every aspect of the dispute and proposing a solution which is not binding on the parties". See J.-P. Cot, *International Conciliation*, (1968) p. 9.

28. This view is widely shared by all major writers on the subject. See, in particular, the discussion by Bowett, *op. cit.* at pp. 181–184; see also G. Fitzmaurice, "The Future of International Law", in *Livre du Centenaire* 1873–1973, *Institut de droit international*, (1973) Annex 4, p. 360; Touval and Zartman, *op. cit. passim.*

29. Merrills, *op. cit.* p. 77.

30. Art, 40; see 21 I.L.M. 479, 495 (1982).

31. Excellent accounts of both the theoretical and practical aspects of mediation are to be found in Touval and Zartman, *op. cit.* note 13 *supra*. See also Northedge and Donelan, *International Disputes: The Political Aspects*, (1971) Chap. 13; Edmead, "Analysis and Prediction in International Mediation", in Raman (Ed.), *Dispute Settlement Through the United Nations*, (1977); Rubin (Ed.), *Dynamics of Third Party Intervention*, (1981) Chap. 1; Waldock, *op. cit.* note 25 *supra*.

32. Amate, *op. cit.* at pp. 25–162.

33. See OAU Off. Doc. CM/1924 (XXXI).

34. Amate, *op. cit.* p. 117. The question of confidence was evidently regarded as an important factor in Kenyan policy on this issue. It is instructive to note the views of the Kenyan representative in the UN General Assembly's Sixth Committee (Mr. F.X. Njenga) during a debate on the role of the ICJ on 4 November 1970: "[Before] confidence in judicial settlement would be complete, it was necessary to ensure that the applicable law served the interests of the whole international community and not merely sectional interests". See UNGA Off. Rec., 24th Sess., Sixth Committee (A/C.6/SR.1213) (4 November 1970), pp. 8–9.

35. Jenks, *op. cit.* p. 104.

36. Amate, *loc. cit.* note 14 *supra*.

37 Bowett, *op. cit.* p. 181; see also Fitzmaurice, *loc. cit.* note 28 *supra*.

38. See note 21 *supra*.

39. See, for example, Andemichael and Nicol, *op. cit.* p. 103.

40. See Amate, *op. cit.* p. 168.

41. I am not here referring to the more recent developments regarding the establishment of an African Court on Human and Peoples' Rights, which I fully support. A protocol to the African Charter on Human and Peoples' Rights establishing this court was adopted by the Assembly of Heads of State and Government during its 34th Ordinary Session in Ougadougou, Burkina Faso, on 9 June 1998.

42. Declaration of the Assembly of Heads of State and Government on the Establishment, within the OAU, of a Mechanism for Conflict Prevention, Management and Resolution; AHG/DECl.3 (XXIX) Rev.1, June 1993.

10

REGULATING THE COMMON UTILIZATION AND MANAGEMENT OF INTERNATIONAL WATERCOURSES: THE SENEGAL REGIME

Introduction

International fluvial law provides one of the most instructive examples of an area of international law to which African States have made a significant and unmistakable contribution. The development of international fluvial law in Africa was first initiated in 1885 with the conclusion of the General Act of Berlin.[1] This evolutionary process has expanded in the post-colonial era. More specifically, the post-1960 period has witnessed the conclusion of new treaties by the new African States relating to the management and utilization of various international watercourses as well as drainage basin systems: the Niger, Senegal and Gambia Rivers as well as Lake Chad in West Africa; the Nile River and Kagera basin in East Africa; and, more recently, the Zambezi in Southern Africa. It has also already been argued in this study that the practice of modern African States in this area of international law has achieved two things: the expansion of international fluvial law in general, on the one hand, and the emergence of certain rules of international law peculiar enough to the African treaty regimes as to be suggestive of an original African contribution to the development of international fluvial law, on the other.[2]

The treaty regime respecting the multilateral utilization and management of the Senegal watercourse system provides a most apt case-study for an appreciation of this contribution. For, apart from the Niger, the Senegal has been under an internationalized regime for a longer period than any other international watercourse in Africa.[3] The three and a half decades that have elapsed since this river was placed under an internationalized regime by the new African riparian States is sufficiently long to allow for at least a preliminary assessment of the development of international fluvial law in the West African sub-region. In this regard, two instruments will be specifically examined here: the Convention Relating to the General Management of the Senegal River Basin (*Convention Relative à l'Aménagement Général du Bassin du fleuve Sénégal*) signed at Bamako, Mali, on 26 July 1963 and the Convention Relating to the Status of the Senegal River (*Convention Relative au Statut du Fleuve Sénégal*) concluded at Dakar, Senegal, on 7 February 1964[4]. The conclusion of these two treaties represented the first attempt by newly independent African States riparian to an international watercourse to lay down the principles of international law to be observed by the riparian States concerned in their management and utilization of the watercourse, both in navigational and non-navigational matters. Indeed, one of the earliest attempts by some of the newly emergent African States to develop among themselves new rules of international law; as Mensah-Brown puts it, "an international law made by Africans for Africans".[5]

The Pre-Independence Position

It may briefly be recalled that the principal reason for convening the Berlin West Africa Conference in 1884 was the desire to resolve what had come to be known as the "Congo Question" and to extend the principles of the freedom of navigation, as laid down at the Congress of Vienna in 1815, and the freedom of commerce to the Congo and the Niger. However, the view had been expressed by some of the European powers that these principles should also be extended to all major rivers in Africa.[6] Lord Granville, for instance, had expressed this desire in the British Government's reply to the German invitation to the forthcoming conference:[7]

> "[H.M.] Government would like gladly to see the fullest freedom both of navigation and commerce secured, not only for the Niger and Congo, but that they would also welcome the extension of the principles, as far as circumstances would permit, to other rivers in Africa."

At the conference, the German delegation also expressed its readiness to see the Vienna principles extended to all major African rivers,[8] but the proposal was not supported by all delegations. Indeed, the view ultimately prevailed that where a river lay wholly within the territorial possessions of one colonial power only, the question of the application of the Vienna principles would not arise. Thus, the French delegation to the Berlin Conference was instructed as follows:[9]

> "*Il est donc entendu que les déliberations porteront uniquement sur les régions du Congo et du Niger. Vous auriez soin notamment d'en exclure, s'il y avait lieu, l'examen des questions relatives au Senegal et a l'Ogoué, en faisant observer que ces cours d'eau traversent les territoires relevant exclusivement de la France et qu'ils ne sauraient dès lors être considérés comme des fleuves internationaux auxquels les prencipes du Congrès de Vienne fussent applicables.*"

The Senegal river was thus excluded from the agenda of the conference and none of the other participants, in fact, challenged France's position in this regard. The result was that the Senegal remained under a non-international regime until after the emergence of the new States of Senegal, Mali, Mauritania and Guinea. Guinea had gained independence statehood in 1958, but it was not until after the independence of the other States in 1960 that the first moves towards the establishment of an international legal regime for the river were undertaken. The regulation and utilization of the Senegal from 1885 to 1959 was thus the exclusive province of the metropolitan authorities in Paris. The only exception was in 1959 itself when the colonial governmental organ set up to manage the regulation of the river briefly came under the joint authority of the autonomous States of the Federation of French West Africa (which, under a new constitutional arrangement, were now members of the French Community) as explained below. France did not limit the utilization of the river to navigation; from the start emphasis was also placed on non-navigational uses. Thus, it may be noted that attempts at the economic exploitation of the river were first undertaken in 1930 under the auspices of the *Services de Production* of the Federation of French West Africa. An administrative organ was later established on 7 July 1934 under the title: *Mission d'études du Fleuve Sénégal* (MEFS). The principal task of this organization, which only became fully operational in the following year, was that of "conducting and executing all research and experimental work throughout the length of the Senegal River aimed at developing [and exploiting] it from the triple standpoint of agriculture, navigation and power production, within the territories of Senegal, Soudan (present-day Mali), Mauritania and Guinea".

In fact, MEFS spent three years making topographical, hydrological and geological studies which never materialized into any concrete projects. It was superseded, in 1938, by the *Mission d'Aménagement de Sénégal* (MAS), which, unfortunately, could not carry out much of its intended work due to the outbreak of the Second World War.[10] The only notable work which had been completed concerned the irrigation of the Guede and Diorbival areas (in the Podor region of the lower Senegal) which were devoted to the cultivation of cotton. After the war, MAS was reorganized with its aims now limited to sectional and relatively uncoordinated research. In this regard one may mention the studies initiated by this body in 1947 relating to the feasibility of using the Felou and Gouina rapids for hydro-electric power production.

Further reorganization was occasioned in 1959 when MAS became a joint organization for the three States of the French West African Federation which had become autonomous: Mauritania, Senegal and Soudan (Mali). The reconstituted organization was broadly mandated to examine matters of navigation, irrigation, power production, fishing, and so on.[11] It may also be said that this was perhaps the nearest to an internationalized regime that the Senegal river was ever subjected to prior to 1963. But even this arrangement was largely ineffectual and collapsed soon after independence in 1960 when Mali withdrew from the organization. Consequently, none of the recommendations that followed from its studies was ever implemented.

One thing ought to be noted here: Guinea's non-participation in this organization. To begin with, it would appear that this French colonial territory was not considered as much of a riparian as the other colonies, the view being that Guinea's only claim was that it was a riparian to the rivers which subsequently combine to form the Senegal river, but did not itself share the waters of the Senegal proper. A similar view was later mildly expressed with regard to Guinea's claim to riparian status to the Niger.[12] It is contended here that this view stands in contradiction to the modern practice of States in the regulation of international rives, which advocates the embracing of not only those States riparian to the river proper, but also those riparian to its tributaries and sub-tributaries, such as Guinea: the drainage basin approach to the regulation and management of international watercourses. But, on the other hand, Guinea's exclusion from the organization may, additionally, be explained within the context of the breakdown of its diplomatic relations with France following the former's categorical refusal to become an autonomous member of the French Community, which other former French colonies had agreed to join, in 1958. It is quite obvious that Guinea could not have been welcome in the Paris-sponsored organization in the politically hostile climate that followed the events of 1958 even if it had wanted to be involved in the regulation and utilization of the Senegal at the time. But all this is of little practical moment since, as has already been noted above, the organization failed to achieve anything of real significance during its brief existence.

Evolution of the International Legal Regime

As has already been intimated above, the origins of the international legal regime of the Senegal lie firmly within the post-independence era. The original suggestion for the elaboration of an international treaty for the Senegal can be traced to President Modibo Keita of Mali who, at the beginning of 1962, made a proposal to his Guinean and Mauritanian counterparts for a summit meeting to discuss "the common utilization of the river, and of the entire basin, as well as the resources therein".

In fact, a series of studies had earlier been conducted, in respect of the above proposals, under the auspices of the Federation of Mali (which had comprised the newly independent States of Senegal and Soudan (or Mali), between 20 June and 20 August 1960. But, like the earlier studies carried out by MEFS and MAS, these efforts came to nothing and were soon discontinued. And, in any case, this was not an internationalization of the river regime. It was ultimately agreed that instead of a trilateral meeting, one involving all four basin States be convened.

The first ministerial conference was accordingly held in the Guinean capital, Conakry, from 10 to 11 July 1962. The conference, attended by the respective ministers of public works and energy together with their technical assistants, was principally concerned with the navigation of the Senegal, between St. Louis and Kayes, and the construction of barrages at Gouina (in Mali) and Dagana (in Senegal). The conference made two main recommendations. The first was that the riparian States devise means for the exploitation of the resources of the river basin and that they establish an inter-governmental organization in this respect. And, second, that the United Nations be requested to appoint a mission to draw up an inventory of works required in the basin in matters of navigation, hydroelectricity, soil conservation, construction of dams, agriculture, ports management and even the sociological aspects of the utilization of the river basin.[13] In fact, the riparian States had already acknowledged – and so the ministerial conference was only reiterating – the role that the United Nations and its relative agencies could play in the financing of any recommended projects.

In short, therefore, the first ministerial summit of the Senegal States urged the rational utilization of the resources of the Senegal basin within the concept of the widely accepted "community of interest" theory, since they viewed the basin as possessing a "single unit" character. The most significant recommendation here was that relating to the creation of an international riparian organization, comprising all the four riparian States, to manage the regulation and exploitation of the river and its resources.

As there was more or less general agreement and similarity of views on the principles which were to guide the utilization of the river and the exploitation of the basin's resources, the drafting and preparation of the statutes did not entail any serious controversy amongst the participants. The resulting treaty regime was established in two stages: first, the second ministerial conference held in Bamako, Mali, signed a treaty on 26 July 1963. Styled the Convention Relating to the General Management of the Senegal River Basin, the agreement was for the most part concerned with the creation of an international riparian organization, *Comité Inter-Etats* or Inter-State Committee.

The adoption of the above treaty was followed by a meeting of technical and legal experts from the four States on 19 and 20 December 1963. Under the direction of the newly constituted Inter-State Committee, this meeting drew up general guidelines for a development of the river basin and made a preliminary survey in a number of sectors: hydroelectric energy production, mineral and industrial development, navigation, irrigation and so on.[14] The legal framework regarding all these issues was more properly defined in the second treaty: the Convention Relating to the Status of the Senegal River, which was adopted at the first sitting of the Inter-State Committee's Council of Ministers in Senegal on 7 February 1964. In addition, this meeting also adopted the Committee's Rules of Procedure.

These arrangements thus laid down, between them, the treaty regime that was to apply to the Senegal basin for almost a decade until 1972, when they were both superseded by a new treaty. In the following sections these treaties will be referred to simply as the "Bamako or 1963 Convention" and the "Dakar or 1964 convention", respectively. The Bamako and Dakar Conventions were, of course, meant to complement each other. In examining their provisions, there will inevitably be need occasionally to draw comparison with other international legal instruments that have contributed to the development of international fluvial law elsewhere in West Africa, in particular the General Act of Berlin of 1885, already referred to above, and the Act Relating to Navigation and Economic Cooperation between States of the Niger Basin, concluded at Niamey, Niger, on 26 October 1963 and the Agreement concerning the Niger River Commission and Navigation and Transport on the Niger, also concluded at Niamey on 25 November 1964.[15]

Regulation and Utilization of the Senegal Basin under the Bamako and Dakar Treaties

(i) Navigational Use

Freedom of Navigation: Meaning of the Term

The principle of freedom of navigation on the Senegal was first invoked in the preamble to the Dakar Convention (1964) which stated, in part:

> "*[Quel] l'exploitation en commun du Fleuve implique le principe de la liberté de navigation et de l'égalité de traitement des [utilisateurs].*"

But it was in Articles 1 and 5 of the treaty that express provisions guaranteeing the twin concepts of freedom of navigation and equality of treatment were to be found. As is the case with most navigation treaties, and in accordance with the established practice in international law, the Dakar Convention embodied both the nautical and commercial aspects of navigation.

In fact, it may be noted that the emphasis here was more on commercial navigation than on any other aspects, for Article 5 partly provided that:

> "*[La navigation] est entièrement libre et ouverte aux ressortissants, aux bateaux marchands et aux marchandises des Etats sur un pied d'égalité en ce qui concerne les droits de port et les taxes sur la navigation, ainsi que les conditions auxquelles est soumise la navigation commerciale.*"

Two points must be noted here. First unlike, say, the Act of Niamey (1963) relating to the Niger, the concept of freedom of navigation as embodied in the Dakar Convention was a narrower one. Article 3 of the Niamey Treaty had been formulated so as to embrace, in addition to commercial navigation, the navigation of pleasure craft as well as that for the transportation of passengers. No similar formulation can be discerned in the Dakar Convention. Secondly, there arises the question of the beneficiaries of this freedom of navigation. The general position in international law is that freedom of navigation in favour of all nations in general is not yet the established rule. But it may also be noted in this regard that whereas the General Act of Berlin of 1885 did legislate for such freedom in favour of all nations at large, the General Act and Declaration of Brussels, five years later, was not as liberal. Furthermore, Article 5 of the Convention of St. Germain in 1919 restricted the class of beneficiaries to the parties to the Convention and Member States of the League of Nations which adhered to it.[16] The Act of Niamey, however, reverted to the wide construction employed in the General Act of Berlin, granting the freedom of navigation to all nations (Article 3). There is a significant difference between the formulation used in the Act of Niamey and that of Article 5 of the Convention of Dakar, the latter employing the words "merchant vessels and merchandise *of the States*" rather than "vessels of *all nations*" as was the case in the former treaty. This linguistic difference cannot be without legal significance. The evidence from the *travaux préparatoires* of the conferences preceding the conclusion of both the Bamako and Dakar Conventions, and provisions of the two agreements themselves, can only be construed as limiting the utilization of the Senegal and its navigation to the four riparian States only.[17] In this regard, attention must also be drawn to Articles 12 and 13 of the Bamako Convention, which expressly stipulate the four riparians as the States entitled to determine the international legal status of the Senegal and its tributaries.

But one cardinal point must be emphasized: it is not enough to identify the beneficiaries of the grant of freedom of navigation without analyzing the various elements which make up the concept of free navigation itself in the conventions under consideration. So, one must examine the rights and obligations of the beneficiaries, on the one hand, and those accruing to the grantor State, on the other, as embodied in the Bamako and Dakar Conventions.

(ii) Extent of the Rights Granted

In determining the extent of the rights granted under this treaty regime, regard must be had to the rules and principles laid down, in particular, in respect of such things as payment of, or exception from, dues and tolls, entry into ports, cabotage, non-discrimination, and so on.

Freedom of Traffic

One of the most significant innovations of the Congress of Vienna in 1815 was the abolition of the practice of requiring boats to call at a given port and break bulk there or to transship their cargoes into vessels of local boatmen: *droits de relâche, d'échelles, d'étape ou de rompre charge.* All major navigation treaties concluded after 1815 – including the General Act of Berlin – incorporated this abolition, though, of course, with minor variations.[18] The abolition of the rights of forced call and transshipment arose out of the need to ensure a full and absolute freedom of traffic, an idea which is itself an essential element of the concept of freedom of navigation, as was subsequently observed in two leading judgments by the Permanent Court of International Justice.[19] It may be said that the post-independence African treaties relating to international watercourses have treated the matter differently inasmuch as they do not incorporate a specific abolition of the *droits de relâche* and so on, as was the case with the earlier European treaties. But this was to be expected since the practice had never been employed on these rivers and the need to expressly abolish it in these treaties does not, therefore, arise. Still, it may be concluded that the idea of freedom of traffic as a necessary component of the concept of freedom of navigation on the Senegal (as is also the case on the Niger) must be presumed. Indeed, this presumption follows from the provision of Article 5 of the Convention of Dakar, which has already been discussed above.

Entry into Ports and Commerce

That the concept of freedom of navigation implies the freedom of commerce is not always stipulated in every navigation treaty. But this is a conclusion that is based on the long-established practice of States (going back even earlier than the Congress of Vienna of 1815), the decisions of international tribunals and the opinions of eminent jurists.[20]

As was noted above, Article 5 of the Convention of Dakar contains the stipulation that freedom of navigation and equality of treatment shall apply in regard to "*les droits de port et les taxes sur la navigation, ainsi que les conditions auxquelles est soumise la navigation commercial*". The importation of the right to engage in commerce into the regime of free navigation would appear to be clearly established in this provision. From this, certain rights can be presumed to follow in favour of the nationals and vessels of the various States engaged in this navigation, namely the right to enter the ports of the State in whose territory the waterway lies, the freedom to make use of the State's plants and docks, to load and unload goods and to transport them, and so on, as was observed in the judgment of the Permanent Court of International Justice in the *Oscar Chinn* case.[21] In short, all those rights without which the freedom of commerce implied in the grant of freedom of navigation will be impaired.

Non-Discrimination: Cabotage

It is a logical consequence of the granting of freedom of navigation that there must be a guarantee of non-discrimination in respect of the nationals, merchandise and vessels of any State. This is now well established in the practice of African States. Thus Articles 7 and 8 of the Dakar Convention both carried the important provision that the taxes and duties payable on goods and vessels shall in no way be discriminatory and that where any tolls are charged on roads, railways and canals constructed to obviate the non-navigable parts of the river, the nationals of the various States shall be treated on the basis of perfect equality.

But one exception to the requirement of non-discrimination has been recognized by the great majority of treaties: *petit cabotage*, the navigation from port to port in the same State (as contrasted with *grand cabotage*, concerning navigation between any places on the same river). On this issue, Baxter made the apt observation that:[22]

> "Since the limitation of cabotage to nationals constitutes a qualification of freedom of navigation on an international river, an express reservation of the power to exclude foreign shipping and persons must be made when the river is thrown open to free use..."

Neither of the Niamey Treaties made reference, express or implied, to this issue in respect of the Niger. There was no such lacuna in respect of the Senegal since it was stipulated, at least, that the regulation of cabotage would at all times be the responsibility of the Inter-States Committee (Article 7 of the Dakar convention). The conclusion to be drawn from this is that, on the Senegal, *petit cabotage* was not reserved to the riparian States.

Exemption from Dues and Tolls

The question of exemption from dues and tolls in relation to the concept of freedom of navigation is a very important one. Indeed, the question of whether or not the granting of freedom of navigation implies navigation without payment of any kind lies at the root of the whole exercise of trying to define what the term "freedom of navigation" means.

Seigniorial duties which used to be charged by the territorial sovereign for the sole fact of using the river (such as *droits de péage*, *de transit*, *de reconnaissance*, and so on) have long been regarded as being inconsistent with the idea of free navigation ever since the days of the French Revolution. But then, these should not be confused with other types of charges, such as those levied on goods carried on board vessels in the form of customs duties or those levied upon shipping in return for services actually rendered, for examples for the improvement and maintenance of navigability, which may be permitted, within limits.

Article 5 of the Dakar Convention, already cited above, made reference to "port duties and navigation taxes". But it was Article 7 that carried a more elaborate stipulation:

> "*La navigation ne sera assujettié à aucune restriction ni redevance basée sur le seul fait de la navigation. Toutefois le cabotage le long du fleuve pourra être l'objet d'une réglementation par le Comité Inter-Etats.*
>
> *Il ne sera etabli aucun péage ni maritime ni fluvial basé sur le seul fait de la navigation ni aucun droit sur les merchandises qui se trouvent à bord des navires.*

Pourront seuls être perçus les taxes ou droits qui auront le caractère de rétribution pour services réndus à la navigation même. Le tarif de ces taxes ou droits ne comportera aucun traitement différentiel."

And, in relation to the roads, railways and canals assimilated to the river regime, it was provided that only such tolls could be levied as were calculated on the cost of expenses on construction, maintenance and management (Article 8). Two observations may be made in this regard. First, the absence of any enumeration of the taxes and duties that were to be permitted under the Bamako and Dakar Treaties, as had been done, for example, under Article 14 of the General Act of Berlin of 1885 and other international navigation pacts. Second, the absence of any provision in the treaties regarding the question of customs duties on goods on board and vessels.

Of course, the absence of any specific enumeration of the permissible taxes under a given regime is not uncommon in treaties of this nature. Indeed, it may be pointed out that within post-independent Africa, the Niamey Treaties themselves did not follow the precedent provided by Article 14 of the General Act of Berlin. Similarly, although the Dakar and Bamako Conventions are silent on the matter, it may be concluded that, following established practice, the imposition of customs duties on goods destined for the riparian State is legally permissible as long as it is not itself discriminatory as regards, say, the different users or country of origin or destination of the goods.

Types of Vessels: Exclusion of Warships

The legal regime established by the Bamako and Dakar Conventions differed from that obtaining on most international rivers in yet another respect: these treaties only legislated for merchant vessels ("*bateaux marchands*"). Thus, Article 5 of the Dakar Convention, unlike Article 3 of the Act of Niamey, made no stipulation whatsoever, for example, for pleasure craft or transport fleet.

The exclusive emphasis on merchant vessels is not surprising. The argument is here advanced that the content of "freedom of navigation" is linked to "freedom of commerce"; the explicit stipulation for merchant vessels, often to the exclusion of other types of vessels, must be viewed as a logical consequence of this linkage. One category of vessels usually excluded in this regard is that of warships. And here the Bamako and Dakar Conventions simply followed the practice established in the majority of navigation treaties in not legislating for the navigation of warships. The position in international law is clear on this issue: where a treaty opens up a river or other waterway to international navigation, passage by warships is not automatically included. It has been argued that the reason for this is that if the content of "freedom of navigation" is accepted as implying the "freedom of commerce", then inclusion of warships would surely be an inconsistency. As Baxter puts it:[23]

> "Warships are seldom expressly mentioned, but language like that of the Articles formulated in the Congress of Vienna, '*sous le rapport de commerce*', points by implication to the applicability of the Articles to merchant vessels alone. *[As] a matter of interpretation, it would seem that any language in a treaty which states that the waterway is open for purposes of commerce should be construed to exclude passage by warships.*" [Emphasis added.]

This remains the case even if the treaty – as was the situation with the Bamako and Dakar Conventions – does not expressly prohibit the navigation of such warships. But it must be pointed out that parties to treaties are, of course, at liberty to expressly provide for the right of warships to navigate the international river in question if they so wish. The most relevant example in this case is Article 22 of the General Act Berlin (relating to the Congo). This article provided that war-ships of signatory States would be permitted to navigate on that river, and were to be exempted from payment of navigation dues. There are also some treaties from Latin America: the Treaties between Argentina and Brazil (1857), respecting the Parana, Paraguay and Uruguay rivers,[24] between Brazil and Paraguay, (1856)[25] and (1858)[26] and between Argentina and Paraguay (1976)[27], and the Treaty between Brazil and Uruguay (1909)[28]. Here it must be submitted, however, that the passage of warships on the Senegal cannot be implied in the absence of any express stipulation to that effect in the relevant treaties.

Territorial Scope of the Freedom of Navigation: Tributaries and Sub-tributaries

In most cases, the definition of "international river" has, since the Congress of Vienna, been construed so as to embrace not only the river itself but also its tributaries and its sub-tributaries. In this respect, where some treaties have insisted on the qualification that such affluents and sub-affluents must themselves be international, other treaties not only dispense with this requirement but rather seek to extend the international regime to tributaries and sub-tributaries located exclusively within the territory of one State. The Senegal treaties belong to the latter category.

That the navigational regime adopted for the Senegal was meant to cover the whole hydrological basin is evident from an examination of a number of provisions in both the Bamako and Dakar Conventions as well as the *travaux préparatoires*. Thus, the resolution drawn up by the first ministerial conference involving all the four riparian States, which has already been referred to above, emphasized, *inter alia*, the "unitary character" of the basin.[29] Similarly, the preambular dispositions of the Bamako Convention laid emphasis on the coordinated exploitation of the entire basin, as did Article 1 of the same treaty. A more explicit definition was contained in Article 13:

> "*Le fleuve Sénégal est declaré par les quatres Etats riverains 'Fleuve international', y compris ses affluents, dans le cadre d'un statut elaboré et ratifié par les quatres Etats riverains.*"

It may be argued that this definition did not go far enough since it left undefined the status of sub-tributaries. This was subsequently remedied in the Dakar Convention which re-emphasized the drainage basin approach. Accordingly, Article 5 extended the freedom of navigation to the river, its branches and issues ("*le fleuve Sénégal et ses embranchements et issues, de l'interiéur des Etats*"). Article 8 went even further, incorporating into the Senegal river system the streams and lakes located in the Senegal basin. The approach adopted in the Dakar Convention accords more properly with the modern approaches in this area of international law, as was pointed out earlier in this discussion. And it is this approach which is to be commended to other riparian States sharing the major international watercourses in Africa – the Nile, the Zambezi, the Congo (or Zaire) rivers as well as the various lakes – which are, or might be, engaged in resource exploitation and management projects over these watercourses.

Roads, Railways and Lateral Canals

One of the most remarkable similarities in the legal regimes established by the various post-colonial treaties for West African international watercourses concerns the assimilation of roads, railways and canals to the river systems. First introduced into international law by Articles 16 and 33 of the General Act of Berlin, this has indeed become standard practice in international fluvial law in Africa, and it found expression in Article 8 of the Dakar Convention. Significantly, the wording of the various treaty provisions relating to this issue (for example, Article 7 of the Convention of St. Germain (1919) and Article 14 of the Agreement of Niamey (1964) has always been remarkably similar, with only minor variations as befit each individual river regime. So Article 8 provided, in part:

> "*[Les] routes, chemins de fer ou canaux lateraux qui pourront être établis dans le but spécial de supplier à l'innavigabilité ou aux imperfections de la voie fluviale sur certaines sections du flleuve, de ses affluents, embranchements et issues pourront être considerés par le Comité Inter-Etats comme des dependances de ces rivières et lacs et seront également ouverts au trafic [international].*"

As the Senegal is by no means wholly navigable, the relevance of this provision in the treaty cannot be doubted. On the assimilated roads, rail routes and canals the cardinal principles of freedom of navigation and equality of treatment were to apply.

(iii) The Right of the State in Whose Waters Free Navigation is Granted

Sovereignty

It is an established rule of international law that even where freedom of navigation is granted to other States, the grantor State concerned still retains sovereignty over that stretch of the river lying within its territory. This remains the case whether or not it has been so stated in the treaty, for conventional freedom of navigation has always been considered largely as an exception to the general rule of absolute sovereignty.[30] Thus, in its Advisory Opinion concerning the *Jurisdiction of the European Commission of the Danube*, the Permanent Court of International Justice upheld Romania's right to exercise sovereignty over the maritime Danube in all respects not incompatible with the powers possessed by the Commission.[31].

Legislation: Jus Edicendi

It automatically follows from the principle regarding retention of their sovereignty by the riparian States that all foreign vessels and nationals are subject to the riparian's laws and regulations, so long as such laws and regulations are not themselves inconsistent with the concept of freedom of navigation and equality of treatment. But here, again, the practice of States is not necessarily uniform. The evidence is that most treaties will stipulate the areas in which the riparian States are entitled to enact envisaged legislation. The Venezuela-Colombia Treaty of 1941 on the demarcation of the frontier and navigation of common rivers is one such treaty.[32] But the Senegal treaties carried no such stipulation. Nevertheless, it can be argued that the riparian States retained the right to pass any reasonable legislation which is favourable to the freedom of navigation and commerce and the common utilization of the river, its tributaries and sub-tributaries in general. One may conclude, from an examination of the provisions of various treaties in this respect, that areas in which the right of a riparian State to legislate is recognized are such as relate to police, customs, health, public security, and control of the boatmen's nautical skill and supervision of the shipping material and so forth. Indeed, guidance may be sought from Article XV of the Helsinki Rules (1966)[33] which provides that:

"A riparian State may exercise rights of police, including but not limited to the protection of public safety and health, over that portion of the river [subject] to its jurisdiction, provided the exercise of such rights does not unreasonably interfere with the enjoyment of the rights of free navigation."

On the other hand, it may be noted that the international organization established by the riparian States, the Inter-State Committee, was accorded certain powers and competencies: executive, administrative and legislative, as well as technical, financial and judicial. The main body of the Committee's attributes was embodied in Article 11 of the Dakar Convention, but other aspects of these attributes could also be discerned from the various provisions in both the Bamako and Dakar Conventions. The question that arises is: what was the legal import of these provisions and how were they to be reconciled with those of the riparian States in the event of a conflict or an inconsistency between them? A brief examination of these powers, in particular the executive and legislative powers, would be in order here.

The Inter-State Committee was clearly endowed with some executive and administrative powers in addition to its consultative authority. Thus, apart from the task of "over-seeing" the regulation and exploitation of the river and its resources, the Committee was empowered to disallow any projects which might, in its judgment, occasion a detrimental effect upon the river regime.[34] As regards its legislative competence, the Committee was empowered to promulgate regulations regarding, or in furtherance of, the application of the principles embodied in the two treaties, as well as its own internal regulations and rules of procedure, and to fix regulations concerning the navigation of the Senegal and its tributaries and sub-tributaries, the financing of such navigation and its maintenance and improvement.

However, two points must be emphasized. First of all, in common with other international watercourses in Africa, and unlike European rivers such as the Danube and the Rhine, the Senegal has never had a system of river police or inspectors as part of the institutional machinery under the internationalized regime. Consequently, the Inter-State Committee lacked the actual authority to enforce these decisions or, indeed, its various regulations, and could only rely on the State authorities to undertake such enforcement in their respective territories. The obvious remedy here would be for the riparian States to establish a river police force or a system of inspection under the authority of the riparian commission. The other interesting question arises with respect to Article 11(a) of the 1964 Convention. This article provided that the common regulations and other decisions promulgated by the Committee were binding upon the States concerned after their approval by those States. This formula, denying as it did the decisions of the organization automatic binding force upon the member States, was a result of the desire to avoid creating a "supra-national" organization which would over-ride the sovereignty of the individual members. But, in theory at least, this could lead to the absurd situation whereby States were obligated to submit their plans for proposed works to the organization (as required by Article 8 of the Bamako Convention and Article 3 of the Dakar Convention) only to have those States escape the binding effect of the organization's resultant decision by simply withholding their approval of such a decision under this provision. Article 11(a) was thus clearly an anomalous provision and, it is submitted, did not provide for any clear mechanism for reconciling conflicts between the regulations and decisions of the organization and those of the riparian States. In practice, no problem appears to have risen in this regard.

Integrated Development

Navigational Uses

It is fairly clear from the relevant provisions of the Bamako and Dakar Conventions that navigation is regarded as a most important aspect of the utilization of the Senegal and its tributaries and sub-tributaries by the riparian States. In fact, the two treaties devoted more attention to the regulation of navigation than to other uses. As was pointed out above, the Dakar Convention expressly provided that "the common exploitation of the river implies the principle of freedom of navigation and the equality of treatment of the users". However, it should also be noted that the Senegal river States only regarded navigation as a pre-eminent, but not necessarily sole use as was always invariably the case in the earlier days of the evolution of international fluvial law on European rivers and under the General Act of Berlin of 1885. For Articles 2 and 3 of the Dakar Convention did give specific reference to the industrial and agricultural exploitation of the river, its tributaries and sub-tributaries.

The preceding section discussed, *inter alia*, the rights of the State in whose waters free navigation has been granted. Yet, Articles 3 and 5 of the Dakar Convention also established two important obligations on the part of these States. First, there was the obligation upon each of the parties to submit to the international riparian authority – the Inter-State Committee – advance plans of any projected works that might substantially affect the conditions relating to the navigability (and also to the industrial or agricultural utilization) of the river (Article 3). In addition to this, Article 6 prescribed a different sort of obligation: not only were the parties placed under an obligation to maintain the navigability of those sections of the river under their respective sovereignty, but they were also enjoined to carry out whatever work may be necessary to improve such navigability.

The first obligation results from the theory of limited territorial sovereignty, already alluded to above, the idea that there is a general obligation incumbent upon States not to undertake works which might affect either the physical integrity of the watercourse (maintenance of the same volume of water and the same current) or the quality or the water without the consent of other riparian States is one that has been subscribed to by the great majority of modern writers: Fauchille, Guggenheim, Andrassy, Berber, Bourne, among many others.[35] This thesis has also been upheld in the judgments of some national courts (for example the United States Supreme Court which, being a federal court adjudicating upon constituent states' disputes, offers a particularly instructive analogy with international tribunals) as well as international tribunals.[36]

Pollution is one obvious problem which arises in this regard. Admittedly, the problem of fluvial pollution cannot be given adequate treatment within the limited scope of this discussion. In any case it is a matter to which none of the international fluvial treaties in Africa have made more than just a passing reference. Neither the Niger treaties nor those relating to the Senegal, the Nile, the Gambia or Lake Chad carry any elaborate stipulations regarding the problem of pollution. This has not always been the case in other continents. It may be recalled, for instance, that in 1974 the Council of Europe adopted a draft Convention for the Protection of International Watercourses against Pollution.[37] An apt example in this respect from Latin America is the Treaty between Argentina and Uruguay concerning the legal regime of the Rio de la Plata (1973).[38]

Article 3 of the Dakar Convention, which followed almost verbatim the provision in Article 4 of the Act of Niamey (1963), provided as follows:

> "*Les Etats riverains engagent à soumettre au Comité Inter-Etats et dès leur phase initiale les projets dont l'exécution est susceptible de modifier d'une manière sensible certaines caractéristiques du régime du fleuve ses conditions de navigabilité ou d'exploitation agricole ou industrielle, l'état sanitaire des eaux, les caractéristiques biologiques de sa faune ou de sa flore.*"

Although the two articles referred to above do not state the matter in explicit terms, it is the contention here that both provision establish the prohibition of any action which would have the effect of altering the natural flow of the water and any industrial or agricultural use likely to cause pollution of the water, unless, of course, the prior consent of the other riparian States has been obtained. In this regard, it may be recalled that the Inter-State Committee was empowered to disallow any projects that might, in its judgment, occasion a detrimental effect upon the river's regime. A possible explanation as to why the various West African treaties are almost silent on the question of pollution is, perhaps, that they were concluded at a time of very little industrial and technological activity in these areas – certainly not the sort likely to occasion fluvial pollution. The "problem" was thus almost non-existent at the time.

The second obligation has been central to the individual and collective plans for the integrated development of the Senegal basin by the four States. As regards navigation, the riparian States have been engaged in integrated projects with the twin-objective of: (a) improving the general navigability of the river; and (b) improving facilities of the two main ports of Kayes and St. Louis, as well as a number of other intermediate ports. So, while each State endeavours to improve the navigability of those sections of the river under its sovereignty, as required by Article 6 of the Dakar Convention, the greater responsibility in this respect has fallen under the successive riparian organizations. Under the direction of these organization, schemes for the integrated development of the Senegal have focused on the construction of two main dams, at Diama (in Senegal) and Manantali (on the Bafing sub-tributary in Mali) which will, *inter alia*, regularize the water flow and improve the navigability of the greater part of the Senegal, assuring land-locked Mali access to the sea all year round. The economic merits and advantages of the integrated approach to the management and development of the Senegal basin cannot be doubted.

It has already been noted that the riparian States had recognized, from the first preliminary conference preceding the establishment of the international legal regime, that the development of the Senegal basin, whether in navigational or non-navigational aspects, could not be achieved without financial aid from the United Nations, other international bodies and individual States.[39] The Inter-State Committee approved the first of such many applications for financial aid to the United Nations at its meeting of 5 to 8 February 1965. The then U.N. Secretary General, U Thant, subsequently discussed the plans for the integrated development of the river basin, and in particular the improvement of navigability, with the Secretary General of the riparian organization, M. Robert N'Daw.[40] But after nearly two decades of surveys, technical research, studies and conferences involving the successive riparian organizations, such donor States as Canada, China, France, Germany and the United States, the United Nations and other international organizations, it was only on 12 December 1979 that the foundation stone of the Diama dam was jointly laid by the Heads of State of Mali, Mauritania and Senegal, now under the auspices of the new international riparian organization created in 1972, the Organization for the Development of the Senegal River (*Organisation pour la Mise en Valeur du Fleuve Sénégal* – OMVS).

Non-Navigational Uses

One of the more obvious non-navigational uses of the Senegal river and its Faleme tributary is their role as international boundaries between Senegal and Mauritania, and Senegal and Guinea, respectively. This issue will not be discussed in any more detail here; it does not belong to the same category of uses which the treaties under discussion intended to regulate. These treaties do not, in fact, make any specific reference to any non-navigational uses except to employ such broad terms as "problems of hydro-electric energy", as in Article 6 of the Bamako Convention, or "agricultural and industrial exploitation" (Articles 3 and 4) and "the rational exploitation of the resources of the Senegal river" (Articles 1 and 11) in the Dakar Convention. This is only to be expected, for it would be pointless for any treaty to attempt an exhaustive enumeration of such uses since the ever changing technological character of the modern world implies equally expanding uses of the waters of international watercourses of this nature. Broad treaty formulations such as these have the advantage of leaving the signatory States with enough latitude to incorporate such expanding economic uses.

It is clear that so far as concerns non-navigational uses, the Senegal river States have always placed almost exclusive emphasis on hydro-electricity and agricultural production.[41] So, for example, the three specialized commissions which constituted the Permanent General Secretariat of the Inter-State Committee related to administrative and juridical affairs, navigation and transport, and hydro-electric energy and agriculture, respectively. These also formed part of the expanded objectives of the Organization of Senegal River States (*Organisation des Etats Riverains du Sénégal* – OERS), a new body which had been established to replace the Inter-State Committee in 1968, but was itself superseded by the creation of the OMVS in 1972. The projects relating to hydro-electric energy production and agriculture are, like the project to improve navigability, heavily dependent on the construction of the various dams planned for the river and its tributaries. Thus, it had been envisaged that, when completed, the Diama dam would enable the irrigation of up to 135,000 acres, while the Manantali dam would irrigate at least 630,000 acres. The importance of these irrigation projects in a region which has witnessed severe drought and progressive desertification in recent times cannot be overemphasized.

Mention may also be made of the importance of the Gouina and Felou falls, both on the Senegal, in the production of hydro-electric energy. The construction of dams are of even more importance in this respect. Thus, it was initially envisaged that the Manantali dam alone would eventually provide some 100 MW of electricity, which would contribute to the general industrial development and expansion of the area.[42]

There are also other non-navigational uses which, though falling within the purview of the agricultural and industrial exploitation envisaged under the various treaties, have not been embraced by the development programs of the Senegal riparian organizations. Thus, none of these organizations has instituted any integrated projects in matters of mineral exploitation and fishing, to name only two such uses, despite the fact that there have been a number of resolutions by these organizations in this respect over the years. At the moment, these areas have remained the preserve of national economic policies. This is, of course, perfectly in order, for both the Bamako and Dakar Conventions (Articles 1 and 2 respectively) reserved to each riparian State the right to exploit the resources in those sections of the river (and its tributaries) within its territory in accordance with its rights of sovereignty, but having due regard to the obligations created by these treaties.

The International Legal Regime of the Senegal under the Labé and Nouakchott Treaties

The international legal regime discussed in the preceding sections was established by the Bamako and Dakar Conventions, respectively. But both treaties have since been superseded by new agreements: first, by the Labé Treaty of 1968 and, secondly, by the Nouakchott Treaties of 1972. Similarly, the international riparian organization originally created under the Bamako Convention, the Inter-State Committee, has since been replaced by another organization.

In fact, the Labé Treaty, entered into by the same four signatories to the earlier treaties, did not in any sense abrogate the Bamako and Dakar Conventions. The main objective of the 1968 agreement was to provide the legal framework for the creation of a new international organization which was to be accorded a much broader role for political, economic, social and cultural cooperation than was the case with the Inter-State Committee, which was a riparian organization *simpliciter*. The new organization, *Organisation des Etats*

Riverains du Sénégal (OERS), was intended to embrace other aspects of economic cooperation and political unity going beyond the mere common exploitation and utilization of the Senegal river. Thus, it must be emphasized, the new treaty necessitated a restructuring of the institutional mechanisms of the previous regime only. It did not occasion any change in the legal principles enshrined in the 1963 and 1964 treaties regarding the regulation and utilization of the Senegal and its tributaries. In effect, the only significant structural change brought about in 1968 was the incorporation of the Inter-State Committee into the new organization as merely one of its specialized organs, designated as the General Secretariat for the Utilization of the Senegal River Basin. It is important to quote the relevant provision of the Labé Treaty *in extenso* in this regard. Article 23 provided:

> "*Le Secrétariat Général à l'Aménagement du Bassin du Fleuve Sénégal est dirigé par un Secrétaire Général chargé de promouvoir et de coordonner les études et les travaux de mise en valeur du Bassin de Fleuve Sénégal, conformement à la convention internationale du 26 juilllet 1963 relative à l'aménagement général du Bassin du Fleuve Sénégal et à la convention international du 6 fevrier 1964 au Statut du Fleuve Sénégal.*
>
> *Des amendements aux conventions internationales susvisées substitueront le Conseil des Ministres de l'OERS au Conseil des Ministres du Comité Inter-Etats pour l'aménagement du Bassin du Fleuve Sénégal.*"

So, it can validly be concluded that the Bamako and Dakar Conventions continued to be the source of international legal rules and principles governing the utilization of the Senegal even after the conclusion of the Labé Treaty in 1968. But the Labé Treaty itself was abrogated on 29 November 1971 and was soon superseded by two new treaties concluded by Mali, Mauritania and Senegal: the Convention Relating to the Status of the Senegal River (*Convention Relative au Statut du fleuve Sénégal*) and the Convention Establishing the Organization for the Development of the Senegal River (*Convention Portant Création de l'Organization pour la Mise en Valuer du Fleuve Sénégal*), both signed at Nouakchott, Mauritania, on 11 March 1972.

The reasons for the demise of the OERS and the consequent abrogation of the Labé Treaty cannot adequately be discussed here. Such a discussion is not pertinent to the declared scope of this chapter. Suffice it to note that the OERS was first paralyzed barely a few months after its establishment. Following the overthrow of President Keita's government in Mali in November 1968, Guinea withdrew its support for the organization, rendering it ineffective for the greater part of 1969. To compound the problem, a bitter political and diplomatic dispute subsequently developed between Guinea and Senegal when the former accused the latter not only of giving sanctuary to certain Guinean political dissidents, but also of collaborating with these dissidents to attack that country. A group of Guinean dissidents had allegedly invaded Guinea in November 1970.[43] Guinea eventually terminated its membership of the organization and renounced the Labé Treaty in virtue of Article 38, which provided for voluntary withdrawal by any member State. In their turn, the three remaining member States agreed upon a formal dissolution of the *OERS* and termination of the treaty on 29 November 1971 and thereafter proceeded to create a new treaty regime amongst themselves. As already indicated above, the new treaties were concluded on 11 March 1972 and have remained in force ever since. The question that may now be posed is: to what extent, if at all, have the Nouakchott Conventions affected the international regime of the Senegal as previously laid down in the Bamako and Dakar Conventions?

On the whole, the principles of international fluvial law relating to the regulation and utilization of the Senegal basin which had previously been embodied in the former treaties remain unchanged by the 1972 agreements. But some general observations may be made in this respect.

As might be expected, the 1972 Nouakchott Convention Relating to the Status of the Senegal River first and foremost reaffirms the principle that the utilization of a common international watercourse implies and entails the freedom of navigation and equality of treatment of users. As in the former Dakar Convention, this is expressed as one of the preambular dispositions. In addition to this, Article 2 of the 1972 Convention reaffirms the parties' determination to establish close economic cooperation in order to ensure the most rational and judicious exploitation of the resources of the river basin and to guarantee the twin principles of freedom of navigation and equality of treatment already referred to above.

One important question that arises in relation to the observations just made above concerns the beneficiaries of the right of navigation. It has already been seen that under Article 5 of the Dakar Convention of 1964 the navigation of the Senegal river was declared to be entirely free and open to the nationals, merchant vessels and gods of the States on a footing of perfect equality. As was intimated above, it might be argued that the wording of this provision was unclear, since the term "States" could be construed as referring either to riparian States only or to all nations at large. However, as has already been argued in this discussion, the latter interpretation would not, generally speaking, be supported by the general legal trend which has developed since the Second World War: this negates the presumption that where freedom of navigation has been declared on an international watercourse, the right is granted to all nations regardless of whether they are riparian to the international watercourse or not. But, of course, there is no rule of international law prohibiting riparian States from providing to this effect in a (navigation) treaty. Indeed, it has been contended that the intention of the signatories to the Dakar Convention of 1964 was to confer the freedom of navigation to all States.[44] I do not share this view. It should be reiterated here that having regard to the evidence from the travaux préparatoires of the conferences preceding the conclusion of both the Bamako and Dakar Treaties, and the provisions of the two agreements themselves, the conclusion must be that the utilization of the Senegal and its navigation were intended to be limited to the riparian States only.[45]

The Nouakchott Convention treats this issue differently and with more clarity. What is important here is that the categorization is one of contracting parties (signatory States) as against third States to the treaty and not one of riparian as opposed to non-riparian States. Thus, Article 6 of the Nouakchott Treaty provides:

> "*Sur les territoires nationaux des Etats contractants la navigation sur le fleuve Sénégal et ses affluents, qui seront designés ultérieurement, est entièrement libre et ouverte aux réssortissants, aux bateaux marchands et merchandises des Etats contractants, aux bateaux affretés par un ou plusieurs Etats contractants, sur un pied d'égalité en ce qui concerne les droits de port et les taxes sur la navigation commercial.*
>
> *Les bateaux marchands et navires etrangèrs, de toute origine, seront soumis à une réglementation commune qui sera elaborée ultérieurement.*"

This provision is unique and has not been adopted in the various other treaties concluded by African States in this area of international law. Its incorporation into the Nouakchott Convention can be explained in the context of the political problem that existed at the time of the conclusion of these treaties between the three contracting States, on the one hand, and the other riparian State, Guinea, on the other. It has already been seen how the gradual deterioration in the political relations between the former and the latter had led to the latter's withdrawal from the former treaty regime and to the subsequent demise of the O.E.R.S. The substitution of the term "Contracting States" (*Etats contractants*) for the more usual "riparian States" (*Etats riverains*) in the article quoted above was quite clearly necessitated by the deliberate desire on the part of the three original parties to the Nouakchott Conventions not to accord the other riparian State, Guinea, an equal right of free navigation unless the latter adhered to the new treaties – which it is entitled to do under the terms of Article 15 of the Convention Relating to the Status of the Senegal River and Article 22 of the Convention Establishing the O.M.V.S. These articles, which have similar wording, state:

> *"Tout Etat riverain du fleuve Sénégal peut adhérer à la présente Convention [à l'Organisation]. A cet effet, il devra adresser une demande écrite à l'Etat dépositaire des instruments de ratification, qui en saisira les autres Etats membres."*

Again, it is important to note here that only those States riparian to the Senegal can adhere to the Nouakchott treaties. In effect, this leaves Guinea as the only State that may become a party to the new international legal regime regulating the Senegal basin, in addition to the three original signatory States. This stands in stark contrast to the current legal position relating to the Niger river, since the international legal regime concerning this watercourse now embraces States which, though broadly speaking lie within the same hydrological basin, cannot be said to be riparian either to the Niger proper or to any of its tributaries or sub-tributaries.[46]

Another respect in which the 1972 Conventions do not follow the precedent of the Bamako and Dakar Treaties concerns the delimitation of certain individual rights of the riparian States in the utilization and exploitation of those sections of the international watercourse lying within their territory. It has already been argued that the internationalization of a watercourse does not entail the total abandonment of the individual riparian States' sovereign rights over their respective sections of the international watercourse. On the contrary, there are to be found in the various international conventions on the subject provisions specifically upholding the sovereign right of the riparian States individually to exploit the sections of the river located within their territory subject, of course, to any terms the particular treaty or treaties may lay down: for example, that any works being undertaken by the national authorities should not interfere with the freedom of navigation accruing to the other riparian States under the regime of internationalization, and so on. Similarly, it is also the practice in most treaties to stipulate that on those sections of the river which are utilized by only one riparian State and are not of significant concern to other riparian States, the State concerned is at liberty to establish a particular regime if such action is deemed necessary for the maintenance of public order and security. There are no corresponding provisions in the Nouakchott Convention except for Article 3 which simply states that:

> *"L'exploitation du fleuve Sénégal est ouverte à chaque Etat contractant suivant les modalités définiés par la présente Convention."*

Compared to the provision in Article 2 of the Dakar Convention referred to above (as also to Article 2 of the Act of Niamey of 1963, relating to the Niger) the stipulation in Article 3 just cited above would not seem to be a clear reaffirmation of the sovereign rights of the riparian States over their respective sections of the watercourse. Nevertheless, the question may be posed: is the legal position established by the Nouakchott Convention in this regard indeed different from that under the Dakar Convention?

It is the contention here that in spite of the absence of any provisions categorically stipulating the sovereign rights of the riparian States over those portions of the watercourse lying within their territories, the existence of such rights must, in fact, be presumed. The basis of this contention has already been outline in earlier arguments in the preceding sections. Vitanyi has expressed the point thus:[47]

> "From the fact that the bed and the water of the waterways which are subject to an international regime form part of the State whose territory they wash it follows that the legislation and the jurisdiction of that State also extend to that portion of its territory."

The implication here is that no limitations on sovereignty are to be presumed and that the restrictions on the territorial sovereignty of the riparian State which are usually incorporated into treaties establishing an international regime must therefore be interpreted strictly. The conclusion to be drawn from this reasoning is that even when a treaty, such as the Nouakchott Convention, does not contain any provisions to this effect, the retention by the riparian States of sovereignty over their respective sections is to be taken for granted.

Conclusion

It cannot be doubted that international fluvial law is the one branch of international law to whose growth the independent West African States riparian to some of the continent's major international watercourses have had occasion to contribute as active participants and not merely as passive recipients of that system of law. It is, of course, true that in one sense, the various multilateral treaties governing the utilization of the Niger, Senegal and Gambia Rivers or Lake Chad, for example, can be seen merely as a continuation of the evolutionary process that began with the conclusion of the General Act of Berlin in 1885. As has already been argued in Chapter 4, the Berlin Act holds a certain significance for the student of the history of international law in Africa. It represented the first occasion whereby European formulated conventional rules of international law, designed for the Euro-centric international legal system of the time, were transplanted to the African continent (quite apart from its role in the colonization and partitioning of the

African continent by European powers). But, on the other hand, it has also been argued in this chapter that some of the themes and concepts embodied in the treaties examined here are original and unique to these treaties and do not merely echo legal concepts and ideas incorporated in some of the earlier European navigation treaties.

The major areas in which the Senegal treaties departed from the earlier practice of European States in this area of international law have already been discussed in the preceding sections and need not be restated here. However, one important point must be reiterated in this regard: one discerns in the Bamako and Dakar Conventions two cardinal principles. These are: first, the principle of equitable and reasonable use of the waters and resources of a shared international watercourse by all co-riparian and co-basin States; second, the integrated approach to the management and development of the resources of both the watercourse itself and the drainage basin as a whole. These are principles that have, significantly, been adopted by all the other West African treaties relating to the regulation and utilization of international watercourses. Perhaps, to this extent, one may validly conclude that the post-colonial practice of the African States concerned here is the most instructive example of the tendency of these States to develop among themselves new rules of international law to govern their relations. Or, in some cases, to reinterpret some of the old rules of European Christendom for the benefit of the "newcomers" to the expanded family of nations. However, I would argue that the modest contribution by the various African States, for example the Senegal basin States of Guinea, Mali, Mauritania and Senegal, to the development of international fluvial law is not for the benefit of only the so-called newcomers. It is also of benefit to the international community as a whole and, in particular, to the ever expanding system of international law.

Notes

1. For an extensive discussion of this issue, see T. Maluwa, "The Origins and Development of International Fluvial Law in Africa: A study of the international legal regimes of the Congo and Niger Rivers from 1885 to 1960", *29 NILR 368* (1982).

2. See Chapter 4 above.

3. The post-independence internationalized regime of the Niger dates back to 26 October 1963 when some nine riparian and co-basin States signed the Act Relating to Navigation and Economic Co-operation between States of the Niger

Basin at Niamey, Niger. However, unlike the Senegal, the Niger had been the subject of internationalization under the General Act of Berlin of 1885 (Articles 26 to 33).

4. For texts of the treaties, see *19 Rev. Jur. et Pol., Ind. et Coop. 299* (1965).
5. A.K. Mensah-Brown (Ed.), *African International Legal History*, (1975) p. 3.
6. On the question of the "transplantation" of the principles relating to the regime of international navigation laid down at the Congress of Vienna in 1815 for the major European rivers to African rivers, see note 1 *supra*.
7. Granville to Lessen, 8 October 1884; Conf. 4205, No. 11.
8. See G.F. de Martens, *NRG*, 2nd Ser., Vol. 10, pp. 212, 264.
9. *Documents diplomatique: Affaires du Congo et de l'Afrique Occidentale*, Ministère des *Affaires Etrangères*, Paris, (1885) p. 45 *et seq*.
10. MAS Bull. No. 31: *Rapport au sujet des possibilités d'aménagement offertés par la vallée du Fleuve Sénégal* (1934); See also, Bull. No. 33: *Note sur les études générales à entreprendre en vue de l'aménagement des vallées du Sénégal et du Niger inférieur*, (1934).
11. See, generally, MAS, *Régularisation et aménagement du Fleuve Sénégal*, (1949).
12. T.O. Elias, "The Berlin Treaty and the Niger River Commission", *57 AJIL 873* (1963) at 878.
13. See generally, Comité Inter-Etats, *Recommendations et procès-verbal de la rencontre de Conakry*, (1962).
14. Comité Inter-Etats, *Ses Perspectives*, (1967) pp. 6–8.
15. Other pre-independence treaties that have had a bearing on the development of international fluvial law in West Africa are the General Act and Declaration of Brussels of 1890 and the Convention of St. Germain-en-Laye of 1919. Both these treaties effected certain changes to the regime established for the Niger under the Berlin Act. On this, see note 1 *supra*.
16. *Ibid.* p. 394.
17. Unpublished conference papers and *travaux préparatoires* relating to the various riparian organizations for the Senegal consulted by the present writer at the *Organisation pour la Mise en Valeur du Fleuve Sénégal* (OMVS) headquarters in Dakar, Senegal, during a research visit in April 1982.

18. See, for example, Articles 13, 14, 26 and 27 of the General Act of Berlin (1885). These provisions were consolidated in the various Peace Treaties of 1919/1920: Articles 321–326, 334 of the Treaty of Versailles; 284–289 of the Treaty of St. Germain; 212–217, 223 of the Treaty of Neuilly; and 268–273 and 279 of the Treaty of Trianon; see also, the Convention and Statute of Barcelona on the Regime of Navigable Waterways of International Concern (1921), 7 LNTS 35; *NRG*, 3rd Ser., Vol 18, p. 690 *et seq*.

19. *European Commission of the Danube* case, P.C.I.J. Ser. B., No. 14, p. 64; *Oscar Chinn* case, P.C.I.J. Ser. A/B, No. 63, p. 83.

20. The following observation was made by the Permanent Court of International Justice in the *European Commission of the Danube* case:

    "The freedom of navigation therefore covers not only shipping passing through a sector of the river corresponding to a port, but also shipping arriving in or leaving a port. [Freedom] of navigation is incomplete unless shipping can actually reach the ports under the same conditions".

    And, in the *Oscar Chinn* case:

    "[Freedom] of navigation implies, as far as the business side of maritime or fluvial transport is concerned, freedom of commerce also".

    See also, P. Guggenheim, *Traité de droit international public*, Vol. 1, (1953) p. 415; B. Vitanyi, *The International Regime of River Navigation*, (1979) p. 143.

21. Note 19 *supra*.

22. R. Baxter, *The Law of International Waterways*, (1964) p. 154.

23. *Ibid.* pp. 154–155.

24. *49 BFSP 1306*.

25. G.F. de Martens, *Recueil Manuel et Pratique Générale*, Vol. VII, (1857) p. 516.

26. *41 BFSP 1274*.

27. G.F. de Martens, *NRG*, Vol III, p. 516.

28. *102 B.F.S.P. 206*.

29. The reference to the "unitary character" of hydrological basins in the 1962 resolution was really only a re-affirmation of the "integrated river basin management approach" which the various U.N. studies in this regard had recommended to States sharing common (i.e. international) watercourses. See, for example, the UN Secretary General's Report to the ECOSOC Committee on Natural Resources, Doc. E/C.7/2 Add. p. 1.

30. See, for example, B. Vitanyi, *op. cit.* p. 233. See also, I.L.A. Report of 50th Conference, (1962) p. 441.

31. P.C.I.J., Ser. B. No. 14, p. 64.

32. *144 BFSP 748.*

33. I.L.A. Report of 52nd Conference, (1966) p. 508.

34. Article 8 of the Bamako Convention; Article 3 of the Dakar Convention.

35. See P. Fauchille, *Traité de droit international public*, Vol. 1, part 2, (1925) p. 451; P. Guggenheim, *Traité de droit international*, Vol. 1, (1953) p. 385; F.J. Berber, *Rivers in International Law*, (1959) p. 155; J. Andrassy, "Le droit international de voisinage", *79 Hague Recueil 71* (1951) at 114; C.F. Bourne, "Procedure in the Development of International Drainage Basins", *22 Univ. Toronto L.J. 172* (1972).

36. See, for example, *Wyoming* v *Colorado*, 259 U.S. 419 (1922); *Kansas* v *Colorado*, 206 U.S. 46 (1907); *New Jersey* v *New York*, 283 U.S. 336 (1931). See also *Lake Lanoux Arbitration* (*France* v *Spain*) 24 Int. L. Rep. 101 (1957).

37. J.G. Lammers, "The Draft European Convention of the Council of Europe for the Protection of International Watercourses against Pollution", 6 *Neth. Yrbk. Int. L. 167* (1975).

38. See, in particular, Articles 6, 48 and 66; 13 ILM 251 (1974).

39. Resolution of Ministerial Conference of 10–11 July 1962; see note 13 *supra*.

40. *2 Africa Res. Bull. 281* (1965).

41. Comité Inter-Etats, *Propositions concernant la coopération pour le développement economique*, Vol. 1 and 2, (1966) *passim*.

42. For example those at Galando (Mali), Solde and St. Louis (Senegal) and Tongue (Guinea).

43. See *Le Monde*, Paris, 14 December 1970; it may also be noted in this regard that earlier political differences between Senegal and Guinea had, in fact, led the latter to suspend, temporarily, its participation in the Inter-State Committee in January 1967; See 4 *Africa Res. Bull.* 669 (1976).

44. B. Vitanyi, *op. cit.* p. 113.

45. This view is based on my perusal of the various unpublished *travaux préparatoires*, conference papers and resolutions relating to the Inter-State Committee made available to me during a research visit to the OMVS Headquarters in Dakar, Senegal, in April 1982.

46. It may be noted that a proposal to include States riparian to the affluents of the Senegal, but not to the main river itself, was rejected by the organization in 1975; See *Proposals for restructuring the OMVS and revising its constitutive treaty*, (OMVS General Secretariat, 1974) p. 32 (Article 27).

47. B. Vitanyi, *op. cit.* p. 223.

VI

IMPLEMENTING NEW INTERNATIONAL LAW

11

SOUTHERN AFRICAN LAND-LOCKED STATES AND RIGHTS OF ACCESS AND TRANSIT UNDER THE NEW LAW OF THE SEA

Introduction

The majority of the Southern African States which comprise the Southern African Development Community (SADC) are heavily depended upon South Africa economically. Indeed, the reduction and eventual elimination of this economic dependence provided the cardinal motivation for the establishment of the Southern African Development Coordination Conference (SADCC), the precursor to SADC, in 1980.[1] One aspect of this dependence is in the area of transport and communications; Botswana, Lesotho, Malawi, Swaziland, Zambia and Zimbabwe are land-locked States (LLS)[2] which have all, to varying degrees, traditionally depended on South African transit routes and seaports for their international trade.

Of course, the right of access to the sea is only one angle from which the legal position of LLS under the new Law of the Sea may be examined. other equally significant issues arise, for example: the right of access for LLS to the living resources in the Exclusive Economic Zones (EEZ) of coastal States, the right of access to the non-living resources of the continental shelf, as well as the outer limit of the continental shelf, the high seas, and so on. All these issues concern, in part, the recognition and ascription of rights of access to, and exploitation of, the resources of the seas among coastal and non-coastal States (or LLS), as well as coastal but geographically disadvantaged States (GDS), whether in the areas of fishing, navigation, deep sea-bed mining, aquatic food-production, etc. However, from a practical point of new, it is the question of access to the sea for transportation and communication purposes that is of more immediate relevance to the Southern African LLS. The reason why access to the sea is of such paramount importance to these LLS (as is also the case with other African LLS) is that trade in Africa is largely externally, rather than internally, oriented. Moreover, the bulk of this international trade is still predominantly carried by sea. Thus access to the sea is synonymous with access to the world market. Now, for the greater majority of developing LLS, the twin characteristics of landlockedness and isolation from the major world markets naturally entail high transportation costs for both the exportation and importation of goods to and from these markets. Furthermore, most LLS often have to contend with the fact that the use of the territory of one or more States for access to and from the sea may be entangled with a host of political considerations; or that they are economically and politically too weak and unable to exert much influence either on the more powerful transit State(s) concerned or on the wider international community generally.[3]

The relevance of these considerations has been amply demonstrated in the bilateral relations between South Africa and some of the LLS in question in the fairly recent past. On a number of occasions before the political developments of the last few years, which culminated in the inauguration of South Africa's first democratically elected government on 10 May 1994, that country did blatantly exploit the dependence of these LLS on its transport and communications network, and access to the sea, for political gain. This was demonstrated in dramatic fashion in January 1986 when Lesotho, which is in a uniquely pernicious position, was virtually blockaded by South Africa. In mid-1987, the then so-called independent South African "homeland" of Bophuthatswana attempted to exploit the dependence of the Republic of Botswana on the South African rail network. There was reason to believe that Bophuthatswana made its demands at the behest of South Africa itself, as a thinly disguised attempt aimed at securing two objectives: first, to extract diplomatic recognition for the "homeland" from both Botswana and Zimbabwe; second, to remind these two northern neighbours, along with other Frontline States, of the heavy dependence of their economies on the South African transport system and their vulnerability to South African counter-sanctions. At the time, the line through Botswana (and Bophuthatswana) carried just over half of Zimbabwe's import and export traffic; a further 35–40 per cent was transported via Beit Bridge on the Zimbabwe-South Africa border, while only 10 per cent was being routed through the Mozambican port of Beira.[4] Earlier, both Zambia and Zimbabwe had also suffered varying degrees of threats of counter-sanctions, including the closure of communications and transit routes through South Africa, for their unrelenting opposition to the apartheid and support for the national liberation movements then engaged in the liberation struggle against the apartheid regime.

The dependence of the Southern African LLS on South African transit routes and seaports cannot be doubted. In fact, with the exception of Angola, the Democratic Republic of Congo, and Tanzania, all SADC States rely on these transit routes and seaports for most (and in the case of Botswana, Lesotho and Swaziland – the BLS countries – practically all) of their exports to overseas markets. This problem was, for the greater part of the 1980s, of course compounded by the South African sponsored destabilization of the transport network of the region, which ensured that use of Angolan and Mozambican ports was for a long time a less than viable alternative, even for the northern-situated SADC LLS, namely Malawi, Zambia and Zimbabwe.[5]

The Right of Access of Land-Locked States under International Law

In view of the problem outlined above, it becomes necessary to examine the right of access to the sea of the Southern African LLS within the wider context of their economic and political relations with the dominant coastal State, South Africa. Although the question whether general international law permits LLS to exercise a right of transit to the sea has stimulated considerable academic debate,[6] it cannot be claimed that it has been definitively settled. In general, opinions range from the position that transit or access to the sea is a *natural right* for all LLS, to the view that they may only exercise a *privilege* of passage authorized by an existing treaty, a special licence, or on the basis of local custom.[7] This divergence of opinion was aptly summarized by O'Connell, a leading authority on the law of the sea, as follows:[8]

> "Authors are divided on the question whether there is or is not a general duty to grant transit rights across national territory to neighbouring States which are unfavourably situated. Those opposed argue that since there are degrees of economic necessity, it is difficult in the abstract to distinguish mere assertions of transit needs from actual dependence upon neighbouring [territory]. The other school argues from the thesis of the economic interdependence of States to a juridical conviction in favour of transit rights, pointing out that not only have such rights actually been created in many instances by agreement but that the area of discretion of sovereigns to impede the passage of goods is now so restricted by treaty that an absolute right of exclusion appears antiquated. Opinion over the last fifty years has hardened in favour of the view that at least in some instances States whose economic life and development substantially depends upon the grant of

transit rights may legitimately claim them. This dependence is most obvious in the case of land-locked States, and they may offer analogies for other instances."

O'Connell and Lauterpacht, among the modern authorities, have adopted this view in contradistinction to the views of other writers, such as Oppenheim and Schwarzenberger, who generally advanced the proposition that there is no general right of transit under customary international law.[9]

Can the Right of Access and Transit be Based on Customary International Law?

It is sometimes argued by LLS that some of the main provisions of multilateral treaties transit rights have passed into the corpus of customary international law; or, to put the matter differently, that the various bilateral treaties governing transit could furnish evidence of customary international law, either in the process of formation or already in existence.[10] The argument sounds plausible enough, and in the view of some writers, the process has already taken place.[11] But, as Vasciannie rightly warns, this position must be treated with considerable caution, for in most cases the evidence on this point is equivocal and inconclusive.[12] In any event, the question whether provisions of multilateral treaties do, in some cases, generate enforceable rights in customary law is linked to two other considerations: whether such treaties are self-executing or not; and the wider question regarding the nature of norm-creating, or potentially norm-creating, multilateral treaties. Prior to the conclusion of the United Nations Convention on the Law of the Sea in 1982 (LOSC), the issue of transit had featured, directly and indirectly, in a number of multilateral treaties: Article 23(e) of the Peace Treaty of Versailles (1919); Article 6 of the Barcelona Convention and Statute on Freedom of Transit (1921); Article V of the General Agreement on Tariffs and Trade (GATT); Article 3 of the General Convention on the High Seas; and Article 1 of the New York Convention on Transit Trade of Land-locked States of 1965.[13]

It is significant that the great majority of commentators agree that none of these provisions in the various multilateral treaties clothe the right of transit with the status of a customary rule, nor is it generally accepted that these provisions have now matured into customary rules of international law. Quite the contrary; for even Article 3 of the High Seas Convention, which contains an elaborate formulation of what some might view as the creation of a right of transit, is regarded by many as not really placing any international legal obligation at all upon coastal States to grant rights of transit and access to LLS.[14] In fact, the article provides as follows:

> "1. In order to enjoy the freedom of the seas on equal terms with coastal States, States having no seacoast should have free access to the sea. To this end States situated between the sea and a State having no seacoast shall by common agreement with the latter and in conformity with existing international conventions accord:
>
> (a) To the State having no seacoast, on a basis of reciprocity, free transit through their territory; and
>
> (b) To ships flying the flag of that State treatment equal to that accorded to their own ships, or to the ships of any other States, as regards access to seaports and the use of such ports.
>
> 2. States situated between the sea and a State having no seacoast shall settle, by mutual agreement with the latter, and taking into account the rights of the coastal State or State of transit and the special conditions of the State having no seacoast, all matters relating to freedom of transit and equal treatment in ports, in case such States are not already parties to existing international conventions."

Quite clearly, the right of access thus remained a matter for bilateral negotiation and arrangement between coastal States and LLS, in conformity with existing international conventions. Moreover, the grant of transit and access rights was to be on the basis of reciprocity. This implied, ultimately, that if a particular coastal State had no need of access through the territory of a land-locked neighbouring State, it would have no particular incentive for granting access to the latter, for it was under no legal obligation to do so. But, of course, it could also be argued that for the coastal State granting access "reciprocity" need not be pegged to similar (and reverse) access through the territory of the LLS as such, but that it could be met with, or "repaid" by, a host of other considerations, for example preferential treatment in trade. In any event, Article 3 is not worded in terms that imply imperative force:[15] thus it is quite possible for coastal States to support the rule in this Article and still maintain that they are not obliged to provide transit facilities as a matter of law.[16]

Subsequent to the High Seas Convention, the battle for the recognition of a legal right to transit and access for LLS was taken to the UNCTAD negotiations, starting with the first conference, First UNCTAD, in 1964. The concerted effort was spear-headed by the African-Asian bloc of LLS, and a special committee was set up to look into the proposal emanating from these States. In fact it was the work of this committee that led to the convening of the conference which, in turn, led to the adoption of the Convention on Transit Trade of Land-locked States or the New York Convention, as the treaty is also generally known, already referred to above. Yet, although this Convention, in general, recognized the need for the transit rights of LLS, and was an attempt at balancing the interests of land-locked countries against those of coastal or transit States, it still did not provide for a general categorical right of access under international law as such. In this regard, it is instructive to note that with the exception of Botswana, all other LLS of the Southern African region subsequently ratified the New York Convention; South Africa did not ratify the Convention either, arguing that there were already existing bilateral instruments regulating the matter. A similar argument was advanced by Portugal, the then colonial power over Mozambique and Angola, the other major coastal States in the region.[17]

On the available evidence, it is highly doubtful that the argument that the various provisions in the pre-1982 multilateral conventions either reflected any existing customary right of transit, or were themselves evidence of an emerging rule of customary international law, can legitimately be defended.[18]

The United Nations Law of the Sea (LOS) Convention

The issue under consideration is now regulated by the provisions in Part X of the LOS Convention, aptly entitled: "Right of Access to and from the Sea and Freedom of Transit". The demands of LLS presented at the various stages leading to the negotiations which culminated in UNCLOS III were essentially three-fold: that they be granted a right of access to and from the sea; that this right be recognized by the international community in general; and that the right not be dependent on the conclusion of bilateral agreements with transit and coastal States. The original negotiating position was contained in a series of "Draft Articles" relating to LLS submitted by Afghanistan, Bolivia, Czechoslovakia, Hungary, Mali, Nepal and Zambia, on behalf of the other LLS.[19] On their part, African LLS subsequently made an effort to present a united negotiating position within the UNCLOS conferences. Consequently, the Organization of African Unity (OAU) adopted a declaration on 19 July 1974 on 'Issues of the Law of the Sea'. The declaration stated in part:[20]

> "[African] States endorse the right of access to and from the sea by the land-locked countries and the inclusion of such a provision in the universal treaty to be negotiated by the Law of the Sea Conference."

The declaration did not, however, represent the united voice which some LLS had hoped for, particularly within the African group itself. For Nigeria, arguably one of the leading coastal States among the OAU member States, struck a discordant note when its delegate to UNCLOS III insisted, while conceding the right of transit of LLS, that:[21]

> "The modalities of the exercise of free transit should be settled by bilateral or regional arrangements or agreements between the transit and land-locked States concerned."

In the final analysis, however, it may justifiably be argued that Part X of the LOS Convention does represent a fairly significant advance upon the previous positions of LLS under the "old" pre-1982 law of the sea. Article 125 is the most relevant of these provisions on the point under discussion. The Article provides, in part:

> "1. Land-locked States shall have the right of access to and from the sea for the purpose of exercising the rights provided for in this Convention including those relating to freedom of the high seas and the common heritage of mankind. To this end, land-locked States shall enjoy freedom of transit through the territory of transit States by all means of transport.
>
> 2. The terms and modalities for exercising freedom of transit shall be agreed between the land-locked States and transit States concerned through bilateral, subregional or regional agreements."

Article 125 represents a classic compromise in multilateral treaty formulation: on the one hand, it appears to recognize a *general* right of access; yet, at the same time, it still places the accent on bilateral or regional negotiation in so far as the practical arrangements for the *enjoyment and exercise* of the right by LLS is concerned. In this case, the question may legitimately be posed: to what extent is the right of access now recognized under international law? In relation to Part X of the LOS Convention, at least, it has been suggested that:[22]

> "There is some scope for the view that the provisions in Part X may be binding under general international law. Specifically, the fact that the main negotiating texts preceding the Convention all contained similar rules on access suggests that participants at the UNCLOS III reached consensus on the rules in Part X from an early stage at the Conference; the argument would be that this consensus reflected widespread agreement on emergent rules of customary law pertaining to free transit."

But, as the same learned writer goes on to argue, this presumption may, in fact, be rebutted both in its own terms and by reference to the actual course of negotiations on transit at the UNCLOS III. At most, what may be said, and what merits emphasis, is that Part X is likely to have considerable impact upon customary law in the future; in particular, because Article 125 is clearly expressed in mandatory terms, its norm-creating character can hardly be denied.[23] Vasciannie's justification for this view is that:[24]

> "[The] terms of Part X are publicized and well known to negotiators from both land-locked and transit countries; they may therefore serve as a model for subsequent agreements, and, as such, they will help in the crystallization of new rules in the area of transit. By way of comparison, it may be recalled that when the Universal Declaration of Human Rights was adopted by the General Assembly in 1948, it was not regarded as a statement of law or legal obligation. Yet, by its very existence, the Declaration created 'an expectation of adherence' which, in turn, generated State practice in favour of human rights norms. Since at least some transit States at the UNCLOS III seemed willing to support the basic right of transit, it is not far-fetched to anticipate that a similar process could occur in the case of Part X."

This somewhat optimistic conclusion would seem to be justified, within limits. But it is worth noting that it is reached *ex abundanti cautela*, and is couched more in terms of the *lex feranda* than the *lex lata* on transit rights.

Unlike Article 3 of the High Seas Convention, Article 125 does not suggest that the existence, recognition or grant of rights of access is dependent upon the sovereign discretion of the coastal or transit State in question; only that the modalities for the exercise of such rights shall be a matter for bilateral or regional arrangements. It would seem, therefore, that Baloro's contention, that LLS have not fared by better under the LOS Convention than under all other previous attempts at multilateral regulation of their transit and access rights, is not wholly tenable.[25] This is not to deny that Part X of the LOS Convention does present certain fundamental problems. For example, Article 125(3) accords transit States the right to take all necessary measures to ensure that the exercise by LLS of the rights and facilities provided for under that part of the Convention do not infringe their legitimate interests; yet, as has correctly been pointed out by other commentators, the Convention itself is silent on the question of who is entitled to determine, and upon what criteria, the existence of such legitimate interests. However, since the Convention provides for machinery for the compulsory judicial and arbitral settlement of most kinds of disputes that may arise under it (Article 291), the ability of transit States to deny LLS transit rights on the basis of capricious and arbitrary considerations may not be as wide as it might at first appear. It would be interesting to see how the practical question of whether the rights of access and transit for the Southern African LLS vis-à-vis South Africa can be claimed as a matter of legal right will be approached in the actual practice of the States concerned, now that the LOS Convention is in force. Here it is apt to observe that although South Africa signed the Convention on 5 December 1984, it took almost thirteen years to the day to be ratified. The new, post-apartheid parliament consented to this ratification only in November 1997.[26]

The Right of Access as a General Principle of International Law

The discussion in the preceding sections was concerned with the argument that there may be a case for the recognition of the existence of a customary rule according LLS a right of transit and access to the sea. Other arguments suggest the existence of a right of access to the sea which is binding *erga omnes* in virtue of a general principle of international law. Briefly, three claims are made in this regard: first, that the right of access is a logical corollary of freedom of the high seas and the common heritage of mankind, both recognized under the LOS Convention, and is as such enforceable even in the absence of treaty undertakings;[27] secondly, that the right is founded upon natural law considerations;[28] and, finally, that such a right can be likened to servitudes in municipal legal systems.[29]

Both Rubin and Vasciannie point out that the argument that a right of access exists as a corollary to the freedom of the high seas is, in fact, logically faulty. The analogous counter-argument posed by these writers is this: that although international law accords both scheduled and non-scheduled flights the right to fly over the high seas, yet only the latter can traverse the airspace of foreign States without permission.[30] Rubin's other argument, however, is difficult to defend. He contends that even if freedom of the high seas implies a right of access to the sea, it does not necessarily mean that LLS have the right to transit *goods* across foreign territory.[31] But, surely, is this not a case of juristic hair-splitting? Traditionally the claims for rights of access have been made precisely in relation to the right of States to engage in commerce with foreign States, and this implies a right to transit goods. Without that, the right of access would be a vacuous "right" of no practical moment. Moreover, it might also be argued that a State cannot enjoy the full attributes of its statehood if it cannot exercise, on a basis of equality with other States, the functions of a State; these include trade, communication and intercourse with the outside world. Thus, where the right of access to and from the sea is denied, then the LLS is denied the opportunity to enjoy full measure of its statehood. In this regard, it would be instructive to consider, for example, the analogous claims made in the *Right of Passage* case.[32] The right of passage acknowledged by the Court in this case was based upon local custom. The question is whether, and to what extent, it has any relevance for similar situations, such as that of LLS (for example Lesotho, which is entirely surrounded by South Africa) that seek access by land to the sea? The observation by Lauterpacht, writing about freedom of transit across the territory of another State generally, is of particular relevance on this point:[33]

> "The operative principle, it is believed, is that States, far from being free to treat the establishment or regulation of routes of transit as a substantial derogation from their sovereignty which they are entirely free to refuse, are bound to act in this matter in the fulfillment of an obligation to the community of which they form a part. It is a principle formulated by Grotius over three hundred years ago in the following words: 'Similarly also lands, rivers, and any part of the sea that has become subject to the ownership of a people, ought to be open to those who, for legitimate reasons, have need to cross them; as for instance, if a people [desire] to carry on commerce with a distant [people]'.
>
> On that view [Grotius'], there exists in customary international law a right to free or innocent passage for purposes of trade, travel and commerce over the territory of all States – a right which derives from the existence of the international community and which is a direct consequence of the interdependence of States."

The argument for the importation of natural law considerations into this question poses its own problems. Attempts to base the normative nature of certain rules of international law on natural law principles are often difficult to reconcile with the general positivist character of modern international law. It is thought that in this particular context, a natural law conception of the right of access would have to ignore the territorial sovereignty of transit States.[34] And so would a conception of a right of access based on the notion of servitudes; the doctrine of State servitudes is no longer so widely and readily accepted under modern international law as it once was, even in the limited context of succession of States to treaties.[35] The conclusion that the doctrine has little bearing on the question whether LLS as a group have a right of access to the sea under general international law is thus fully justified.[36]

Conclusion

The picture that emerges from this brief discussion is not an altogether happy one for the Southern African LLS. The claim that rights of access and transit exist at customary international law is not supportable by the evidence from the relevant multilateral treaty arrangements and other manifestations of State practice. At the same time, the provisions in Article 125 in Part X of the LOS Convention cannot be regarded as an expression of existing customary law in this respect, nor yet categorical evidence of an emerging customary rule. As was stated above, until the provisions in question crystallize into norms of customary law through repeated adoption in State practice the claim that the right of access is now part of the *lex generalis publicum* will remain highly untenable. Even the recent entry into force of the entire LOSC does not resolve the question categorically. For, as was observed above, one major weakness in the Convention is that individual LLS and coastal States still need to reach specific agreement on the terms and practical modalities of free transit across the territory of the latter, and yet the Convention is silent as to what happens in the event of failure to reach such agreement. This leaves some scope for disputes. The legal position of Southern African LLS, therefore, can only best be assured by particular bilateral or regional arrangements with South Africa and the other coastal States in the region, quite apart from whatever rights and privileges may be claimed on the basis of the LOS Convention.

This conclusion cannot provide much comfort for the LLS concerned. For it will be recalled that during the dark days of high apartheid and the dubious "total onslaught" strategy, the existence of such bilateral or regional treaty obligations did not stop South Africa from imposing a total blockade over a land-locked neighbour wholly dependent upon its transit routes and seaports; or from dislocating and destabilizing large sections of the transport and communications network of its northern neighbour, Mozambique, through the proxy "low intensity conflict".[37] Of course, one cannot begin to suggest here that the new democratic government in South Africa is ever likely to follow the dubious regional agenda which informed the strategic choices of the apartheid regime, and one is rather tempted to conclude that the recent political changes in South Africa render these experiences no more than sad historical blots on the evolution of international law and the international rule of law in the Southern African subregion. But, to use the old adage, history has a way of repeating itself. The reality is that the eradication of apartheid and racist minority rule in South Africa will not, of itself, ensure the disappearance of a problem which could recur in the relations between the States of the region (or in respect of other LLS elsewhere in the world). This is not to deny that, generally speaking, practice has shown that States are more inclined to respect, rather than to defy, the requirements of LLS for rights of transit and access; and that few have been the occasions when parochial self-interests have motivated transit or coastal States to deny LLS these rights. However, this potentially enduring problem can only be resolved by the universal and unequivocal adoption of the right of access as a basic right of LLS within the ever-growing corpus of norms of international law. The ratification of the LOS Convention by South Africa is not enough. Its unequivocal recognition of the right of access to the sea for its neighbouring LLS would be the most positive and reassuring move towards this desirable objective.

Notes

1. The Southern African Development Coordination Conference (SADCC), was established in Lusaka in March 1980, with the adoption of the Lusaka Declaration, at a summit meeting attended by the Heads of State and Government (or their representatives) of Angola, Botswana, Lesotho, Malawi, Mozambique, Swaziland, Tanzania, Zambia and Zimbabwe. The organization was subsequently reconstituted, through a formal treaty, as the Southern African Development Community (SADC), with the added membership of the recently independent Namibia, on 17 August 1992; South Africa became the eleventh member on 29 August 1994. SADC now comprises 14 countries, with the added membership of Democratic Republic of Congo, Mauritius and Seychelles. In this discussion, the former acronym "SADCC" will only be used when referring specifically to the pre-1992 period, and only where the context requires such usage.

2. The term "land-locked State" (LLS) is used in the sense in which international lawyers generally understand it, namely "a State which has no sea-coast and which must, therefore, rely on one or more neighbouring States for access to the sea". There are currently fifteen LLS in Africa: Botswana, Burkina Faso, Burundi, Central African Republic, Chad, Ethiopia, Lesotho, Malawi, Mali, Niger, Rwanda, Swaziland, Uganda, Zambia and Zimbabwe. For some of the leading discussions on the legal position of LLS under the Law of the Sea in general, see Z. Cervenka (Ed.), *Land-locked Countries of Africa*, (1973); S. Vasciannie, *Land-locked and Geographically Disadvantaged States in the International Law of the Sea*, (1990); M.I. Glassner, *Access to the Sea for Developing Land-locked States*, (1970); A.M. Sinjela, *Land-locked States and the UNCLOS III Regime*, (1983).

3. An earlier discussion of some of the issues raised here is to be found in J. Baloro, "Rights of Access to the Sea: International Legal Aspects of Land-locked SADCC States' dependency on the Republic of South Africa", unpublished mimeo.,

(University of Swaziland, date unknown). As regards the right of access of these States to the living resources in South African coastal waters and EEZ, see R.K. Sizani, "The Law of the Sea Convention and the Rights of the neighbouring African Land-locked States to fish in the South African fishing zone", *3 African J Int'l & Comp L 507* (1991).

4. Starting in early February 1987, the Government of Bophuthatswana demanded that train crews from Botswana and Zimbabwe should obtain entry visas prior to using the rail line which crossed the "homeland" territory bordering on Botswana. The dispute was only resolved when Bophuthatswana agreed that South African crew would now collect traffic at the Rakhuna terminal, near Ramatlabama border post (on the Botswana-Bophuthatswana border) from the Botswana and Zimbabwean crew, instead of Mafeking, well within the "homeland" territory. See Keesing's *Contemporary Archives*, Vol. XXXIII, (October 1978) pp. 35434–35435.

5. SADC's response in this regard has been to direct its attention to the development of alternative transit routes based in part on the concept of the "northern corridor", namely improving the viability of the rail/road routes to the Mozambican and Tanzanian ports, and thus reducing dependence on South African transit routes and ports.

6. See, for example, L. Caflisch, "Land-locked States and their access to and from the Sea", 49 BYIL 71 (1978); A.P. Rubin, "Land-locked African countries and rights of access to the sea" in Cervenka, *op. cit.* note 2 *supra*. See also Sinjela, *op. cit.* note 2. For an earlier discussion see H. Tabibi, *The Right of Free Access to the Sea*, (1966); see also *Question of Free Access to the Sea of Land-locked Countries*, UN Doc. A/CONF. 13/29 and Add. 1 (1958), in UNCLOS I, *Official Records*, Vol. I, p. 306. See also T. Franck *et al.*, "The New Poor: Land-locked, Shelf-locked and Other Geographically Disadvantaged States", *7 N Y U J Int L & Politics 33* (1974).

7. Vasciannie, *op. cit.* note 2 *supra*, p. 197. See also Glassner, *op. cit.* note 2 p. 16 *et seq*.

8. D.P. O'Connell, *International Law*, Vol. I, (2nd ed., 1970) pp. 237–238.

9. O'Connell, *ibid.*; E. Lauterpacht, "Freedom of Transit in International Law", *44 Trans Grotius Soc 313* (1958–1959) L. Oppenheim, *International Law*, Vol. I, (8th ed., H. Lauterpacht), (1955) pp. 675–676; G. Schwarzernberger, *A Manual of International Law*, (1960) p. 103 *et seq*.

10. See, for example, the argument advanced by Nepal at UNCLOS III: UNCLOS III, *Official Records*, Vol. II, p. 238.

11. See especially J.E.S. Fawcett, "Trade and Finance in International Law", *123 Hague Recueil 215* (1968); also J. Symonides, "Geographically Disadvantaged States and the New Law of the Sea", 8 *Polish Yrbk Int L* 55 (1976).

12. Vasciannie, *op. cit.* note 2, p. 198.

13. For a full discussion of these conventional developments see Glassner, *op. cit.* n. 1 pp. 16–38; Vasciannie, *ibid.* pp. 198–209.

14. Thus, with respect to this provision, it has even been argued that the actual obligations of the coastal States are apparently envisaged as moral rather than legal; see Cervenka, *op. cit.* note 2 *supra*, especially essay by Cervenka, "The Right of Access to the Sea of African Land-locked Countries", *passim*. See also Baloro, *op. cit.* p. 10. An argument in favour of the existence of a customary right would run as follows: first, that the preamble to the High Seas Convention proclaims the Convention to be "generally declaratory of established principles of international law"; second, that since Article 2 proclaims that all States (including LLS) shall enjoy the freedom of the high seas, the logical conclusion must be that the Convention could not ascribe such a fundamental right while taking away its realization.

15. Rubin, *op. cit.* p. 188.

16. This was the view adopted by the US delegation to UNCLOS I: see statement by Arthur H. Dean, Head of the US Delegation to UNCLOS I, to the Senate Foreign Relations Committee, 20 January 1960, cited in M. Whiteman, *Digest of International Law*, Vol. IV, (1963) pp. 632–633.

17. The 1969 Customs Union Agreement between Botswana, Lesotho, South Africa, Swaziland and (as a more recent signatory) Namibia guarantees the parties freedom of transit through each other's territory (Art. 16). Similarly, the United Kingdom-Portugal Treaty relating to the Use of the Port of Beira and Connected Railways of 17 June 1950 guaranteed unimpeded movement of goods between the Portuguese colony of Mozambique and the land-locked British colonial territories (now Malawi, Zambia and Zimbabwe). A similar agreement between the United Kingdom and Portugal guaranteed Swaziland's access to the port of Laurenço Marques (now Maputo).

18. For an authoritative statement of the circumstances under, and extent to, which particular rules contained in the provisions of multilateral treaties may be regarded as evidence of emerging customary norms, see the International Court of Justice's judgment in the *North Sea Continental Shelf Cases*, I.C.J. Rep. [1969] p. 42. See also L.P. Lee, "The Law of the Sea Convention and Third States", *77 AJIL 541* (1983), in which the criteria laid down in the *North Sea*

Continental Shelf Cases are discussed in relation to the Law of the Sea Convention as a whole.

19. See, generally, *Study of the Question of Free Access to the Sea of Land-locked Countries and of the Special Problems of Land-locked Countries Relating to the Exploration and Exploitation of the Resources of the Seabed and the Ocean Floor beyond the Limits of National Jurisdiction*, UN Doc. A/AC/ 138/37 (1971).

20. UN. Doc. A/CONF. 62/33; in UNCLOS III, *Official Records*, Vol. III, p. 63.

21. UNCLOS III, *Official Records*, Vol. XXI, p. 245.

22. See Vasciannie, *ibid.* p. 208.

23. *Ibid.* p. 209.

24. *Ibid.*

25. Baloro, *op. cit.* p. 14. Of course, as is generally admitted, it cannot be pretended that the provisions of Part X of the LOSC will necessarily resolve all problems faced by LLS, but its generally positive aspects cannot be totally denied either.

26. It has been suggested by some commentators that the main reason for Pretoria's earlier reluctance to ratify the Convention probably arose out of the contentious issue of the right of access (particularly to its EEZ resources) of the neighbouring LLS. On this, see D.J. Devine, "South Africa and the Law of the Sea: Problems Common, Uncommon and Unique", in T.W. Bennett *et al.*, *The Law of the Sea*, (1986) p. 40 *et seq.* It may also be important to bear in mind that the Convention is unique in the sense that it was negotiated as a "package deal", and that many of its provisions are either norm-creating or declaratory of customary law. The provision respecting freedom of transit is, in the view of some commentators, arguably a candidate for this status. In a statement to the National Assembly on 28 October 1994, the South African Minister of Transport had indicated in fairly clear terms that South Africa would certainly take into account the interests of its land-locked neighbours, in terms of the obligations set out under the Convention, when the time comes to ratify it.

27. Thus, for example, Principle 1 of the *Principles Enunciated by the Preliminary Conference of Land-locked States*, UN Doc. A/CONF. 13/13/C. 5/L/ 1. For a historical perspective of this argument, see G. Scelle, *Manuel de droit international public*, (1941), Part 1, p. 389.

28 The idea of access as a "natural right" was first advocated by Hugo Grotius in his *De Jure Belli ac Pacis*, (1625), II, 2, 3. This idea was also taken up by the *Conseil Executif Provisoire* of the French Republic in its decree issued on

16 November 1792 demanding freedom of navigation on the Scheldt; see J.H. Verzijl, *International Law in Historical Perspective*, Vol. 3, (1970) p. 103.

29. Scelle, *op. cit.* 389; cf. Portugal's argument in the *Case Concerning Right of Passage Over Indian Territory*, I.C.J. Pleadings, Vol. I, pp. 628–629; 714 *et seq.*

30. See Articles 5 and 6 of the Chicago Convention on International Civil Aviation (1944): 15 UNTS 295; Vasciannie, *op. cit.* p. 216; Rubin, *op. cit.* p. 55.

31. Rubin, *ibid.*

32. See note 30 *supra.*

33. Lauterpacht, *op. cit.* note 9 *supra*. For the reference to Grotius, see his *De Jure Belli ac Pacis*, (1625), II, 2, (Carnegie Classics of International Law edition, 1925), pp. 196–197.

34. Some writers in fact argue that the principle of territorial sovereignty has been qualified to permit a right of transit. See, for example, Lauterpacht, *ibid.*

35. See the brief analysis of this notion in the preceding discussion on the devolution of the Niger Treaties in Chapter 4. The notion of State servitudes has been advocated by a number of leading legal scholars, for example: H.D. Reid, *International Servitudes in Law and Practice*, (1932); H. Lauterpacht, *Private Law Sources and Analogies of International Law*, (1927) pp. 119–124; Oppenheim, *op. cit.* pp. 535–543; O'Connell, *op. cit.* pp. 544–552. See also J. Viall, "The transit of persons to and from Lesotho (Pt. II)", *1 CILSA 187* (1968). But see A.D. McNair, "So-called State servitudes", *6 BYIL 111* (1925).

36. See, for example, Vasciannie, *op. cit.* p. 217.

37. It is generally acknowledged that South Africa was, until the beginning of the 1990s, largely behind the Mozambique National Resistance (Renamo) movement which was responsible for the widespread destruction of human life and the dislocation of the transport network in the southern part of the country in the course of the long drawn-out low intensity conflict (or civil war) which raged on in that country for almost seventeen years, starting in 1975. See J. Hanlon, *Apartheid's Second Front: South Africa's war against its neighbours*, (1986) *passim*; also R. Rothberg *et al.* (Eds.), *South Africa and Its Neighbours: Regional Security and Self-Interest*, (1985).

12

ENVIRONMENT AND DEVELOPMENT IN AFRICA IN THE 1990s: SOME LEGAL ISSUES

Introduction

The environment has been among the foremost concerns of the international community over the last two decades. Two important milestones have marked this period. First, the convening of the first United Nations Conference on the Human Environment (UNCHE) in Stockholm, Sweden, which culminated in the adoption of the Stockholm Declaration of 16 June 1972. This conference marked the first real attempt to put the environment on the international agenda and, more importantly, pronounced upon the relationship between the protection and enjoyment of human rights and the quality of the environment.[1] Second, the convening, twenty years later, of the United Nations Conference on Environment and Development (UNCED) in Rio de Janeiro, Brazil, from 3 to 14 June 1992, which also resulted in the adoption of a declaration, the Rio Declaration on Environment and Development.[2] Quite apart from the symbolic significance of celebrating the twentieth anniversary of the Stockholm Declaration, UNCED served both to reaffirm the relevance and normative value of the principles of international environmental law that had grown up in the intervening period and to reiterate the importance attached to the relationship between the environment and development by political leaders, non-governmental organizations and scientific and academic groups. At least, that had been the expectation.

The debate about the need to protect the environment has, of course, transcended virtually every discipline of human knowledge. But, perhaps, the most striking feature of this debate has been the increasing acceptance of the necessary linkage between what were in previous times usually regarded as total separate issues: development and environment. As the World Commission on Environment and Development (WCED), also generally known as the "Brundtland Commission", so aptly put it in its report, *Our Common Future*, presented to the United Nations in 1987:[3]

> "There has been a growing realization in national governments and multilateral institutions that it is impossible to separate economic development issues from environment issues; many forms of development erode the environmental resources upon which they must be based, and environmental degradation can undermine economic development."

In fact, this view, that environmental quality management and protection and the development process are intimately linked, long predates the WCED statement quoted above. Thus, it had been observed in the Report of the Panel of Experts which had been convened by the Secretary General of the United Nations Conference on Human Environment as early as 1971:[4]

> "From a broad standpoint it may be said that one of the ultimate goals of economic development is the creation of a healthy, pleasant, desirable environment. In this sense, any actual or potential conflict between the two processes could disappear and everything that would be done in favour of environment would simply be computed as economic development."

These sentiments were reiterated in Rio. As some commentators have already observed, if nothing else, UNCED demonstrated the tremendous complexity of global environmental problems, which arise in a wide range of activities, in a wide range of media, and which concern diverse groups seeking potentially conflicting environmental or developmental objectives.[5] Accordingly, *Agenda 21*, the UNCED program of action for sustainable development adopted at Rio, seeks to establish different but related program areas, objectives and activities for different areas of "environment" and "development".[6] But what do these concepts mean in the context of these debates?

Some Definitional and Conceptual Issues

The Right to the Environment and the Meaning of "Environment"

A convenient starting point would be the acknowledgement that both "environment" and "development" are now familiar concepts in the wider debate concerning international human rights. At any rate, international human rights lawyers have, especially during the last decade and a half, engaged in exciting, if contentious, debates about the nature and content of "new" species of human rights. Included in this scheme of "new" human rights are the right to development and the right to the environment.[7] To be sure, the very existence of these rights continues to be contested by some human rights theorists and commentators, especially those rooted in Western human rights scholarship. Moreover, even those who acknowledge the existence of the two particular rights mentioned above as human rights quickly point out that while, on the one hand, there may be a necessary linkage between them, there would also seem to exist a tension between the right to development and the right to the environment, on the other hand.

The term "environment" has been described as both ambiguous and self-explanatory. In Caldwell's words, "it is a term that everyone understands and no one is able to define".[8] None of the major treaties, declarations, codes of conduct or guidelines adopted by the international community attempts to define the term, at least not directly. No specific mention or definition of it appears in the United Nations Charter, no doubt due to the fact that environmental concerns were not thought important enough to merit inclusion in the Charter at the time of its drafting and adoption in 1945. Thus, as some commentators have rightly observed, the only chance reference to the environment in the Charter is to "good neighbours" in the second paragraph of the Preamble and "good neighbourliness" in Article 74.[9] Neither the Universal Declaration of Human Rights of 1948 (UDHR) nor the subsequent International Covenant on Civil and Political Rights of 1966 (ICCPR) changed the situation. However, the International Covenant on Economic, Social and Cultural Rights (ICESCR), adopted in the same year, incorporated some provisions that have a direct relevance to the environment. In terms that are clearly more anthropocentric than ecological, Article 11 (1) provides, in part:

> "The States Parties to the present Covenant recognize the right of everyone to an adequate standard of living for himself and his family, including adequate food, clothing and housing, and to the continuous improvement of living [conditions]."

After further recognizing the right of everyone to the enjoyment of the highest attainable standard of physical and mental health, in Article 12(1), the Covenant goes on to enumerate the steps required to achieve the full realization of this right. Among these is the "improvement of all aspects of environmental and industrial hygiene" (Article 12(2)(b)). It was left to the

Stockholm Declaration to expound on the emerging consensus. However, on its part, the Stockholm Declaration provided no clear definition of the term "environment", but merely referred obliquely to "man's environment as that which gives him physical sustenance and affords him the opportunity for intellectual, spiritual, moral and social growth". But, more to the point, it further noted that "both aspects of man's environment, the natural and the man-made, are essential for his well-being and enjoyment of basic human rights – even the right to life itself".[10] Although the Stockholm Declaration did not go as far as proclaiming a right to the environment, it did at least draw attention to the nexus between a healthy environment and the enjoyment and satisfaction of certain basic human rights. Thus, Principle 1 of the Stockholm Declaration states that "[man] has a the fundamental right to freedom, equality and adequate conditions of life, in an environment of a quality that permits a life of dignity and well-being..."

Among the more recent international human rights instruments, it is the African Charter on Human and Peoples' Rights of 1981 that, for the first time, explicitly recognizes that "All peoples shall have the right to a general satisfactory environment favourable to their development" (Article 24). This formulation is admittedly vague, and leaves a large scope for argument as to what constitutes a "general satisfactory environment". Moreover, the African Charter does not explicitly stipulate a corresponding duty on the part of States regarding this right. The Additional Protocol to the American Convention on Human Rights in the Area of Economic, Social and Cultural Rights ("Protocol of San Salvador") of 1988 goes a little further. Article 11 provides as follows:

> "1. Everyone shall have the right to live in a healthy environment and to have access to basic public services.
>
> 2. The States Parties shall promote the protection, preservation and improvement of the environment."

Neither of these treaties defines the term "environment", at least for the purpose of construing this right in the human rights context.[11] The Rio Declaration does not offer a definition of "environment" either, but broadly enjoins States to cooperate in the spirit of global partnership to conserve, protect and restore the health and integrity of the earth's ecosystem.[12] However, by the time the so-called Earth Summit was convened in Rio, some consensus had crystallized on at least two positions among the greater majority of international human rights lawyers, scholars and advocates: first, the existence of a right to the environment; secondly, the firm linkage of this right to the concept of sustainable development. In this regard, although the term "environment" has eluded specific elaboration in the various human rights instruments, the provisions cited above indicate that what States seek to secure in acknowledging a human right to the environment is not the right to an "ideal" environment, which is probably difficult both to define and achieve, but rather "the right to have the present environment conserved, protected from significant deterioration and improved in some cases".[13]

The Right to Development and the Concept of "Sustainable Development"

The human rights discourse in the late seventies and early eighties was also partly dominated by arguments relating to the right to development. Although there was widespread acceptance of the need for development, especially of the underdeveloped countries of the Third World, opposing views existed regarding the claim that this need was founded on the notion of a "right" to development, as an inalienable human right. Third World States, generally supported by the former Soviet Union and Eastern European communist countries, saw this right as part of a larger argument for reparation for past colonial exploitation and plunder. Western countries, on the other hand, would only accept a general obligation to cooperate with these States to promote development, but not on the basis of a recognition of an alleged right to development.

The current acceptance of the right to development as both a collective and individual right, at least in the literature on human rights as well as in the relevant pronouncements of some States, owes much to the contribution of African and Africanist scholars engaged in the human rights debate. As with the right to the environment, here one finds that all the earlier international human rights instruments, including the United Nations Charter, are silent on the matter. The numerous references in these instruments to economic, social and cultural development or progress do not, in any case, add up to an explicit recognition of a right to development as such. Indeed, as is well-known, it was only in 1972 that the Senegalese jurist, Keba M'baye, later a judge at the International Court of Justice, first proposed the recognition of this right.[14] Subsequently, as Chairman of the Commission on Human Rights in 1977, he was instrumental in seeing the first formal recognition of a human right to development in international instruments. The United Nations General Assembly, for example, adopted a resolution acknowledging the right to development on 23 November 1979.[15] Seven years later, on 4 December 1986, the General Assembly finally adopted the Declaration on the Right to Development by a vote of 146 in favour, 1 against and 8 abstentions.[16] Article 1 of the Declaration provides as follows:

"1. The right to development is an inalienable human right by virtue of which every human person and all peoples are entitled to participate in, contribute to, and enjoy economic, social, cultural and political development, in which all human rights and freedoms can be fully realized."

Article 3 goes on to state that "States have a duty to cooperate with each other in ensuring development and eliminating obstacles to development." It is also relevant to notice that, in 1981, the African Charter on Human and Peoples' Rights became the first international human rights treaty to recognize the right to development explicitly, and to place a duty on States to protect this right. According to Article 22 of the Charter:

"1. All peoples shall have the right to their economic, social and cultural development with due regard to their freedom and identity and in the equal enjoyment of the common heritage of mankind.

2. States shall have the duty, individually or collectively to ensure the exercise of the right to development."

Thus, although some controversy still exists as to the precise meaning and content of this right, and despite the continuing rejection by a minority of scholars and commentators of the very existence of such a right,[17] there would seem to be no doubt that contemporary international law regards the right to development as one of the "new" human rights. The right to development stresses the indivisibility of human rights, and the inter-linkages between civil and political rights, on the one hand, and economic, social and cultural rights, on the other.

As already noted above, the inextricable relationship between environmental protection and development, especially for developing countries, was recognized at the Stockholm conference, and some of the principles adopted at that conference take account of this. But the immediate problem was how to accommodate the political and economic implications of restricting industrial, agricultural, fisheries, and other developmental activities of States in order to ensure protection of the environment and conservation of resources. Prior to Stockholm, developing countries had tended to regard environmental problems as belonging to the industrialized or developed world. Given this attitude, Third World countries insisted on placing priority on development and viewed with suspicion attempts by the industrialized countries to place equal, or higher, emphasis on environmental issues. Clearly, in the eyes of the Third World delegate who is quoted as having declared at the Stockholm Conference, "Let me die polluted"[18], there could be no justification by developed States in diverting funds from development assistance to prevention or reduction of environmental degradation. It was partly in an effort to address these concerns that some of the principles adopted at Stockholm attempted to reconcile this apparent tension between development and environment. Thus, Principle 8 states that economic and social development is essential for ensuring a favourable environment [for man] and the improvement of the quality of life; Principle 11 recognizes that environmental policies should enhance, and not adversely affect, the development of developing countries, and so on and so forth.

It was only from the early 1980s that the international community began to adopt strategies that took account of the reality that the environment could not forever in all cases sustain unlimited development. The International Union for the Conservation of Nature (IUCN) led the way with the adoption of its *World Conservation Strategy* in 1980, which was premised on sustainable utilization of species and ecosystems.[19] In 1982, the UN General Assembly adopted Resolution 37/7, the "World Charter for Nature", which aimed, *inter alia*, at optimal sustainable productivity of all resources coupled with conservation and environmental protection.[20]

The WCED took up these issues, synthesized the emerging consensus and proffered a definition of (sustainable development) as "development that meets the needs of the present without compromising the ability of future generations to meet their own needs".[21] The WCED took the position that development and economic growth can be accommodated within certain ecological limits and proceeded to identify seven requirements for sustainable development: (a) a system that allows citizens to take part in political decision-making; (b) an economic system that is self-reliant and able to generate surpluses and technical knowledge; (c) a social system that can resolve the tensions of disharmonious development; (d) a production system based on respect for ecological development; (e) a technological system capable of finding new solutions; (f) sustainable international trade and finance; (g) a flexible self-corrective administrative system.[22] Furthermore, it is now generally acknowledged that the notion of "sustainable development" requires the maintenance, rational use and enhancement of the natural resource base that underpins ecological resilience and economic growth, and implies progress towards international equity.[23] The Rio Declaration adopted an even more unequivocal position on the relationship between environment and development. Thus Principle 4 of the Rio Declaration states:

> "In order to achieve sustainable development, environmental protection shall constitute an integral part of the development process and cannot be considered in isolation from it."

Principle 25 of the Rio Declaration goes on to assert that peace, development and environmental protection are interdependent and indivisible.[24] It is important to note, however, that between Stockholm and Rio, African countries did engage in this debate and did adopt their own initiatives. In particular, two principal instruments should be mentioned: the 1989 Kampala Declaration on Sustainable Development in Africa and the 1991 Cairo Common Position on African Environment and Development Agenda.

Environment and Development: the Conceptual Nexus

The relationship between the environment and development has got at least two aspects to it: the "causative" and the "corrective". On the one hand, one may say that the development process itself can be, and has been, the cause of environmental degradation and, conversely, that lack of development can also be one of the causes of such degradation. On the other hand, it may be argued that the process of correcting or arresting environmental degradation is in itself not a separate human activity totally unrelated to the development process, but rather part of that process. Thus, environmental protection and management ought to be considered as part of development planning.

This is not to ignore the real tension that exists between the right to development and the right to the environment. And this tension did resurface in the run up to the Rio Conference, in the opposing perspectives adopted by the Group of 77, on the one hand, and the developed countries, on the other. In an echo of Stockholm, the North blamed the South for exacerbating environmental and developmental problems by overpopulating the world; the latter counter-argued that global pollution and environmental degradation were largely due to the North's apparent extravagant and wasteful way of living. There was a general consensus among developing countries that since Stockholm environmental concerns had received more attention than development issues, and that Rio offered an opportunity to reverse this order. They demanded that development should thus be set as a precondition for environmental regulations, and not vice-versa.[25] On their side, African countries had reiterated their common position in this regard in the 1989 Kampala Declaration on Sustainable Development in Africa and the 1991 Cairo Common Position on African Environment and Development Agenda already referred to above. Principle 3 of the Rio Declaration went some way towards meeting this demand.

In any case, this discussion proceeds on the assumption that the case for regarding the inseparability of the two processes, development and environment protection, has been sufficiently expounded by so many other scholars, commentators, professional or expert groups, as to need no further elaboration here. The present writer accepts as valid the two general propositions which can be discerned from the various pronouncements on this issue: first, that many, or perhaps most, forms of development erode the environmental resources upon which they must be based; second, that in order to achieve sustainable development, there is need to integrate economic and ecological considerations into decision-making.[26] From this, it may be argued that economic and ecological concerns should not be regarded as being necessarily in opposition to each other, but rather that they must, in fact, aim at compatibility.

By common consensus, the African continent best, and most tragically, exemplifies this relationship. On the causative side, some of the interlocking factors which have both affected the pace of development and accelerated the degradation of the environment in Africa have been identified as: (i) poverty and hunger, which lead to environmental degradation, worsening agricultural output, and eventually more poverty and hunger; (ii) a neglect of new investment by the industrialized nations in the wake of such growing poverty; (iii) high infant mortality, lack of education and medical care, which in turn generate even more poverty; (iv) high and uncontrolled population growth, urban squalor, inadequate food supplies, inadequate housing, the mushrooming of slums and shanty towns, unemployment, the proliferation of disease, and so on.[27] I do not propose to examine all these factors and the many others that have not even been mentioned here. The objective here is merely to make a general survey of some of the legal and policy issues that have emerged in the African experience in the area of environment law and policy over the last decade, and to identify the manner in which these legislative and policy constraints relate to, and affect, the development process and vice versa. In particular, attention will be directed at two areas of the legislative process: (i) constitutional and institutional machinery; and (ii) legislation relating to population and human settlements.

The limitation of the present discussion to the two areas intimated above is, of course, deliberate. On the one hand, as has already been observed, the relationship between the environment and development could be examined from various standpoints: the problems of energy and mineral resources, agriculture and food security, industry, species and ecosystems, land use, air, water and marine pollution, industrial and chemical waste, the role of the international economy, and so on. A discussion intended as a general survey such as this one does not provide the context for a comprehensive and meaningful analysis of all these issues. On the other hand, the problems selected for this discussion in many ways represent the very starting point for any analysis of the role of law in the environment-development debate. The constitutional and institutional setting forms the basis for legislative activity in the State; human settlements and population issues lie at the core of human activity, and development and environment are about human aspirations and activities.

Environmental Protection Legislation in Africa

There can be no doubt that law is critical to the regulation of the use of resources and the biosphere. The last two decades, in particular, have witnessed the emergence of clearly identifiable legal norms that can be characterized as forming the corpus of environmental law. These legal norms may not always provide answers to our complex environmental problems, but they do assist in providing mechanisms for negotiating the necessary accommodation, settling disputes, and ensuring, in the case of *international* environmental law, the implementation of treaties and customs. We are here concerned not so much with international environmental law but rather the municipal or *national* environmental laws enacted in the various African States.[28]

It is perhaps instructive to recall the observations made by two African legal scholars some twenty-five years or so ago. In his survey of the development of international environmental law and policy in Africa back in 1972, Ogundere stated:[29]

> "[Africa] has taken rapid strides in the last decade to develop, on the international level, solutions to certain environmental problems, mainly relating to fauna, flora and water resources. In the next decade, Africa should concentrate on the problems of over-population, urbanization and pollution."

And, writing some three years later, Adeniji observed, some what differently, that:[30]

> "The problems concerning environmental protection [are] new challenges in Africa, and the existing legal and administrative structures preclude rapid or all-embracing solutions. [What] is needed is the development of new legal, social and institutional tools that are capable of seeking and determining effective solutions to the problems generated by the current definitional dimensions of environmental protection, for which the present laws and institutions are not adequate."

Much of the debate going on in Africa on this subject reflects the persistent perception that the inadequacies identified by these two commentators more than two decades ago continue to characterize the legal and legislative landscapes in most African countries today.

Environmental law and legislation have been described as important management tools for environmental planning and control of development.[31] This view was given clear recognition in the Lagos Plan of Action adopted at the Organization of African Unity's Economic Summit in Lagos, Nigeria, in April 1980. Indeed, Article 58 of the African Economic Community Treaty which emerged from the Lagos initiative requires members to "promote a healthy environment". A generous reading of the African Charter on Human and Peoples' Rights would also suggest that a healthy environment is, under the treaty, regarded as a fundamental human right (Articles 16 and 24). The critical role of law in the protection of the environment was also recognized both by the WCED and its Experts Group on Environmental Law in the following terms:[32]

> "Both municipal and international law have too frequently lagged behind events. Today, legal regimes are being rapidly outdistanced by the accelerating pace and expanding scale of impacts on the environmental base of development. Human laws must be reformulated to keep human activities in harmony with the unchanging and universal laws of nature."

Environmental legislation as such is not, of course, a wholly post-independence phenomenon in Africa. The basic patterns of existing legislation and legal systems in Africa are largely a legacy of the colonial era. The colonial regimes did enact legislation relating to environmental conservation, although the pre-occupation of colonial administration was with the preservation of the African fauna and flora. One can also identify a whole range of colonial legislation which was, directly and indirectly, concerned with such environmental issues as sanitation, health, protection of marine resources and so on. Although a good proportion of these laws has remained on the statute book, inevitably a lot more legislation has been enacted since independence. Such post-independence legislation has been, in part, designed to take into account such factors as the industrial or economic orientation of the new States, socio-cultural values in relation to land tenure systems and other factors often ignored by the colonial legislator.

Yet, both the colonial and post-colonial laws seem to share one common characteristic: the exclusive emphasis on use- or rule-oriented laws, more concerned with policing, prohibitions and sanctions, rather than resource- or management-oriented laws which put the accent on the rational exploitation and protection of environmental resources and integrated development planning as part of environmental management. The bias towards use-oriented legislation continues to characterize environmental policy-making in all African States.[33]

If, then, legislation concerning the environment, or at least some aspects of it, has been in existence in most African States since the colonial times, why do these laws seem not to have played a particularly visible role in securing the conservation of environmental resources and arresting environmental degradation? In my view, part of the explanation lies in the wrong emphasis placed upon use-oriented laws instead of resource-oriented legislation, as has just been noted above. In addition, there are at least two other factors: the inadequacy of law enforcement machinery, and the lack of standards and controls for maintaining environmental quality.[34] Of course enforcement measures or quality control in themselves may not serve much purpose if the orientation of the laws which they seek to enforce is environmentally unsound or inadequate. The starting point, therefore, has to be the formulation of the right kind of laws: legislation which aims at securing "development without destruction".

Selected Environmental Legislation

(i) Constitutional and Institutional Machinery

Generally speaking, the inclusion of constitutional provisions embodying environmental rights is, at the present time, a very rare phenomenon. There are two possible approaches to the constitutional regulation of environmental protection: one is the entrenchment of a fundamental right, and the other is the incorporation of a statement of public policy.[35] In the former instance, the fundamental rights provision is a provision granting each individual a personal guarantee, a subjective right. In the latter case, the constitutional provision operates as a statement of State policy. The main difference between the two types of constitutional provisions in that the former guarantees a right enforceable by any aggrieved individual by filing a complaint against the State, before a constitutional court or other similarly designated tribunal; the latter is an objective provision that requires attention by the government, but cannot be invoked by the individual as such. Constitutional provisions entrenching fundamental rights, often to be found in that section of the constitution known as the "bill of rights", limit governmental intrusion into the private sphere. Constitutional provisions embodying directive principles of State policy, on the other hand, encourage government action in a certain direction; by guiding rather limiting legislative action. They have thus been described as "intentional norms" or "constitutional directives", as opposed to justiciable fundamental rights.[36] In any event, it is important to note the apt observation by Brandl and Bungert, that:[37]

> "Most environmental constitutional provisions are not prototypes of fundamental rights, nor are they prototypes of statements of public policy; but, rather, that the formulation of each environmental provision falls somewhere along a continuum between the subjective fundamental right at one extreme, and the objective statement of public policy at the other."

Now, as already noted, the incorporation of constitutional provisions relating specifically to environmental protection or providing for environmental rights is not a widespread phenomenon, at least not in Africa. In Africa, the pioneering example was set by Ghana. Article 9(1)(e) of the Constitution of the Third Republic of 1979 contained a declaration on a National Environmental Policy and enjoined the government to take the necessary legislative measures to improve the environment. This constitutional development in Ghana was the culmination of the policies drawn up by earlier governments. For example, the National Redemption Council had already issued a decree in 1974 creating a statutory body known as the Environmental Protection Council.[38] The main functions of this body were, *inter alia*, to formulate policy with regard to environmental matters, coordinate national and international liaison with respect to these matters, and to advise the government on all such issues.

More recent trends in Africa point to an increasing acknowledgement of the need to incorporate environmental rights in constitutional schemes. Three examples from the Southern African region will suffice here: the Namibian Constitution of 1990, the Malawian Constitution of 1995 and the South African Constitution of 1996 all have provisions relating to the environment. Malawi and Namibia have followed the statement of public policy approach, while South Africa has incorporated an environmental right as part of its bill of rights.

Article 95 of the Namibian Constitution (which falls under Chapter 11: "Principles of State Policy") provides that:

> "The State shall actively promote and maintain the welfare of the people by adopting, *inter alia*, policies aimed at the following: [...]
>
> (1) maintenance of ecosystems, essential ecological processes and biological diversity of Namibia and utilization of living natural resources on a sustainable basis for the benefit of all Namibians, both present and future; in

particular, the Government shall provide measures against the dumping or recycling of foreign nuclear and toxic waste on Namibian territory."

Employing somewhat different phraseology, Section 13 of the Malawian Constitution, which also lays down what are termed "Principles of National Policy", provides as follows:

> "The State of Malawi shall actively promote the welfare and development of the people of Malawi by progressively adopting and implementing policies and legislation aimed at achieving the following goals: [...]
>
> (d) *The Environment*
>
> To manage the environment responsibly in order to –
>
> (i) prevent the degradation of the environment;
>
> (ii) provide a healthy living and working environment for the people of Malawi;
>
> (iii) accord full recognition to the rights of future generations by means of environmental protection and the sustainable development of natural resources; and
>
> (iv) conserve and enhance the biological diversity of Malawi."

A number of brief observations may be made with regard to these provisions. In the first place, it has been argued by many commentators that the introduction of an environmental statement of public policy serves no meaningful purpose if it functions merely as a programmatic phrase that would require implementing legislation.[39] The concern here is mainly that if the provision merely commands in a general way that something be done, without giving specific indications as to when, how, and what should be regulated, the statement will not differ meaningfully from constitutional provisions which generally enable the legislature to act. In the more forceful words of Brandl and Bungert:[40]

> "An environmental statement of public policy that does not require the legislature to comply with specific mandates has no constitutional value but serves only as an expression of political, ideological, or ethical attitudes. Such an unenforceable environmental provision, conveying nothing but public sentiment or political intent, is a poor substitute for the specific environmental laws that a state may fail to enact."

But, of course, it cannot be denied that environmental statements of public policy have their own advantages. In acting as guidelines for the legislature, they may propel both the legislature and executive to act, and may raise the environmental consciousness or awareness of both government and society. Indeed, as Brandl and Bungert acknowledge[41], this type of declaration may elevate environmental protection into "a sacrosanct principle of government" – and one may note in this regard that the Malawian provision is part of what are described in the 1995 Constitution as "Fundamental Principles" (Chapter III).

Moreover, it is also instructive to note that the Namibian and Malawian provisions have adopted a commendably progressive approach which has not as yet been replicated in other constitutions elsewhere in Africa: first, the constitutional recognition of the linkage between environmental protection and sustainable development; second, the broadening of the scope of environmental management to include the conservation and enhancement of biological diversity; and, finally, the commitment to respect for the environment rights of future generations. The debate about our legal and moral obligations to respect the environmental rights of future generations is a critical and complex one, but one that cannot be joined in the present discussion.[42]

As already observed above, the South African Constitution of 1996 deals with the environmental question by enshrining an environmental clause, as a fundamental human right, within the entrenched bill of rights (Chapter 2). Section 24, the environmental clause, is complemented by other provisions which have a bearing on environmental law as well, for example, the clauses governing rights to administrative justice, access to information, property, economic activity, and so on.

The inclusion of an environmental clause in the South African bill of rights is a positive development. To begin with, it can be argued that this provision reflects one of the major currents of thought in the human rights and environmental law debates, namely that environment problems can best be approached within the context of an expanded notion of human rights which embraces environmental rights. Proponents of this approach would thus argue that logically the proper place to locate environmental rights in the constitution is in the bill of rights, or that part of the constitution enshrining fundamental individual rights and freedoms. But the South African approach goes further. For, as one of the leading South African commentators on this subject has observed, the other provisions referred to earlier in this constitution take account of the other, alternative, argument in this debate: that optimal environmental management will be achieved by reliance on administrative law rights as well (*locus standi* or legal standing; public participation; access to information; and so on).[43] Moreover, the provision also seeks to establish a linkage between environment and sustainable development; the commitment to conserve and enhance the biological diversity a whole; and recognition of the environmental rights of future generations. It moves away from the anthropocentric bias which was evident in the environmental clause in the interim constitution of 1993. The reference to health in the previous provision meant that the focus was on people, at the expense of basic environmental integrity.[44] It can only be hoped that the incorporation of an environmental right as one of the entrenched fundamental rights in the South African constitution will in time be emulated by other countries on the African continent. The entrenchment of an environmental right in a constitution ensures the existence of a mechanism for resolving conflicts, and amounts to a declaration that such rights stand on an equal footing with other fundamental rights and freedoms.[45]

The institutional machinery for the execution of national environmental policies differs widely, but some general trends can be identified. First, there are those States which have, at one time or another, established single implementation agencies, for example a Ministry of the Environment, or some such designation. Quite a number of countries in Africa fall into this category, for example Malawi, Morocco, Senegal, South Africa, Zambia and Zimbabwe, to mention only a few.[46] Second, there are those States, the majority in Africa, which deal with environmental matters on a sectoral basis, with various ministries or departments taking charge of different aspects: health, trade and industry, agriculture, water resources, mining and energy, soil, land, human settlements and so on. Among these States, there are two further categories: situations in which there is a central coordinating council or agency to liaise with all relevant ministries or departments; and those cases in which no single coordinating agency is in place. Single coordinating agencies can be either a particular designated ministry (as in the case of Botswana's Ministry of Local Government, Lands and Housing) or a Government appointed statutory body (as is the case with Ghana's Environmental Protection Council and Swaziland's National Trust Commission, more recently replaced by the Swaziland Environmental Authority). On the other extreme is a country like Mozambique which, for a half a decade since independence in 1975, had no established mechanism for coordinating environmental policy at all. In fact, it was only 1980 that environmental matters were for the first time incorporated into the country's National Development Plan (1980–1982). Ten years later, the country's new constitution of 1990 actually enshrined within it a commitment to the general principle of sustainable development which ensures the right to a balanced environment and the duty of all to maintain it (Article 72).

The constitutional and institutional machinery briefly described above is far from satisfactory. The absence of any constitutional provisions respecting environmental protection may not, in itself, be deemed such a critical deficiency as long as there is other legislation elsewhere in the legal system to redress the position. Unfortunately, an examination of the environmental practice of most African countries reveals some fundamental flaws. In this regard, three propositions will be advanced here. In the first place, there is need for States not only to embody some commitment to environmental protection in their constitutional machinery, but also to move away from the idea of the State as merely possessing powers to act with regard to the protection of the environment, towards the idea of States falling under a duty so to act. It is the view here that there must be recognized, on the part of all human beings, a fundamental right to an environment adequate for their health and well-being.

The other problem relates to the haphazard way in which environmental policy is coordinated, if at all, in the great majority of African States. Sectoral coordination involving a myriad of government ministries, departments and other statutory agencies is both wasteful and bureaucratically unsound, especially when coupled with the absence of a central coordinating environment unit. Closely related to this issue is the lack of machinery for the environmental impact assessment of development projects in most of the States in Africa. The most common practice is to carry out such assessment only in relation to what are perceived to be "major" projects, instead of routinely integrating this into the development planning process itself. The consequences of such an approach can be quite costly. As the Economic Commission for Africa has observed, the difficulty in establishing a mechanism for environmental impact assessment of development projects is partly due to lack of manpower and, more to the point, the desire of the government to establish politically visible economic development projects within the shortest possible time.[47]

Having regard to the above considerations, two further propositions may be advanced. The first concerns the need for African States to reorganize the institutional machinery relating to environmental protection such that there is ultimately a single body with overall responsibility for coordinating environmental policy in all its different aspects: legislative, administrative, technical, social and economic. Secondly, the machinery for environmental impact assessment ought to be strengthened and made a mandatory aspect of all development projects and industrial activities (including those undertaken by public or private firms or corporations). In a lot of countries environmental impact assessment has been employed only on a periodic basis mainly at the behest of external donor agencies, as a condition for aid, for large-scale development projects. Thus, to take one example, Swaziland has never had any legal requirements for routine environmental impact assessments, although the Swaziland Environment Authority is empowered to undertaken supervisory tasks in this regard.

(ii) Population and Human Settlements Legislation

It has been asserted that environmental stress is, among other things, the product of three main factors which are themselves interdependent: population, social organization or life style and technology. According to this view, population size contributes to environmental stress because people are both resource users and waster producers.[48] Yet, that population size is also an environmental problem has only just begun to command the attention of African States, and it is now appreciated that the issue is not about numbers, but about a State's ability to sustain its people on the available resource base. It is now widely recognized that population growth and development are linked in complex ways. On the one hand, economic development generates resources that can be used to improve education and health, and thus generate more development in the community. On the other hand, high population growth that eats into the resources available for economic and social development can hinder improvements in education and health, and thus slow down or arrest further development.[49] But it is also important to bear in mind the warning that although ecological dysfunction is often rooted in demographic pressure, the relationship between cause and effect is not as automatic as it may often seem. Thus, Engelhard and Abdallah have observed that:[50]

> "In Africa at least, there is a tendency to see a causal relation between greater demographic growth, a deteriorating ecological environment and a decline in per capita agricultural output. But the reverse is worth serious consideration too. In some cases, it has been the rural exodus and the waning of traditional herding methods which have upset the physical environment and destroyed systems of production – and with no compensation either."

The population problem in Africa is too well known to need restating here. The rural population nearly doubled between 1950 and 1985, occasioning a corresponding decline in land availability, both for basic settlement and subsistence and commercial farming.[51] The population explosion in rural Africa continues to generate serious environmental problems: health, nutrition, potable water supplies, sanitation and drainage. In such situations, there is often a drift of the population from rural to urban centres. But such rural to urban migration brings with it new manifestations of environmental stress: overcrowded cities, the mushrooming of slums and shanty towns, health problems, unemployment, social disruption to life styles, crime, and so on. All these factors lead to economic decay and social depression in both the rural and urban areas. In brief, to the extent that unchecked population growth inhibits economic growth and development, and creates environmental problems which are in turn compounded by the lack of economic growth, excessive rates of population growth pose obvious challenges for both economic development planners and environmental policy-makers in Africa.

Environmental legislation can be made to play a vital role in the effort to combat the environmental problems in this area. No African country has any legislation prohibiting rural to urban migration, nor is such legislation desirable. However, in most of these States, this migration challenge is being addressed through the provision of economic incentives to people to remain, or return to, the rural areas where they can lead more economically productive lives. Thus, Botswana, Burundi, The Gambia, Malawi, Swaziland and Zambia, to name only a few, have well established rural development programs which aim at securing this objective. Some countries also grant certain privileges to rural-based industries, for example tax relief or special loan schemes.

On the legislative side, every State has some code or statute (the so-called "Town and Country Planning Acts") which generally govern land use planning, especially in urban development areas. But it must be submitted that the invocation of blanket land use legislation cannot of itself provide adequate solutions: the different aspects of the problem, population growth, urbanization, and health and sanitary conditions, must be addressed separately by specific pieces of legislation. And in devising the necessary legislative and administrative machinery in all these areas, legislators and policy-makers have to take into account the socio-cultural values of the communities concerned. In some parts of rural Africa, for example, there continues to be a wide-spread belief that more people are needed for development; thus, the more children a family has the wealthier it regards itself. For, among other things, children are sometimes regarded as a family's labour force. Such attitudes are compounded by the persistent practice of polygamy in some communities. Attempts to implement family planning and birth control programs in most African States have been frustrated by these socio-cultural beliefs and values. In the absence of meaningful and effective legislation the human settlements and population control problems briefly described here will continue to erode the limited developmental and environmental resource base in all these States. These problems require the most urgent attention.

Conclusion

The debate about the proper role of environmental legislation in the areas of development, resource management and environmental protection is likely to occupy the minds of scholars and policy-makers alike for some time to come. One discerns in this debate two seemingly irreconcilable points of view. On the one hand, there is the argument that environmental laws do not really matter, and further that they can be an obstacle to progress rather than a useful tool for environmental management and protection. On the other hand, there is the view that environmental legislation can be instrumental in solving the enormous environmental problems of the modern world, especially those of the developing countries.

It is the latter view which the present writer advocates, and much of the foregoing discussion has been aimed at articulating the validity and relevance of this view. It is the argument here that if African States, as is also the case with all other nations, are to avoid the impending catastrophe posed by the ever-increasing degradation of the environment, there is need to formulate an effective body of environmental law. For it is only through the machinery of such a body of law that the activities of States can be checked and minimum standards for national legislation regarding environmental management and protection set.

For the reasons stated earlier, this discussion has been predicated on a selective approach. But even on the basis of this selective study, two points stand out quite clearly. First, that the importance of the relationship between environment and development cannot be disregarded. Rather, it is argued that these two processes should be viewed as two interrelated aspects of the same common human goal: the enduring quest for a better life and survival for all. To this end, therefore, it is suggested that both lawyers and policy-makers should regard environmental law as an integral part of a comprehensive system of resource management and economic development planning.

The second major observation that has been made in this discussion is that the problem in Africa is not so much the absence of relevant environmental legislation as the lack of proper orientation and enforcement of the existing laws. For, as was pointed out above, legislation of one kind or another relating to the environment has been on the statute books of all African States since the colonial era. What has been lacking in most cases, however, is the correct orientation in the content and focus of these laws such that they become an integral aspect of the entire system of what may broadly be termed "ecomanagement". This requires nothing short of a radical change in the general conception of the whole body of environmental laws; one must go beyond the traditional outlook upon these laws as merely another set of rules and principles in the wider legal system.[52] Alongside this need to change the orientation of existing laws is the requirement that African States strengthen the machinery for the environmental impact assessment of all development activities. As was observed earlier, this entails that environmental protection measures be incorporated into the process of development planning and project implementation from inception. Furthermore, it entails the incorporation of principles of sustainable development in all relevant legislation more comprehensively.

The developing countries of Africa cannot ignore the innumerable environmental problems which they are presently confronted with, and the idea that the resolution of these problems can be set aside until a certain level of economic development has been achieved must be quashed unreservedly. It is true that concern for the environment has increased over the last decade in many developing countries, including those in Africa. The adoption of National Conservation Strategies (NCSs) by a number of African States (for example, Botswana, Zambia and Zimbabwe) from the mid-1980s bears testimony to this. But one should also issue the warning that the danger here is that these NCSs seem to lie outside the mainstream of policy formulation in these countries. Their very existence could lead decision-makers into the idle belief that environmental concerns have been satisfactorily addressed. It is imperative, therefore, that once drawn up, such NCSs be subjected to a period of public debate and scrutiny involving all interested parties – government, relevant interest groups, environmental non-governmental organizations and all other sections of civil society – leading to the adoption of guidelines to public and private interests, specifying what is expected of them, and a program of specific actions to be undertaken by the State.[53] It may also be the case, as some authorities have argued, that the emergency of strong public advocacy for environmental action on rural and agricultural problems in developing countries may be more important than any other factor in achieving sustainable development.[54] However, beyond this environmental awareness, what is essential is not only a profound change in the political dynamics of developing countries in order to bring renewed attention to the connection between poverty and environmental degradation, but an equally profound reorientation and rearrangement of some of the prevailing notions about the role of law in the scheme of environmental matters and, more particularly, in helping solve the problems occasioned by the conflicting demands of environment and development.

And, finally, a word on population policy. Most environmental legislation in Africa has not dealt with the population issue squarely. To be sure, some countries have to a lesser or greater degree focused on such matters as urban-rural migration, family planning to improve health and productivity. and on analyzing demographic trends to assist in the formulation of appropriate development policies and programs. However, what is required is a new emphasis on population policy which takes account of our present understanding of the negative effects of population pressures on achieving environmentally sustainable development. The issues of population growth control and alleviation of population pressures, where they exist, must therefore be addressed as part of rational environmental and development planning in African countries. In all this, the underlying concern must be that both the right to development and the right to a healthy and satisfactory environment have at their core the dignity of the individual. This principle of human dignity, in turn, provides the core principle which underpins the argument, and justification, for all human rights.

Notes

1. Stockholm Declaration on the Human Environment, adopted by the UN Conference on the Human Environment at Stockholm, 16 June 1972, Section I of the Report of the United Nations Conference on the Human Environment, UN Doc. A/CONF.48/14 and Corr. 1 (1972), reprinted in 11 ILM 1416 (1972) [hereinafter "Stockholm Declaration"].

2. Rio Declaration on Environment and Development, adopted by the UN Conference on Environment and Development at Rio de Janeiro, 14 June 1992, UN Doc. A/CONF.151/5/Rev.1 (1992), reprinted in 31 ILM 876 (1992) [hereinafter "Rio Declaration"].

3. World Commission on Environment and Development (WCED), *Our Common Future: Report of the World Commission on Environment and Development*, (1987) p. 3 [hereinafter "WCED Report"].

4. See M. Ozorio de Almeida, "Economic Development and the Preservation of Environment", *Development and Environment: Report and Working Papers of a Panel of Experts Convened by the Secretary General of the U.N. Conference on the Human Environment*, (1971) p. 107 at 109.

5. See, for example, S.D. Murphy, "Prospective Liability Regimes for the Transboundary Movement of Hazardous Waste", *88 AJIL 24* (1994). See also, generally, M. Pallemaerts, "International Environmental Law from Stockholm to Rio: Back to the Future?" and I. Porras, "The Rio Declaration: A New Basis for International Cooperation", in P. Sands (Ed.), *Greening International Law*, (1994) pp. 1–19; 20–34.

6. *Agenda 21: Programme of Action for Sustainable Development*, UN Doc. A/CONF.151/26 (3 Vols., 1992).

7. P. Alston, "Conjuring up new human rights: A proposal for quality control", 78 AJIL 607 (1984) at 612; see also same author's "Making Space for New Human Rights: The Case of the Right to Development", *1 Harvard Human Rights Yrbk. 3* (1988).

8. L.K. Caldwell, *International Environmental Law and Policy*, (1980) p. 170.

9. G. Palmer, "New ways to make international environmental law", 86 *AJIL* 259 (1992) at 260.

10. See note 1 *supra*, Preamble, para 1.

11. The WCED Report merely remarked that "the environment is where we all live"; see note 3 *supra*, p. xi. The European Community's Action Programme on the Environment, however, proffered the following definition: "[The] combination of elements whose complex inter-relationships make up the settings, the surroundings and the conditions of life of the individual and of society as they are and are felt". See Council Regulations (EEC) No. 1872/84 of June 1984 on Action by the Community Relating to the Environment.

12. See note 2 *supra*, Principle 7.

13. A. Kiss & D. Shelton, *International Environmental Law*, (1991) p. 25.

14. K. M'baye, "Le droit de développement comme un droit de l'homme", *5 Rev Droits de l'Homme 523* (1972). See also J. Donnelly, "In Search of the Unicorn: The Jurisprudence and Politics of the Right to Development", in A. Carty (Ed.), *Law and Development*, (1992) p. 165 at 170; S.R. Chowdhury *et al.* (Eds.), *The Right to Development in International Law*, (1992) *passim*; R. Rich, "The Right to Development: A Right of Peoples", in J. Crawford (Ed.), *The Rights of Peoples*, (1988) at 39; I. Brownlie, *The Human Right to Development*, A Commonwealth Secretariat Study (1989).

15. UNGA Res. 34/46, U.N. Doc A/C.3/34/SR 24–30.

16. UNGA Res. 41/128, G.A.O.R. 41st Sess., Supp. 53, p. 186.

17. See, for example, U.O. Umozurike, "The African Charter on Human and Peoples' Rights", *77 AJIL 902* (1983) at 907 where he states that "The right to development [appears] not to have attained the definitive status of a rule of law despite its powerful advocates. The negative duty not to impede the development of States may go down well; the positive duty to aid such development, in the

absence of specific accords, is a higher level of commitment that still rests on non-legal considerations".

18. Quoted in Kiss & Shelton, note 13 *supra*, at p. 48.

19. The adoption of this document subsequently inspired, in part, the preparation and adoption by a number of African States of their own national conservation strategies, for example: Zambia (1985), Zimbabwe (1987) and Botswana (1990). On its part, Lesotho adopted a National Environmental Action Plan in 1989. The IUCN's "Strategy" has now been revised and published as *The Earth: A Strategy for Sustainable Living*, (1991).

20. UNGA Res. 37/7, 9 November 1982, reprinted in 22 ILM 455 (1983).

21. See note 3 *supra*, p. 43.

22. *Ibid.* p. 65.

23. See, R.D. Munro and J.G. Lammers, *Environmental Protection and Sustainable Development*, (1986).

24. Note 2 *supra*, p. 880.

25. R. Panjabi, "Idealism and self-interest in international law – The Rio Dilemma" *23 California Western Int'l L J 177* (1992/93) at 196.

26. I have discussed this issue at slightly more length in my "Environment and Development in Africa: An Overview of Basic Problems of Environmental Law and Policy", *1 African J Int'l & Comp L 650* (1989) at pp. 656–659; see also the extensive literature cited therein, especially note 18.

27. See note 3 *supra*, pp. 70–71.

28. Environmental law, which aims at conserving and protecting the environment, is not a strictly defined area of law that is wholly distinguishable and separate from other areas of law. There are wide areas of conceptual overlap between environmental protection provisions and, say, criminal, property, construction, and water law. International environmental law is primarily concerned with the rights and duties of States in their relations with each other; it deals with the conservation and management of the environment and with the control of environmental pollution in an international context. Municipal environmental law, on the other hand, is primarily concerned with regulating environmental matters within each given State and in identifying the rights and obligations of the members of a given national political community in their relations not only with the State but with each other as well.

29. J.D. Ogundere, "The Development of International Environmental Law and Policy in Africa", *12 Natural Res J 255* (1972) at 270.

30. K. Adeniji, "The Legal Challenge of Environmental Pollution to Africa: A Case Study in the Regional Approach to Environmental Problems", *4 Anglo-Amer. L R 312* (1975) at 330.

31. See, generally, J. Mayda, "Environmental Legislation in Developing Countries: Some Parameters and Constraints", *12 Ecology L Q* 997 (1985). See also *Development of Environmental Protection Legislation in the ECA Region*, UN Doc. E/CN.14/ECU/5 [hereinafter "ECA Report"].

32. See note 3 *supra*, p. 330.

33. See ECA Report cited in note 31 *supra*, p. 74.

34. *Ibid.* p. 24.

35. For a detailed discussion of the theoretical issues in this regard, see E. Brandl and H. Bungert, "Constitutional Entrenchment of Environmental Protection: A Comparative Analysis of Experiences Abroad", *16 Harvard Environ. L Rev 1* (1992) at p. 8 *et seq.* See also, D. Shelton, "Human Rights, Environmental Rights, and the Right to Environment", *28 Stanford J Int'l L 103* (1991). E. Weiss, *In Fairness to Future Generations: International Law, Common Patrimony and Intergenerational Equity*, (1989), refers to over thirty countries whose constitutions contain an environmental clause. See also J. Glazewski, "The environment, human rights and a new South African constitution", *7 SAJHR 167* (1991).

36. Brandl and Bungert, *ibid.* p. 16; see also the literature cited therein.

37. *Ibid.* p. 18 (footnote reference omitted).

38. R. Gour-Tanguay (Ed.), *Environmental Policies in Developing Countries*, (1977) para. 841340/01.

39. See, for example, H. Sendler, "Grundprobleme des Umweltrechts", *23 Juristisches Schulung 255* (1983) at 258.

40. Brandl and Bungert, *op. cit.* p. 93.

41. *Ibid.* p. 96.

42. See, for example, the brief exchange in *84 AJIL 190* (1990) between A. D'Amato, "Do We Owe a Duty to Future Generations to Preserve the Global Environment?" at 190; E. Weiss, "Our Rights and Obligations to Future Generations for the Environment", at 198; and L. Gundling, "Our Responsibility to Future Generations", at 297. See also Weiss, note 35 *supra*; also same author's

"The Planetary Trust: Conservation and Intergenerational Equity", *11 Ecology L Q 495* (1994); B. Norton, "Environmental Ethics and the Rights of Future Generations", *7 Soc. Theory & Prac. 319* (1981).

43. See, for example, discussion by J. Glazewski, "The Environment and the Interim Constitution", *1 SA J Environ. Law & Pol. 3* (1994). For a brief but illuminating discussion of environmental rights from both a human rights perspective and a procedural or administrative law perspective, see R. Desgane, "Integrating Environmental Values into the European Convention on Human Rights", *89 AJIL 263* (1995).

44. Glazewski, *ibid.* p. 6. The environmental clause which now appears in the South African Constitution of 1996 is formulated in a more expanded fashion than the earlier provision in the interim Constitution of 1993 so as to ensure, *inter alia*, basic environmental integrity, sustainable development and use of resources.

45. Brandl and Bungert, *op. cit.* p. 87.

46. See ECA Report, note 31 *supra*, p. 15.

47. *Ibid.* p. 21.

49. WCED Report, note 3 *supra*, pp. 95–116

50. WCED Report, *ibid.*

51. P. Engelhard & T. Abdallah, "Environment, development and poverty – what ENDA thinks", in *The Courier*, No. 133 (May–June 1992) p. 73.

52. U.N. Dept. of International Economics and Social Affairs (DIESA), *World Population Prospects: Estimates and Projections as Assessed in 1984*, (1986) *passim.*

53. Mayda, *op. cit. passim.*

54. See S. Moyo (Ed.), *Zimbabwe's Environmental Dilemma: Balancing Resource Inequities*, (1991) p. 20.

56. H. Leonard and D. Morell, "Emergence of Environmental Concern in Developing Countries: A Political Perspective", *17 Stanford J. Int'l L 281* (1981) at 313.

APPENDIX

Bilateral Treaties Concluded by the United Kingdom and Other Parties Still in Force in Malawi

Note

The compilation of this list has been based, largely, on information available in the *Malawi Treaty Series*, an official record of the international treaties and other obligations of the Republic of Malawi. The *Malawi Treaty Series* does not purport to be a total and complete record of all of Malawi's international obligations in force at the time of any publication. Accordingly, the omission of reference to any treaty in the *Series* cannot as such be held to constitute non-recognition by the Malawi Government of any of its obligations under such treaty. The record given here reflects the position as it stood at 18 October 1983, when publication of the *Series* was discontinued: See, Malawi Govt. File Ref. No. EA/50/1/10/Vol.II. Multilateral treaties, also published in the *Series*, have not been included here.

Austria

Federal Republic of Austria – United Kingdom: Legal Proceedings in Civil and Commercial Matters, done at London, 14 March 1932.

(Extended beyond 6 January 1967 by Exchange of Notes: Zomba, 31 December 1966 and Nairobi, 28 February 1967).

Belgium

United Kingdom – Belgium: Mutual Surrender of Fugitive Criminals, signed at Brussels, 6 December 1901.

(Extended beyond 6 January 1967 by Exchange of Notes: Zomba 6 January 1967 and Bujumbura, 12 February 1968).

[See Extradition Treaty of 29 October 1901]

Bolivia

Great Britain – Bolivia: Mutual Surrender of Fugitive Criminals, signed at Lima, 22 February 1892.

(Extended beyond 6 January 1967 by Exchange of Notes: Zomba, 6 January 1967 and La Paz, 5 June 1967).

Denmark

United Kingdom – Kingdom of Denmark and Iceland: Legal Proceedings in Civil and Commercial Matters, signed London, 29 November 1932.

(Extended beyond 6 January 1967 by Exchange of Notes: Blantyre, 24 May 1967 and Nairobi, 30 May 1967).

France

United Kingdom – France: Avoidance of Double Taxation and the Prevention of Fiscal Evasion with respect to Taxes on Income, signed at Paris, 14 December 1950.

(Extended beyond 6 January 1967 by Exchange of Notes: Zomba, 6 January 1967 and Blantyre, 6 January 1967).

Germany

United Kingdom – Germany: Mutual Surrender of Fugitive Criminals, signed at London, 14 May 1872 (as amended by the Agreement between the Government of the United Kingdom and the Government of the Federal Republic of Germany for the Extradition of Fugitive Criminals, signed at Bonn, 23 February 1960).

(Extended beyond 6 January 1967 by Exchange of Notes: Zomba, 3 January 1967 and Blantyre, 21 April 1967).

United Kingdom – Federal Republic of Germany: Consular Agreement, signed at Bonn, 30 July 1956.

(Extended beyond 6 January 1967 by Exchange of Notes: Zomba, 18 December 1965 and Blantyre, 7 December 1966 together with the announcement published in a communication of 21 December 1967 in Bonn).

United Kingdom – Germany: Legal Proceedings in Civil and Commercial Matters, signed at London, 20 March 1928.

(Extended beyond 6 January 1967 by Exchange of Notes Zomba: 22 October 1966 and Blantyre, 22 June 1967).

Greece

United Kingdom – Greece: Legal Proceedings in Civil and Commercial Matters, done at London, 27 February 1936.

(Extended beyond 6 January 1967 by Exchange of Notes: Zomba and Athens both dated 6 January 1967).

Government of the United Kingdom – Government of Greece: Exchange of Notes: Consular Fees on Certificate of origin, done at London, 21 June 1929.

United Kingdom – Greece: Mutual Surrender of Fugitive Criminals, done at Athens, 24 September 1910.

(Both treaties extended beyond 6 January 1967 by Exchange of Notes: London, 31 December 1966 and 14 June 1967).

Iraq

United Kingdom – Iraq: Extradition, done at Baghdad, 2 May 1932.

(Extended beyond 6 January 1967 by Exchange of Notes: Zomba, 6 January 1967 and Baghdad, May 1967]).

[See Extradition Treaty of 3 January 1934]

Israel

United Kingdom – Israel: Extradition, done at London, 4 April 1960.

(Extended beyond 6 January 1967 by Exchange of Notes: Zomba, 5 January 1967 and Blantyre, 22 February 1967).

Luxembourg

Great Britain – Luxembourg: Mutual Surrender of Fugitive Criminals, signed at Luxembourg, 24 November 1880.

(Extended beyond 6 January 1967 by Exchange of Notes: Zomba, 6 January 1967 and London, 3 March 1967).

Monaco

Great Britain – Monaco: Extradition, signed at Paris, 17 December 1891.

[Date of Instrument of Extension unknown.]

Netherlands

United Kingdom – Netherlands: Mutual Surrender of Fugitive Criminals, signed at London, 26 September 1898.

(Extended beyond 6 January 1967 by Exchange of Notes: Lusaka, 21 November 1967, and Blantyre, 28 June 1968)

United Kingdom – Netherlands: Avoidance of Double Taxation and the Prevention of Fiscal Evasion with respect to Taxes on Income, signed at London, 15 October 1948.

(Extended beyond 6 January 1967 by Exchange of Notes: Blantyre, 7 June 1969, and Lusaka, 18 June 1969).

Norway

United Kingdom – Norway: Avoidance of Double Taxation with respect to Taxes on Income, done at London, 2 May 1951.

(Extended beyond 6 January 1967 by Exchange of Notes: Zomba, 7 April 1965 and Oslo, 12 July 1965).

Peru

United Kingdom – Peru: Mutual Surrender of Fugitive Criminals, signed at Lima, 26 January 1904.

(Extended beyond 6 January 1967 by Exchange of Notes: Blantyre, 9 August 1967 and Lima, 26 September 1967).

Portugal

United Kingdom – Portugal: Defining Respective Spheres of Influence in Africa, signed at Lisbon, 11 June 1891.

United Kingdom – Portugal: Use of Port of Beira and Connected Railways, signed at Lisbon, 17 June 1950.

United Kingdom – Portugal: Nyasaland-Mozambique Frontier, signed at Lisbon, 18 November 1954.

(Extended beyond 6 January 1966 by Exchange of Notes: Zomba, 15 November 1965 and Blantyre, 3 January 1966).

Great Britain – Portugal: Mutual Surrender of Fugitive Criminals, signed at Lisbon, 17 October 1892.

(Extended beyond 6 January 1967 by Exchange of Notes: Zomba, 4 January 1967 and Blantyre, 27 March 1968).

San Marino

United Kingdom – San Marino: Extradition, signed at Florence, 5 October 1899.

(Extended beyond 6 January 1967 by Exchange of Notes: London, 6 January 1967 and San Marino, 5 July 1967).

Sweden

United Kingdom – Sweden: Prevention of Fiscal Evasion with Respect to Taxes on Income, done at London, 30 March 1949.

(Extended beyond 6 January 1967 by Exchange of Notes: Zomba, 7 April 1965 and Stockholm, 17 June 1965).

Switzerland

Great Britain – Switzerland: Mutual Surrender of Fugitive Criminals, signed at Berne, 26 November 1880.

United Kingdom – Switzerland: Treaty Supplementing Article XVIII of the Treaty of Extradition of 26 November 1880, signed at London on 29 June 1904.

United Kingdom – Switzerland: Treaty Supplementary to the Extradition Treaty of 26 November 1880, signed at Berne, 19 December 1934.

(All extended beyond 6 January 1967 by Exchange of Notes: Zomba, 6 January 1967 and, Nairobi, 19 December 1967).

United Kingdom – Switzerland: Avoidance of Double Taxation with Respect to Taxes on Income, signed at London, 30 September 1954.

(Extended beyond 6 January 1967 by Exchange of Notes: Zomba, 7 April 1965 and London, 3 May 1965).

United States of America

United Kingdom – United States: Extradition, done on 22 December 1931.

United Kingdom – United States: Avoidance of Double Taxation and the Prevention of Fiscal Evasion with Respect to Taxes on Income, done on 6 June 1946 (amended 25 May 1954 and 19 August 1957).

(Both extended beyond 6 January 1967 by Exchange of Notes: Blantyre, 28 December 1965 and 17 April 1967).

INDEX

INDEX OF CASES